Towards a European Ius Commune in Legal Education and Research

Editors:
Michael Faure,
Jan Smits &
Hildegard
Schneider

Towards a European Ius Commune in Legal Education and Research

Proceedings of the conference held at the occasion of the 20th anniversary of the Maastricht Faculty of Law

INTERSENTIA

METRO

Ius Commune Europaeum

Editors:
Michael Faure
Jan Smits
Hildegard Schneider

Towards a European Ius Commune in
Legal Education and Research

ISBN 90-5095-250-X
D/2002/7849/43
NUR 820 en 840

Lay-out: Bureau JA Vormgevers, Tilburg

PREFACE

In October 2001, the Faculty of Law of Maastricht University celebrated its 20th anniversary. On this occasion, a conference was held under the broad title *Towards a European Ius Commune in Legal Education and Research.* In many respects, this conference was the successor of the conference held in Maastricht ten years earlier.[1] Not only was it devoted again to the state of the main legal disciplines from the perspective of the emerging common law of Europe, it also raised questions about the way to teach the law to future generations of students. Even some of the same scholars and practitioners as in 1991 were asked to contribute to the conference.

To devote an international conference to more or less the same subject as ten years ago deserves some explanation. The reader should not be tempted to think that this volume - that contains most of the papers presented at the conference - is only a 'follow-up' of the previous one. Several reasons account for the still growing importance of the '*ius commune*' debate, both in education and in scholarship and both in relation to the Maastricht Faculty of Law.

First, it should be admitted that a 'hidden' agenda of the 1991 conference was to consider the establishment of a 'European Law School'. The developments of the last decade have only emphasized the need for such an educational programme. The legal profession has undergone fundamental changes. Providing legal services has become a global matter. An internationally operating lawyer cannot rely any more on his knowledge of the national legal system only. He must be aware of international and European legal developments. He must be trained in comparative legal methodology. He must be able to use English or other foreign languages in negotiations with clients. On European Community level, legislation was created which enables lawyers to provide legal services across the national borders and establish themselves in another Member State. National legal education has to adapt to this new generation of lawyers who are not anymore concentrated on the own jurisdiction but are global players on the international legal market.

1 B. de Witte and C. Forder (eds.), *The Common Law of Europe and the Future of Legal Education*, Deventer, Kluwer, 1992.

In 1995, a European Law School was actually created in Maastricht. The four year programme tries to educate young lawyers for this new legal market. It provides students apart from the necessary knowledge of Dutch law with a decent training in European law and comparative law. The new *ius commune europaeum* forms the fundamental core of the educational programme of the European Law School. Needless to say that all courses are taught in English.

Second, over the last two years, it has become crystal clear that Europeanization of legal education is no longer a matter of individual universities alone. With the *Bologna* Declaration of 1999, the Ministers of Education of many European states far beyond the borders of the European Union tried to encourage more transparency and comparability of the educational systems in Europe by stimulating the introduction of a bachelor and master structure all over Europe. It still remains to be seen to what extent the European law faculties make use of this opportunity to make their curriculum more fit for the new legal market.

Third, as to substance, there is not a single legal discipline that has not experienced an increasing influence of Europe. Over the last decade, it has become virtually impossible to deal with issues of national law without paying attention to the European or international aspect. This is reflected in the growing internationalization of the academic debate: more and more, legal scholars find their partners not in their own country, but abroad. Thus, the contours of a truly European legal science are created. The contributions to this volume by specialists in the various fields make this abundantly clear.

Fourth, it should be pointed out that in 1991, METRO (the Maastricht Institute of Transnational Legal Research) was still in its infancy. Actually, the 1991 conference was one of the first conferences organized by this research institute. Since then, many seminars, workshops, congresses and – most importantly – publications have followed. Even more, Maastricht has joined forces with several other universities in order to strengthen its research potential. Thus, most of the research now formally takes place within one of the two so-called 'Research Schools', one of them devoted to Human Rights, the other to '*Ius commune*'. Both the Research Schools are recognized by the Royal Dutch Academy of Sciences.

In view of the above, it is to be expected that the Maastricht Faculty of Law can make it well into the following decade with the subjects it has always put high on the agenda: a high level of legal education and of internationalization. There is no reason to doubt that in 2011, a third conference can be devoted to the then still emerging common law of Europe.

In this volume, the contributions are centered around several themes: general issues, good governance, criminal law, ecotax, family law, civil liability, contract law and civil litigation and legal culture. For each theme, specialists in the field were asked to write a discussion paper. That paper is followed by one or more responses by other specialists. This formula ensured a stimulating discussion in the various workshops. We hope the reader finds it equally stimulating to read the contributions.

The papers deal on the one hand with the future of legal education in Europe by focusing – *inter alia* – on the free movement of lawyers from an EC perspective and by presenting the European law school as a model for a competitive transnational co-operation. Many of the other contributions focus on the 'state of the *ius commune*' in the various fields, mentioned above. Some of the papers are rather positive descriptions of the state of harmonization in the particular field. In other papers, the authors are tempted to present normative statements on the desirability of harmonization in the particular area. The reader will notice that there are substantial differences in both respects as far as the various areas are concerned. In some cases, there is relatively little '*ius commune*', but scholars are strongly pleading in favor of more harmonization. In other cases, there is today little harmonization and scholars are moreover skeptical towards the possibility of an emerging *ius commune* in the particular domain. Also, even in the areas where some plaid in favor of more harmonization, there does not seem to be any unanimity. For all the areas discussed in the book, it has been attempted to at least provide this 'state of the *Ius commune*' and the pros and cons of further harmonization in the particular field.

The advantage of this focus on the harmonization in the various areas of the law, rather than on a very abstract level, is that it becomes clear that it is apparently not possible to come to general, although tempting, conclusions concerning the desirability of harmonization. In some areas, there seem to be strong areas in favor of harmonization, in others less. Of course it would be tempting to see a dividing line there between on the one hand areas which are strongly linked to national preferences and values or strongly routed institutional or regulatory attitudes and on the other hand areas where traditionally more flexibility can be discovered and thus probably less routes in national values and preferences. Examples of the first, where therefore harmonization might be more difficult, would be the more public law oriented topics, such as criminal law, taxation and good governance, whereas one could at first blush think that the link with national values and preferences might be less outspoken within the areas of the laws which are more linked to private law, such as with contract law. However, it may be dangerous to argue along these lines of generalization. Take the example of tort law: one could at first blush argue that this is an area which is quite well suited for harmonization, since the links with national values and preferences might be less outspoken. However, in reality the differences between the legal systems in a domain like e.g. compensation for non pecuniary losses still seemed to be quite large, which make it doubtful that e.g. particularly this area of the compensation for pain and suffering is a good candidate for harmonization. On the contrary, one might be tempted to believe that family law would be an area which is very much linked to national values and preferences, but the report dealing with family law in this book shows that exactly in this domain, remarkable progress has been achieved as far as harmonization is concerned.

It is obviously not the ambition of this book to come up with general conclusions on the desirability of harmonization in any of these particular areas. However, we hope that the concentration of contributions dealing with the state and desirability of harmonization in many areas of the law in one book may have the advantage of showing that the harmonization debate merits differentiated answers since the demand for harmonization in the different fields of the law may be different as well.

Finally, we would like to thank a number of persons that contributed to the coming into being of this book. Christopher Fretwell, former MIC student at Maastricht University, took care of the language editing of most of the contributions. Marjo Mullers and Marina Jodogne of METRO provided highly appreciated support, both in the organization of the conference itself and in the editing process.

The editors

TABLE OF CONTENTS

CIVIL LIABILITY

Ulrich Magnus

Ton Hartlief

LIST OF AUTHORS

Prof. Dr Daan Asser, Leiden University

Prof. Dr. Katharina Boele-Woelki, Utrecht University

Prof. Dr. Sabine Gleß, Max Planck Institut für ausländisches und internationales Strafrecht, Freiburg

Prof. Dr. Stefan Grundmann, University of Erlangen

Prof. Dr. Ton Hartlief, Maastricht University

Prof. Dr. Aalt Willem Heringa, Maastricht University

Prof. Dr. Ewoud Hondius, Utrecht University

Prof. Dr. André Klip, Maastricht University

Prof. Dr. Kalle Määttä, University of Helsinki

Prof. Dr. Hector L. McQueen, University of Edinburgh

Prof. Dr. Ulrich Magnus, University of Hamburg

Prof. Dr. Dieter Martiny, University of Frankfurt/Oder

Prof. Dr. Peter-Christian Müller-Graff, University of Heidelberg

Prof. Dr. Knut Wolfgang Nörr, Eberhard Karls Universität, Tübingen

Prof. Dr. Remco van Rhee, Maastricht University

Prof. Dr. Michael Rodi, University of Greifswald

Prof. Dr. Hildegard Schneider, Maastricht University

Prof. Dr. Jan Smits, Maastricht University

Stefan Ubachs, Maastricht University

Prof. Dr. Luc Verhey, Maastricht University

Prof. Dr. Ellen Vos, Maastricht University

Prof. Dr. Pierre Widmer, University of Lausanne

Prof. Dr. Alain Wijffels, University of Louvain-la-Neuve and Leiden University

General

Aalt-Willem
Heringa

TOWARDS A EUROPEAN LAW SCHOOL! A PROPOSAL FOR A COMPETITIVE, DIVERSIFIED MODEL OF TRANSNATIONAL CO-OPERATION

1. Introduction

Ten years ago the Faculty of Law of the University of Maastricht organized a conference under the title: The common law of Europe and the future of legal education.[1] Two of the questions at the various meetings and before the different panels were: what is the status of a common law of Europe; and, if it can be said to exist, albeit in different forms and shapes and at different stages of development with regard to the different areas of the law, how should the existence of a common law of Europe influence legal education in European law faculties.

These questions were at that time, and presently still are, interesting academic questions; but they are also very much practical issues. Could and should there be a place for a harmonized European legal education, maybe not in all law faculties but in at least some of them; shouldn't we aim at training 'European' lawyers: what is a truly European lawyer? That is: how should an innovative European law curriculum (the common law of Europe) look? Is there a place and a firm basis in legal doctrine, for a European version of the American Law School?

2. European Developments in the Area of Legal Education

It goes without saying that many law faculties in Europe have introduced major changes to their curricula in the past ten years. European law, in the strict sense of the term, has been awarded an indispensable place in the curriculum; many courses devoted to national law have undergone changes.[2] It simply proved necessary to introduce European developments as well. It is simply, to give but one example, a

1 The proceedings of this conference have been published in B. de Witte and C. Forder, (eds.), *The common law of Europe and the future of legal education*, Deventer, Kluwer, 1992.

2 This also led to an introduction of foreign languages in national curricula, since prestigious law journals and academic writings are in English. The English language therefore has become an indispensable language whenever European law, international law and comparative law is taken up in a curriculum.

necessity when dealing with national human rights protection to devote major attention to the European Convention of Human Rights and its Court as well as to EU and EC developments.

So, national curricula, aimed at educating national lawyers, have been Europeanized. The more so because of an increasing co-operation on the European level between faculties and because of exchange programs such as the Socrates program and the system of ECTS credits. Many faculties have set up special courses for these exchange students; in faculties such as mine, these courses are being taught in English.[3] Out of necessity they were devoted to issues such as European law, international law, and comparative law. They were also open to one's own national students. All this gradually contributed to an increasing transnational trend and input in previously almost exclusively national legal curricula.

3. A European Legal Education?

In our 1991 conference the purpose was to signal this trend and also to look to the future: what lessons do we have to learn from this development? The perspective of the conference was to see whether it could be said that the time had come for a major change. Next to the national studies of the law, that evidently focus primarily on national concepts and doctrines, it might be time to investigate the feasibility of a truly European curriculum. As opposed to the national law faculties the primary focus then had to be on European law and on the 'common law' of Europe.

The answer to this question was certainly not a simple, straightforward one. First of all, many obstacles were noted: could it be said that there was already a coherent body of European and common law in all areas of the law, of sufficient quantity and quality so as to facilitate its own curriculum? Or, should a student be taught and immersed in a national legal system with its concepts and doctrines, before he can embark upon European and, even more difficult, upon comparative law and the search for common legal principles and doctrines.

A second problem, which can easily be said to exist still, is the absence of a common perspective on what a legal study should entail: the studies in the European countries still differ significantly; as do the national requirements for the legal profession. And, a simple practical aspect, there is no European common view as to a European legal education. National faculties of law therefore have to deal with their own national requirements: to give an example: for a Dutch student to qualify for the bar, he should have studied for four years at a Dutch law faculty ('240 ECTS credits),[4] of which approximately 210 credits[5] must have been spent in studying the various areas of the law. That does not seem to facilitate a truly European legal education.

A third problem raised was about the nature of a good lawyer: does it really matter if a lawyer has not been specifically trained in comparative law and

3 In the academic year there were 48 such English taught courses on offer!

4 This equals 168 studypoints under Dutch law; 48 per annum.

5 Equalling 140 Dutch studypoints.

European law, but instead is very familiar with one legal system? This familiarity with one legal system, accompanied with his legal tools, should provide him with the best expertise for becoming a good European lawyer. Moreover, how many European lawyers do we really need: isn't the major part of a lawyer's business about dismissals, divorces, tort and national administrative law?

There are, therefore, many obstacles and arguments which we have to surmount and counter.

The present state of affairs in Europe seems to me to be the following:

- increasingly law faculties have inserted European law courses into their curriculum;
- in addition some law faculties have gone even further. They have not only added extra courses on European law, but they have introduced into their national law a number of courses with European and comparative elements. They have, so to speak, Europeanized the curriculum;
- many post-graduate programmes have been developed on European law and comparative law; and seemingly attract many students;[6]
- national legislation about the requirements of a law curriculum still shows major differences between the EU member states. It also poses an important obstacle for national law faculties to develop a truly European law curriculum;
- the expansion of European law; the ever increasing trends in harmonization, transnational co-operation and in comparative research show that what seemed a distant future perspective, has come a lot closer and seems much more real and realistic.

4. The European Law School in Maastricht

Taking these factors as a starting point I will give some information about a Maastricht programme we have developed. Subsequently I intend to shed some light about how to proceed even further and where to go from there.

I will do so by providing you with my perspective: it can be characterized by calling it a diversified, competitive model of European legal education.

Let me first explain how we proceeded in my faculty since the 1991 conference, whose findings, reservations and points to ponder we took very much to heart. Alongside the main legal curriculum we have on offer for Dutch law, we developed another, Europeanized curriculum: it had to meet the requirements related to the Dutch bar: it was evident that the students we had in mind had to find work in the legal environment of larger companies and specifically the larger law firms and also the large Dutch ministries. This implied the necessity of a training in Dutch law as well. Added to this practical reason was an academic one: our perception that it seemed unworkable and unwise to start out with a purely European law curriculum. In order to do so, the fullness of European law in its broadest meaning still did not seem ripe and well developed enough to form the

6 In Maastricht: the Magister Iuris Communis: Master on European and Comparative Law.

basis of a legal curriculum. What we had to do therefore was to develop an intensified program: Dutch law plus!

Under the Dutch rules governing the admission to law faculties we have to admit anyone who successfully finishes his secondary education. No selection based on test scores or motivation. The first year of study is therefore designed to select the students; on the basis of this legal reality we offer all students an identical first year: this year provides for an introduction into the law in general and Dutch law in particular; it includes European law and wherever possible comparative law. This gives the faculty a chance to select students as to their capabilities and the students to find out what they really want. It is difficult to grasp what studying the law means before going to law-school, let alone to have any clue about a common law of European and comparative law. So, we decided to let the students settle into a law curriculum that is grounded in Dutch law but impregnated with European and comparative law.

It is after the first year that the students have to make a choice: those who think they will like the European and comparative aspects as well as the Dutch law, will be admitted into the European Law School. It therefore starts in the second year. In this second year, students still follow major courses in Dutch law, in order to make them Dutch lawyers who have a thorough knowledge of Dutch law and who can, on the basis of this expertise, subsequently be involved in comparative law. However, they also have to take extra courses on comparative law, legal English and foreign legal systems. These courses are extra: they test the students' willingness to work harder; they also test their ability; and they inform the students as to what comparative law and European law and the common law of Europe really mean.

The third and the fourth year of the curriculum are a fully fledged 'common law of Europe' curriculum. In all areas of the law (contracts, property, tort, constitutional law, administrative law, company law, labour and social security law, criminal law, procedural law) students are being taught the European aspects as well as the fundamental doctrines and concepts in the main European legal systems. Added to that are also courses on European law in its narrow meaning: institutions and substantive law.

5. Educating European Lawyers

What exactly is being taught in these comparative 'common law of Europe' courses? What is the central approach? Well, to tell you the truth, in that respect a great diversity exists as well.

It is important to realize first of all that it is not our intention to educate specialists in European law, but lawyers that are European lawyers. Students who have acquired an open mind for foreign legal systems; are capable of understanding mixed legal systems and solutions such as are being developed within Europe. It is the tools that we intend to convey to the students and not primarily a detailed knowledge of national legal systems and of European law. Marcel Storme has argued in that respect that: we must train lawyers without frontiers, lawyers who are trained on national but also on European lines. And he also argued that: a law faculty must not teach law: it must train lawyers. That was our intention: training European lawyers.

Our approach has been to teach Dutch law in the first two years; based on the assumption that it is (still) necessary to have a training in one legal system before one can engage in comparative law and European law. In order not to get confused through the variations in details and legal rules, one must be trained in one coherent legal system so as to understand the basic concepts and the underlying system. In this 'national phase' European law evidently must be integrated as well, because in many aspects European law is part of national law.

The final two years are devoted to the comparative aspects: the actual training of the students in these final two years is different compared to the first two.

It is fundamental that the training will be focused more and more on lawyering skills; these skills will be taught through comparative law. Without underestimating the need to acquire knowledge about the legal systems under comparison it is not our primary aim to teach all the details of the national legal systems. That would be impossible. But what can be done is to make students aware of the existence of basic differences and similarities; dissimilarities in approaches and methods of legal reasoning. The lawyering tools that can be derived from it are: creativity; an understanding how uniformity of law on the European level can be promoted whilst taking into account national peculiarities; a familiarity with foreign legal concepts and legal languages; capability of doing research in a foreign legal system and the capability to consult a foreign lawyer; the development of an open mind where it concerns the quest for legal solutions to social problems. For these purposes comparative law has proven to us to be a successful method, whenever it is being used in combination with a basic expertise and understanding of one national legal system.

It is imperative however that this general comparative approach is being utilized for all areas of the law. In some areas European legal systems have more in common than in others. For company law for instance a lot has already been harmonized on the European level; in the context of administrative law or contracts on the other hand many divergences still exist. That does not imply that the comparative method is useless, on the contrary. Despite the many divergences, common principles can be detected. Or, the comparative method can be resorted to in order to try to develop new or common 'European' concepts. The European notion of transparency is for instance a European translation of national constitutional values related to the '*rechtsstaat*' concept. Comparative law is therefore a tool to develop European law.

The above means that we intend to train lawyers without a specialization in one specific area; that does not mean they do not have a specialization: their specialization is the European nature of their qualifications.

Students must and will acquire lawyering tools by searching for common principles underlying and inherent to the legal systems that are compared. This approach will take us away from black-letter law and make students aware of approaches to the law, and will help them in acquiring a critical understanding. It is my experience that a principled comparative law approach should be structurally built into courses. What will be improved in particular is the students'

understanding of the law. The reason is that their eyes will be open to the system which any legal order is; and how this system is structured around basic principles in order to make it coherent, accessible, equal and understandable. In that sense comparative law is a teaching method, and one which is not only a method, but also relates to content! Furthermore, comparative law can bridge the gap between positive law and legal theory. The wisdom acquired from a comparative study of the law is a greater asset than a soon to be outdated knowledge of rules and regulations. A general comparative teaching of the law will make better lawyers and lay the groundwork for transnational (European and global) lawyering.[7] For the purposes of the comparative method, looking for (common) principles and approaches I quote from the preface to a book called Before the Law[8]: 'Law is presented as a field of argument: continually changing; multi-faceted; responding to social, political and economic forces; evolving in different ways in different cultures and historical eras'. Well, that is also an asset of a principled comparative approach. And it does more: it also shows the students the various 'black letter' answers in the systems that are under comparison. But by doing so, it simultaneously shows that different responses are possible; that law is indeed a field of argument'.
There was also, in the Dutch context, another reason for developing the European Law School curriculum as I have been describing to you. I felt the need to offer an advanced legal training to those students who are capable of doing more than is required under a study of Dutch law. We select the better and the more motivated students and allow them to opt for the advanced and challenging European Law School courses. In my opinion, the complexities involved with comparative law, the need also to compare on a conceptual level, require that high standards are set.

6. Achievements and Problems

We witness in our programme that many of our aims have indeed been and can be achieved. That does not mean that there remains nothing to be wished for or that no problems still await resolution. Before I inform you of the problems we have encountered and the future developments with respect to European legal education, please allow me first to briefly summarize the merits of the European Law School programme:

1. lawyers with a broad perspective on law;
2. lawyers trained in conceptual thinking and in lawyering skills;
3. lawyers capable of transnational legal thinking and familiar with foreign legal concepts and terminology and aware of all the traps that can confront lawyers who happen to stumble upon a foreign legal system;
4. general lawyers that have followed a sophisticated legal curriculum;

7 See A.W. Heringa, 'Common principles as a project and a teaching method', *Maastricht Journal of European and Comparative Law*, 6, 1999, 4, p. 327-330.

8 J.J. Bosignore, E. Katsh, P. d'Errico, R.M. Pipkin, S. Arons and J. Rifkin, *Before the Law, An Introduction to the Legal process*, 6th ed, Boston-New York 1998, p. X.

5. lawyers that probably compensate a less detailed knowledge of one particular national legal system with a broad overview of legal problems, transnational legal thinking and Europeanization/globalization of the law.

Now for some of the problems we have encountered.

A first difficulty relates to languages. The best way to engage in comparative research is by being able to read the legal texts in their original form. That would mean for a full-scale comparative program that many languages would have to be mastered. Luckily, a primary limitation is a restriction of the national legal systems to be compared. But even such a restriction still leaves a problem. It is generally accepted that the major European legal systems must be the subject of comparative law courses: English law, French law, German law. Even with this limitation, three languages are relevant. In practice, the requirement that our students are able to speak, write and read English, and are also able to read French and German is seemingly difficult to meet. Therefore, we are very reluctant to make the students read (lengthy) texts in French and German; we even offer them a subsidized French language course.

The linguistic aspect will be difficult for a law faculty to resolve; however we are convinced that a good European lawyer is one who not only feels at home in various legal systems but also with foreign (legal) languages.

A obvious related problem concerns the need for professors and lecturers who have a good knowledge of their own legal system, as well as of comparative law, European law and foreign systems. This implies in my opinion the necessity to have studied or worked abroad and to also focus in research on comparative law, European law and foreign legal systems. A mixed staff, consisting of lawyers originating from different legal systems, a true internationalization of the staff, seems, to say the least, also to be very helpful. This aspect leads me therefore to one of my conclusions: that co-operation between law faculties is required in order to successfully organize and teach a European law programme.

It also underlines the necessity that a European law school programme needs to be combined with research. It is imperative that a faculty that has undertaken such an ambitious programme needs to channel its research resources towards this end. There is an immense amount of work to be done; Professor Van Gerven will present in a contribution to this book, his important case-books project. Also on a more general introductory level there is a need for comparative materials and introductions in comparative issues. There is an abundance of materials available on the Internet; an increasing number of sites give access to legal sources in many countries. It remains necessary however to make assistance available for the students as to how to read foreign materials, in understanding the legal concepts and doctrines. In helping them understand the basic common concepts et cetera. For these purposes, a lot of research must be done.

To sum up it appears necessary to: undertake the development of educational materials; carry out research in the area of comparative law and common principles; develop courses in comparative and European law; encourage co-operation between law schools in these fields; select of students as to their abilities to study in foreign languages about foreign legal systems; and to open up, in and through education, national legal attitudes and legal minds: comparative law tends not to be considered an indispensable tool of the trade by national lawyers.

7. A proposal for a European Law School Model

This is all work that has to be done anyway: however one might perceive the precise future of legal European education; these challenges simply have to be met. In all law courses in my opinion one should introduce comparative aspects, foreign readings, European aspects, et cetera. Apart from this general and all encompassing challenge, I think that all over Europe a number of law faculties ought to be working towards the development of a model of a European Law School. I have presented the Maastricht model, but our model is by no means perfect or the only and ultimate possibility. I would propose a mitigated free competition. A free competition in the sense that those law faculties that want to take up this challenge should do so and should work out their perspectives as to how European legal education should look. With a mitigated competition I mean that these faculties should exchange ideas and should form small networks of co-operation and shared expertise.

My model is therefore a diversified model: some law faculties go further than others; some have a European legal education as I understand this concept, and others do not. They confine themselves to a focus on national law. Those who take up the challenge seek co-operation and mutual assistance. This model therefore is one that is open to further development and improvement. It also underlines the necessity for comparative law through transnational co-operation. Students should also experience the European and comparative features of their training by a students exchange; an internationally mixed student body and teaching staff. Also the development of teaching materials could be carried out in these small workable co-operative networks. These features are nothing new or revolutionary: they have been the elements of Erasmus and Socrates networks and, in our case, co-operation between law faculties. It is, however, my proposal that the European Law School networks, is small; that co-operation is intense and that efforts are made towards offering one curriculum. Or at least, a curriculum that is basically common to the participating partners, but can and will show national accents and variations as well. I would leave the intensity of the co-operation to the partners. It will therefore differ from one network to another.

However, to paraphrase the Belgian author Elschot, between desires and their realization lie practical difficulties and legal problems. The major legal problem concerns the necessary legal recognition, until now, of a law curriculum under national laws. This means, for the time being: either that a European Law School curriculum will differ in the various countries as to the required component of national law; the co-operation I have proposed therefore would be limited to the European Law School part of the curriculum; or that the national countries agree to afford a recognition to European Law School programmes, even though they do not fully correspond to the present national requirements. This national recognition could be furthered by sponsorship from the European Commission.

Law faculties, co-operating in the way I have proposed, ought also to exert pressure upon their national authorities to support and to the extent possible, recognize the new, truly European, law degree.

This approach implies a degree of trust on the part of the national authorities and bar associations in the co-operation of the law faculties. The requirement that a truly European programme has to be set up, under the guidance of a project of co-operation of law faculties of different countries, must be a sufficient guarantee for quality and for a thorough and intense legal training.

A diversified, competitive model, needs adequate support from the Commission and the States to give this baby a good start. The guarantees for quality and a true European nature lie in the international co-operation and student and staff exchange.

8. Other Proposals

In a similar vein Ingo von Münch has written about a European law degree.[9] He also underlines the necessity for a European law degree, because it seems odd to have European law and not an accompanying law degree. He is also very specific as to the necessary steps that must be taken:

1. A blueprint for a curriculum must be developed. I hesitantly agree; however, I also submit that the Maastricht curriculum provides a good example and I do not expect that a curriculum poses major problems. A relative and sufficient consensus seems to exist. Courses about contract, tort, property, constitutional and administrative law, company law, criminal law, European law, human rights, international law, legal procedure, legal skills, do indeed seem self evident. So, I would not spend too much time in an effort to draft a curriculum that fits all participants. It seems self-evident that the main areas of the law will be on offer, in a European and comparative perspective. I also suspect that a national flavour will be added, but that will only be fruitful. If a blueprint is made I suggest it ought not be too detailed; in my model diversity is to be expected and desirable. Let's not inhibit the progress by working solely on blueprints.

2. A free decision of law faculties to participate. I fully agree to allow the faculties to decide if they want to participate or not.

3. The new curriculum will have to be additional for the national students, not a substitute for the national law programme. Therefore the national law programme must be limited so as to make room. That is in my opinion the least that should be done. It is, in all modesty, the Maastricht solution. I have, however, proposed that a further step should be taken by looking for a way

9 I. von Münch, 'Europarecht ohne Europäisches Rechtsstudium?', *Zeitschrift für Europäisches Privatrecht*, Heft 1, 2001, p. 1-3.

towards a special recognition. If such a recognition might be possible, a law faculty might even consider only to offer the new European law school curriculum and become a truly European law faculty.

4. An evaluation of the European Law School programmes, in order to ensure equal standards. It is my conviction that one should not strive for equal standards but for minimum standards. I would however leave this primarily to the law faculties in their co-operation and competition. In order to attract students and moral and legal recognition for their programme, they need to ensure good standards. Let competition and co-operation and the exchange of ideas do their work before we engage upon laborious and centralized evaluations!

5. A student exchange; this requirement is self-evident and essential!
These proposals are more in line with my reflections on the future of European legal education, than the idea advanced by Marcel Storme.[10] He proposes to create some 50 large law schools in Europe: top-class law schools, he adds. Though I might agree with the number and the qualification, I have difficulty with the idea, that they should be created. I believe they should develop! They should prove that they are the top; that their curriculum is the best; that they have the best professors and also a truly European composition of their staff; that their students are the best and that they do the best job in selecting and training them; that they have a well regulated and well structured student exchange built into the programme; that they offer good traineeships et cetera.

Evidently, alongside these European faculties, or national faculties that have such a top programme on offer, there shall, for a long time to come, still be place for national law schools and programmes aimed at national law and national lawyers (although these programmes in my view also must have a truly European flavour). What is also important is that the model should not be exclusive: further experiments ought to be welcomed. In that respect I can fully accept the situation for the next decades that the European Law School programmes are different, have different perspectives and undertake comparative and European law from different angles. That makes me doubt the feasibility and desirability of Von Münch's first proposal that one curriculum must be developed. I think that a basic consensus exists; for the rest I would welcome diversity as a fruitful way to help us develop our thinking about the model of the future European legal education.

9. Conclusion

To sum up my proposals for this model, like-minded law faculties should form small manageable networks that agree to:

10 M. Storme in *IN-LAW*, Report of the conference 'European Lawyers in the 21st Century', Tilburg University September 21-23, 2000.

- each set up a European law program;
- co-operate as to the content and teaching of these programs;
- facilitate student exchange; students follow comparative law courses also with the foreign partner; comparative law will benefit from courses followed elsewhere; each university will have its own approach and emphases et cetera even in comparative law courses.

As a result diversity will be achieved, various trans-European Networks will be established and agreement will be reached between the European countries to recognize the diplomas obtained even though all the national conditions are perhaps not being met. And all of this as a first step towards the creation of a diploma of a European lawyer.

Hildegard
Schneider

THE FREE MOVEMENT OF LAWYERS IN EUROPE AND ITS CONSEQUENCES FOR THE LEGAL PROFESSION AND THE LEGAL EDUCATION IN THE MEMBER STATES

1. Introduction

In the 20 years since the faculty of law was founded in Maastricht the professional life of lawyers and legal education in Europe has become more and more international. When I studied law, during the mid-seventies, the legal education in all Member States of the European Community was still very nationally orientated. European law was considered an interesting but still quite exotic subject to be chosen as a specialisation. Legal education concentrated on the national legal system. The different legal professions were to a large extent operating on the national legal markets only.

It was, however, precisely in this period that the European Court of Justice took its first two very important decisions which opened the European market for the legal profession, at least for the advocates. These were the rulings in the cases *Reyners* and *Van Binsbergen*.[1] Also in the seventies, the first directives for professionals including a directive regulating cross-border services for advocates were accepted by the Council of Ministers.[2]

Since this period, the legal profession has undergone fundamental changes. Providing legal services has become a global matter. An internationally-operating lawyer can no longer rely on his knowledge of the national legal system alone. He must be aware of international as well as European legal developments.

In the following, I want to give an overview of this development. Special attention shall be given to the most important cases of the European Court of Justice regarding the legal profession. Very often these cases were not only of importance for the legal profession as such but can be considered as landmark decisions for the

1 Case 2/74, *Reyners v Belgium* [1974] ECR 631 and case 33/74, *Van Binsbergen v Bestuur van de Bedrijfsvereniging voor de Metaalnijverheid* [1974] ECR 1299.

2 Council Directive 77/249/EEC *OJ* L 78, 26.3.1977, p. 17 (The Lawyers Service Directive).

development of Community law in general.[3] The majority of the cases concern the right of establishment and the provision of cross-border legal services. More recently, the applicability of competition rules on the liberal profession including the legal profession has, however, become a new issue.

The second part of this article will be devoted to the relevant secondary European legislation concerning the legal profession in a cross-border context. Three directives are of major concern for the free movement of lawyers: the Lawyers' Service Directive from 1977,[4] the Recognition of Diplomas Directive from 1989[5] and the Lawyers' Establishment Directive from 1998.[6]

Not only the professional rules have changed under the influence of European law. The national legal educational systems as well have started to adapt to the new generation of lawyers who are not focused solely on the own jurisdiction solely but are global players on the international market. If we look back at the Dutch faculties of law of the beginning eighties the changes are remarkable. Twenty years ago, the *Erasmus* programme had not even started. International student exchange at undergraduate level was still in its infancy. Studies abroad, at least for law students, were limited mainly to postgraduate programmes. It was extremely rare that a new law student would decide to complete his educational programme fully outside his own jurisdiction.

Today, undergraduate student exchange is part of the daily features of university life and it has become more and more common that students choose for either a Master or even a full study abroad.[7] Future law students are no longer bound to their own legal education. They are able to choose between the best, the fastest, the cheapest and the most internationally orientated legal education offered at various faculties in the different Member States. The European Law School programme at the faculty of law in Maastricht has already proven that it can attract not only Dutch but also foreign students.[8] The Hanse Law School starting now in Groningen has been set up with the same intentions. With the growing awareness of a European legal market the competition between the different educational systems will further increase.

With the *Bologna* Declaration of 1999, the Minister of Education of many European states far beyond the borders of the European Union tried to encourage more transparency and comparability of the educational systems in Europe by stimulating the introduction of a bachelor and master structure all over Europe. As the European universities are confronted with the *Bologna process* at this very moment, I

3 For example: Case C-340/89, *Vlassopoulou v Ministerium für Justiz, Bundes- und Europaangelegenheiten Baden-Württemberg* [1991] ECR I-2357; Case C-19/92, *Dieter Kraus v Land Baden-Württemberg,* [1993] ECR I-1663 and Case C-55/94, *Gebhard v Consiglio dell'Ordine degli Avvocati e Procuratori di Milano* [1995] ECR I-1465.

4 Council Directive 77/249/EEC *OJ* L 78, 26.3.1977, p. 17 (The Lawyers Service Directive).

5 Council Directive 89/48/EEC *OJ* L 19, 24.1 89, p. 16.

6 Directive 98/5/EC *OJ* L 77, 14.3.1998, p. 36.

7 At the faculty of economics at the Maastricht University the percentage of foreign student has already passed the 50% in some area studies.

8 See the submission of A.W. Heringa in this book, p. 3-13.

would like to give some final, in some respects, critical comments as to the possible consequences for the internationalisation of the legal curricula by the implementation of such a system here in the Netherlands.

2. The Case-law of the European Court of Justice

One of the main goals of the EC Treaty from its very beginning has been the creation a common market for all economic activities. This has included the free movement of professionals. National rules which had the effect of preventing persons from providing professional services or establishing themselves in another Member State had to be progressively abolished. The barrier to mobility, constituted by the requirement of a national diploma, can as much be seen as an obstacle to completing the internal market as e.g. different safety standards for technical goods.

Many such obstacles have been removed through the interpretation of European law by the European Court of Justice. This has been the case in particular where the restrictions were based on nationality. The first landmark decision of the European Court of Justice in this area for lawyers was *Reyners v Belgium*.[9] The case concerned a Dutch national, resident in Belgium, having qualified in Belgium as a lawyer, who was refused admission to the Belgium Bar on the grounds of his nationality. The next important decision of the ECJ in the same year was the *Van Binsbergen* ruling.[10] This concerned a lawyer of Dutch nationality, resident in Belgium, seeking to practise before the Dutch courts. He was refused permission to do so on account of a Dutch legal requirement of national residence.

In both cases one of the issues was the direct effect of an EC-Treaty provision. Already in 1963 the Court had in the case *Van Gend & Loos* principally ruled on the possible direct effect of Treaty provisions.[11] In the *Reyners* case the court held that Article 52 (now 43) of the EC-Treaty had direct effect from the end of the transitional period.[12] Before doing so, the Court stated that Article 55 (now 45) EC-Treaty exception referring to the exercise of official authority did not apply to the profession 'advocat', even though its members might occasionally perform functions concerned with such an exercise of official authority. Accordingly, if a national of a Member State was otherwise fully qualified for the admission to the legal profession in the host Member State, he could not be refused on the basis of lacking the nationality of that State. Consequently, the nationality requirement for advocates had to be abolished in all Member States.[13]

9 Case 2/74, *Reyners v. Belgium* [1974] ECR 631.

10 Case 33/74, *Van Binsbergen v Bestuur van de Bedrijfsvereniging voor Metaalnijverheid* [1974] ECR 1299.

11 Case 26/62, *Van Gend & Loos v Nederlandse Administratie der Belastingen* [1963] ECR 1.

12 The transitional period ended on the 31 december 1969.

13 At that moment a nationality requirement existed next to Belgium also in France, Luxembourg, the Netherlands, Italy and de facto in Germany. See also H. Adamson, *Free Movement of Lawyers*, 2nd edition, London, Butterworth, 1998, p. 35 with some comments regarding the notarial professions and the application of Article 55 (now 45) of the EC Treaty.

In the *Van Binsbergen* judgment the court held that Article 59 (now 49) of the EC-Treaty had direct effect. The Netherlands could, therefore, not require permanent residence on the part of a lawyer providing services in that State. With respect to the freedom to provide services, the Court of Justice has since that decision in 1974,[14] developed a justification test similar to the *Cassis de Dijon* 'rule of reason' in the freedom of goods context.[15] In a subsequent case *Webb*, the Court elaborated further on the requirement of 'objective justification of restrictive rules'.[16] In *Säger*, the Court ruled that Article 59 (now 49) EC Treaty required the:

> 'abolition of any restriction, even if it applies without distinction to national provider of services and to those of other Member States, when it is liable to prohibit or otherwise imped the activities of a provider of services established in another Member State where he lawfully provides similar services'[17].

Doctrinally, it has been heavily argued and discussed after the decision in the case *Säger* whether the same principles also apply to the freedom of establishment.[18] This question was finally decided by the ECJ in the affirmative in two lawyer's cases in the nineties.[19]

Chronologically, however, the next important decision for lawyers was *Thieffry* decided in 1977.[20] This case concerned the refusal by the Paris Bar to recognise, for admission to the profession of advocate, a Belgium law degree which had previously been recognised for academic purposes by the University of Paris as a diploma equivalent to a French law degree. The Court held that in these circumstances the Paris Bar was obliged to consider the Belgium degree as equivalent to the French and accept admission to the Bar.

Personally, I also agree with the final result of the decision of the Court of Justice, I always found the reasoning of the Court quite misleading, as it seems that the Court did not see any difference between the recognition of a diploma for professional purposes and the recognition of a diploma for academic means. The distinction is, however, of great relevance. If a Dutch university, for example, recognises a foreign law degree for the sole purpose that the holder of the diploma can start a postgraduate Masters programme, this form of recognition shall and

14 Case 33/74, *Van Binsbergen v Bestuur van de Bedrijfsvereniging voor de Metallnijverheid,* [1974], ECR 1299.

15 Case 120/78, *Rewe-Zentrale AG v Bundesmonopolverwaltung für Branntwein,* [1979], ECR 649.

16 Case 279/80, *Webb,* [1981], ECR 3305; see also the Cases 110-111/78, *Van Wesemael,* [1979], ECR 35.

17 Case C-76/90, *Säger,* [1991] ECR I-4421, see also Case 275/92, *Schindler* [1994], I-1039.

18 H. Schneider, *Die Anerkennung von Diplomen in der Europäischen Gemeinschaft,* Antwerp, Intersentia, 1995. p. 43.

19 Case C-19/92, *Dieter Kraus v Land Baden-Württemberg,* [1993] ECR I-1663 and Case C-55/94, *Gebhard v Consiglio dell'Ordine degli Avvocati e Procuratori di Milano* [1995] ECR I-1465. See also S. O'Leary, 'The Free Movement of Persons and Services', in P. Craig & G. de Burca (eds.), *The Evolution of EU Law,* Oxford, Oxford University Press, 1999, p. 377 (401), L. Daniele, 'Non-Discriminatory restrictions in the Free Movement of Persons', *ELR,* 1997, p. 191-200.

20 Case 71/76, *Thieffry v Conseil de l'ordre des advocats à la Cour de Paris* [1977] ECR 765.

should not have any direct consequences for the admission of the candidate to the Dutch Bar. It is a recognition only for academic purposes.

Meanwhile, this case has lost practical relevance in so far as the admission of a lawyer like Thieffry would today be considered under the relevant secondary legislation.[21]

The next lawyer's case concerned a German lawyer named Klopp who had not only the necessary German qualifications but also fulfilled all requirements for admission to the Paris Bar.[22] In fact he was dual qualified. Nevertheless, his admission to the French Bar was refused on the ground that he wanted to retain professional residence in Germany as well as establish himself in Paris. This double residency was considered contrary to the French rule of *unicité de cabinet*, requiring an advocat to have only one professional residence. The Court held, that to maintain this rule in a transfrontier context would prevent lawyers from other Member States from exercising their right of establishment by integrating in the legal profession of another Member State. Having and retaining a professional residence in Germany could not be a reason for refusing the applicant's admission to the Paris Bar. Furthermore, the Court declared that the existence of a second professional residence in another Member State did not present any obstacle to the application of rules of professional conduct in the host Member State.

This decision of the Court was not only important for lawyers with dual qualification who wanted to establish themselves in two Member States. Indirectly, it also had influence on the internal application of the one office, *unicité de cabinet*, requirement which not only existed in France but also in other Member States. After the Court's ruling it seemed to be quite anomalous to prohibit a national lawyer from having two offices on national territory while he might be allowed to have two offices in two different Member States provided that he fulfilled the professional qualification requirements. Such a form of reverse discrimination seemed not anymore acceptable. Most Member States have therefore abolished this requirement.

Until the end of the eighties, in the majority of cases with regard to the freedom of establishment, the national restrictions in question were in some way classifiable as directly or indirectly discriminatory.[23] The Court was either not faced with a case of a purely non-dicriminatory nature or at least tried to avoid a clear and definite answer.[24] National requirements concerning qualifications and diplomas may, however, have the effect of hindering nationals of other Member States in the exercise of their rights of establishment or to provide services guaranteed to them

21 See the Diplomas Directive 89/48/EEC and the Establishment Directive 98/5/EC.

22 Case 107/83, *Ordre des Avocats au Barreau de Paris v. Klopp* [1984] ECR 2971. See further L. Gormley, 'Freedom to practice at the Bar of more than one Member State, *ELR* 1984, p. 439-441.

23 Case 2/74, *Reyners v Belgium*, [1974], ECR 631; Case 71/76, *Thieffry*, [1977], ECR 765; Case 11/77, *Patrick*, [1977], ECR 1199; Case 107/83, *Klopp*, [1984] ECR 1971.

24 Note for example Case 182/83, *Robert Fearon v Irish Land Commission* [1984] ECR 3677 and Case 221/85, *Commission v Belgium (Clinical Biology Services)* [1987] ECR 719.

by Articles 43 and 49 ECT (formally Articles 52 and 59 ECT) without being directly or indirectly discriminatory on grounds of nationality or residence.

In *Vlassopoulou v Ministerium für Justiz, Bundes- und Europaangelegenheiten Baden-Württemberg*,[25] the Court was confronted with this problem. Irene Vlassopoulou was a Greek lawyer registered at the Athens Bar. In addition to her Greek diplomas she had a German doctorate in law. Furthermore, she had been working at a German law firm and received permission to deal with foreign legal affairs concerning Greek law and Community law in accordance with the German *Rechtsberatergesetz* in 1984. She practised German law under the responsibility of one of her German colleagues. In May 1988, Mrs. Vlassopoulou applied to the Ministery for admission to the German Bar as *Rechtsanwältin*. Her application was refused on the ground that she did not have the necessary German qualifications, laid down in the *Bundesrechtsanwaltsordnung*. Basically, those qualifications were acquired by studying law at a German university, passing the First State examination, completing a preparatory training period and then passing the Second State examination. The German Ministry clearly stated that Article 52 (now 43) of the EC Treaty did not give the right to exercise her profession in Germany with a Greek qualification. Furthermore, when Mrs. Vlassopoulou made her application in May 1988, no directive on the mutual recognition of diplomas giving access to the profession of lawyers had yet been adopted. This directive only came into existence in December of the same year.[26] The Court, however, was in the moment of its decision fully aware of the existence and the content of the Diploma Directive (89/48/EEC).

The German and Italian government therefore claimed before the European Court of Justice, that in absence of Community rules for coordinating conditions of access to the profession of lawyers and mutual recognition of legal diplomas, a Member State was still entitled to make admission to the Bar dependent on the fulfilment of non-discriminatory conditions laid down by national law. The Court, however, did not follow this line. In the *Vlassopoulou* judgment,[27] the Court ruled, that Member States were required to consider any education and training received by the migrant. The Member State must, in case of equivalence, recognize the qualification obtained in another Member State and take into account relevant practical professional experience of the migrating professional. The *Vlassopoulou* decision is clearly influenced by the so-called horizontal approach to the recognition of diplomas, an approach favoured by the Commission since the mid-eighties and finally codified in Directive 89/48/EEC on the mutual recognition of diplomas.[28]

The final, and very important steps towards a general prohibition of any restriction, whether of discriminatory or non-discriminatory nature, were finally

25 Case C-340/89, *Vlassopoulou v Ministerium für Justiz, Bundes- und Europaangelegenheiten Baden-Württemberg* [1991] ECR I-2357.

26 The Council adopted the Directive on a General System for the Recognition of Higher Education Diplomas on 21 December 1988, Council Directive 89/48/EEC *OJ* L 19, 24.1.1989, p. 16.

27 Case C-340/89, *Irene Vlassopoulou v Ministerium für Justiz, Bundes- und Europaangelegenheiten Baden-Württemberg*, ECR [1991], I-2357.

28 Council Directive 89/48/EEC *OJ* L 19, 24.1 89, p. 16.

taken in the *Kraus and Gebhard* decisions.[29] In the *Kraus* case, a restriction based on the compulsory authorization of the use of a foreign academic title, namely the LL.M. degree of the University of Edinburgh, was to be decided upon. Kraus was a German lawyer who had followed a postgraduate programme in Edinburgh and received there the title Master of Laws (LL.M.). Returning to Germany he informed the competent authorities there about the acquired title and its nature but refused to apply for the then still compulsory authorization to use it. The national authority decided that the individual authorization was still absolutely necessary for the lawful use of the title. Penalties could otherwise be due. Kraus appealed against this decision and a preliminary ruling was requested by the national administrative Court.

In its judgment of 13 March 1993,[30] the Court held that national measures liable to hinder or make less attractive the exercise of fundamental freedoms can only be justified if the Member State is able to demonstrate an objective justification and comply with the principle of proportionality. The Court accepted that the protection of the public for the abuse of academic titles could be considered as a legitimate interest justifying certain restrictions.

The Court, however, made it very clear that the authorization procedure has to fulfil a proportionality test. This means the authorization procedure must in the first place be intended solely to verify whether the postgraduate academic title obtained in another Member State was properly awarded, following a course of studies which was actually completed, in an establishment of higher education which was competent to award it. Next, the authorization procedure must be easily accessible to interested parties, and should not, in particular, be dependent on the payment of excessive administration fees.[31]

Although the importance of the facts of this case, the use of a foreign academic title with or without national authorization, can to some extent be questioned, there is no doubt of the fundamental character of this ruling for the further development of Community law in general.[32] Furthermore, it has to be considered that a post-graduate title is compulsory in some Member States for entering the civil service on a certain level or to be accepted to a doctorate programme.[33] In such a situation the hindering effect of a compulsory authorization of a foreign academic title and a burdensome procedure becomes obvious.

The case *Gebhard v Consiglio dell' Ordine degli Avvocati e Procuratori di Milano*,[34] finally, raised very important questions about the difference between cross-border legal service and establishment. Reinhard Gebhard was a German national qualified

29 Case C-19/92, *Kraus v Land Baden-Württemberg* [1993], ECR I-1663 and Case C-55/94, *Gebhard v Consiglio dell'Ordine degli Avvocati e Procuratori di Milano* [1995] ECR I-4165.

30 Case C-19/92, *Kraus v Land Baden-Württemberg* [1993], ECR I-1663, para 32.

31 Case C-19/92, *Kraus v Land Baden-Württemberg* [1993], ECR I-1663, para 38 and 39.

32 See also E. Johnson and D. O'Keefe, 'From discrimination to obstacles of free movement: recent developments concerning the free movement of workers', *CMLRev.* 1994, p. 1313.

33 This is e.g. the case in Greece.

34 Case C-55/94, *Gebhard v Consiglio dell'Ordine degli Avvocati e Procuratori di Milano* [1995] ECR I-4165.

only as German *Rechtsanwalt*. He had been admitted to the German bar and had maintained his registration there. In fact, however, he has been resident in Italy and had practised law there for several years. After having practised for more that ten years in association with an Italian law firm, he started his own business. At that moment a complaint was made by some Italian professionals to the Milan Bar Council, including those with whom he had previously worked. In this complaint it was stated that he had used the title *avvocato* on his letter-heading, had appeared under the title *avvocato* before the local courts and had practised from a law firm under his own name. The Milan Bar Council imposed on Gebhard the sanction of suspension from pursuing his professional activity for six months. Gebhard appealed against this decision to the *Consiglio Nazionale Forense* and argued, in particular, that the Lawyers' Service Directive 77/249/EEC of 22 March 1977[35] entitled him to pursue his professional activities from his own chambers in Milan.

The *Consiglio Nazionale Forense* stayed the proceedings and referred two questions on the interpretation of Directive 77/249 to the ECJ for a preliminary ruling. Unfortunately, the national court did not ask any questions regarding the applicability and possible direct effect of certain provisions of the Diplomas Directive 89/48/EEC which Italy had failed to implement in time.[36] The Court held that

> 'the concept of establishment within the meaning of the Treaty is a very broad one, allowing a Community national to participate, on a stable and continuous basis, in the economic life of a Member State other than his State of origin and to profit there from, so contributing to economic and social interpenetration within the Community in the sphere of activities as self-employed persons'.[37]

In contrast, where the provider of services moves to another Member State, the provisions of the chapter of services, in particular the third paragraph of Article 60, envisage that he is to pursue his activity on a temporary basis.[38] The temporary nature of the activities in question has to be determined in the light, not only of the duration of the provision of the service, but also of its regularity, periodicity or continuity. The Court further elaborated, that the fact that the provision of service is temporary does not mean that the provider of services within the meaning of the Treaty may not equip himself with some form of infrastructure in the host Member State (including an office, chambers or consulting rooms) in so far as such infrastructure is necessary for the purposes of performing the services in question.[39]

The Court, however, came to the conclusion that Gebhard who, as a national of a Member State, pursued a professional activity on a stable and continuous basis

35 The Lawyers' Service Directive (1977) *OJ* L 78, p. 17.

36 The Directive had to be implemented until the 4 January 1991.

37 Case C-55/94, *Gebhard v Consiglio dell'Ordine degli Avvocati e Procuratori di Milano* [1995] ECR I-4165, para 25.

38 Case C-55/94, *Gebhard v Consiglio dell'Ordine degli Avvocati e Procuratori di Milano* [1995] ECR I-4165, para 26.

39 Case C-55/94, *Gebhard v Consiglio dell'Ordine degli Avvocati e Procuratori di Milano* [1995] ECR I-4165, para 27.

in another Member State did not fall under the provisions relating to the freedom to provide of services but under the chapter relating to the right of establishment.[40]

The Court held, however, that national measures liable to hinder or make less attractive the exercise of fundamental freedoms guaranteed by the Treaty must fulfil four conditions: they must be applied in a non-dicriminatory manner, they must be justified by imperative requirements in the general interest; they must be suitable for securing the attainment of the objective which they pursue; and they must not go beyond what is necessary in order to attain it.[41]

This clearly shows that the Court accepted that in an internal market, non-discriminatory national restrictions also fall under the scope of establishment provisions and can only be justified by overriding requirements in the general interest as long as these national provisions fulfil the proportionality test. With this judgment a certain development in the Court's case law came to a final conclusion. The *Gebhard* formula has been used since several times in different contexts.[42]

In the most recent decisions of the Court of Justice concerning the legal profession, both dating from 19 February 2002, the questions related to the right of establishment were of comparatively minor importance.[43] Only in the *Wouters* case was the issue actually raised.[44] As such both cases do not concern the free movement of lawyers directly. The main issue in both cases was the applicability of competition rules to professional associations such as the national bar associations. In the *Wouters* case, the question was whether the prohibition of multi-disciplinary partnerships between members of the Bar and accountants violated competition rules. In the *Arduino* case, the ECJ had to decide upon the question whether a draft decision of the *Consiglio Nationale Forense* (National Legal Council) regarding the scale of lawyers' fees, which had to be finally approved by a ministerial degree, came within the scope of the prohibitions of Article 81 (1) and Article 10 of the EC Treaty. Both cases are of major importance for the further development of professional rules on the national and international level.

In the *Arduino* decision the Court first repeated the long established *Van Eycke* formula that principally, the Articles 5 and 85 (now 10 and 81) of the EC Treaty were infringed where a Member State required or favoured the adoption of agreements, decisions, or concerted practices contrary to Article 85 or reinforced its effects, or where it divested its own rules of the character of legislation by delegating responsibility for taking decisions affecting the economic sphere to private

40 Case C-55/94, *Gebhard v Consiglio dell'Ordine degli Avvocati e Procuratori di Milano* [1995] ECR I-4165, para 28.

41 Case C-55/94, *Gebhard v Consiglio dell'Ordine degli Avvocati e Procuratori di Milano* [1995] ECR I-4165, para 37.

42 In the Case C-212/97, *Centros* [1999], ECR I-1459 the Court had employed that formula for the first time in the context of the establishment of companies.

43 Case C-309/99, *J.C.J Wouters et al. v Agemene Raad van Advocaten*, 19 February 2002 and Case C-35/99, *Criminal Proceedings v. Manuele Arduino*, 19 February 2002. Only in the *Wouters* Case questions regarding the freedom of establishment and the freedom to provide services were actually raised. See further A. Vossestein, Case Note, *CML Review* 39, 2002, p. 841-863.

44 Case C-309/99, *J.C.J Wouters et al. v Agemene Raad van Advocaten*, 19 February 2002.

economic operators.[45] The ECJ generally accepted the applicability of competition rules to the liberal professions. The Court, however, came to the conclusion that the conditions defined by the *Van Eycke* formula were not fulfilled by the Italian legislation in question. The Court, therefore, decided that the competition rules did not preclude a Member State from adopting legislation which approved, on the basis of a draft produced by a professional body of members of the Bar, a tariff fixing minimum and maximum fees for the members of the profession.

In the *Wouters* decision the ECJ concluded first that the registered members of the Bar of the Netherlands carried on an economic activity and were, consequently, undertakings for the purpose of Articles 85, 86 and 90 (now 81, 82 and 86) of the EC Treaty.[46] Furthermore, the Court came to the conclusion, contrary to the intervening German, Austrian and Portugese governments, that a professional organization such as the Bar of the Netherlands had to be regarded as an association of undertakings and that a regulation concerning partnerships between members of the Bar and other members of liberal professions adopted by a body such as the Bar of the Netherlands, had to be regarded as a decision adopted by an association of undertakings within the meaning of Article 85 (1) (now 81(1)) of the EC Treaty.[47]

Surprisingly, the Court then concluded, however, that the Bar of the Netherlands could reasonably have considered that a regulation which prohibited any multi-disciplinary partnerships between members of the Bar and accountants was necessary for the proper practice of the legal profession in the Netherlands. The Court accepted the necessity of the Dutch national measure, even if, as the Court affirmed, multi-disciplinary partnerships of lawyers and accountants were allowed in some Member States.[48] With this ruling and the reference to 'proper practice' as a sort of general interest and to a necessity requirement the Court seems to have introduced a sort of 'rule of reason' in competition law.[49] With the same argument and the same reference to 'proper practice' as justification for the national provisions, the Court also denied a violation of Article 52 and 59 (now 43 and 49) EC Treaty.[50] The consequences of this step taken by the ECJ for the future development of competition law and not only with regard to the liberal profession

45 Case C-35/99, *Criminal Proceedings v. Manuele Arduino*, 19 February 2002, para 35 refering to Case 267/86, *Van Eycke* [1988] ECR 4769, para 16; Case C-185/91, *Reiff* [1993] ECR I-5801, para 14; Case C-153/93, *Delta Schiffahrts- und Speditionsgesellschaft* [1994] ECR I-2517, para 14; Case C-96/94, *Centro Servizi Spediporto* [1995] ECR I-2883, para 20,21 and Case C 35/96, *Commission v Italy* [1998] ECR I-3851, 54.

46 Case C-309/99, *J.C.J Wouters et al. v Agemene Raad van Advocaten*, 19 February 2002, para 49 refering also to the joined Cases C-180/98 to C-184/98, *Pavlov and Others* [2000] ECR I-6451, para 77 with regard to medical practioners.

47 Case C-309/99, *J.C.J Wouters et al. v Agemene Raad van Advocaten*, 19 February 2002, para 64 and 71.

48 Case C-309/99, *J.C.J Wouters et al. v Agemene Raad van Advocaten*, 19 February 2002, para 108.

49 Case C-309/99, *J.C.J Wouters et al. v Agemene Raad van Advocaten*, 19 February 2002, para 97-109.

50 Case C-309/99, *J.C.J Wouters et al. v Agemene Raad van Advocaten*, 19 February 2002, para 119-123.

can not yet be fully appreciated. In any case, again a lawyer's case has proven to be a landmark decision for the development of Community law in general.

3. Secondary Community Legislation and the Recognition of Diplomas

3.1. The Vertical Approach

Through the years the Community has followed different strategies with regard to the recognition of diplomas.[51] Back in the 1960s the European Community chose to follow a vertical or sectoral approach to the recognition of professional qualifications. Initially, several such directives - relating in particular, to occupations and sectors in commerce, industry and small craft industries - were adopted in order to facilitate access to specific occupations by guaranteeing, subject to certain conditions, recognition in the host Member State of work experience gained in the home Member State. This type of directive has been called transitional measures because of pending mutual recognition of diplomas. Although their status was originally be intended to be only transitional they remained for quite a period of time.[52] Only very recently a considerable consolidation of these 35 transitional directives was achieved through the so-called third General System Directive 1999/42/EC.[53] No directives, however, had been adopted in that period dealing with the traditional regulated professions, e.g. lawyers, accountants, engineers, doctors or architects.

In the seventies, the Community's approach to the problem of recognition of diplomas for the traditional regulated professions became vertical: that is to say, recognition was provided individually, profession by profession, with a minimum harmonization or co-ordination of the education and training required for each profession in the Member States. The principal procedure was to pass two directives simultaneously, one based on Article 57 (1) (now 47 (1)) of the EC Treaty regulating the recognition of the diplomas and a second directive based on Article 57 (2) (now 47 (2)) concerning the co-ordination of education. The first sectoral directives dealing with a traditional profession concerned doctors (1975). These directives set the pattern for subsequent directives dealing with other 'medical, allied and pharmaceutical professions': nurses (1977),[54] dentists (1978),[55] veterinary surgeons (1978),[56] midwives (1980)[57] and pharmacists (1985).[58]

51 See H. Schneider, *supra* note 18.

52 P.M. Storm and R.H. Hooghoudt, 'Doorwerking in Nederland van het vrije verkeer van personen en diensten', *RM Themis*, 1980, p. 473.

53 European Pariament and Council Directive establishing a mechanism for the recognition of qualifications in respect of professional activities covered by the Directives on liberalization and transitional measures and supplementing the general systems for recognition of qualifications, COM(96) 22 final of 8 February 1996.

54 Directive 77/452/EEC, *OJ* 1977, L 176, p. 1.

55 Directive 78/686/EEC, *OJ* 1978, L 233, p. 1.

56 Directive 78/1026/EEC, *OJ* 1978, L 362, p. 1.

57 Directive 80/154/EEC, *OJ* 1980, L33, p. 1.

58 Directive 85/433/EEC, *OJ* 1985, 253, 37.

For each profession there are two directives: the Mutual Recognition Directive and the Co-ordination Directive. The Mutual Recognition Directive specifies the general and specialist diplomas awarded in each Member State which must be recognised by the other Member States. It makes special provision for those who have already been licensed to practise without possessing one of the specified diplomas. Furthermore, the Directive deals with matters such as the use of academic and professional titles, certificates of good character, criminal and disciplinary offences, certificates of personal health and the wording of professional oaths. In addition, the Directive includes special provisions with regard to transfrontier medical services.

The Co-ordination Directive lays down the minimum education and training required for the award of a mutually recognised diploma. The original Doctors' Directives were accompanied by Council Decisions setting up an Advisory Committee on Medical Training and a Committee of Senior Officials on Public Health. The advantage of this vertical recognition system is that a professional who has acquired a certain diploma listed in one of the directives can establish himself freely through the whole Community without any further educational requirements.

Apart from directives for the medical professions sectoral directives were adopted for lawyers (1977) and architects (1985).[59] In contrast to the directives for the medical professions, however, the Lawyers' Service Directive deals not with harmonization of the legal educational systems nor with permanent establishment in the host Member State but only with transfrontier 'legal services'. The Directive was as such designed as a very limited measure to cover only the temporary provision of services. This includes general advisory work in the host Member State as well as the right for visiting lawyers to represent clients before the courts. At first sight, this right to represent clients before the courts of the host Member State even seems to be considerably limited by Article 5 of the Lawyers' Service Directive. This provision requires the service-providing lawyer to act in conjunction with a host State lawyer while representing his clients before courts. The Court of Justice, however, has ruled in a *Commission's* case against Germany that this requirement does not apply in all cases where the assistance of a lawyer is not a mandatory requirement under domestic legislation and where, consequently, a party would be entitled to defend his own interest or even to entrust that task to a person who is not a lawyer.[60] The Court confirmed this interpretation of Article 5 of the Lawyers' Service Directive again in a case against France.[61]

3.2. *The Horizontal Approach*

Experience has shown that the process of drafting, agreeing upon and implementing sectoral directives is long and laborious. In some cases, e.g. the directives for architects and pharmacists, it took more than eighteen years to pass the direc-

59 Directive 85/384/EEC, *OJ* 1985 L 223, p. 15.
60 Case 427/85, *Commission of the European Communities v. Germany* [1988] ECR 1123.
61 Case 294/89, *Commission of the European Communities v. France* [1991] ECR I-3591.

tives in the Council. In some cases, regarding for example, engineers, the Council could not come to an agreement at all. Furthermore, it has been proven that the already existing sectoral directives could only with great difficulties be adapted to new developments. The sectoral harmonization method was, therefore, been abandoned by the Commission in the mid-eighties. Instead, a new strategy of mutual recognition without prior harmonization for the mutual recognition of diplomas was introduced with Directive 89/48/EEC.

3.2.1. The First General System Directive 89/48/EEC

The roots of Directive 89/48/EEC can be traced back to the European Council on 25 and 26 June 1984 in Fontainebleau. There it was noted that the Community, in spite of its high ideals did not mean very much to the people of Europe. Urgent action was needed to make a reality of a 'Europe without frontiers'. The Heads of State and Government deeming it indispensable to respond to the expectation of the peoples of Europe, called upon the Communities institutions to introduce a 'general system for ensuring the equivalence of university diplomas in order to bring about the effective freedom of establishment within the Community'. The Commission responded to this appeal with a proposal for a directive submitted to the Council on 9 July 1985 which subsequently became Directive 89/48/EEC.

Directive 89/48/EEC is a manifestation of the 'europhoria' which followed the Single European Act and the prospect of the completion of the internal market by the end of 1992. This goal was initially set out in the Commission's White Paper on Completing the Internal Market.[62] The White Paper proclaimed the need to eliminate legal and economic barriers among the Member States in order to create a single integrated market. The new strategy was a broader shift towards mutual recognition without prior harmonization as a means of eliminating barriers to the establishment of the internal market. The aim of the Directive was to speed up the process of giving effect to the freedom of establishment for the professions in the European Community. The basic philosophy underlying the Directive was the principle of mutual trust in the quality of the educational systems and the professional training in the other Member States.

Meanwhile, in addition to Directive 89/48/EEC, the Council adopted Directive 92/51/EEC, which follows the same horizontal approach. It covers the recognition of diplomas of post-secondary courses of less than three years and vocational training certificates. In 1999 the Council has adopted a third Directive based on the horizontal approach.[63] One of the aims of this Directive was to clarify and simplify Community legislation in the area of the so-called 'transitional measures' relating in particular to commerce, industry and small craft industries.

62 COM(85) 310, June 1985.

63 European Pariament and Council Directive establishing a mechanism for the recognition of qualifications in respect of professional activities covered by the Directives on liberalization and transitional measures and supplementing the general systems for recognition of quailfications, COM(96) 22 final of 8 February 1996.

The horizontal approach is based on the assumption that any professional who is fully qualified in one Member State possesses the qualifications needed to practice the same profession in another Member State. The diploma of such a professional has to be recognized according to Article 3 of the Directive. Only where the training undergone differs substantially from that required by the host Member State, the latter may require the shortfalls to made up. Therefore, Article 4 of the Directive contains the so-called compensation mechanisms. The compensatory instruments chosen are either an aptitude test or an adaptation period.

Unlike under the Directives on transitional measures, recognition of professional experience gained in the home Member State does not, in itself, entitle the migrant to immediate authorization to take up and pursue the same profession in the host Member State. His professional experience, however, has to be taken into account by the competent authorities in the host Member State when determining what further training has to be completed or what form of aptitude test has to be passed in order to compensate for any substantial differences between the education and training undergone by the migrant and that required in order to practice in the host Member State.

In this regard, the ruling of the Court of Justice in the *Vlassopoulou* decision could be considered as an interpretation of the principles laid down in Directive 89/48/EEC on a general system for the recognition of higher educational diplomas, even if the *Vlassopoulou* ruling was given without a direct reference to the Directive.[64] Very recently this '*Vlassopoulou* principle' was even codified in Directive 2001/19/EC on professional recognition.[65]

3.2.2. Directive 89/48/EEC and the Legal Profession

Directive 89/48/EEC includes special rules for the legal profession. Generally, the migrant can choose between the two different compensatory mechanisms, aptitude test and adaptation period. In the case of the legal profession it is up to the host Member State, however, to make that choice. Most Member States have chosen the aptitude test as the compensatory instrument for the legal profession. Only Denmark seems to have taken an exceptional stand and recognises foreign lawyers after an adaptation period. 'Legal professions' in the sense of the Directive means lawyers (advocates), accountants, patent attorneys, tax advisors and, under certain conditions, notaries. Notaries form a special category. Not all the Member States have passed a law for notaries. Many Member States relied on the exception

64 Case C-340/89, *Irene Vlassopoulou v Ministerium für Justiz, Bundes- und Europaangelegenheiten Baden-Württemberg*, ECR [1991], I-2357.

65 Directive 2001/19/EC of the European Parliament and of the Council of 14 May 2001 amending Council Directives 89/48/EEC on the general system of professional qualifications and Council Directives 77/452/EEC, 77/453/EEC, 78/686/EEC, 78/687/EEC, 78/1026/EEC, 78/1027/EEC, 80/154/EEC, 80/155/EEC, 85/384/EEC, 85/385/EEC, 85/432/EEC, 85/433/EEC and 93/16/EEC concerning the professions of nurse responsible for general care, dental practioner, veterinary surgeon, midwife, architect, pharmacist and doctor (SLIM Directive), *OJ* L 206 of 31.7.2001, p. 1.

contained in Article 45 EC Treaty and in all countries were the Latin notary profession exists, a nationally requirement is still in evidence.

According to a First Commission's Report on the state of implementation of the Directive some 620 lawyers obtained recognition under the Directive until autumn 1995. Recognition mostly took place after having passed an aptitude test. Direct recognition without any compensation was granted for migrant lawyers between England and Wales and the Republic of Ireland. Since then, more than 2000 lawyers have been recognised. According to Article 7 of the Directive a lawyer who achieves recognition according to Article 3 is allowed to use the professional title of the host member State corresponding to that profession. This means e.g. a Dutch lawyer who passes the aptitude test before the Law Society in London will be able to use the foreign title ,solicitor' acquired by recognition alongside his home title of 'advocat'.

It has to be noted that a lawyer can only rely on the Directive if he is a fully trained professional. This means he has to have completed not only the academic legal education but also the necessary professional training required in the Member State of origin.[66] Article 5 only encourages Member States but does not obliged them, to allow the applicant to undergo the necessary professional training which he has not undergone in his Member State of origin.

3.2.3. Implementation of Directive 89/48/EEC

Directive 89/48/EEC required Member States to take the appropriate measures to comply with it by 4 January 1991.[67] The majority of the Member States were late passing the necessary measures.[68] Ireland, Denmark and the United Kingdom were the first to pass general legislative acts.

Two contrasting methods of implementation were adopted. Some of the Member States implemented the Directive by one general act of legislation, completed, in some cases, by detailed regulations for specific professions. This was done in Denmark,[69] Ireland,[70] Italy,[71] the Netherlands,[72] Portugal,[73] Spain[74] and the United Kingdom.[75]

66 Only Spain does not have a compulsory professional trainingsperiod for advocates. A Spanish lawyer can, therefore, rely on the directive 89/48/EEC directly after the conclusion of academic studies.

67 Art. 12 of Directive 89/48/EEC.

68 Of the then 12 Member States only Ireland had adopted the necessary measures by the 4th January 1991.

69 Act concerning access to pursue certain professions in Denmark for nationals of the European Communities and the Nordic countries, No 291 from 8 May 1991, see further H. Schneider, *supra* note 18, p. 219 *et seq.*

70 Statutory Instrument S. No. 1 of 1991, see further H. Schneider, *supra* note 18, p. 222.

71 Legge communitaria per il 1990, Gazzetta Ufficiale from 12 January 1991, see further H. Schneider, *supra* note 18, p. 224.

72 Algemeene Wet erkenning EG-hoger-onderwijsdiploma's from 19 January 1994, Stb. 1994, 29 and 30, see further H. Schneider, *supra* note 18, p. 229.

Other Member States used a sectoral implementation approach, implementing the Directive with different acts for each profession involved. This method was used by Germany,[76] France,[77] Luxembourg[78] as well by Belgium and Greece.[79] The Netherlands also passed some sectoral measures.[80] In the case of Belgium and Greece, however, the Court of Justice has established their failure to implement the Directive in time. Both Member States had passed only a very limited number of sectoral implementation measures in an appropriate time.[81] A case against the Netherlands was dropped after the Dutch implementation law was finally published. Nevertheless, the Netherlands can be considered as being very late with the implementation of the first General System Directive. This was especially true for the Dutch implementation for the legal profession.[82]

The Member States which joined the Community in 1995, on the contrary, had finished their task with great success. The three Member States had all adopted implementing measures by the date of accession. Austria and Sweden have implemented the Directive in the sectoral way, while Finland has passed a general law and a corresponding regulation.[83]

3.3. The Establishment Directive for Lawyers

In principle, the Commission had abandoned the vertical approach in the mid-eighties, with only one exception. The Commission has been prepared to draft specific directives if two preconditions have been fulfilled: An agreement must have been reached within the profession and the national authorities must show their

73 Decreto-Lei no 289/91 from 10 August 1991, Diario da Republica no. 183, see further H. Schneider, *supra* note 18, p. 230.

74 Real Decreto 1665/1991 from 25 October 1991, BOE 280 from 22 November 1991, see further H. Schneider, *supra* note 18, p. 232.

75 Statutory Instrument 1991 No 824 Professional Qualifications, The European Communities (Recognition of professional Qualifications) Regulation 1991, see further H. Schneider, *supra* note 18, p. 233.

76 Gesetz über die Eignungsprüfung für die Zulassung zur Rechtsanwaltschaft, BGBl 1990, Teil I, 1349 und Verordnung für die Zulassung zur Rechtsanwaltschaft BGBl 1990, Teil I, 2881, see further H. Schneider, *supra* note 18, p. 291.

77 Loi No 90-1259 from 31 December 1990, see further H. Schneider, *supra* note 18, p. 324.

78 Loi du 10 août 1991, Mémorial No 58 from 27 August 1991, see further H. Schneider, *supra* note 18, p. 332.

79 See H. Schneider, *supra* note 18, p. 208.

80 For the legal profession exist next to the general law (Algemene Wet erkenning EG hoge onderwijsdiploma's, Stb. 1994, 29) also two instruments passd by the Dutch Bar, Verordening op de Prove van Bekwaamheid from 13 September 1996, *Stcrt.* 1996, 197 and Regelement des Nederlands Orde van Advocaten from 14 October 1996, *Advocatenblad* 22 November 1996, 1112.

81 Case C-365/93, *Commission v Greece* [1995], ECR I-499 and Case C-216/94, *Commission v Belgium* [1995] ECR I-2155.

82 This late implementation is now going to be repeated in the case of the Establishment Directive 98/5. Again a procedure of the Commission before the ECJ has been started.

83 See H. Schneider, *supra* note 18, p. 293.

support for such an initiative.[84] These conditions were fulfilled for an establishment directive for lawyers. At the invitation of the Commission, the Council of the Bars and Law Societies of the European Community (CCBE) drafted a directive which was accepted by the CCBE in October 1992 after seventeen years of negotiations.[85] The lawyers of all the Member States - with the sole exception of Luxembourg - principally agreed on the fact that a specific directive for lawyers was needed. The CCBE took the view that the general system has not worked satisfactorily for the lawyers' profession in all aspects: Directive 89/48/EEC does not solve the question of the right to practise on a permanent basis under the home Member State title. Furthermore, experience has shown that the aptitude test as required by the majority of the Member States has often constituted a real obstacle to the freedom of establishment for lawyers. Internationally active lawyers want to be able to move easily between different Member States and establish themselves there without going through a burdensome recognition procedure by passing an aptitude test. They mostly are not interested in acquiring the professional title of the host Member State as long as they can establish themselves easily under home title.

The Commission published its own proposal based on the CCBE draft at the end of 1994.[86] This first Commission's proposal differed considerably on two very essential points from the original CCBE draft. According to the CCBE draft, lawyers are allowed to establish themselves under 'home title' in another Member State on a permanent basis, while the original proposal of the Commission included the obligation for the migrant to integrate fully into the profession of the host Member State after a period of five years. The Commission's Draft Directive was heavily criticized.[87] The five year limitation on the right to practise under home title in other Member States, one of the Commission's alterations, could not be considered to be in accordance with Article 43 (formally 52) of the EC Treaty.

After the Gebhard judgment in 1995, the draft Directive made, however, more rapidly progress through the European legislative machinery.[88] The original provision of a right to practise under home title on a permanent basis was reintroduced. The Directive was finally adopted on 16 February 1998 and published in the *Official Journal* on 14 March 1998.[89] Its full title is 'Directive 98/5/EC of The European

84 See Lord Cockfields explanations towards the European Parliament in October 1988: 'We would not, however, exclude subsequent specific complementary directives once the geneal system is in operation, provided that the profession concerned supported the move and was already in agreement as to the content of the further directive, and that it could be shown that a specific directive would maker movement between Member States more easy'. *OJ* 2-370/114, 26 October 1988.

85 This agreement of the CCBE became known as the Lisbon compromise or as one author called it 'the miracle of Lisbon'.

86 COM(94) 572 final of 21 December 1994.

87 House of Lords Select Committee of the European Communities, *Establishment of Lawyers, HL Session 1994-95*, 14th Report London, HMSO, 1995, p. 10 and 69; H. Adamson, *Free Movement of lawyers*, 2nd ed., London, Butterworth, 1998, p. 90 *et seq.*; H. Schneider, *supra* note 18, p. 284.

88 H. Adamson, *Free Movement of lawyers*, 2nd ed., London, Butterworth, 1998, p. 94.

89 *OJ* L 77, 14.3.1998, p. 36.

Parliament and of the Council to Facilitate Practice of the Profession of Lawyer on a Permanent Basis in a Member State other than that in which the Qualification is Obtained'. Luxembourg which had opposed the Directive from its very beginning, lodged an action with the ECJ for annulment of the Directive. Luxembourg argued that it should have been adopted unanimously by the Council. The proceedings were rejected by the ECJ by decision of 7 of November 2000[90] and the Directive considered valid. According to Article 16 the Directive 98/5/EC had to be implemented by 14 of March 2000. Since then, Austria, Denmark Finland, Germany, Greece, Italy, Sweden, Spain, the United Kingdom and Norway as a Member State of the European Economic Area have implemented the Directive.[91]

Article 2 of the Directive 98/5 EC gives the right to a lawyer to pursue on a permanent basis in another Member State under his home country professional title the activities further specified in Article 5 of Directive 98/5. According to Article 5 (1) of the Directive a lawyer practising under home state title may carry on all professional activities carried on by the lawyer of the host State, namely advice on home State law, Community and international law, and host State law. The possibility to advice on host state law was one of the issues heavily discussed during the negotiations in the Council. Articles 5 (2) and (3) contain some limitations on the full rights of practice. Article 5 (3) repeats the provisions of Article 5 of the Lawyers' Service Directive relating to practice before courts of the host State. The precise formulation, however, is modified according to the case law of the ECJ, in particular the judgment *Commission v Germany*.[92] Consequently, a migrant lawyer does not have to work in conjunction with a local lawyer in any case where the litigant could act in person or where representation other than by a host State lawyer is allowed.

Article 10 of Directive 98/5 lays down the procedure for a migrant lawyer wishing to achieve full integration into the profession of the host State. A migrant lawyer can also prefer to continue indefinitely to practise under home title. Article 10 (2) only clarifies that a lawyer practising under home title may at any time apply for recognition under the Diploma Directive 89/48/EEC. As such the recognition will take place according to Articles 3 and 4 of Directive 89/48/EEC. Articles 10 (1) and 10 (3) provide two new alternative routes to the already existing recognition mechanism according to Directive 89/48/EEC. They have the clear purpose of avoiding the requirements of an aptitude test. Direct recognition has to take place according to Article 10 (1) if the migrant lawyer has practised for a period of three years in the host Member State and he can show that he has 'effectively and regularly' pursued an activity in the law of that State including Community law. In such a case, the migrant lawyer is exempted from any compensatory instrument such as the aptitude test of Article 4 of Directive 89/48/EEC. If a lawyer does not fulfil the requirements of Article 10 (1) completely, he may fall back on Article 10 (3). Instead of complete exemption from the conditions of Article 4 of Directive 89/48/EEC, the migrant lawyer 'may obtain' from the competent authority admission to the

90 Case C-168/98, *Luxembourg v European Parliament and Council*, ECR [2000].

91 See overview on the website of the CCBE: <http://www.CCBE.org>.

92 Case 427/85, *Commission of the European Communities v. Germany* [1988] ECR 1123.

profession of the host State without having to meet the conditions of Article 4 of Directive 89/48/EEC. This provision gives the competent authorities a certain degree of discretion.

The reference to Community law as part of the national law of the host Member State seems to include the possibility that a migrant lawyer who solely practised Community law for a period of three years, without any involvement in national law, can nevertheless demand according to Article 10 (1) direct integration into the profession of the host Member State.

Articles 11 and 12 of the Directive regulate the possibility of joint practice in different variations including the joint practice of several lawyers of different Member States and joint practice between migrating lawyers and host State lawyers.[93] The manner in which such lawyers practise jointly in the host Member State shall be governed by the law and regulations of that State.

The effects of Directive 98/5/EC for the legal profession in detail can not yet fully be seen. One will have to wait a couple of years to see more clearly how many lawyers will indeed use it and to what extent the mobility in the profession will increase. It seems, however, already quite obvious that compared to twenty years ago, the professional legal market has undergone an enormous and fundamental change and that this development certainly will not stop but on the contrary continue and further increase. This has, as I have already stated, direct consequences for the legal education, its structure and its content.

4. Consequences for the Legal Education

If we look at the length and the structure of the legal academic and professional education in the Member States as it exists today we can see quite considerable differences regarding the study and training periods in total.[94] In particular, the organization and duration of the professional training period in order to become a fully qualified lawyer (advocate) vary dramatically between the different Member States. Spain has, for example, no compulsory professional training period at all. Consequently, the academic education of five years corresponds with the total length of legal education in that Member State. Other countries have on the contrary very long professional trainings requirements.[95]

93 See further H. Adamson, *Free Movement of Lawyers*, 2nd ed., London, Butterworth, 1998, p. 121.

94 The number of years given in the overview are based on the norms regulated and not on the statistics of factual lenght of study periods. Here differences between the Member States are again quite extreme.

95 See the national reports in the special issue: 'Legal Education and Training in Europe', *International Journal of the Legal Profession*, vol. 2, number 1, 1995. Further M.J. Allmayer-Beck, 'Professional Training of Lawyers in the European Union', in Bundesministerium des Justitz der Republik Österreich (ed.), *The Significance of Idenpendent Legal Professions in an Integrated Europe*, Manz, Stämpfli, Wien, Bern, 1999, p. 141 and J. Lonbay, 'Differences in the Legal Education in the Member States of the European Community', in B. de Witte and C. Forder (eds.), *The Common Law of Europe and the Future of Legal Education*, Deventer, Kluwer, 1992, p. 75-93.

Country	Academic education and title	Academic education in years
Belgium	licence en droit/Licenciaat in de rechten	5
Denmark	cand. jus.	5
Germany[96]	Referendarexamen	3,5 (4)
Finland	universitydegree L.L.M. lakimies	5
France	Maîtrise	4
Greece	university degree	4
Ireland	law degree	3
Italy[97]	laurea giurisprudenza	4 (5)[98]
Luxembourg	no nat. legal education	4 oder 5
Netherlands	Meester in de rechten	4
Austria	Magister Juris Doctor Juris	4 5
Portugal	lic. en direito	5
Sweden	jur kand	4/5
Spain	lic. en derecho	5
United Kingdom	law degree, LL.B.	3 (4 years in case of law & languages)

96 In Germany just very recently a reform of the legal education has been excepted on federal level. Whether this will lead to a fundamental difference for the length of the legal education in practice can not yet be predicted. Until now, the lenght of the legal education in fact was considerably longer than the regulated 6 years: BT-Drucksache 14/8629.

97 Italy has quite recently adopted new legislation regarding the legal education by adopting a Bachelor-Master structure. Legge 19 Octobre 1999, N-370 'Disposizione in material di università e di ricetca scientifica e tecnologica'.

98 New system: first three years lead to a degree called 'laurea' and the second one, lasting two years, will lead to a degree called 'laurea specilistica'.

Country	Length of professional education	Complete length of the legal education in years
Belgium	3	8
Denmark	3	8
Germany	2,5	6
Finland	4	9
France	3	7
Greece	1,5	5,5
Ireland	2	5
Italy	2	6
Luxembourg	3	7 or 8
Netherlands	3	7
Austria[99]	Magister juris: 7 Doctor juris:6	11 11
Portugal	1,5	6,5
Sweden	5	9/10
Spain	0	5
United Kingdom	3	6 (7 In case of law & language LL.B)

On the other hand, the majority of the Member States have a four to five years academic legal curriculum. It should, however, be remembered that in most continental Member States (e.g. Austria, Denmark, Germany, Italy, France, Greece) there are huge differences between the official and the real duration of studies. The years given in the overview can, therefore, be considered as being more theoretical than realistic. Although some Member States tried in the past seriously to take

99 Reforms in Austria have also been strongly discussed and therefore it can be expected that the length of the Austrian legal education will certainly be shortened considerably in the near future.

measures aimed at reducing the real duration to the theoretical period of studies, they were not always successful.[100]

Only Ireland and the United Kingdom have a first law degree lasting three years. This degree gives access to the professional training. It is important to note, however, that the faculties in the United Kingdom which offer a so-called 'law & language programme' have organised this in a four-year bachelor structure. Mainly students following this type of bachelor programme are those who participate as *Erasmus/Socrates* students in an exchange programme. There also exists four-year British law programmes organised jointly with some continental faculties. These programmes lead to a double academic qualification.[101] If one looks at the European legal education as whole, it must therefore stongly be pointed out that there is very little convergence around a first degree after 3 years in Europe.[102]

This brings me to my final remarks on the development of a European Space for Higher Education, also known as the so-called *Bologna* process. I can give here only a very short historic overview.[103]

In May 1998, the Ministers responsible for higher education in France, Germany, Italy and the United Kingdom met to celebrate the Sorbonne university's eight-hundredth anniversary. In the course of the celebration and a concurrent conference, they signed a 'Joint declaration on the harmonization of the architecture of the European higher educational system'. This became known as the *Sorbonne* declaration. One has to note here that in France the Attali report including recommendations for educational reforms in France had just been published in May 1998 and that in Germany the *Hochschulrahemengesetz* was amended in August 1998. In the new *Hochschulrahmengesetz* bachelor's and master's degrees were introduced as the traditional German degrees are less known and, therefore, less attractive for foreign students. The option was given to choose between four years undergraduate cycles with a one year master programme or three years bachelor degrees with a two years master programme was given to the German faculties.

In the *Attali* report the existence or emergence of a single European model of higher education was proposed, based on a sequence of studies and degrees of 3-5-8 years and a Bachelor-Master-Doctorate structure. The *Sorbonne* Declaration, however, only recommended that studies should be organised in an undergraduate cycle leading to a first qualification and a graduate cycle leading to a master degree. Although an extensive debate has taken place based on the assertions in the *Attali* report, an indication on the duration of these cyles was not provided. The only indication being that the undergraduate programme should have a minimum of

100 See G.R. de Groot and H. Schneider, 'Juristenausbildung am Vorabend des 21. Jahrhunderts, in U. Hubner and W. Ebke (eds.), *Festschrifft für Bernhard Großfeld*, Heidelberg, Verlag Recht und Wirtschaft GmbH, 1999, p. 307.

101 For example a French/English degree that offers the possiblity to undergo the professional training in both of the jurisdictions.

102 See also the Project Report of Guy Haug, *Main Trends and Issues in Higher Education Structures in Europe*, prepared for the Bologna meeting on 18 June 1999, p. 5.

103 See also E. Hackl, *Towards a European Area of Higher Education: Change and Convergence in European Higher Education*, EUI Working Papers, RSC No. 2001/09.

three years. Furthermore, Guy Haug,[104] clearly underlined in a report 'Main Trends and Issues in Higher Education Structure in Europe' which was prepared for the *Bologna* meeting of the Ministers of Education that a model strictly following the pattern 3-5-8 does not exist. No country in Europe has such a system across the board in all sectors of higher education or all disciplines.[105] Bachelor programmes with four or even more years exist even in the United Kingdom, while there are master programmes with a one-year as well as a two-years duration.

A year after the *Sorbonne* Declaration, in June 1999, Minister for Education from 29 European countries met in Bologna, to sign this document, the so-called *Bologna* Declaration. Many of the signatories are countries from Central and Eastern Europe. It has therefore strongly to be underlined that this *Bologna* Declaration is not a legal instrument passed in the context of the European Union or even the European Community. The binding character of this declaration is therefore very limited, especially as many of the Ministers involved by the setting up of this Declaration had, from the perspective of their national constitutional system, no legitimacy to bind the national legislators and authorities in this area of law. This clearly is the case as far as federal States are concerned where the legislative power as regards educational matters rest at State/*Länder* level (e.g. Belgium and Germany).

The *Bologna* Declaration is, in my opinion, a very typical form of soft law with all its democratic deficits. Soft law is according to Francis Snyder ‚rules of conduct which, in principle, have no binding force, which nevertheless may have practical effects'.[106] If we see the effects of the *Bologna* Declaration then it certainly fulfils these criteria. In addition to the Netherlands, also Austria, France, Germany, Italy and Norway have started to adapt their systems to a Bachelor – Master structure. In some of the Nordic and Central and Eastern European Country the bachelor-master model is already used.

It is quite remarkable, however, that at the European Council meeting under the Portuguese Presidency in Feira in March 2000, the Member States of the European Union could not come to an agreement for 'the Establishment of a European Area of Education'. On the other hand, in May 2001 another Education Summit outside the European Union context took place in Prague in order to review the *Bologna* Process.

Meanwhile the Netherlands have started to implement the *Bologna* Declaration. In my opinion unfortunately, the Dutch government has chosen for a 3 + 1 structure for the majority of university education including law. The bachelor is

104 Principal Adviser, European Association of Universities (CRE), Geneva/Paris.

105 Project Report of Guy Haug, *Main Trends and Issues in Higher Education Structures in Europe*, prepared for the *Bologna* meeting on 18 June 1999, p. 5.

106 F. Snyder, *Soft Law and Institutional Practice in the EU Community*, EUI Working Paper, No. 93/5, p. 2.

supposed to take three years, the master programme one year. This form of implementation will not be in line with the majority of the continental European States. [107]

I call this development unfortunate because I do not think that it is an adequate reaction on the *Bologna* process. Until now, the minimum legal education in the Netherlands for the first law degree has been four years. These four years are necessary for the so-called 'civil effect' in order to enter the professional training.

The Dutch three years bachelor degree of the future will not give this civil effect and will therefore not be sufficient for access to professional training. Consequently, students will have to follow a master course in order to have access to the traditional legal professions and to the European legal market as layers. This form of master course will, however, not be a specialized academic graduate LL.M. degree like in the United Kingdom or in the United States, for which students can be selected and mostly will have to pay. On the contrary, this Dutch master will still be part of the basic legal education leading to the 'civil effect'. The use of the English name 'master' is therefore very misleading.

Finally, I call the Dutch way of implementation very unfortunate, as it will in my opinion lead not only to even less transparency of academic titles,[108] but even - and this may be worse - to less international exchange of students on the undergraduate level. For the Dutch law faculties it will become very difficult in the future to send undergraduates abroad in the framework of the *Socrates* exchange because traditionally this exchange took place during the fourth year. This fourth year will, in the future, be organised in the form of a special one year Master programme. It does not seem very likely that half of this year can be spent abroad, if a special degree has to be issued at the end of that period. Longer periods, like a one-year exchange, will be impossible if not organised in the form of a joint degree. This development might have serious consequences for the already more than ten years existing 'law and language programme (*Europees Recht en Taal Studies*, ERTS) at the faculty of law in Maastricht.

It has, however, finally to be stressed again that nothing is against the creation of a European Area of Education. The opportunity should, however, be used to create further internationalization of legal education and more academic mobility and not to destroy student exchange networks and international legal educational programmes built up in the last twenty years. A bachelor-master structure in the form of 3 + 1 can, in my opinion, only be defended for budgetary reasons but certainly will not contribute towards a more coherent European Higher Education Space.

107 See Final Report of the CRE Project, *Towards Accreditation Schemes for Higher Education in Europe?*, February 2001. The majority of states will choose for five year education, either in the form of 3 + 2 or 4 + 1. See e.g. § 19 of the German Hochschulrahmengesetz.

108 A three years Dutch bachelor law degree will not be comparable to a three years British law degree as the later gives access to professional training while the Dutch one will not.

Ewoud Hondius

THE EUROPEAN PRIVATE LAW MOVEMENT AND THE CHANGES IT REQUIRES IN LEGAL EDUCATION AND RESEARCH

1. Introduction

Today, we celebrate the first twenty years of the Faculty of Law of the University of Maastricht. Twenty years of innovation in teaching and research have been the fruits of this endeavour. In this paper, I wish to explore the changes in legal education and research which the next decade will require in terms of the commitment of staff, students and the administration. Maastricht likes to reckon in decades. The first decade of its existence saw the introduction of the functional approach in law teaching (1.1.). A decade later, in 1991, came the foundation of the European Law School (1.2.). The coming decade - on which this paper will focus - should be devoted to the introduction of European law in the regular curriculum (1.3.). What the decades of the future will bring, may only be speculated about (1.4., 1.5.). Let us take a better look at these decades, before coming to the subject of this paper.

1.1. 1981 – Functional Approach

In 1981, the University of Limburg, as it was then called - now: the University of Maastricht - began to offer a law curriculum.[1] The curriculum was highly innovative in being based on small groups, the absence of lectures, one examination for all, and a functional approach to the subject-matter. The ideas behind this new approach were not entirely novel, as the University of Limburg had earlier started a medical faculty based on the same ideas.

Classes were small. Students were put together in groups of ten. The groups would set their own educational target; 'instructors' would only be present at the group meetings to answer questions put to them by students. Their task was not to lecture. The subject-matter was not broken down in the traditional way into private law, administrative law, criminal law, et cetera, but in a functional way. In the

1 See B. De Witte and C. Forder (eds.), *The common law of Europe and the future of legal education*, Deventer, Kluwer, 1992.

medical faculty, students would deal with 'pain in the back' or 'pain in the neck', instead of traditional subjects. Likewise, law students would learn about housing law or - in the more abstract - regulation. Once every couple of months there was a single examination for all students, the idea being that students would gradually be in a position to obtain better results.

The ideals of 1981 are no longer adhered to in full by the present law faculty. 'Small' groups do no longer consist of ten students only. Lectures have been re-introduced. The functional approach is still the cornerstone of the curriculum, but it is under increasing pressure - it requires instructors to write their own textbooks every year, which imposes an increasing burden on the staff. And the single examination for everyone has been abolished. Still, it was and remains a highly interesting experiment, and parts of the Maastricht approach have found their way to other law faculties in the Netherlands and abroad.

1.2. 1991 – the European Law School

In 1991, Maastricht once again introduced a novelty: the European Law School. The idea was to bring students from various European nations together and to instruct them not in Dutch, English, French or German law, but in the principles common to these and other European legal systems. The language of instruction is English. The curriculum has the disadvantage that it is perhaps too futuristic: a common European private, administrative or criminal law simply do not (yet) exist. There are pockets of community law in these areas, but most of the law is still domestic. It has therefore been questioned whether it is a good pedagogical principle to focus the curriculum on utopia. Personally, I do not share the criticism. For centuries, European lawyers have been educated not with their own legal system, but rather with Roman law. Why then could present-day students, instead of being instructed in the law of the past, not be instructed in the law of the future?

1.3. 2001 – European Law in the Curriculum

The present decade witnesses the increasing impact of European law on the regular curriculum. Whereas an interest in European private law, administrative law, criminal law or the like was still considered somewhat eccentric some ten years ago, this is no longer the case. Those who covet the most interesting jobs nowadays would do well to study European law. Lecturers who are well versed in European law are extremely difficult to keep, since they are in high demand in all major areas of society. This development has major consequences for the regular curriculum (although not the European Law School, where it has already been taken care of). In some of the coming Chapters I hope to explore the development of a harmonized European private law in more depth. At the end of the paper I will try do draw some conclusions from the growing impact of European law for present-day legal education and research.

1.4. 2011 – Global Law

Although this paper will only deal with the coming decade, we should perhaps briefly venture into the longer-distance future. There is not much fantasy necessary to predict that the decade after the present one, that of the 2010s, will witness another revolution. At present, many lawyers find the focus on Europe already quite a challenge. In the 2010s, with the European Union having maybe upwards of twenty Member States, there will be a growing interest in the other parts of the world. Focussing on Europe will begin to appear provincial, just as an accent on domestic law is viewed nowadays.

1.5. 2021 – the Withering away of Law – was Marx Right After All?

What the 2020s will bring us becomes more speculative. It would not surprise me if the 2020s would bring us some withering away of traditional legal doctrine. After internationalization has completed its victory over Ihering's provincialism, a new challenge will be that of interdisciplinary research. Already at the present time there is much talk of interdisciplinary education and research, but traditional legal education and research remain highly mono-disciplinary. The new approach will require law faculties to give up the idea that their law students should know every single part of the main parts of the curriculum. Without doing away completely with knowledge, methods and philosophy will gain in importance.

2. Achievements in the Past Decade

Having set the scope of this paper, I now turn to its first leg, devoted to the development of a European private law. The past decade, running from 1991-2001, has witnessed a spectacular growth of interest in developing a European private law. This has happened not only on the official level - directives (2.1.), communications (2.2.) and case-law (2.3.), but also on that of private efforts: Lando (2.4.), Gandolfi (2.5.), Trento (2.6.), Spier and others (2.7.) and Van Gerven (2.8.) are some of the best known of such projects.

2.1. From Directive to Regulation

The European Union has four instruments available for harmonization: treaties, regulations, directives and recommendations. Until recently, directives were the main vehicle for the harmonization of private law. The many directives on consumer protection are a good example. Their main advantage was, and is, that they enable member states to integrate a directive's substance in the form of national legislation. The drawbacks are twofold: first, transposition is needed to implement these instruments, and second, the adaptation into domestic law may lead to major divergences. It is therefore of some importance that, of late, regulations seem to be in better favour in Brussels. Where directives are concerned, the European Court is now more strict in surveying their correct transposition.

2.2. *The Communication on Contract Law*

Although the 11th of September 2002 will probably be remembered much longer, 11 July 2002 was an important day for the development of European Private Law. On that day, the Commission published its 'Communication of the Commission to the Council and the European Parliament on Contract Law'.[2] With this Communication, the Commission seeks a discussion as to the desirability, the feasibility and the necessity of a European Law of Obligations, not only as between academics but also in business circles. To this effect, the Commission first sketches the present state of affairs. So far, the discussion is very academic, between partisans and antagonists, between those who advocate codification and those who seek a Restatement, technicians and advocates of a legal cultural identity. Four options are offered to us by the Commission. In the first place, we can simply do nothing and leave the conclusion of contracts to market forces, which may arrive at industry-wide model contracts for cross-border transactions. A second solution is to promote the development of Principles, such as the Principles of European Contract Law of the Lando Commission. In this respect, the Commission sees a role for itself (p. 17). In this respect one may also think of Europe-wide general conditions. A third option is the improvement of the quality of existing European regulation. In this respect, the Commission mentions two examples: the SLIM-project - which stands for 'Simpler Legislation for the Internal Market' - and the possibility of extending the scope of application of a number of consumer protection directives to non-consumer transactions. A fourth and last option exists in promoting a text with provisions on general questions of obligations (p. 19). Here, the Commission is considering a directive, regulation or recommendation, which may run from fully optional to wholly mandatory. The latter solution would replace domestic law, while an optional regulation would come next to it. The Commission does not exclude the existence of even more options.

Those who begin reading the Communication without any pre-existing ideas, will not fail to be disappointed. Is this all there is to say? The Communication numbers 64 pages, but 43 of these are annexes. In the remaining 21 pages, the Commission does mention four interesting options, but nowhere does it come to any conclusions. Could not the Commission have given some guidance to the discussion? And yet, to end with this impression, would not be correct. The major importance of the Communication is that it has put the subject of a European Civil Code on the political agenda. Something which so far had nearly only touched academics, may now turn into a political issue on which trade and industry and other pressure groups will take a stance.

Which of the four options will be preferred by which group seems self-evident. The Lando Commission (2.4.) has always, like its sister working group which drafted UNIDROIT's Principles for International Commercial Contracts, been in favour of a Restatement. The Study group for a European Civil Code directed by Christian von Bar may have opted for a Code (the fourth option), but the fact that

[2] COM(2001) 398 final, <http://europa.eu.int/comm/off/green/index_nl.htm>.

this group is in fact the heir to the Lando Commission and the presence in its midst of a fair number of Restatement proponents, makes a compromise between the two strands plausible. Gandolfi's Academy (2.5.), finally, which like the Lando Commission is quoted in the Communication, quite clearly sees its draft as a draft codification and not as a Restatement. Gandolfi is only unclear as to the entry into force of his Code: 'le groupe de travail ne s'est pas expressément posé le problème de la voie par le truchement de laquelle l'avant-projet pourra devenir un code en vigueur pour les citoyens de l'Union européenne' (p. LVII). In short the discussion of academics, a solitary legrandist notwithstanding, will be focussed on the choice between a Code and a Restatement. My own preference lies with a Restatement (the second option): it would be contrary to all forms of respect (*comity*) to force a code down the throats of the English and the Irish.[3]

The non-thinking part of trade and industry will most probably prefer the option of not doing anything (option 1); the thinking part will look ahead and will choose between a Code and a Restatement. It finally appears useful not to opt for only one solution, but rather to extend the scope of application of a number of directives and to simplify the chosen terminology.

The Communication did achieve what it purported to do: it led to a highly interesting discussion. A major event was the conference organized by SECOLA (Society for European Contract Law) in Leuven, just two weeks before the Laeken Summit. The volume of conference papers, unpublished so far but available on the internet, contains reactions to the Communication from Josef Drexl (who favours total harmonization), Geraint Howells, Massimo Bianca (who is in charge of sales in the Gandolfi group), Christian von Bar ('Even law professors must learn to play in teams'), Mauro Bussani, Jürgen Basedow, Ugo Mattei ('The new European Code should be hard, minimal, not limited to contracts, and process oriented'), Hans-Peter Schwintowski ('Das *Europäische Zivilgesetzbuch* könnte ein zweiter Baustein – after the euro, EH – auf dem Wege zur Verinnerlichung der Idee *Europa* in den Herzen der europäischen Bürger sein'), Roger Van den Bergh ('Forced Harmonization of Contract Law in Europe: Not to be continued'), Hugh Collins, Norbert Reich, Stefan Grundmann and Wolfgang Kerber, U. Drobnig, Walter van Gerven, Jan Smits, Thomas Wilhelmsson, the European Consumer Law Group, and Bernard Tilleman and Bart Du Laing. Several of these reactions may also be found on the European Commission's website.

2.3. Case-Law of the European Court of Justice

Recent case law of the European Court of Justice shows the increasing importance of private law. Two examples are Heininger and TUI. In Heininger, a couple had taken out credit to the amount of DM 150,000 (approx. € 75,000) in 1990 for the purchase of an apartment. Eight years afterwards, the Heiningers cancelled the credit agreement, alleging that they had been led into the agreement by an intermediary who had visited them on his own initiative. This meant – according to the

3 See chapter 3 under (2) below.

Heiningers - that the German Door-to-Door Sales Act applied, and since the bank had not observed its duty to inform the borrower of his cooling-off period, that period still ran. The German courts totally disagreed with the Heininger contention, but they at least allowed them to ask the opinion of the European Court. The Court of Justice, in its wisdom, allowed the Heininger claim.[4]

TUI is perhaps even more interesting.[5] An Austrian family had booked a holiday in Turkey, where their ten-year old daughter Simone fell ill from salmonella. Simone had to remain in bed for the remaining part of the holiday and the parents claimed compensation. Compensation was duly awarded, but the amount did not include anything for the loss of enjoyment ('entgangene Urlaubsfreude'). The appellate court, the *Landesgericht* Linz, asked the Court of Justice whether this interpretation of the package travel directive was correct. According to the Court this was not the case. The notion of 'non-material damage' should be interpreted in a uniform way, preferably in a broad sense, so as to allow the compensation for 'entgangene Urlaubsfreude'.

The development of a European jurisdiction reminds one of the growth of American law. In the 1980s Cappelletti directed a European University Institute based research project into the question of what Europeans could learn from American federalism. In a recent English language publication, the Dutchman Van Erp has taken up this question again.[6] On the basis of the case law of the American *Supreme Court*, Van Erp analyses to what extent the European Court contributes to the development of European Private Law. In both instances, the author discerns a two-tiered approach:

> 'Ónly after examination of its own authority under the EC Treaty can the Court decide if it will create a substantive rule of private law itself or leave the matter to the courts of the member states, be it within certain limits. As such, this approach is not different from the common analysis of the US federal common law cases, where also a two-pronged test is used' (p. 57).

2.4. The Lando Commission; its Unidroit Counterpart and the Von Bar Succession

Of the various private efforts at harmonization of private law in Europe, Ole Lando's Commission on European Contract Law is no doubt one of the best known. The Commission started its well-documented work in the 1980's. It resulted in the publication, in 1995, of the first part of its Principles of European Contract Law, consisting of General Provisions, Terms and Performance of the Contract, Non-Performance and Remedies in General, and Particular Remedies for Non-Per-

4 Case C-481/99, *Heininger/ Bayerische Hypo- und Vereinsbank.*

5 Case C-168/00, *Leitner/TUI.*

6 J.H.M. van Erp, *European Union Case Law as a Source of European Private Law/A Comparison with American Federal Common Law, preadvies Nederlandse Vereniging voor Rechtsvergelijking,* Deventer, Kluwer, 2001, p. 1-58.

formance.[7] In 2000, Part II followed (integrated with Part I).[8] Meanwhile, in 2001 a third part has been finished. It consists of chapters on assignment, assumption of debt, compound interest, conditional obligations, illegality, joint liability, prescription and set off. This Part, which will once again integrate Parts I and II, is expected to be published in 2002.

By a strange coincidence, the Commission on European Contract Law was not the only group to embark upon a harmonization project. In Rome, the Institute for the Unification of Law (UNIDROIT) started a very similar project, which in 1994 resulted in the publication of Principles for International Commercial Contracts[9]. There has always been some competition between the two projects, and probably for the better. But the most striking conclusion from a comparison between the two is their obvious similarity. Not only are the adopted solutions often the same or similar, but the very choice of subjects dealt with, the style of drafting and the order of the chapters are all very much alike. This in itself is not so strange, if only because of the personal connections - at least five members served on both Commissions. Two formal points on which the two sets of Principles differ relate to their scope of application. The UNIDROIT Principles only deal with commercial contracts, whereas the PECL are applicable to all contracts, including consumer transactions and private contracts. An obvious difference is that the Lando Principles only cover (Western) Europe, while UNIDROIT has a global scope of application. This geographical feature does perhaps explain why the PECL's highly acclaimed system of national Notes could not work in the case of UNIDROIT.

On one point, the UNIDROIT Principles have met with more success than PECL: UNIDROIT and the President of its Working Group, Michael Joachim Bonell, have always succeeded in having the better publicity. This, and the fact that in the end the UNIDROIT Principles were published first, may explain the apparent edge that they still have with regard to their practical application. Indeed, there is a growing number of arbitral awards based on the Principles for International Commercial Contracts, and they have also influenced new legislation in Central and Eastern Europe.[10]

One of the weaknesses of the Lando project is that it is very much a one-man effort. At one time it was hoped that Hugh Beale would prove to be the successor once Ole Lando - born in 1922 - stepped down, but his appointment as a Law Commissioner prevented him from taking over. With the Commission on European Contract Law having held its final meeting in Copenhagen in February 2001, the

7 O. Lando and H. Beale (eds.), *Principles of European Contract Law/Part I,* Dordrecht, Nijhoff, 1995.

8 O. Lando and H. Beale (eds.), *Principles of European Contract Law/Parts I and II,* The Hague, Kluwer, 2000.

9 *Principles of International Commercial Contracts,* Rome, UNIDROIT, 1994, also available in many other languages, including Arabic, Dutch, French, German, Italian and Spanish. See M.J. Bonell, *A New Approach to International Commercial Contracts/The UNIDROIT Principles of International Commercial Contracts,* The Hague, Kluwer, 1999.

10 See for Lithuania: V. Mikelenas, 'Unification and Harmonization of Law at the Turn of the Millennium: the Lithuanian Experience', *Revue de droit uniforme,* 2000, p. 243-260.

question was raised as to how to deal with practical issues such as copyright. For this purpose, a four-member commission has been appointed, consisting of Eric Clive (Scotland), Ole Lando (Denmark), André Prüm (Luxembourg) and Claude Witz (France).[11] More importantly, another group has presented itself - and been accepted - as the spiritual heir to the Lando Commission.

In 1997, under the then Dutch presidency of the European Union, a conference on a European Civil Code was held in Scheveningen, the seaside resort of The Hague. Although the conference was not in favour of drafting a European Code which would be binding upon all Member States, it was precisely that which Christian von Bar agreed to look into. The Study Group which Von Bar and his colleagues has set up includes several members of the former Lando Commission. Von Bar succeeded in securing sufficient funds to set up a number of teams of young researchers in Germany and the Netherlands.[12]

2.5. *Gandolfi*

So much publicity has been given to the *Principles of European Contract Law*, that one nearly forgets that there are other projects as well. Perhaps the second best known project is the one initiated by the Italian Romanist Giuseppe Gandolfi. In about 1990, Gandolfi started with his major work, a Code of Contract Law, based on the Italian *Codice civile*.[13] Until recently, the project was chiefly known for the fact that one of its members was acknowledged to have belonged to a mixed committee of the English and Scottish *Law Commissions* and to have elaborated a draft Contract Code. Gandolfi immediately saw to it that this 'MacGregor Code' was published and so spared it the fate of oblivion.[14] Another consequence was that next to the *Codice civile* the MacGregor Code would serve as the guideline for the work of the Gandolfi Academy. In 2002, the Academy published its Draft Code ('avant-projet').[15] The subject-matter is close to that dealt with by the Lando Principles. On three points, the Gandolfi Draft Code is different however. First, whereas the Lando Principles are a team effort, the Gandolfi Code has been drafted by one man, Giuseppe Gandolfi, albeit guided by his *Académie des privatistes européens*. Then, an attractive feature, the text enters into discussion with the two sets of Principles and with the ideas of Gandolfi's colleagues: 'Les contributions des Académiciens'. Finally, the project has been drafted in French.

11 The group also serves as the Editing Group.

12 See Ch. von Bar, 'Die Study Group on a European Civil Code', in *Festschrift Dieter Henrich*, Gieseking, 2000, p. 1-12.

13 Why the Italian Code (1942), and not the more modern Dutch Civil Code (1992)? Gandolfi's answer: because the Dutch Code has not yet generated case law and a code without cases like potatoes without gravy. (comparison by EH).

14 H. McGregor, *Contract code drawn up on behalf of the English Law Commission*, Milan/London, 1993.

15 G. Gandolfi (ed.), *Code européen des contrats/Avant-projet, Livre premier*, Milano, Giuffrè, 2001, 576 p.; see H.-J. Sonnenberger, 'Der Entwurf eines Europäischen Vertragsgesetzbuchs der Akademie Europäischer Privatrechtswissenschaftler - ein Meilenstein', *Recht der Internationalen Wirtschaft*, 2001, p. 409-416.

2.6. *Trento*

Another private project, is the Trento Common Core of European Private Law project, directed by Mauro Bussani and Ugo Mattei. The project is based on the ideas of the two Rudi's: Rodolfo Saco and the late Rudi Schlesinger. Every July, a large band of young - at heart - lawyers gather in the beautiful North Italian town of Trento. Each meeting begins with a plenary session,[16] but then it is back to the core business: the development of a common core of private law. Two volumes have so far been published. The first volume to be published as a fruit of the project, is the one on Good Faith edited by Zimmermann and Whittaker.[17] The volume comprises thirty cases, which all are dealt with from the point of view of sixteen jurisdictions - fifteen EU jurisdictions including Scotland (but excluding Luxembourg) plus Norway. This analysis is preceded by a general introduction by the two Editors, historical surveys by Schermaier on Roman law and Gordley on *ius commune,* and a comparative paper on the American reception of *good faith* by Summers. The book ends with concluding remarks by Zimmermann and Whittaker. What kind of cases does the book deal with? An example is the following:

> 'case 1, courgettes perishing: Barchester Chemicals Ltd is a producer of agricultural and domestic fertilisers. Cecil is a market gardener and buys directly from Barchester's a quantity of one of their products, "Growright 100", for use on his courgettes. Owing to the high content of salt in this product, the plants' vegetation perishes: it is clear that this would not have happened if Cecil had been advised to give the plants large quantities of water at the time of administering the product. What claims does Cecil have against Barchester?' (p. 171).

This has nothing to do with good faith, a Dutch reader may object, and indeed that is what the Dutch reporter Van Erp observes (p. 192). All the same, he concludes that Barchester was bound to inform Cecil, as is the case under Belgian, French and German law, but then on the basis of good faith. The common law reaches the same result by the technique of implied terms. This is in line with the general conclusion, that of the thirty cases, eleven are solved in exactly the same way in all jurisdictions, nine are solved in exactly the same way in most of the jurisdictions and only in ten cases are there clear differences. Surprisingly, to the Editors, it is not the common law, which is the odd man out.

> 'Instead, we often find a smaller legal jurisdiction out on a limb, this being particularly noticeable as regards the Nordic legal systems and Irish law. One possible reason for this may be that where a legal system by its size tends to engender less litigation there are fewer occasions on which courts are presented with facts suitable to test or to clarify the application of exiting legal rules' (p. 655).

16 See the collection of papers read at plenary sessions in M. Bussani and U. Mattei (eds.), *Making European Law/Essays on the 'Common Core' project,* Università degli Studie di Trento, 2000.

17 R. Zimmermann and S. Whittaker, *Good Faith in European Contract Law,* Cambridge, Cambridge University Press, 2000, 720 p.

A disadvantage of team work such as that in the Trento project, is that it may take a long time to finish. This is apparent from the fact that the national reports in the Zimmermann/Whittaker volume were concluded in 1997. Fortunately, the general report does reflect later developments. The disadvantage is also discernible in the second volume which was published on *Enforceability of Promises*.[18] The Editor of this volume is the American comparatist and legal historian James Gordley. The volume looks into the question of to what extent promises are binding. In modern continental law, this question is usually answered in the affirmative, as opposed to Roman law and the *common law* with its *consideration* requirement. The book comprises fifteen cases, which are dealt with from the point of view of twelve European jurisdictions (Denmark, Finland, Luxembourg and Sweden are missing, but Scotland once again receives special attention). Contrary to the Editor's expectation, the differences are larger than he had anticipated. An example is the gift. In most European jurisdictions its validity is still dependent upon the fulfilment of a form requirement. Usually, the form required is a notarial deed, but in Portugal, Scotland and Spain an ordinary deed is sufficient. In England, the promisor should make a 'deed under seal' - it is sufficient (but not in Ireland) that he declares the deed to have the object of being such a deed, or he must establish a trust. Gordley did find *something* in common: 'We did find that, generally, these results reflect similar underlying concerns' (p. 371).

2.7. *Spier and Koziol and Others*

One of the more active private groups engaged in the development of 'Principles' of European Private Law is the Spier/Koziol group.[19] Before publishing a set of Principles, the group sets out to discover common ground between the various jurisdictions. The questionnaire method used is very much akin to that of the Trento Common Core project, discussed in 2.6. It is highly commendable that the group does not keep the results of the questionnaire approach to itself, but is willing to share the finds with others through publication. In my earlier Survey, I already mentioned three of the group's publications. By 2002, another four were published. Number four deals with causation.[20] It contains ten national reports and a comparative analysis. The national reports deal with the same 24 cases each. The ten jurisdictions covered are Austria (Koziol), Belgium (Cousy, Vanderspikken), England (Rogers), France (Galand-Carval), Germany (Magnus), Greece (Kerameus), Italy (Busnelli, Comandei), South Africa (Neethling), Switzerland (Widmer) and the United States (Schwartz). The comparative analysis demonstrates how much the jurisdictions have in common, but also how much they differ on other points.

18 J. Gordley (ed.), *The Enforceability of Promises in European Contract Law*, Cambridge, Cambridge University Press, 2001, 478 p.

19 See J. Spier and O.A. Haazen, 'The European Group on Tort Law ("Tilburg Group") and the European Principles of Tort Law', *Zeitschrift für Europäisches Privatrecht*, 1999, p. 469-493. Meanwhile, the centre of the group has gravitated to Vienna (Helmut Koziol).

20 J. Spier (ed.), *Unification of Tort Law: Causation*, European Centre of Tort and Insurance Law, The Hague, Kluwer, 2000, 161 p.

I have given this overview by way of example. Outside the realm of Contract and Tort Law, various other private projects may be mentioned. Principles have also been developed for the Law of Trusts by the Kortmann group.[21] A set of draft directives on Procedural Law has been drafted by a group chaired by Marcel Storme.[22] The development of European Principles has even been proposed for Family Law.[23]

2.8. Casebooks

'I had a dream'. The Leuven - and formerly: Maastricht - based Walter Van Gerven would probably add: 'that there shall be a time when lawyers all over Europe share a common thesaurus of case law'. An era when Donoghue v Stevenson, Hühnerpest en Jeand'heur are not just known locally in England, Germany and France, but in all European countries. Van Gerven's dream has resulted in two case books. The first to appear was 'Tort Law'.[24] Here four jurisdictions are compared on the basis of annotated cases. These jurisdictions are England, France, Germany and Europe. Other European jurisdictions are mentioned only occasionally. Earlier, one single Chapter from this book had already been published separately - 'Scope of Protection' (1998). When that Part was published, the question could be raised how many thousands of pages the final volume would contain. The Editors have been able to limit the size to a little under 1,000 pages, first by limiting the number of decisions from other jurisdictions than the four major ones, and second, by referring to Maastricht University's website[25] for further information and for the text in the original language. The Chapters added as compared with the earlier book include General Topics, Liability for One's Own Conduct, Causation, Liability for the Conduct of Others, Liability not Based on Conduct, Defences, Remedies, Impact of Supranational and International Law.

This is a highly readable book. Tort law really comes to life through cases. A disadvantage, as with the teamwork involved in the Trento series mentioned above in 2.6., is that the outcome is very much dependent upon the punctuality of all contributors. This is very much evident in the second volume to appear in the series, the one on Contract Law, edited by Hugh Beale.[26] The book deals with the notion of Contract, the relation with Tort and Restitution, pre-contractual liability, the binding force of contracts, offer and acceptance, validity, *vices de consentement*, unfair contract terms, interpretation, *imprévision*, remedies, third parties and

21 D.J. Hayton, S.C.J.J. Kortmann and H.L.E. Verhagen (eds.), *Principles of European Trust Law*, The Hague, Kluwer Law International - W.E.J. Tjeenk Willink, 1999.

22 M.L. Storme (ed.), *Approximation of Judiciary Law in the European Union*, Dordrecht, Kluwer, 1994.

23 M.V. Antokolskaia, W.A. de Hondt and G.J.W. Steenhoff, *Een zoektocht naar Europees familie-recht*, Report Nederlandse Vereniging voor Rechtsvergelijking, Deventer, Kluwer, 1999.

24 W. Van Gerven, J. Lever and P. Larouche (eds.), *Tort Law, Common Law of Europe Casebooks*, Oxford, Hart, 2000, 969 p.

25 <http://www.rechten.unimaas.nl/casebook>.

26 H. Beale and others (eds.), *Contract Law. Casebooks on the Common Law of Europe*, Oxford, Hart, 2002, 993 p.

assignment. As in the Tort volume, these subjects are illustrated by cases taken mainly from English, French and German law. Other cases have been taken from Australia, Belgium, Italy (6), the Netherlands (4), and Switzerland, but Austria, Greece, the Nordic countries, Portugal, Scotland and Spain remain unrepresented. Unlike the Tort volume, the one on Contract Law does not have a companion website with the original text. This is a handicap for those readers who prefer a text in the original language.

A third casebook yet to appear is a volume on 'Judicial Review of Administrative Action'

Van Gerven is not the only Editor of casebooks. The 'Casebook Europäisches Privatrecht' comprises 19 cases of the European Court of Justice in the area of private law.[27] Cases reported are for instance Francovich, Cassis de Dijon and Bosman. The interest of the casebook lies in the fact that these cases are annotated from a European, English, German, French and Italian perspective. Earlier, the same publishers published a 'Casebook Europäisches Verbraucherrecht'.[28] These are only some recent examples of casebooks which will most certainly contribute to a growing common thesaurus of European cases.

3. Non-Achievements

The achievements then, at first sight, seem overwhelming. A decade of efforts, especially at NGO level, have resulted in a common core of academic writing on most parts of private law in Europe. Still, much remains to be done. In this Chapter, I will indicate some non-achievements of the past decade.

3.1. Constitutional Competence

First of all, surprisingly, there is no consensus as to a firm basis for codification of private law in the European Treaty. The 1997 Scheveningen Conference, the results of which were published in the *European Review of Private Law*, clearly indicated the diversity of scholarly opinion on this point, with a slender majority being of the opinion that the Treaty offers no such competence.

3.2. Comity

The minority, which is of the contrary opinion, nonetheless would not wish to force a European Civil Code down British and Irish throats. The principle of comity argues against this. An alternative to the Code movement of Von Bar and others would perhaps be a Restatement. The Code v Restatement discussion is an ongoing debate, even within groups such as the Von Bar commission.

27 R. Schulze, A. Engel and J. Jones (eds.), *Casebook Europäisches Privatrecht*, Baden-Baden, Nomos, 2000, 425 p.

28 H. Schulte-Nölke, R. Schulze and J. Jones (eds.), *A Casebook on European Consumer Law*, Oxford, Hart, 320 p.

3.3. The Business Community

When in 1980 the Vienna Sales Convention (CISG) was adopted, the academic community welcomed this major achievement towards world trade. But world trade itself could not have been less interested. After the entry into force of CISG, most major businesses would opt out of the Convention. Only those businesses who were unaware of the Convention would be bound by it. This lack of interest in CISG has never failed to amaze academics. Why not be glad to have a neutral set of rules when one party is based in China and the other in Germany?

A similar unpleasant surprise - from an academic point of view - is the lack of interest of European trade and industry in the private efforts at harmonization presented above. So rare is the interest of the business community, that whenever there is an arbitral award in which the Unidroit Principles are referred to this is reported all over as another example of the importance of these Principles.

3.4. The Academic Community

Above I have suggested that the academic community is enthusiastic about the harmonization movement. I should now perhaps add that first not all scholars feel comfortable with the movement towards European harmonization and second that there is some outright hostility. First, perhaps the majority of University lecturers up until the present time prefer to stick to domestic law, often because of unfamiliarity with European law. I suggest that these lecturers will soon be forced by directives and case-law to readjust their classes or else they will find themselves out of place. The second group is more interesting. It consists of those who are familiar with the movement but rather - or in their views: because of that - are very much against the present ways of harmonization. Such opponents include a number of English authors - Hugh Collins,[29] Tony Weir[30] - , transatlantic-born jurists - the Canadian Legrand[31] -, and even some Dutch authors, such as Jan Smits[32] from Maastricht University. I would suggest that it is the essence of academia that there be debate, so the opponents actually do contribute to harmonization by making the partisans aware of their faulty reasoning.

4. We shall Overcome?

What to do with the non-achievements summarized above? The constitutional impediment only looks like a minor one: if a qualified majority so wishes, the Giscard d'Estaing commission could work out an amendment to the European

29 H. Collins, 'European Private Law and the Cultural Identity of States', *ERPL*, 1995, p. 353-365.

30 T. Weir, 'Die Sprachen des europäischen Rechts: Eine skeptische Betrachtung', *ZEuP,* 1995, p. 368.

31 P. Legrand, 'Against a European Civil Code', 60 *Modern Law Review*, 1997, p. 44-63.

32 J. Smits, *The Making of European Private Law*, Antwerp, Intersentia, 2002.

Treaty. The comity principle can be taken care of by offering member states a Restatement - or a Model Code - instead of making them swallow a code.

How to make business aware of the advantages of harmonization? Seminars and the like seem to be the proper answer. Easily readable commentaries equally may serve to raise the business interest. The academic community will finally be forced by market forces to provide the legal education and to do the legal research which lives up to today's requirements.

5. Some Concerns

Although there are ways to overcome the present non-achievements, there is reason for some concern.

5.1. Case-Law

First, although there is a growing body of community case-law on questions of private law, it is still very limited as compared with domestic case-law. What is now very important is that *domestic* case-law on questions of European private law be reported in other jurisdictions and other languages. Only in this way may lawyers of other nationalities learn of such cases.

5.2. Geographical

There is a number of ongoing research projects on private law in Europe, mentioned elsewhere in this paper. It is of major importance that these projects already take into account the forthcoming arrival of a number of new member states.

5.3. Subject-Matter

There is now little doubt that Contract Law is a major target of harmonization. Contract Law is close to two other areas: Securities and Tort Law. Once one harmonizes Contract Law, Securities are bound to follow. This then raises the difficult question whether or not the rest of Property Law (including transfer of Real Estate) should follow suit. Only in the case of *Intellectual* Property is harmonization self-evident. With the decreasing demarcation between Contract Law and Tort Law, it seems inevitable, as the Lando and Unidroit working groups found, that some Tort Law will also have to be harmonized. The problem here is the intermingling with Social Security, which so far remains very different in European jurisdictions.

When we talk about Contract Law nowadays, this includes Commercial Contract Law. As the Italians realized long ago, the distinction between a separate Civil Law and Commercial Law is no longer desirable.

Two growth areas of harmonization, after the Tampere summit, are Civil Procedure and Private International Law. On the other hand, the recent formation of a Study Group on European Family Law will still have great barriers to over-

come. The law of Succession will likewise prove resistant to Europeanization for some time to come.
Finally, we should always be aware of the growing co-operation between Private Law and Anti-trust Law, which are already harmonized, and Administrative Law, which is not.

5.4. Technical

In the preceding text I have already mentioned a number of technical problems which will keep us occupied over the present decade, such as the form of harmonization: Regulation v. Directive, Code v. Restatement. There are other technical problems, such as the question of a single fabric - should we accept the increasing dichotomy between domestic law and European law within one legal system.

6. Role of Academics

This conference is about a European *ius commune* in legal education and research. Let me briefly and rather sketchily explore the role of academics in this development. Of first and foremost importance is the training of future generations of students. Erasmus has paved the way; the *Bologna* Declaration aims to do the same, but Dutch experience shows that the development of bachelor and master programmes may actually endanger some of the exchange programmes arrived at in the last century.

Academic staff should now engage in exchange themselves. I will develop this theme in the next Chapter. It is important to engage in an exchange of intellectual ideas in Europe. To this end, we should learn to express ourselves in other European languages.

In our teaching, we should promote the common stock of legal thinking: Savigny, Maitland and Pothier. We should also promote the development of a common stock of landmark cases and in the drafting of common projects. More generally, common research projects may be the cornerstone to increased harmonization.

7. The Maastricht Charter

The past Chapter leads to a set of rules which, with respect to the organizers of this conference, I would like to call the *Maastricht Charter of Legal Education*. The Charter embraces the following principles:

7.1. Every Law Student shall study at least one Semester Abroad

It is essential that every law student shall spend at least one out of his or her six semesters of bachelor studies abroad. Only in this way will it be ascertained that the student is sufficiently aware of the peculiarities of his or her own legal system. A European Law Faculty in one's own country is not exactly the same, although it offers a somewhat similar experience. Likewise, taking courses in a language which is different from one's native tongue may be helpful in developing awareness, but only a five-month period abroad will fully succeed in the objective.

7.2. For Promotion to Senior Positions, Staff shall teach at least one Semester Abroad

Perhaps even more important is an obligation for senior staff to spend some time abroad teaching. It does not help very much if students are aware of their system's peculiarities and staff are not. Exchange agreements under Socrates arrangements may provide for financial possibilities for such exchanges.

7.3. Every Researcher shall publish at least once Annually Abroad

What is valid for legal education is also true for research. Only when publishing the results of one's research in foreign languages will researchers become aware of the shortcomings of their own language. It is of special importance to native speakers of English, who because of their language having become the *lingua franca* of international fora are very much in danger of becoming blind to the intricacies of their own tongue.

7.4. Every Lecturer (Teacher and/or Researcher) shall take part in continuing Legal Education, with Conferences abroad counting Double

It is a strange phenomenon that for many liberal professions, such as those of attorney and medical doctor, continuing education - 'éducation permanente' - is now compulsory, but for teachers and researchers of law it is not. In fact, most universities now offer their staff excellent financial opportunities to take part in such courses, but they are not compulsory.

7.5. Every Lecturer shall be entitled to a Sabbatical to be spent Abroad

Only when lecturers are offered regular possibilities to get to grasps with new developments, will their teaching and research remain of a good quality. A system of sabbaticals after the American model should be introduced to enable them to retrain.

7.6. Universities shall set aside Funds for Comparative Research Projects

Universities are now increasingly co-operating in international research projects. The University of Maastricht, with its co-operation in a project on mixed legal systems, its participation in the research school *ius commune* and in many other schemes, is a good example.

8. Conclusions

Private law is rapidly becoming European in outline. This requires a fundamental shift in both legal education and legal research. The Maastricht Charter purports to lay down a first blueprint for this shift in paradigm.

Peter-Christian
Müller-Graff

PRIVATE LAW SOCIETY IN THE CONSTITUTION OF THE EUROPEAN UNION – THE CONTEXT OF COMMON PRIVATE LAW IN EUROPE

1. Introduction

Private law society in the constitution of the European Union is a subject which seems to go beyond the areas of private law covered so far at this conference, but it is a necessary continuation of considering a common private law for the European Union. To this end it is surely essential to discuss the question of the common principles of private law in technical detail as was done during these days at this place,[1] as was pursued at the great conference of this faculty ten years ago[2] and as was carefully scrutinized in, for example, the notes for the Principles of European Contract Law by the Commission on European Contract Law.[3] However, working on the details of private law rules does not answer the question of the ends of such an endeavour. Not even the well-known practical arguments often put forward, in particular the aspect of overcoming specific transaction costs of legal counselling in transnational transactions, tell the whole story. My thesis is that within the European Union, European private law in general, and European contract law in particular, can hardly be considered to be a purpose in themselves, but receive their vocation and limits from the role of civil society in the constitution of Europe. After last September we have every reason to return to and ponder anew on the role of transnational civil society and to consider this substantial question at least as intensely as we discuss the issues of a new formalized European constitution and of the relationship between the institutions of the European Community.[4]

1 Universiteit Maastricht.

2 Conference organized by the Faculty of Law of the Rijksuniversiteit Limburg at Maastricht on the occasion of its 10th anniversary, in September 1991; for the reports see B. de Witte and C. Forder (eds.), *The common law of Europe and the future of legal education*, Deventer, Kluwer, 1992.

3 See O. Lando and H. Beale (eds.), *Principles of European Contract Law*, Parts I and II, prepared by the Commission on European Contract Law, Kluwer Law International, 2000.

4 See, e.g., P.-Ch. Müller-Graff, 'Der Post-Nizza-Prozess. Auf dem Weg zu einer neuen europäischen Verfassung?', *integration*, 2001, p. 208 *et seq*; S. Volkmann-Schluck, *Die Debatte um*

In order to develop and illustrate this thesis the following observations are subdivided into four main questions. Firstly: what is the meaning of private law society in the light of *civil society*? (2.); secondly: what is the meaning of the *constitution* of the European Union in this context? (3.); thirdly: is there a *basis* for the emergence of a *transnational European* private law society in *European Community law*? (4.); and fourthly: what are the *perspectives* for a European private law society and a common private law within the European Union? (5.).

2. Private Law Society as an Element of a Civil Society

Turning first to the idea of private law society in the light of the general theory of civil society we encounter, first of all, in the German speaking world the well-known but also somewhat shimmering term 'Privatrechtsgesellschaft' as created by Franz Böhm more than three decades ago.[5] According to his understanding the term embodies one of the great objectives of the French Revolution of 1789, namely the constitutional call for private autonomy in social life.[6] The realization of this idea became one of the great achievements experiencing a triumphal march through the Western European nation states and territories from the end of the 18th century against feudal rights, privileges, guild systems and public authorities.

2.1. The Idea of Private Law Society ('Privatrechtsgesellschaft')

The term 'Privatrechtsgesellschaft' has made a remarkable revival in scholarly publications in the German speaking world in recent years.[7] But why and with what content? Franz Böhm was mainly interested in the political and constitutional model, in which the 'Privatrechtsordnung' ('private law order') was entrusted with the self organization of a society composed of freely and autonomously planning individuals. It is a model in which administration of public power serves solely the protection and preservation of society and in which the state carries this power as a fief of a society unable to act on its own.[8]

eine europäische Verfassung, Centrum für angewandte Politikforschung, 2001; I. Pernice, 'Die Europäische Verfassung', in *Tradition und Weltoffenheit des Rechts*, Festschrift für Herbert Steinberger, Springer, 2002, p. 1319 *et seq.*

5 See F. Böhm, 'Privatrechtsgesellschaft und Marktwirtschaft', *ORDO*, Bd.XVII, 1966, p. 75.

6 F. Böhm, 'Privatrechtsgesellschaft und Marktwirtschaft', *ORDO*, Bd.XVII, 1966, p. 79.

7 See, e.g., C.-W. Canaris, 'Verfassungs- und europarechtliche Aspekte der Vertragsfreiheit in der Privatrechtsgesellschaft', in *Wege und Verfahren des Verfassungslebens*, Festschrift für Peter Lerche, München, C.H. Beck, 1993, p. 873 *et seq.*; K. Nörr, *An der Wiege deutscher Identität nach 1945: F. Böhm zwischen ordo und Liberalismus*, de Gruyter, 1993; F. Bydlinski, *Das Privatrecht im Rechtssystem einer 'Privatrechtsgesellschaft'*, Springer, 1994; F. Bydlinsky, 'Privatrechtsgesellschaft' und Rechtssystem', in *Unternehmen, Recht und Wirtschaftsordnung*, Festschrift für Peter Raisch, Heymanns, 1995, p. 7 *et seq.*; W. Zöllner, *Die Privatrechtsgesellschaft im Gesetzes- und Richterstaat*, O. Schmidt, 1996. For an economic point of view, see K. Mayer and J. Scheinpflug, *Privatrechtsgesellschaft und Europäische Union*, Mohr, 1996.

8 In the original text this model is described as a model, in dem der Privatrechtsgesellschaft 'die Lenkung einer Gesellschaft frei und autonom planender Individuen' anvertraut ist, die

More concrete aspects are emphasized in the modern use of the term *'Privatrechtsgesellschaft'* such as the gradual discovery and emergence of rules originating from private autonomous conduct as opposed to rules stemming from the legislator or courts (e.g. F. Bydlinski).[9] Such private sources can be seen particularly in the autonomous shaping of contracts, standard terms, professional standards, technical norms, courses of dealing, practices, customs and trade usages. Another aspect of the *'Privatrechtsgesellschaft'* is emphasized with the assertion of the freedom to shape the content of a contract against legislative and judicial requirements (e.g. C.-W. Canaris[10] or W. Zöllner).[11] But even these more concrete approaches assume that private autonomy - in the sense of self-determination and self-responsibility - serves as the most beneficial soil for a free, prosperous and peaceful community.

One might easily object to these ideas, arguing that they are rooted in idealistic assumptions which are far from the realities of the world and that this idealistic remoteness is shown by the increasing modern tide of legislative and judicial norms, by the increasing discovery of public aspects in all areas of life together with steady demands for collective and public action and by constitutional social welfare tasks (in German: *grundgesetzlicher Sozialstaatsauftrag*). However, it is precisely one of the questions of modern theories of civil society to ask to what extent such phenomena are reasonable and necessary for successful community life (in German: *gelungenes Gemeinschaftsleben*).

Evidently not every existing social phenomenon is reasonable or necessary. (1.) The mere increase of legislative and judicial norms does not in itself answer the question of whether this development is convincing in relation to the alternative of autonomous self-regulation. Such scepticism is documented by many efforts to contain this flood, e.g., in Germany by the *'Deregulierungskommission'*,[12] by the *Sachverständigenrat 'Schlanker Staat'*[13] (slim state) and by ministerial checklists for assessing the necessity of a given piece of legislation.[14] And it must be said such

'Verwaltung der Herrschaftsmittel ... ausschließlich dem Schutz und der Erhaltung der Gesellschaft dient' und 'der Staat ... diese Majestät sozusagen von der nicht handlungsfähigen Gesellschaft zu Lenen (trägt)'; see *supra* note 5, p. 80.

9 See F. Bydlinsky, *Das Privatrecht im Rechtssystem einer 'Privatrechtsgesellschaft'*, Springer, p. 59 *et seq.*, 73 *et seq.* and 80 *et seq.* A parallel can be drawn to Ph. Selznick, *The Moral Commonwealth - Social Theory and the Promise of Community*, University of California Press, 1992 (Paperback 1994), who writes (albeit in a very abstract way) on p. 449: 'Common law is not made by judges or by any other sovereign power. Rather it is an expression of community, a product of shared history and common life'. See also p. 469.

10 See *supra* note 7.

11 See *supra* note 7, p. 20.

12 Deregulierungskommission, *Marktöffnung und Wettbewerb - Gutachten*, Poeschel, 1991.

13 See R. Scholz and K.G. Meyer-Teschendorf, 'Reduzierung der Normenflut durch qualifizierte Bedürfnisprüfung', *ZRP*, 1996, p. 404 *et seq.*

14 See, e.g., Prüffragen für Rechtsvorschriften des Bundes - Beschluß der Bundesregierung v. 11.12.1984 mit Anhang; Richtlinien für die Wahrnehmung und Organization öffentlicher Aufgaben im Freistaat Bayern, Bekanntmachung der Bayrischen Staatsregierung v. 26.6.1994 Nr.B III 3-155-9-1.

efforts have only met with mixed success.[15] (2.) The casual discoveries of the public effects of private conduct, in particular the conduct of enterprises, do not exclude an assessment of a system of self regulating autonomous initiatives and decisions as being in principle a system which profoundly serves the public interest. W. Zöllner has even created the somewhat strong formula for the role of private autonomy: '*Je mehr Privatautonomie, desto weniger Staatsbevormundung*'[16] (The more private autonomy, the less subordination under the state). (3.) The objective of the welfare state as well as the call for social human rights do not and should not imply the refusal of the fundamental principle of self-determination and individual responsibility.

2.2. The Relation to the Theory of Civil Society

This principle serves as the bridge from the long-standing idea of '*Privatrechtsgesellschaft*' to the modern theories of civil society as developed in the most coherent way by the sociologist P. Selznick in his book 'The Moral Commonwealth'.[17] His theory emphasizes the beneficial potential of the non-etatist political community for all concerned. It comprises in essence the idea of autonomous individuals who are conscious of and bound by the community. Viewed from this liberal communitaristic perspective (or better: communitarian liberal perspective) the idea of '*Privatrechtsgesellschaft*' is directed at *one* of the basic elements of civil society, namely at the legally effective self-determination of an individual in relation to other individuals, business partners, organizations and overarching communities.

It is evident that civil society is more than this. In particular the idea of civil society encompasses the initiatives and activities of non-governmental organizations which collect certain individual interests and thoughts together and which generate elements and yardsticks for substantiating the mysterious category of the *public good* (in German: *Gemeinwohl*) - non-governmental organizations such as political parties with their programmatic objectives, scientific communities with their codes of conduct and their methods of consensus-building, churches with their doctrines, pressure groups ranging from trade unions to industrial associations with their specific guidelines, counselling committees for governments and ministries with their proposals. Embedded in and inspired by the entirety of these voices, regional, national and transnational legislators, governments and judiciaries gain their specific definition and tone.

Efforts to polarize liberalism and communitarism fail to hit the point, since the stipulated individual awareness of and responsibility for other individuals cannot seriously be thought of without individual freedom and autonomy.[18] Hence Selznick is right when he states that a successful community requires the develop-

15 See as an assessment P.-Ch. Müller-Graff, 'The Quality of European and National Legislation', *EuZW*, 1998, p. 325 *et seq.*

16 See W. Zöllner, 'Die politische Rolle des Privatrechts', *JuS*, 1988, p. 329.

17 P. Selznick, *The Moral Commonwealth. Social Theory and the Promise of Community*, University of California Press, 1992, paperback 1994.

18 See *supra* note 17 (paperback), p. 63 *et seq.*

ment and strengthening of the autonomy of individuals.[19] A living civil society (*'gelebte Zivilgesellschaft'*) and hence a *Privatrechtsgesellschaft* is the basis of the mutual oath of individuals on which the formal act of establishing a constitution is solidly based.[20]

3. Private Law Society and the Constitution of the EU

This leads to the second question, the relationship between a private law society and the *constitution* of a community and - in the present context - to the relation between a private law society and the constitution of the European Union.

3.1. The Topic of a Constitution of the EU and Primary Law

Mentioning the constitution of the European Union may provoke a preliminary question. Does such a constitution exist at all? And, if not, should it be created? The answer depends upon the expectations hung onto the term 'constitution'. Due to a broad variety of understandings and interests the sometimes feverish and well-known public and academic discussion on 'a European constitution' is often confused and confusing.

The existence of a constitution of the Union is partially denied[21] and the necessity of creating one is either stipulated[22] or rejected.[23] Partially it is held that the Treaties on which the Union is based already form a constitution in a substantial sense. This is a strong position among scholars of European Community law[24] and the European Court of Justice[25] and at least a former position of the Federal Constitutional Court[26] in Germany. From this point of view the present Post-Nice

19 See *supra* note 17 (paperback), p. 207 *et seq.* and 215 *et seq.*

20 See *supra* note 17 (paperback), p. 477 *et seq.*

21 See, e.g., R. Scholz, 'Einführung: Maßstäbe für Erfolgsbilanz und Balanceverlust', in R. Scholz (ed.), *Europäische Union - Schon eine 'Union des Rechts'? - Zwischen Erfolgsbilanz und Balanceverlust*, Bachem, 1996, p. 30; D. Grimm, 'Braucht Europa eine Verfassung?', *JZ*, 1995, p. 568.

22 See, e.g., O. Graf Lambsdorff, 'Europa braucht eine Verfassung', *Handelsblatt*, Nr. 145, 31.7./1.8.1998, p. 6; J. Fischer, 'Vom Staatenverbund zur Föderation - Gedanken über die Finalität der europäischen Integration', *integration*, 2000, 149 *et seq.*

23 See, e.g., Ch. Koenig, 'Ist die Europäische Union verfassungsfähig?', *ZEI-Report*, Oktober 1999, p. 8.

24 See, e.g., H.P. Ipsen, *Europäisches Gemeinschaftsrecht*, Mohr, 1972, p. 64; P. Pescatore, in *Europäische Gerichtsbarkeit und nationale Verfassungsgerichtsbarkeit*, Festschrift für Hans Kutscher, Nomos, 1981, p. 335; R. Bieber and J. Schwarze, *Verfassungsentwicklung in der Europäischen Gemeinschaft*, Nomos, 1984, p. 20; P.-Ch. Müller-Graff, 'Verfassungsziele der EG/EU', in M. Dauses (ed.), *Handbuch des EU-Wirtschaftsrechts*, München, C.H. Beck, 2000, A I 90; M. Zuleeg, in H. von der Groeben, J. Thiesing and C.-D. Ehlermann (eds.), *Kommentar zum EU-/EG-Vertrag*, 5th ed., Baden-Baden, Nomos, 1997, Art.1 Rdz.10; I. Pernice, 'Vertragsrevision oder europäische Verfassungsgebung?', *FAZ*, 7.7.1999, p. 7; Th. Oppermann, *Europarecht*, second edition, München, C.H. Beck, 1999, p. 182.

25 ECJ 1991, I-6079 note 19.

26 BVerfGE 22, 293.

debate deals only with the question of a new constitution.[27] It is not surprising that many of those who are close to European Community law have no problems with this understanding. Indeed, the daily public operations of the European Community would be without legitimacy if the EC Treaty did not provide for the authorization and control of those actions. It is well known that the EC Treaty confers public powers upon the European Community and provides for procedural, political and judicial mechanisms for the control of their use. This is precisely the substantial function of a constitution in the historical constitutionalization in Europe.[28] With a sharp analytical eye the Federal Constitutional Court recognized as early as 1967 that the EEC Treaty is '*gewissermaßen die Verfassung der Gemeinschaft*'[29] ('so to speak the constitution of the Community'). And in 1991 the European Court of Justice labelled the EEC Treaty as '*die grundlegende Verfassungsurkunde der Gemeinschaft*'[30] ('the basic constitutional document of a community of law'). This is well analysed, even if semantic purity suggests that one should not confuse linguistically and mentally a state constitution with a transnational constitution.

3.2. Constitutionality in the Modern Theory of Civil Society

However, the question remains whether European primary law is also constitutional in the sense of the modern theory of civil society. Doubts remain if one follows Selznick´s theory which distinguishes between the formal enactment of a constitution and the intrinsic reason of the obliging or compulsory nature (*Verbindlichkeit*) of a constitution.[31] For Selznick´s theory of civil society the intrinsic reason for a constitution as the good overall organization of a people is not the formal act, but an implied and real covenant between citizens – a covenant in the form of a 'constitutional' promise for mutual respect and mutual assistance in good times and bad (in the words of Winfried Brugger: '*sich gegenseitig zu achten und gemeinsam füreinander einzustehen, in guten wie in schlechten Zeiten*').[32] As a matter of course such a covenant does not require the oath of individuals on a meadow in the Alps, as was allegedly the case with the '*Rütlischwur*'. However, the depth of individuals' consent to the transnational European Union and the density of the elements for a successful community life[33] – namely common history, common culture, common communication, common identity – is obviously limited. This does not exclude the emergence and existence of a transnational European civil society and constitution, but its coherence has to be realistically thought of as being different from the coherence of a national civil society and its constitution.

27 See P.-Ch. Müller-Graff *supra* at note 4.
28 See, e.g., F. Hartung, *Deutsche Verfassungsgeschichte*, 1950.
29 See *supra* note 26.
30 See *supra* note 25.
31 See *supra* note 17, p. 477 *et seq.*
32 'The Moral Commonwealth – Zur Verfassung von Gesellschaft und Staat aus der Sicht des Kommunitarismus', *KritV*, 2001 at V 7.
33 For these elements see P. Selznick *supra* at note 17, p. 360 *et seq.*

Viewed from these requirements for a successful transnational community life, primary law is not so much a key-stone of the constitution of a transnational community but the foundation stone.

4. Private Law Society in Primary Law of the EC

This insight leads to our third question: does *European primary law* contain a *basis* for a European private law society or, in other words, for private autonomy? Here a triad (in German: *ein Dreiklang*) can be heard: basic freedoms, human rights and citizenship of the Union.

4.1. The Basic Freedoms in the Internal Market

The key point is to be found in the *basic freedoms* of the internal market. They draw together the fundamental concept of integration of the EC Treaty in the form of *individual rights*. It is well known that historically this concept emerged after more ambitious institutional approaches towards European integration failed in 1954.[34] The far-reaching public perspectives of this concept include peacekeeping, gaining prosperity and fostering solidarity in a transnational community.[35] Nevertheless, the concept is primarily focused on the interaction of economic forces and initiatives in the interest of achieving common prosperity. However, the founding states did not leave the realization of these objectives to traditional patterns of international economic co-operation, but instead relied on the economic welfare theory of comparative cost advantage which is based on the free movement of productive factors and products within a common economic territory.[36] It is also well known that this philosophy was transformed into European primary law, specifically into the four basic freedoms of border-crossing: the movement of persons, capital, goods and services.[37] The European Court of Justice deserves the merit of transforming the explicit prohibitions of impediments to transnational movement into directly applicable subjective rights of individuals and enterprises to engage in border-crossing activities.[38]

As a result the substantial European primary law is based on the functional idea, by way of border-crossing private initiative, of serving the prosperity goal, realizing the peace objective and offering the chance that the transnational civil context creates a potential for fostering solidarity. The present assumption is that

34 The failing ambitious project was the European Defence Community.

35 See P.-Ch. Müller-Graff, 'Einheit und Kohärenz der Vertragsziele von EG und EU', *Europarecht Beiheft*, 1998, 2, p. 67 *et seq.*

36 See, e.g., W. Molle, *The Economics of European Integration*, Ashgate, Dartmouth, 4th ed., 2001, p. 11 *et seq.*

37 See Articles 23 *et seq.*, 39 *et seq.*, 43 *et seq.*, 49 *et seq.*, 56 *et seq.* EC-Treaty; as a comprehensive analysis of recent developments see P.-Ch. Müller-Graff, 'Die Verdichtung des Binnenmarktrechts zwischen Handlungsfreiheiten und Sozialgestaltung', *Europarecht Beiheft*, 1, 2002 p. 16 and 36 *et seq.*

38 See ECJ 1963, 1 (*Van Gend & Loos*).

various single, autonomously initiated and performed, mutually advantageous, border-crossing business and labour contacts generate a transnational web of relations and assessments - perhaps even new circles of marriage and an additional identity - and all this in a more fundamental, sustainable and lasting way than might be achieved by inter-governmental or supranational co-operation between states.

The vitality and attractiveness of this concept for an organized transnational area of interaction is presently demonstrated by its extension to candidate states, in particular its adoption by the East Central European States.[39] After an initial period of varying transformations the orientation towards this concept is visible and guided in particular by the construction plan of the association agreements[40] and by the countless road signs of the European Commission for the preparation of the national legal orders of the candidate states to the rules of the internal market.[41] As a result, the precursors of the emergence of a transnational civil society grow into the depths of East Central Europe, although the scepticism of the citizens of the Union is rather high according to polls taken in spring.

4.2. Human Rights

The basic freedoms which open the gate for a European private law society are flanked by measures of individual protection against the actions of European Community institutions and their national implementation, in other words by *human rights*. Although not explicitly mentioned in the EC Treaty and embodied only in a solemn declaration in Nice[42] they are nevertheless articulated, case by case, as general principles of law by the European Court of Justice.[43] As a result Community law recognizes - without the legal need of a Charter of Human Rights - nearly the whole array of fundamental rights as embodied, for example, in the German Grundgesetz; in particular: the respect for personal rights,[44] herein included the

39 See, e.g., P.-Ch. Müller-Graff (ed.), *East Central Europe and the European Union: From Europe Agreements to a Member Status*, Baden-Baden, Nomos, 1997; M. Maresceau (ed.), *Enlarging the European Union*, New York, Longman, 1997.

40 As an analysis see, e.g., M. Maresceau, '"Europe Agreements": A New Form of Co-operation between the European Community and Central and Eastern Europe', in P.-Ch. Müller-Graff (ed.), *East Central European States and the European Communities: Legal Adaptation to the Market Economy*, Baden-Baden, Nomos, 1993, p. 209 *et seq.*

41 See, in particular, the Commission's White Paper on the Preparation of the Associated Countries of Central and Eastern Europe for Integration into the Internal Market, COM(95) 163 final, 3 May 1995; as an analysis see M.-A. Gaudissart and A. Sinnaeve, 'The Role of the White Paper in the Preparation of the Eastern Enlargement', in M. Maresceau (ed.), *Enlarging the European Union*, New York, Longman, 1997, p. 41 *et seq.*; later on: 'Road Maps' and 'Accession Partnerships'.

42 Charter of Fundamental rights of the European Union, (2000) *OJ* C 364/1.

43 For the former development see, e.g., P.-Ch. Müller-Graff, 'Europäische Verfassung und Grundrechtscharta: Die Europäische Union als transnationales Gemeinwesen', *integration*, 34, 2000, p. 40 *et seq.*

44 ECJ 1969, 419 note 7 (*Stauder*).

right of privacy;[45] equal protection[46] and the freedom of religion;[47] the freedom of speech and publication;[48] the protection of the family[49] and the freedom of association;[50] the protection of mail[51] and the freedom of profession;[52] the protection of the home[53] and of property[54] as well as efficient legal protection.[55]

4.3. The Citizenship of the Union

Eventually the triad of primary law fundamentals for a transnational private law society and, by that, for a civil society in general is completed by an institute which already points to a political community, namely the citizenship of the Union. Although it serves only as an encompassing term for the rights and obligations that are granted by Community law to the citizens of the Member States,[56] the institute creates a specific common civil status which transcends respective national citizenship. It constitutes common civil ground in relation to the Community and a distinction to citizens of third States. One can therefore agree with Ulrich Everling that citizenship of the Union is a task for the Union to understand itself not only as a Community for technocratic purposes, but as a political Community of law. In the idea of the citizenship of the Union one can partially discover the transformation of the European Union into a community of solidarity and destiny.

5. Perspectives of a European Private Law Society

This touches on the fourth and last question, namely the *perspectives* of a European private law society in *primary and secondary Community law.*

5.1. The Orientation to a Transnational Civil Society

In the interest of a successful Union no immediate nor actual reason for deviating from the idea and principle of fostering the transnational civil society is visible. This is valid as far as no regulatory policies or mandatory law are necessary to protect a civil society against itself. Privately generated relations between individuals and enterprises provide the chance not only to base a transnational area on social

45 ECJ 1992, I-2575 note 23 (*Commission of the European Communities v Federal Republic of Germany – Protection of public health*); 1994, I-4737 note 17 (*Aids-Test*).

46 ECJ 1962, 653 (*Equalization of ferrous scrap*); 1994, I-1853 note 26 (*Codorniú*).

47 ECJ 1976, 1589 (*Prais*).

48 ECJ 1984, 19 note 34 (*VBVB-VBBB*); 1991, I-2925 note 43 (*ERT*).

49 ECJ 1989, 1263 note 10 (*Migrant workers*).

50 ECJ 1995, I-4921 (*Bosman*).

51 ECJ 1989, 2859 note 18 (*Hoechst*).

52 ECJ 1979, 3727 note 31 (*Hauer*); 1986, 2897 (*Keller*); 1987, 4097 (*Heylens*); 1994, I-4973 note 78 (*Banana market*).

53 ECJ 1989, 2859 note 17 (*Hoechst*).

54 ECJ 1979, 3727 note 17 (*Hauer*); 1994, I-4973 note 78 (*Banana market*).

55 ECJ 1986, 1651 note 18 (*Johnston*); 1987, 4097 (*Heylens*).

56 See Article 17 EC Treaty.

connections, but also to tame the exaggeration of conflicts between nationally defined collective interests and entities. Without this basis the developed primary law construction of Europe remains without a sense of its own foundation - with the exception of the Common Foreign and Security Policy which can be pursued (and presently seems to be pursued) as a classical alliance without any supranational element or connection to the internal market.

5.2. The Further Development of the Private Law Society

However, even on the basis of this well-founded principle, questions arise for the perspectives of the three above-mentioned elements of primary law, among which the basic freedoms must and will continue to play the central role.

5.2.1. The Role of the Basic Market Freedoms

Concerning the future of the *basic freedoms* under the aspect of a transnational European private law society, permanent overarching issues exist, in particular the questions as to whether their scope is jeopardized or has to be strengthened and whether their realization is to be accompanied by restrictions of general freedoms of action (catch-word: regulation in secondary law).[57] In this respect two lines of development are visible: firstly, the increasing consolidation and strengthening of the basic freedoms and, secondly, the gradual shift of regulatory policies and regulation from the national level to European restrictions of general freedoms of action.

5.2.1.1. Consolidation

Increasing consolidation has occurred in numerous new rules adapted into the *EC Treaty* at Maastricht and Amsterdam. The primary law framework for a European private law society was extended piece by piece. With the emergence of Monetary Union[58] (Maastricht) the free movement of capital and payment was transformed into clear subjective rights.[59] The explicit obligation of the European Community and the Member States to pursue an economic policy which is - on the basis of the internal market - conducted in accordance with the principle of an open market economy with free competition[60] (Maastricht) strengthened the constitutional decision for the basic freedoms and competition.[61] The explicit insertion of a European Community competency for industrial policy (Maastricht) is simultaneously counterbalanced by expressly prohibiting the European Community from

57 See H. Giersch, 'Europa 1992: Nicht auf dem Verordnungswege', *FAZ*, 8.10.1988, p. 15.

58 Articles 105 *et seq*. EC Treaty.

59 See Article 56 EC Treaty.

60 See Article 4 EC Treaty.

61 See P.-Ch. Müller-Graff, 'Die wettbewerbsverfaßte Marktwirtschaft als gemeineuropäisches Verfassungsprinzip?', *Europarecht*, 1997, p. 433 and 439 *et seq*.

introducing any measure which could lead to a distortion of competition.[62] The introduction of the role of services of general economic interest as part of the principles of the EC Treaty (Amsterdam) is simultaneously accompanied by affirming the necessity that they comply, in principle, with the rules on undistorted competition.[63] The inclusion of the area of freedom, security and justice[64] (Amsterdam) emphasizes the objective of the free movement of persons without internal border controls.

In addition to this development of primary law texts the European *judiciary is continually* extending the scope of the basic freedoms in order to overcome specific single access impediments, e.g. restrictions on buying spectacles in another Member State,[65] discriminatory taxation,[66] obstacles to changing from one soccer club to another amongst Member States,[67] refusing to register the branch of an English private limited company in Denmark[68] or restricting conditions on the application for employment in a private bank.[69]

Together with this line of consolidation a further phenomenon is evident: namely the contribution of Community *legislation* to overcome impediments of different kinds. Secondary law paves the way for a more intense use of basic freedoms where primary law does not help: e.g., encouraging consumers to engage in transnational transactions by way of harmonizing different standards of consumer protection;[70] supporting enterprises to participate in public tenders in other Member States by way of eliminating restrictive rules and practice;[71] creating the possibility for competition in telecommunication and in the supply of electricity by way of easing transnational activities.[72] On the other side European Community legislation provokes the question as to whether over-regulative actions are being taken at the expense of civil society.

62 See Article 157 par. 3 EC Treaty.

63 See Article 16 EC Treaty.

64 See Article 61 EC Treaty.

65 ECJ 1998, I-4075 (*Decker*).

66 E.g., ECJ 1997, I-2471 (*Futura*); 1998, I-4635 (*ICI*); 1999, I-7447 (*Eurowings*); 1999, I-7641 (*Vestergaard*); 2000, I-2787 (*Baars*).

67 ECJ 1995, I-4921 (*Bosman*).

68 ECJ 1999, I-1459 (*Centros*).

69 ECJ 2000, I-4139 (*Angonese*).

70 See, e.g., P.-Ch. Müller-Graff, 'EC-Directives as a Means of Private Law Unification', in A.S. Hartkamp *et al.* (eds.), *Towards a European Civil Code*, Nijmegen, Den Haag, Ars Aequi Libri, Kluwer Law International, 1998, p. 71, 75 *et seq.* and 83.

71 See, e.g., I. Seidel, 'Öffentliches Auftragswesen', in M. Dauses (ed.), *Handbuch des EU-Wirtschaftsrechts*, München, C.H. Beck, 2000, H IV.

72 See, e.g., for telecommunication Ch. Engel, 'Kommunikation und Medien', in M. Dauses (ed.), *Handbuch des EU-Wirtschaftsrechts*, München, C.H. Beck, 2000, E V; for electricity R. Lukes, 'Energierecht', in M. Dauses (ed.), *Handbuch des EU-Wirtschaftsrechts*, München, C.H. Beck, 2000, M.

5.2.1.2. Transfer of Regulatory Policies to the Community

This leads to a second important line of development: the transfer of regulatory policies and regulation from the Member States to restrictions of the general freedom of action generated by Community law: for example, national protection of the electricity sector is overcome at the price of numerous single provisions in directives; national food safety law is modified by the implementation of detailed approximation directives; and national consumer protection is replaced by filigree directives. As a consequence, the issue of protection of individual autonomy by fundamental rights potentially gains momentum,[73] although the practical importance of human rights protection at the level of the European Community level similar to that of the national level cannot yet be seen.

5.2.2. The Role of Human Rights Protection

The increasing role of *human rights protection* in view of regulatory internal market legislation of the Community has its roots in a paradoxical mechanism. Strengthening transnational freedoms is partially achieved by more regulation by the Community. The proper protection of individuals in these cases is primarily the task of the judiciary of the Community. In this context human rights are an issue only in so far as actions of the Community are not yet struck down by the violation of other principles of law such as lack of competency (as in the tobacco case),[74] lack of sufficient reasoning (as in the Air France case)[75] or disproportionality.[76]

Does the Nice Charter on Human Rights[77] strengthen the judicial protection provided by the European Court of Justice and is there a need to transform the Charter into primary law? Answering the first question is somewhat speculative, answering the second question requires careful evaluation of the status quo. It can be seen that the resistance against a primary law solution in Nice has its roots in a number of different concerns: a concern of unitarizing effects of a jurisprudence on fundamental rights for all Member States in contradiction to the idea of subsidiarity; concern about the tacit transfer of competencies to the European level in contradiction to the call for a clear delineation of competencies; and concern of potentially strengthening the European judiciary in relation to the political institutions of the EC in contradiction to political primacy. These are serious concerns that do not need and cannot properly be discussed here.

73 See, e.g., P.-Ch. Müller-Graff, 'Basic Freedoms – Extending Party Autonomy across Borders', in S. Grundmann, W. Kerber and S Weatherill (eds.), *Party Autonomy and the Role of Information in the Internal Market*, Warsaw, De Gruyter, 2001, p. 133 and 148.

74 ECJ 2000, I-8419 (*Germany v. Parliament and Council*).

75 Court of First Instance 1998, II-2405, 2447 *et seq.* at notes 94 *et seq.* (*British Airways and British Midland/Commission*).

76 E.g., ECJ 1986, 2519 note 21 (*Commission/Germany*).

77 See *supra* note 42.

5.2.3. The Future of the Citizenship of the Union

Eventually the *citizenship of the Union* will be enriched by any new legal guarantee for an individual or any new legal obligation of an individual in the framework of the EC and, by that, may cultivate the soil on which the European private law society can prosper.

5.3. Community Private Law for the European Private Law Society

A last question now confronts us: Does the European private law society require an adequate detailed legal framework for its conduct? In other words, does it require private law based on Community law (Gemeinschaftsprivatrecht)? Does it, perhaps, require the enactment of a European Civil Code? It is well known that this is a live issue in scholarly work,[78] in working groups,[79] in statements of the European Parliament[80] and, partially, in the recent Communication of the Commission on European contract law.[81] And indeed a European codification would not only create an economically beneficial common private law in Europe but could also widen the array of European symbols: a symbol for the European civil society side by side with the Euro as the tangible symbol of the internal market, with the European passport as the symbol of citizenship of the Union and with the European Treaties as the symbol of a mutually binding common political will and constitution.

It is therefore fair to ask whether a European codification of private law should be one of our current tasks?[82] Nobody can dispute that for a long time the *forces* unleashed by basic transnational market freedoms have worked towards approximation and, through that, towards a new form of a European *ius commune*. It is also plausible that common or uniform rules for contract law, for securing transactions, for liability and for other legal instruments of compensation allow more reliability for planning and for conduct than the complex combination of rules on the conflict of laws in connection with potentially different substantial laws. Indeed, the private self-determination of economic life is already generating adequate transnational rules on a large scale: new types of contracts, international standard terms, individual courses of dealing, professional standards, technical norms, trade usages, lex mercatoria and rules for arbitration.

78 See, e.g., V. Rizzo (*a cura di*), *Diritto Privato Comunitario*, Edizione Scientifische Italiane, 1997; A.S. Hartkamp *et al.* (eds.), *Towards a European Civil Code*, second edition, Nijmegen-Den Haag, Ars Aequi Libri, Kluwer Law International, 1998; P.-Ch. Müller-Graff (ed.), *Gemeinsames Privatrecht in der Europäischen Gemeinschaft*, 2nd ed., Baden-Baden, Nomos, 1999.

79 For the Commission on European Contract Law see *supra* note 3; see also: Academy of European Private Lawyers, *European Contract Code*, preliminary draft, 2001; *Studiengruppe für ein europäisches Zivilgesetzbuch.*

80 (1989) *OJ* C 158/400 (26.6.1989); (1994) *OJ* C 205/518 (25.7.1994).

81 COM(2001) 398 final (11.7.2001).

82 Thereby recalling the controversy on the creation of a German Civil Code in the 19th century between A.F.J. Thibaut, *Über die Notwendigkeit eines allgemeinen bürgerlichen Rechts für Deutschland*, Heidelberg, Mohr und Zimmer, 1814 and C.F. von Savigny, *Vom Beruf unserer Zeit für Gesetzgebung und Wissenschaft*, Heidelberg, Mohr und Zimmer, 1814.

However, economic life is also increasingly encountering the *limits* set by mandatory law which has been adopted by the Community in favour of a well-balanced protection of the public good. This points to the problems and limits of a private law society, namely to the protection of the private law society against itself. As a consequence an epochal harmonization of regulatory law takes place - that is similar to the territorial rules in the German Customs Union in the 19th century being overcome or to the state case law in the American internal market being overcome by the UCC in the 20th century. Within the European Community it is not the political Community which seeks an adequate private law, but the economically acting civil society. Hence there seems to be a more realistic option than a great leap into a European codification of private law which would entail the abolition of the great national civil codifications such as the Civil Code, the ABGB or the BGB: namely the development of Community private law alongside national codifications (which, however, would not remain untouched in their scope and content) in the form of an emerging European commercial law, comparable perhaps to the former emergence of the Allgemeine Deutsche Handelsgesetzbuch of 1861 or the US-American Uniform Commercial Code in the last century. In fact, it can already be observed that the overwhelming number of EC-directives in private law are focused on enterprises, among them particularly consumer protection directives which usually deal with questions in the relationship of a consumer to an enterprise. Hence it is no surprise that in Germany the implementation of directives concerning private law has found its way not only into the Civil Code and into special consumer law statutes outside the Civil Code, but also, with different intensity, into any of the first four parts of the Commercial Code. Hence some creative fantasy should be given to the idea of a European Commercial Code (ECC).

In all these considerations one elementary point should not be neglected. The basic text which is adequate for the European private law society and which decisively generates it already exists. It is the EC Treaty which is conceptually founded on the idea of a common market and, by that, on the border-crossing basic market freedoms. They - the basic freedoms - come close to fulfilling *Jean Monnet's* word that the task is not to bring States into a coalition but to unite people.[83] Hence they - the basic freedoms - constitute the Magna Charta of the European private law society also for the future of the new century.

83 J. Monnet, *Erinnerungen eines Europäers*, Baden-Baden, Nomos, 1998, p. IV.

Good Governance

Luc Verhey

GOOD GOVERNANCE: TOWARDS A EUROPEAN IUS COMMUNE?

1. Introduction

'Good governance' is a fashionable notion these days. Until recently, it was seldom heard in the political and constitutional debate on the future of Europe. In a short period of time, this has changed.[1] The growing popularity of 'good governance' can be explained by recent developments. Since the fall of the Santer Commission, caused by the First Report of the Committee of Independent Experts, there seems to be a broad consensus that changes in decision-making and implementation procedures at European level need to be made in line with the general principles of 'good governance'.

However, it would be wrong to view the European debate on good governance as having been prompted by the fall of Santer only. It should be seen in the broader context of an increasing inability of the EU to act effectively, visibly and credibly. As the Commission recently stated in its White Paper on European Governance (hereafter: the White Paper), 'many people are loosing confidence in a poorly understood and complex system to deliver the policies that they want'.[2] The need to change European governance must furthermore be seen against the backdrop of closer ties between the EU and future Member States and third countries. In discussions and negotiations on, for instance, enlargement and foreign aid, the position of the EU is less credible if the EU itself fails to comply with the basic conditions of good governance.[3]

The great difficulty is to reach a consensus on the precise content of the notion of 'good governance' at European level and the way in which it is to be made operational. As a result of this, there is a considerable risk that the debate on 'good governance' will not progress beyond vague intentions. In this respect, it is of great

1 See for example Ch. Joerges, '"Good Governance" Through Comitology, in Ch. Joerges and E. Vos (eds.), *EU Committees: Social Regulation, Law and Politics*, Oxford, Hart Publishing, 1999, p. 311 *et seq*. The notion of 'good governance' also plays a significant role in the recently published *White Paper*. See para. 3.

2 *European Governance, A White Paper*, Brussels, 25.7.2001, COM(2001) 428 final, p. 3.

3 *White Paper*, p. 26.

importance that the Prodi Commission, shortly after taking office, identified the reform of European governance as one of its four strategic objectives for the coming years.[4] From that time onwards, the Commission worked hard to put this objective into practice. In the beginning of the year 2000, a White Paper was published on the reform of the Commission,[5] which included an action plan.[6] The programme can be seen as a direct reaction to the reports by the Independent Committee of Experts. However, this programme only deals with the Commission's own role. In the White Paper on European Governance mentioned earlier, the Commission goes much further by proposing an ambitious set of reforms relating to rules, processes and behaviour that affect the way in which powers are exercised at European level. It proposes 'opening up the policy-making process to get more people and organizations involved in shaping and delivering EU policy'.[7] Pursuant to this general objective, the Commission has formulated several proposals to reform the EU decision-making process.

The aim of my own paper is relatively modest. First, several brief observations will be made on the constitutional context of the debate on 'good governance'. Special attention will be paid to the relation between 'good governance' and the process of institutional reform. Subsequently, the paper will describe and analyse a number of key elements in the White Paper. In so doing, I will conform to the order of the issues as discussed by the Commission. There is no room for exhaustive examination of all the issues. I will limit myself, therefore, to an overview of the most important proposals and some brief comments. The final paragraph will contain some concluding remarks.

2. Constitutional Context

The debate on 'good governance' must be placed with the context of the EU's constitutional framework. This the Commission fully recognizes. In the White Paper on European Governance, the Commission points out that the Union faces a double standard: not only is there a need for urgent action to adapt governance under the existing treaties, but also for a broader debate on the future of Europe in view of the next Inter-Governmental Conference, where further institutional change will be the subject of intense debate.[8] This has prompted the Commission to adopt a dual approach. On the one hand, it formulates proposals to change the way the Union operates under the existing treaties. On the other, it stresses the interrelation between those proposals and the need for institutional change: 'reforming European governance also sketches a path towards future Treaty changes at the next Inter-

4 Brussels 9.2.2000, COM(2000) 154 final.

5 Reforming the Commission, *A White Paper – Part I*, Brussels, 5.4.2000, COM(2000) 200 final/2. See P. Craig, 'The Fall and Renewal of the Commission: Accountability, Contract and Administrative Organization', *ELJ*, 2000, p. 98-116.

6 Brussels 1.3.2000, COM(2000) 200 final.

7 *White Paper*, p. 3.

8 *White Paper*, p. 3.

Governmental Conference – it presents the outlines of a model for the Union's future political organization'.[9]

However, as many years of experience have shown, developing a consistent constitutional model for the EU is a highly complex matter. Because of the variability and ambiguity of its institutional framework, the EU cannot be considered a traditional 'state'. The constant tension between intergovernmentalism and supranationalism renders the EU unique, but also prevents a proper understanding of the way the EU exercises public power compared to traditional constitutional models.[10] The specific nature of the process of European integration seems to call for an unorthodox approach.

The EU is frequently characterized as a multi-level governance system. In such a system, integration is a 'polity-creating process in which authority and policy-making are shared across multiple levels of government – sub-national, national and supranational'.[11] None of the actors in this process is considered to be dominant. Although national governments are major players in policy making, they do not have a monopoly on control. Supranational institutions, the Commission and the European Parliament in particular, also exercise influence on policy-making. The members of these institutions do not, at least not primarily, look after the interests of the Member State from which they originate, but act in the interest of the EU as a whole. However, neither institution is dominant. The Member States, as represented in the Council and numerous committees, play a key role in EU decision making.

This unique and highly complex way of exercising public power at EU level greatly influences the debate on the constitutional future of the EU. Development of new, less state-oriented theories and concepts has been advocated.[12] Traditional constitutional parameters are considered to be of limited use, sometimes even to be dangerous. Weiler, for example, regards the constitutionalization of Committee procedures, which at present is an important part of the decision-making and implementation process within the EU, as a 'normative disaster'.[13] In his view, the

9 *White Paper*, p. 34. See further par. 6.

10 G. de Burca, 'The Institutional Development of the EU: A Constitutional Analysis', in P. Craig and G. de Burca (eds.), *The Evolution of EU Law*, Oxford, Oxford University Press, 1999, p. 64.

11 G. Marks, L. Hooghe and K. Blank, 'European Integration from the 1980s: State-Centric v. Multiple-Level Governance', *JCMS*, 1996, p. 341 and 342. See also P. Craig, 'The Nature of the Community: Integration, Democracy, and Legitimacy', in P. Craig, G. de Burca (eds.), *The Evolution of EU Law*, Oxford, Oxford University Press, 1999, p. 16 *et seq.*

12 P. Craig, *supra* note 11, p. 19 *et seq.* See also R. Dehousse, 'European governance in search of legitimacy: the need for a process-based approach', in O. De Schutter, N. Lebessis and J. Paterson (eds.), *Governance in the European Union*, Luxembourg, Office for Official Publications of the European Communities, 2001, p. 169 *et seq.*; E.M.H. Hirsch Ballin, 'Vervlochten constituties. Nederland in de Europese rechtsorde', in A.K. Koekkoek (ed.), *Bijdragen aan een Europese grondwet, Publikaties van de staatsrechtkring* (staatsrechtconferenties nr. 5), Deventer, W.E.J. Tjeenk Willink, 2000, p. 11 *et seq.*

13 J.H.H. Weiler, 'Epilogue: 'Comitology' as Revolution – Infranationalism, Constitutionalism and Democracy', in Ch. Joerges and E. Vos (eds.), *EU Committees: Social Regulation, Law and Politics*, Oxford, Hart Publishing, 1999, p. 346.

case law of the European Court[14] is premised on the classical belief in the ability and necessity of assigning and maintaining legal powers to well-defined subjects only. It thus excludes discretionary powers of committees, *de facto* obscuring the autonomy of these committees as exists in practice and, consequently, the constitutional value of accountability. Instead, the Court 'would have to recognize the infranational[15] character of the *Comitology*, which defies the normal constitutional categories laboriously constructed in the context of a supranational understanding of the Community'. In his opinion, an infranational adjudication:

> 'would reverse the current set of priorities and put values before structure. Equality of access, transparency, political accountability should trump considerations of, say, delegation and attribution'.

At first glance, this approach of 'putting values before structure' seems to square well with the concept of 'good governance'. The debate focuses on identifying the main principles of 'good governance' and how these should be given effect under the working methods of the Community rather than on bringing the institutional structure in line with common constitutional standards. However, values and structures are not opposites. On the contrary, it seems to be impossible to put principles of good governance, such as accountability and transparency, into practice without a clear and consistent institutional structure that conforms to generally accepted principles of democracy and the rule of law. To a considerable extent, these principles directly relate to the structure as such. Giving priority to values over structures is therefore undesirable: they are intertwined and inseparable.

The importance of state-oriented constitutional principles for the debate on European governance should not be underestimated. Although the EU is not a 'state' in the traditional sense, this does not mean that the classical constitutional values will not apply. As De Burca stated:

> 'it is not necessarily only the constitution of a state, but of any political entity exercising public power, which ought to guide and constrain its institutions by reference to observable rules of good government, such as that they should be accessible and reasonably accountable to those on whose behalf they act'.[16]

It is not plausible to assume that those rules would be totally different from traditional constitutional values. Parallelism with national constitutional traditions

14 Known as the Meroni-doctrine. See ECJ Case 9/56 (1957-58), ECR 133.

15 Weiler's theory is that there are three modes of governance within the EU: the international, the supranational and the infranational. In his view, infranational governance covers implementing and executive measures, standard setting and the like, of the kind which are the daily fare of *Comitology*. Not the Community or the Member States are the key players, but rather 'both at Union and Member State levels, administrations, departments, private and public associations, and certain, mainly corporate, interest groups.' See J.H.H. Weiler, *The constitution of Europe. 'Do the new clothes have an emperor?' and other essays on European integration*, Cambridge, Cambridge University Press, 1999, p. 270 *et seq*, esp. p. 273.

16 G. de Burca, *supra* note 10, p. 65.

seems to be confirmed by Article 6 TEU; it provides that the Union is founded on the principles of liberty, democracy, respect for human rights and the rule of law, 'principles which are common to the Member States'.

The challenge for the EU consists in identifying more precisely the content of the constitutional principles shared by Member States and transform these into constitutional rules governing the EU, with due regard to the peculiarities of the EU legal order.[17] An important issue will be the degree to which these peculiarities, as have developed in the past, can be taken into account. There seems to be a considerable risk that the transposition of constitutional standards to EU level will be the end product of an unclear and ambiguous compromise between intergovernmentalism and supranationalism. Such a compromise could not only cause serious practical problems, but also prevent that essential constitutional values are sufficiently safeguarded.

A major problem, of course, is that Member States fundamentally disagree on the constitutional model for the future political organization of the EU. It is not realistic to expect that this problem will be resolved in the short term. However, a pragmatic, case-by-case approach of institutional aspects does not seem to be an attractive alternative. An example of this is the recent position of the Dutch government. In a White Paper sent to the Dutch parliament, the Dutch government wrote that it 'does not opt for a blueprint, i.e. a detailed plan prescribing the definitive shape of the European house'. Instead, it prefers reforms based on 'the demands and needs ensuing from the actual problems facing Europe'.[18] Although, from a political perspective, such an approach is understandable, it creates the risk that different, perhaps even contradictory, solutions are chosen in individual cases. For example, in the same document, the Dutch government proposes both that the President of the Commission be elected by the people and that political accountability of individual commissioners before the European Parliament be increased. These proposals are a puzzling mixture of elements of presidential and parliamentary systems and therefore virtually irreconcilable.[19] It shows that, although difficult to achieve, there remains an urgent need to develop a consistent, long-term vision of a constitutional model for the EU, based on the constitutional traditions of the Member States.

3. Principles of Good Governance

Although the Commission recognizes the institutional dimension of European governance,[20] this is not the prevailing perspective of the White Paper. It is primarily focused on changing European governance under the existing Treaties. It seems logical therefore, from the Commission's perspective, that the White Paper

17 W. van Gerven, 'Ethical and political responsibility of EU Commissioners', *CML Rev.*, 37 2000, p. 6.

18 Tweede Kamer, vergaderjaar 2000-2001, 27407, nr. 9, p. 7.

19 *Ibidem*, p. 6. For this reason, Dutch politics have always rejected direct election of the Prime Minister.

20 See para. 6.

starts by identifying principles of good governance that could serve as a guideline for the necessary changes. However, one could argue that this is an unfortunate approach. Without a clear idea of the constitutional context, the precise meaning of 'good governance'[21] and its principles, as well as the way in which these should work out in practice, remains difficult to determine.

Until recently, the principles of good governance were not systematically codified at European or international level. However, on the basis of, especially, Article 6 TEU, such principles are increasingly formalized into written rules and codes of conduct. Article 41[22] of the EU Charter of fundamental rights provides for a general right to good administration.[23] This provision, not found in the European Convention on Human Rights, on which the Charter has largely been based, reads as follows:[24]

> 'Article 41:
> 1. Every person has the right to have his or her affairs handled impartially, fairly and within a reasonable time by the institutions and bodies of the Union.
> 2. This right includes:
> - the right of every person to be heard, before any individual measure which would affect him or her adversely is taken;
> - the right of every person to have access to his or her file, while respecting the legitimate interests of confidentiality and of professional and business secrecy;
> - the obligation of the administration to give reasons for its decisions.
> 3. Every person has the right to have the Community make good any damage caused by its institutions or by its servants in the performance of their duties, in accordance with the general principles common to the laws of the Member States.[25]
> 4. Every person may write to the institutions of the Union in one of the languages of the Treaties and must have an answer in the same language'.[26]

In addition to this general provision, the Commission has formulated the key principles to be observed: independence, responsibility, accountability, efficiency and transparency.[27] These objectives serve as a general guideline for the reform programme inspired by the work of the Committee of Independent Experts, in

21 The Commission has defined the notion 'governance' as 'rules, processes and behaviour that affect the way in which powers are exercised at European level, particularly as regards openness, participation, accountability, effectiveness and coherence'. See the *White Paper*, p. 8, note 1.

22 See also Article 42 in which the right of access to documents is laid down. However, this right has already been protected in Article 255 EC. See also Article 1 TEU.

23 The notion 'administration' seems to be a less broad than 'governance': it only concerns executive powers.

24 This right, like others rights in the Charter, can be limited under the conditions of Article 52 (1). Limitations must be provided for by law and must respect the essence of the right. In addition, limitations, which are subjected to the principle of proportionality, may only be set if they are necessary and genuinely meet objectives of general interest as recognized by the Union or 'the need to protect the rights and freedoms of others'.

25 See Article 288 EC.

26 See Article 21 EC.

27 Reforming the Commission, *A White Paper – Part I*, Brussels, 5.4.2000, COM(2000) 200 final/2, p. 7.

which the Commission is now involved. In its second report, the Committee made a number of general recommendations aimed at enhancing integrity, responsibility and accountability in European political and administrative life.[28] In turn, the Committee drew inspiration from examples elsewhere, especially the OECD Principles[29] and the Standard Principles of Public Life of the British Nolan (now Neill) Committee.[30]

The Commission recently formalized these principles by adopting a Code of good administrative behaviour.[31] This code is considered to be essential to ensure respect for the right to good administration as laid down in the Charter (see above). The notion 'quality service' plays a key role: it calls for the Commission and its staff to be 'courteous, objective and impartial'. Its administration must be 'open, accessible and properly run'. The Code, which expressly provides that it is binding, obliges the Commission to respect general principles of good administration in its relations with the public. These principles are the following: lawfulness, non-discrimination, proportionality and consistency.

The Commission has also announced the setting-up of a Committee on Standards in Public Life, apparently based on the British example.[32] The Committee's role will be to provide advice on ethical standards at the European Institutions, thus contributing to the further development and implementation of principles of good governance.

The notion of 'good governance' must be seen in the context of the foregoing. In its White Paper, the Commission formulates (once again) some key principles of good governance to guide specific proposals of change:[33]

- *Openness*. The institutions should work in a more open manner and, together with the Member States, should actively communicate on what the EU does and the decisions it takes;
- *Participation*. In order to ensure more confidence in EU policy and institutions, broad participation must be ensured throughout the policy chain - from conception to implementation;
- *Accountability*. Roles in the legislative and executive processes need to be clearer. Moreover, all EU institutions, as well as the Member States, must explain their actions and assume responsibility for them;

28 Committee of Independent Experts, *Second Report on Reform of the Commission*, Brussels 10.9.1999, vol. 2, chapter 7, p. 108 *et seq.*

29 Principles for Managing Ethics in the Public Service, adopted by the Council of the OECD, 23.4.1998, <www.oecd.org>. See also the Second Report, *supra* note 28, p. 113.

30 Nolan Committee's *First Report on Standards in Public Life*, Cm 2850, 1995. This Committee identified seven principles that generally apply to MPs, Ministers and civil servants, executive agencies (quangos) and NHS bodies: selflessness, integrity, objectivity, accountability, openness, honesty and leadership.

31 Code of good administrative behaviour, (2000) *OJ* L 267/20.10.2000.

32 Reforming the Commission, *A White Paper - Part II*, Brussels 1.3.2000, COM(2000) 200 final, p. 3. See also Committee of Independent Experts, *Second Report*, *supra* note 28, p. 121.

33 *White Paper*, p. 10.

- *Effectiveness.* Policies must be effective and timely, delivering what is needed on the basis of clear objectives and an evaluation of future impact and past experience;
- *Coherence.* Policies and actions must be coherent and readily comprehensible.

In the Commission's view, these principles underpin democracy and the rule of law in the Member States, applying to all levels of government - global, European, national, regional and local. Furthermore, their application reinforces the principles of proportionality and subsidiarity. According to the Commission, this means 'that before launching an initiative, it is essential to check systematically (a) if public action is really necessary, (b) if the European level is the most appropriate one, and (c) if the measures chosen are proportionate to those objectives'.[34]

It is difficult to disagree with the Commission *in abstracto.* The above principles are indeed important elements of good governance, which may serve as guidance for improving the way the EU operates in practice. As past experience has shown, however, is very difficult to reach agreement at European level on the implementation of the principles. The debate on public access to documents of the European Parliament, the Council and the Commission has revealed fundamental differences of opinion between the Member States as to how the principles of openness and transparency are to be given effect.[35] It is relatively easy to subscribe to the noble intentions expressed by such principles. Really important is, however, how they will function in concrete cases.

It must be said that in any case one major element seems to be missing. In the list of principles devised by the Commission, the notion of the rule of law is underexposed. Such principles as lawfulness, legality, equal treatment, fairness, integrity, objectivity and impartiality, although perhaps self-evident, are not included. These principles should not be observed exclusively by the judiciary,[36] but must also be addressed to the executive and the legislature. In consequence, the rule of law and the principles derived from it must be regarded as an integral part of 'good governance'.

4. Improving Participation

In an effort to improve European governance at different levels, the Commission presents a range of proposals. Classified under four headings, their aims are:

- to improve involvement of the public in shaping and implementing EU policy;
- to improve the quality and enforcement of EU policies;

34 *White Paper,* p. 11.

35 Regulation (EG) Nr. 1049/2001, Brussels 30.5.2001. See D.M. Curtin, 'Citizens' fundamental right of access to EU information: an evolving digital *passepartout?*', *CML Rev.*, 2000, p. 7 *et seq.*

36 See Conclusions Rule of Law Conference, Noordwijk 23-24 June 1997. The introductory report of this conference: E.A. Alkema *et al.* (eds.), *The role and independence of the judiciary and the administration of justice in the perspective of the rule of law*, Leiden, 1997.

- to enhance a stronger link between European governance and the EU's global role;
- to refocus the role of the institutions.

The following section contains some general comments on the first heading. The other three headings will be discussed in subsequent sections.

The Commission feels that the processes of preparation and adoption of EU policy must be more transparent and better than at present take into account the opinions of interested parties. For this reason, the Commission wishes to improve the involvement of regional and local authorities as well as civil society in shaping and implementing policy within the EU.[37] Each Member State should provide 'adequate mechanisms for wide consultation when discussing EU decisions and implementing EU policies with a territorial dimension'. However, there is an additional role for the Commission: it should organize:

> 'a systematic dialogue with the European and national associations of regional and local government, while respecting national constitutional and administrative arrangements'.

At first sight, this policy of involving local and regional authorities seems largely self-evident. However, if the Commission wishes to achieve these goals, interference, in any case indirectly, in the constitutional legal order of the Member States will be difficult to avoid. The policy challenges the legitimization of national governments as Member-State representatives and may call into question existing constitutional rules and practices. Admittedly, the Commission assures that national constitutional and administrative arrangements[38] will be respected, but this may become a problem if the arrangements leave too little room for involving local and regional interests properly. The example shows that the scope of the White Paper is much broader than one would infer from its title: not only does it concern European governance, but also and to a considerable extent national governance.

In addition to national authorities, civil society as a whole should be more involved in EU policy-making.[39] The Commission refers to the role of the Economic and Social Committee as laid down in Article 257 EC, as recently amended.[40] It also points out that both the Commission and the European Parliament are already in the habit of consulting interested parties through different instruments. However, the Commission stresses that more should be done. What is needed, according to

37 *White Paper*, p. 12.

38 See, for example, Article 113 of the Dutch Municipalities Act, which obliges national government to consult municipal authorities on policy with a local dimension, 'unless public interest requires otherwise'. See also Article 114 *et seq.*

39 *White Paper*, p. 14-18.

40 Agreed in Nice. The second sentence of the text reads as follows: 'The Committee shall consist of representatives of the various economic and social components of organized civil society, and in particular representatives of producers, farmers, carriers, workers, dealers, craftsmen, professional occupations, consumers and the general interest'.

the Commission, is 'a reinforced culture of consultation and dialogue'.[41] Remarkable is its statement that 'creating a culture of consultation cannot be achieved by legal rules which would create excessive rigidity and risk slowing the adoption of particular policies'. The Commission prefers 'a code of conduct that sets minimum standards, focusing on what to consult on, when, whom and how to consult'.[42] In addition to these minimum standards, the Commission intends to develop more extensive 'partnership arrangements'. This entails additional consultations of civil-society organizations which, analogous to public institutions, comply with principles of democracy and the rule of law (openness, representativity). Finally, the Commission stresses the importance of the many European and international networks. It wishes to develop 'a more systematic and pro-active approach to working with key networks to enable them to contribute to decision shaping and policy execution'.[43]

Again, it is difficult to object to the Commission's general intentions. The present working methods, by which involvement of interested parties is far from obvious, are indeed cause for alarm. Less evident is the apparent reluctance to legal rules on general principles of consultation. It is a regrettable misconception that legal rules inevitably result in excessive rigidity and slow procedures, as the Commission seems to assume. The rigidity or flexibility of a legal rule depends on its structure and content, not on the instrument as such. The Commission does not make clear why a code of conduct is to be preferred and what its content should be.

Generally speaking, the legal perspective of good governance seems to receive too little attention in the White Paper. It would have been possible, for example, to consider developing general rules governing administrative decision making (including consultation), enforcement and judicial review, as a follow-up to Article 41 of the Charter.[44] Perhaps a European general administrative statute is a step too far at this stage, for political and legal reasons,[45] but the importance of developing general rules at least for certain areas should not be underestimated. A strong legal position of citizens *vis-à-vis* EU institutions and Member States could boost confidence in European governance, thus contributing significantly towards the objectives of the White Paper.

With regard to codifying general rules, the EU should take advantage of experience with comprehensive codifications in a number Member States, such as Germany and the Netherlands. Moreover, it has to be borne in mind that, apart from the extensive case law of the European Court of Justice, a number general principles have already found their way to the Code of good administrative behaviour discussed above.[46] This code identifies 'guidelines for good adminis-

41 *White Paper*, p. 16.

42 *White Paper*, p. 17.

43 *White Paper*, p. 18.

44 E.M.H. Hirsch Ballin, 'Een grondrecht op behoorlijk bestuur', *NTB*, 2000, 10, p. 305 *et seq.*

45 J. Schwarze, *European administrative law*, London/Luxembourg, Sweet and Maxwell, Office for official publications of the European Union, 1992, p. 1446 *et seq.*; J.H. Jans *et al.* (eds.) *Inleiding tot het Europees bestuursrecht*, Nijmegen, Ars Aequi Libri, 1999, p. 370-372.

46 (2000) *OJ* L 267/20.10.2000.

trative behaviour' with a view to the Commission's performance, such as the duty to:

- act objectively and impartially;
- provide information on administrative procedures as required;
- ensure that an opportunity be given to interested parties to make their views known, where EC law provides that interested parties should be heard;
- state the reasons on which its decisions are based and communicate them to the persons and parties concerned;[47]
- notify interested parties of the possibility of lodging an appeal and how to go about it.

In addition to this, the code contains guidelines relating to correspondence, telephone and electronic communication, as well as the protection of personal data and confidential information.

However, elements of this kind are not found in the Commission's proposals presented in the White Paper, which lacks a comprehensive legal approach. It is necessary, therefore, to broaden the perspective of good governance. Attention should be paid to the codification of general principles of administrative law as an important contribution towards good governance. An essential part of such codifycation would be a broadening of the possibilities for citizens to apply for judicial review at European level. At present, these possibilities are limited and therefore not always available in cases where citizens are directly affected by EU decisions.[48]

5. Improving the Quality of Policies and Regulation

A second component of the Commission's proposals concerns the improvement of the quality of EU policies of regulation and delivery.[49] The Commission has found serious deficiencies here. As a consequence of the reluctance on the part of the Council and the European Parliament to allow the Commission more room for policy execution, legislation often contains an undesirable level of detail, which has resulted in a lack of flexibility and has undermined effectiveness. In some instances, rules are also poorly enforced.

In order to improve the current situation, the Commission identifies basic factors for determining whether and, if so, which measures should be taken. First, proposals must be prepared on the basis of an effective analysis of the appropriateness of intervention at EU level (subsidiarity) and the need for regulatory intervention. The objectives and consequences of any proposal must be clearly identified. Second, a more realistic view of the impact of legislation must be developed. Legislation is often only part of a broader solution, combining formal rules with

47 See Article 253 EC.

48 See Article 47 of the EU-Charter on Human Rights. This article provides for a right to an effective remedy and the right to a fair trial.

49 *White Paper*, p. 18-26.

non-binding rules, such as recommendations, guidelines or self-regulation. In the Commission's view, use of divergent policy tools must be promoted. Third, the Commission writes that, whenever legislation is needed, more attention should be paid to the choice of instrument. Regulations should only be considered in cases in which uniform application and legal certainty across the EU is needed. More frequent use should be made of framework directives. In all instances in which legal rules are established, 'primary' legislation should be used for essential elements only, such as basic rights, obligations and implementation, leaving it up to the executive to fill in the technical details through implementing 'secondary' rules.

Apart from, and in addition to, the use of such regular instruments as legislation, the Commission wishes to promote alternative tools and working methods in specific cases, namely 'co-regulation' and 'the open method of co-operation'. Co-regulation combines binding legislative and regulatory action with actions taken by the actors most concerned in order to improve compliance. However, this method is only suited for cases 'where fundamental rights or major political choices are not called into question'.[50] Secondly, the Commission favours an 'open method of co-operation'. The precise content of the method remains unclear; the Commission defines it as:

> 'a way of encouraging co-operation, the exchange of best practice and agreeing common targets and guidelines for Member States, sometimes backed up by national action plans ...'.[51]

It seems to be an instrument that combines regulatory action and implementation in on-going consultation with interested parties at Member-State level. The Commission warns, however, that:

> 'the use of the method must not upset the institutional balance nor dilute the achievement of common objectives in the Treaty. In particular, it should not exclude the European Parliament from a European policy process'.

Finally, the Commission announces several other measures to improve regulation and policy. It will:

- simplify further existing EU law and encourage Member States to simplify national rules giving effect to EU provisions;
- publish guidelines on the collection and use of expert advice;
- define criteria for the creation of new regulatory agencies and the framework within which they operate;[52]
- promote a stronger assessment and feedback culture in order to learn from past successes and failures;

50 *White Paper*, p. 21.
51 *Ibidem*.
52 See further para. 8.

- enhance enforcement of EC law, among other things by establishing criteria for the investigation of alleged breaches of EC law.

Last but not least, the Commission encourages the Council and the European Parliament to make greater efforts to speed up the legislative process.

The set of measures proposed by Commission is impressive and of an ambitious nature. There is no question that it contains many elements essential for improving the legitimacy of European governance. However, many proposals must be further developed and will have to be implemented. In this context, advantage should be taken of experience at national level, because many deficiencies pointed out by the Commission have also occurred in the Member States.

The common objective of the Commission's proposals is to improve the quality of EC legislation and policy-making. This requires a comprehensive overall approach in dealing with the various stages of the process, from analysing the need for EU intervention to evaluating EU policy and feedback. Such an approach could lead to a general legislative policy, consisting of a framework of criteria and guidelines. This framework should not be a straitjacket, but rather a set of coherent guidelines for the legislature and the executive to hold onto, aimed at improving the quality and consistency of rules and policies.

An example of such an approach can be found in the Netherlands. In 1991, the Dutch government presented an extensive policy plan 'for the further development and implementation of a general legislative policy, aimed at improving the constitutional and administrative quality of government policy'.[53] Although the composition of the government has changed since then, the essentials of this policy are still in place. A primary part concerns quality criteria applying to legislation.[54] These criteria are the following:

a. *Lawfulness and realization of principles of justice.* Legislation must be in conformity with the law, especially international and EC law, the Constitution and general principles of justice, such as the principle of legal certainty;
b. *Effectiveness and efficiency.* Effectiveness implies that the law, at least to a considerable degree, must lead to attainment of the targets set by the legislator. Efficiency relates to the requirement that there must be a balance between the costs and benefits ensuing from the effect of the law;
c. *Subsidiarity and proportionality.* Where possible, responsibility should be left or entrusted to local authorities and social organizations. Instead of intervening immediately and unilaterally, the government should establish a more indirect policy in interaction with society;
d. *Feasibility and enforceability.* It must be possible to enforce compliance with the aid of legal responses to non-compliance and by taking measures. Extremely important factors are the capacity and expertise of the executive and judicial

53 Legislation in perspective (Zicht op wetgeving), Tweede Kamer, vergaderjaar 1990-1991, 22008, nrs. 1-2.

54 Tweede Kamer, vergaderjaar 1990-1991, 20008, nrs. 1-2, p. 18 *et seq.*

authorities. Too often these two factors have been considered the tail end of the legislative process.

e. *Coordination*. Unnecessary or unwelcome diversity of rules or practices concerning the same or related topics should be avoided. Moreover, there must be coherence between rules, which, although operating from different angles, are applicable to one and the same case.

f. *Simplicity, clarity and accessibility*. High drafting standards must be set for the organization and design of the law and the formulation of legal provisions.

These general criteria have been further developed. To a large extent, they are laid down in the 'Legislative Drafting Rules' (*Aanwijzingen voor de regelgeving*), as laid down by the Dutch Prime Minister.[55]

Although, in part, the above criteria are the same as those used at European level, in the Netherlands they constitute a comprehensive set of standards that have been codified and developed into concrete and practical guidelines. They have a broader scope than the guidelines for EC legislation and are more detailed.[56] Substantial knowledge has been gained as to their performance. It is worthwhile considering the appropriateness of developing criteria and guidelines along the same line at European level. It shows that the EU can learn from national experiences.

After this general comment, more specific observations will now be made. The Commission legitimately advocates using primary legislation more frequently to regulate essential elements only, leaving it up to the executive (the Commission itself) to fill in the details.[57] The Commission rightly points out that, in national systems, the problem of too detailed and too complex a legislation would be addressed through implementing rules which are monitored by national parliaments rather than through statutes adopted by the Parliaments themselves.[58] When elevating this to the European level, an essential condition would be the existence of effective mechanisms of parliamentary control. This is consistent with the Commission's argument 'that the European Parliament should enhance its control on the execution of EU policies and the implementation of the budget'.[59] The question is whether this suffices to justify delegation of large discretionary powers to the executive. The Commission is aware that a situation must be created in which 'legislation defines the conditions and limits within which the Commission carries out its executive role'[60], but remains rather vague. It fails to mention present

55 Regulation by the Prime Minister 18.11.1992 nr. 92M008 337, *Stcrt.* 230. This regulation came into force at 1.1.1993 and was amended several times.

56 Resolution Council EC 8.6.1993, (1993) *OJ* C 166, 17.6.1993, Resolution on a draft interinstitutional agreement on common guidelines for the quality of drafting of Community legislation, (1998) *OJ* C 098, 9.4.1998.

57 See Article 202 EC.

58 *White Paper*, p. 18.

59 *White Paper*, p. 30.

60 See *White Paper*, p. 31.

limitations imposed by EC case law.[61] These should be observed by the ECJ in the future as well. Main elements which in any case remain to be regulated by the legislator itself are the rights and obligations of individuals, the scope of the powers of the executive and the most essential conditions under which these powers can be exercised, judicial remedies, rules governing liability and sanctions, as well as supervision of compliance with legal rules.

A second observation regards the proposed alternative methods of policy-making, such as connecting with 'networks', the use of 'co-regulation' and the 'open method of co-ordination'. Methods of this kind seem to have in common that they are aimed at 'wider ownership' of the policies in question by involving 'those most affected'. The overall goal is that policies become more effective as a result. Although the Commission presents these methods as a contribution to good governance, there is a risk of the opposite effect. With regard to the use of such methods, there are no legal rules guaranteeing such fundamental constitutional values as representativity, transparency and accountability. Under these circumstances, care must be taken that these methods will not replace or adversely affect regular constitutional guarantees. The Commission recognizes these risks, but fails to propose any specific remedies.[62] My view is that restraint should be exercised when using such methods.

6. Refocusing Institutions: a Revitalized Community Method?

The Commission recognizes the institutional dimension of European governance, which makes up the final part of the White Paper. The Commission rightly states that the phased integration which has characterized the Union's development, has tended to cut policies into sectoral slices with different objectives and different tools. The capacity to ensure coherence has diminished over time. For this reason, the Commission rightly advocates an overall policy strategy.[63] To this end, the institutions and the Member States should adapt their *modus operandi* under the existing Treaties as well as promote further institutional reform.

However, the White Paper does not contain much detail on how this must be achieved. The Commission's ambitions are directed towards 'reinvigoration of the Community method'. According to the Commission, the method provides a means to arbitrate between different interests by passing them through two successive filters: 'general interest' as guarded by the Commission; and 'democratic representation', both at European and national level, as guarded by the Union's legislature, i.e. the Council and European Parliament.[64] In the Commission's view, it will continue to serve as independent guardian of the Treaty.[65] A more targeted use of its right of initiative must be promoted. The role of the European Parliament must be strengthened; co-decision must be extended to other areas and control by the

61 Case 22/70 (1970), ECR 1161 (*Koester*).
62 *White Paper*, p. 20 and 21.
63 *White Paper*, p. 28.
64 *White Paper*, p. 8.
65 See Article 213 EC.

European Parliament enhanced.[66] Both the Council and European Parliament should focus more on political direction, leaving implementation to the executive.

To reinforce the Community method, the Commission outlines a model for the Union's future political organization:[67]

- division of powers between the legislature and the executive. The Commission assumes that, at European level, a separation of the two roles will make it easier to apply the principles of subsidiarity and proportionality. Whereas the Council and the European Parliament should enjoy equal roles in the co-decision procedure, which is not the case under the current Treaty, the Commission should be allowed to assume 'full executive responsibility';
- clear principles identifying how competence is shared between the Union and its Member States. In this respect, the Commission advocates a multi-level approach: in such a multi-level system of governance 'the real challenge is establishing clear rules for how competence is shared – not separated'.

The method of division of powers seems to depend, therefore, on the specific situation; at the 'horizontal' level (in the relation between the institutions) powers have to be 'separated', whereas at the 'vertical' level (in the relation between Union and Member States) they are 'shared' rather than separated.

At first sight, the ambitions of the Commission seem relatively modest. It does not propose a fundamental overhaul of the institutional structure. Its priority lies in clarifying the way in which the present framework functions. However, the picture is far from complete, which makes the Commission's White Paper proposals still rather vague. However, this could change in the near future. In the White Paper, the Commission announces that it will actively contribute to the wider process of constitutional reform. More detailed, and perhaps more far-reaching, proposals by the Commission can therefore be expected at a later stage. The White Paper gives the impression that the Commission intends to both strengthen the position of the European Parliament and enhance its own executive powers. However, in the Commission's view, the position of the Council should be weakened.

The *Commission* is holding on to its role of independent guardian of the general interest of the Community, which raises the question as to the precise meaning of this claim. Looking after the general interest should not be a mission on which the Commission has a monopoly. The interest of the Community as a whole is, or rather should be, the concern of other EU institutions as well. It must also be recognized that looking after the general interest is not a neutral activity. As daily practice shows, different perceptions of 'the general interest of the Community' are possible. The choices that need to be made in EU context are inevitably of a political nature. In this sense, the Commission cannot be considered to be an independent body. The principle of 'independence' has a different meaning in this respect; it

66 *White Paper*, p. 30.

67 *White Paper*, p. 34 and 35.

obliges the members of the Commission not to allow themselves to be influenced by national interests.[68]

The perceived independent position of the Commission should not be an obstacle to full accountability. Since the fall of the Santer Commission, it is generally felt that accountability mechanisms need to be improved. What kind of mechanisms should prevail is unclear, however. In its Second Report, the Committee of Experts has opted for the parliamentary model. In the Committee's view, the Commission 'must familiarize itself with a more stringent notion of the accountability inherent in parliamentary control'.[69] Not only should individual members of the Commission be accountable, they must also be politically answerable to the European Parliament 'for their own personal, managerial and operational shortcomings in the exercise of their high office as well as important shortcomings in the functioning of their departments, even when the blame for these cannot be laid upon them personally'. This responsibility should be enforced through 'significant strengthening of the hand of the Commission President'.[70] Article 217, par. 4 EC Treaty as formulated in the Treaty of Nice, seems to be a first step in this direction: it provides that an individual member of the Commission must resign if so requested by the President upon the consent of the Commission as a whole. Of course, the European Parliament could ask the President to make use of this power in specific cases, but a system of full political responsibility based on a formal power of the European Parliament to discharge individual Commissioners does not as yet exist.

There is no *communis opinio* about future developments.[71] It remains to be seen, therefore, how the Commission's position will develop. The White Paper does not offer express choices. In general terms, the Commission subscribes to enhancing Parliament's role in supervizing the performance of the Commission's executive role, but this is not worked out in detail. It confines itself to announcing that it will reflect on this topic in the light of the next IGC.[72] In my view, the consistent line of the Committee of Independent Experts, briefly described above, should be followed.

68 Committee of Independent Experts, Second Report, *supra* note 28, p. 117. It is sometimes called into question whether this is reality. See C. Landfried, 'Regulation of Biotechnology by Polycratic Governance', in Ch. Joerges and E. Vos (eds.), *EU Committees: Social Regulation, Law and Politics*, Oxford, Hart Publishing, 1999, p. 186.

69 Second report, *supra* note 28, p. 111.

70 *Ibidem*, p. 133. See also W. van Gerven, 'Het voor en tegen van een Europese Grondwet', in A.K. Koekkoek (ed.), *Bijdragen aan een Europese grondwet, Publikaties van de staatsrechtkring* (staatsrechtconferenties nr. 5), Deventer, W.E.J. Tjeenk Willink, 2000, p. 42 *et seq.*

71 Some authors even seem to object to further 'parliamentarization' of the Commission or at least advocate delegation of policy-making powers to institutions other than the Commission (agencies) 'to preserve policy continuity against the changing preferences of variable parliamentary majorities'. See G. Majone and M. Everson, 'Institutional reform: independent agencies, oversight coordination and procedural control', in O. De Schutter, N. Lebessis and J. Paterson (eds.), *Governance in the European Union*, Luxembourg, Office for Official Publications of the European Communities, 2001, p. 129.

72 *White Paper*, p. 31.

The Commission's White Paper is more outspoken on the role of the *European Parliament*. As mentioned earlier, the Commission is in favour of the EP enhancing its control of the implementation of EU policies. In its view, this means 'departing from the present emphasis on detailed accounting with more policy-oriented control based on political objectives'.[73] Moreover, the areas in which co-decision applies, should be reviewed in order to reinforce the role of the EP.

The strengthening of the EP has traditionally been hampered by intergovernmentalist influences and the absence of a strong European identity.[74] The prevailing view is that the citizens from the various Member States do not share a common history, language, culture and ethnic background and for his reason, do not constitute a '*demos*'.[75] As a result, the democratic legitimatization of the EP is viewed as weak. Conferring more powers on the EP would be no solution or in any case not an appropriate one.[76] However, there seems to be no alternative. The fact that the EP was given an electoral mandate by the EU citizens will always be a dominant factor. No other EU institution, not even the Council, has such a strong democratic basis. In view of the need for a more democratic EU, it would be both unrealistic and undesirable to try to prevent the EP from becoming stronger.

This, however, does not detract from the need to improve the performance of the EP in the way suggested by the Commission: more political outlines and less technical details, not only with regard to legislation, but also to its control function. The EP should not lose itself in investigating highly specific cases, but concentrate on general assessment of policy implementation.[77] One of the most important instruments is laid down in Article 193 EC. Pursuant to this article, in the course of its duties, the EP may, at the request of a quarter of its members, set up a temporary Committee of Inquiry to investigate alleged contraventions or maladministration in the implementation of Community law. In order to use this instrument effectively, the EP could perhaps draw inspiration from the experience within nation states, for example with the American Congressional Committees or the British Select Committees.[78]

The role of the *Council of Ministers* is perhaps the most complicated one. On the one hand, it is a EU institution, participating in supranational decision-making. On the other, the members of the Council act from a strong intergovernmental perspective. It is unclear what its role will be in the long term. In particular the future relation between the Commission and the Council is of vital importance. As the Committee of Independent Experts has pointed out, two extreme models may

73 *White Paper*, p. 30.

74 P. Craig, *supra* note 11, p. 11 *et seq.*

75 *Ibidem*, p. 28. See also J.J. Weiler, The constitution of Europe, Do the new clothes have an emperor? And other essays on European integration, Cambridge, Cambridge University Press, 1999, p. 324 *et seq.*

76 R. Dehousse, *supra* note 12.

77 See Ch. Joerges, '"Good Governance" Through Comitology?', in Ch. Joerges and E. Vos (eds.), *EU Committees: Social Regulation, Law and Politics*, Oxford, Hart Publishing, 1999, p. 327 and 328.

78 S. de Smith and R. Brazier, *Constitutional and Administrative Law*, London, Penguin Books, 1998, p. 292-296. They refer to more specific literature.

be distinguished: i) the Commission as a technocratic agency, with the Council as the body required to ratify Commission action, and ii) the Commission as a kind of federal government, with a bi-cameral parliament and the Council performing the role of upper chamber representing the interests of the Member States.[79]

The White Paper does not expressly discuss this issue. Generally speaking, the Commission wishes to put the Council and the EP on an equal footing with regard to both adoption of legislation and supervision of the Commission's executive role. This could imply that, ultimately, the Commission would opt for some kind of federal construction. Most likely, such a long-term perspective has been inspired by present deficiencies in the decision-making process. In the Commission's view, there is a lack of consistency in the different sectoral Councils. According to the Commission, the Council, in particular the General Affairs Council composed of the Ministers of Foreign Affairs, 'has lost its capacity to give political guidance and arbitrate between sectoral interests'.[80] Efforts made thus far to improve effective co-ordination have, at least in the eyes of the Commission, not been successful enough.

With the explosive expansion of the EU action radius, it is probably an illusion to think that the Ministers of Foreign Affairs could play a dominant role in resolving disputes between domestic departments. In most sectors, Foreign Affairs departments lack the expertise and experience to intervene in an authoritative way. An even bigger problem, perhaps, is co-ordination within the Council. The future enlargement of the EU will render the decision-making process even more complex. This raises the question as to whether the Council will be able to preserve its present role. In view of future enlargement and the strong will to continue the process of integration, development towards some kind of federalism, at least in the long term, seems inevitable.

7. Committees and Agencies

The institutional dimension of 'good governance' cannot be properly assessed without paying attention to two important phenomena which have developed almost entirely outside the official institutional framework established in the Treaties: committees and agencies.

At EU level, there is a large number of *committees*,[81] often referred to under the general heading of 'Comitology'. Originally, committees came about as a result of a strong resistance within Member States to unconditional delegation of powers by the Council to the Commission pursuant to Article 202 EC. Different procedures have been introduced in order to force the Commission to consult a committee (often consisting of Member States' representatives) before adopting implementation decisions. If the Commission chooses not to follow the opinion of a committee, it is in many cases obliged to refer its draft decision back to the Council. In practice, committees have proven to be very powerful.

79 Second Report, *supra* note 28, p. 134.
80 *White Paper*, p. 29.
81 E. Vos, 'The Rise of Committees', *ELJ*, 1997, p. 210-229.

The system of 'Comitology' has often been criticized from a constitutional perspective. Major objections are its extreme complexity and haphazardness, lack of transparency and openness in operation, the time-consuming nature of applying Comitology procedures, absence of general procedural and administrative standards applicable to committees and, last but not least, the diminishing influence of the EP on decisions in which, in effect, committees play a decisive role.[82] However, committees can also be seen as an attempt to restore the institutional balance between the Member States and the EU.[83] Furthermore, the ECJ has decided that the committee system is not contrary to institutional balance as laid down in the EC Treaty, since the ultimate decision-making power is not vested in the committees, but remains with either the Council or the Commission.[84] Finally, mention should be made of the Comitology decision by the Council, which partly redresses some of the objections raised, especially lack of transparency.[85]

However, it is obvious that much of the criticism has not yet been met. It seems that the Commission now tries to make use of this criticism, particularly as regards the problem of impairment of the EP,[86] to get rid of the Comitology system. As mentioned earlier, it proposes to revitalize 'the Community method', thus restoring the situation in which each institution concentrates on its core tasks.[87] In consequence, the Commission also wishes to see the need to preserve existing committees to be called into question. However, future assessment of the Comitology system should take account of the need for expert advice with regard to implementing EU policies. Moreover, as compensation for the loss of many committees, the Commission wishes to introduce 'a simple legal mechanism', allowing the Council and the EP, as the legislature, to monitor and control the actions of the Commission, on the basis of the principles and political guidelines adopted under Community law.[88]

Admittedly, the Commission's approach could lead to a clearer division of powers and to speedier decision-making. Simplification of the Comitology system should therefore be promoted. However, it must be borne in mind that the committees not only meet the need for expertise, but also contribute towards creating support for those who will have to execute EU policy. The proposal by the

82 G. de Burca, *supra* note 11, p. 72-75.

83 E. Vos, *supra* note 81, p. 224.

84 Case 22/70 (1970), ECR 1161 (*Koester*). This jurisprudence was firmly criticized by J.H.H. Weiler, 'Epilogue: 'Comitology' as Revolution - Infranationalism, Constitutionalism and Democracy', in Ch. Joerges and E. Vos (eds.), *EU Committees: Social Regulation, Law and Politics*, Oxford, Hart Publishing, 1999, p. 339 *et seq.*

85 Council Decision of 28 June 1999, laying down the procedures for the exercise of implementing powers conferred on the Commission (1999/468/EC), *OJ* L 184, p. 23. See K. Lenaerts and A. Verhoeven, 'Towards a legal framework for executive rule-making in the EU? The contribution of the new Comitology-decision', *CML Rev.*, 2000, p. 645-686.

86 However, Joerges has argued that the functioning of the EP itself is at least part of the problem. For a more effective control of Committee activities he suggests that the EP revise its monitoring strategy. See Ch. Joerges, *supra* note 1, p. 328.

87 See *supra* par. 6.

88 *White Paper*, p. 31.

Commission therefore seems to be contrary to the intention, expressed elsewhere in the White Paper, to enhance involvement of national authorities and other interested parties.[89] Furthermore, the Commission has not worked out how it is to compensate for Committees that will be discontinued. It remains completely unclear what is meant by 'a simple legal mechanism' to control the actions of the Commission.

If the Comitology system is compared with parallel phenomena in at least some Member States, committees could have two distinct functions. In the first place, committees could serve as advisory bodies made up by independent experts who advise to the Commission on the basis of their scientific knowledge and social and political experience. In the second place, committees could take the role of deliberative bodies: a forum consisting of representatives of Member States and/or civil society which can be consulted by the Commission on matters of implementation of EU policy and legislation. Given this dual role, the present Comitology system should be subjected to far-reaching reform. The number of the committees could probably be brought down significantly. The obligation to refer proposals back to the Council if they do not accord with the opinion of the relevant committee, notably the regulatory and management committees, should, in principle, be repealed. As regards implementation measures, such an obligation detracts fundamentally from the executive role of the Commission. It is therefore to be preferred that the powers of the committees be limited to advice and consultation. Contrary to the Commission's alleged intention, committees must continue to play an important role in preparing and implementing EU policy. The Commission must attach great importance to committee opinions and publicly account for the extent to which such opinions have or have not influenced its decisions. Furthermore, the question of the need for additional rules governing the activities of committees, particularly regarding their composition and working procedures, must be looked into.[90]

A second type of organization that is becoming increasingly popular at EU level are *agencies*.[91] They were created to assist EU institutions, especially the Commission, in carrying out specific administrative tasks in a broad range of fields, such as the environment, training, and living and working conditions. The EC Treaty does not provide for a specific legal basis for the creation of agencies. They are almost all based on the general power of the Council, laid down in Article 308 EC, to take the appropriate measures should action by the Community, in the course of the operation of the common market, prove to be necessary. Delegation of powers to agencies is only allowed under very strict conditions. Up to now, the Court has rejected delegation of discretionary powers to independent bodies, such as agencies. Only clearly defined executive powers may be delegated, the exercise of which must always remain subject to supervision by the Commission.[92]

89 See *supra*, par. 4.

90 R. Dehousse, *supra* note 12, p. 183.

91 G. de Burca, *supra* note 10, p. 75 *et seq.*, E. Vos, 'Reforming the European Commission: what role to play for EU agencies', *CML Rev.*, 2000, p. 1113-1134.

92 Case 9/56 ECR 133 (*Meroni*). This decision has been criticized by G. Majone and M. Everson, *supra* note 71, p. 143 *et seq.*

The role of agencies has been the subject of intense debate.[93] Agencies are considered advantageous in the sense that they are able to reduce the workload of the Commission, making it possible for the Commission to concentrate on strategy policy. Moreover, it has been suggested that clearly identifiable agencies are more visible to the outside world than obscure Commission divisions or committees, which contributes to greater transparency and accountability. Sometimes agencies are promoted because of their political independence, which places them in a better position to preserve policy continuity against the changeable preferences of variable parliamentary majorities.[94] On the other hand, agencies have been strongly criticized, because they lack a constitutional basis and are not subject to constitutional guarantees. In particular, the transparency of and accountability for the activities of agencies have been called into question.

In its White Paper, the Commission proposes the creation of additional autonomous EU regulatory agencies in clearly defined areas.[95] When exercising decision-making powers, agencies should operate with a degree of independence, however, the EU legislature should set limits to their activities and powers and provide for openness. Agencies' competences may in no way affect the balance of power between the traditional EU institutions. In the Commission's view, this implies that the following conditions must be met:

- agencies are only granted power to take decisions in individual cases in connection with the application of regulatory measures: they cannot adopt general measures of their own accord;
- agencies cannot be given responsibility for matters for which the EC Treaty has conferred a direct power of decision on the Commission;
- agencies cannot be granted decision-making powers in politically sensitive areas, i.e. situations in which they would have to arbitrate between conflicting public interests, exercise political discretion or carry out complex economic assessments;
- agencies must be subject to an effective system of supervision and control.

The Commission wishes to further develop these conditions; in 2002, it plans to define 'the criteria for the creation of new regulatory agencies in line with the above conditions and the framework[96] within which they should operate' as well as set out 'the Community's supervisory role over such agencies'.

As the Commission rightly states, a variety of national regulatory agencies already exists across the Member States.[97] The Commission's intention to strengthen

93 E. Vos, *supra* note 91, p. 1119.

94 G. Majone and M. Everson, *supra* note 71, p. 129.

95 *White Paper*, p. 24.

96 See the proposal for a Council regulation, laying down a statute for executive agencies to be entrusted with certain tasks in the management of Community programmes: Brussels, 13.12.2000 COM(2000) 788 final. These agencies operate under the control and responsibility of the Commission.

97 *White Paper*, p. 23.

the role of agencies at EU level runs, in effect, parallel to developments within the Member States and is therefore a logical step, in any case from a national perspective. However, the role of national agencies and the conditions under which they operate within the national context differ substantially from one to the other. As national experiences show the quality of the general framework will be crucial for the legitimization of these bodies. The White Paper remains rather vague in this respect. As mentioned earlier, the conditions for creating regulatory agencies at EU level are a step in the right direction, but do need further elaboration. It is essential to develop 'an effective system of supervision and control'. Delegation of powers to agencies requires a specific legal basis and may in no way prevent the Commission from being held accountable and responsible by the EP for the general policy and performance of such bodies. In this respect, appropriate legal powers to effectively control agencies must be available to the Commission.

Political supervision in itself is not sufficient, however. As suggested above, codification of general rules of administrative law at EU level should be considered.[98] These rules should also apply to decision making by regulatory agencies. Judicial review by an independent tribunal of individual decisions taken by agencies[99] should be seen as an indispensable guarantee. These and other legal safeguards are rather self-evident and have been advocated by many authors. They have not been received much attention in the White Paper, however.

8. Concluding Remarks

In summarizing I wish to make some concluding remarks. The White Paper of the Commission contains a rich variety of helpful ideas and intentions to improve European governance. It expresses great ambitions for both the short and the long term. However, in many places, either the ideas proper or the way in which they are to be implemented remain rather vague. At the abstract level, the White Paper often states the obvious and fails to specify how 'good governance' is to be made operational. At this stage, this is perhaps understandable for practical and strategic reasons, even inevitable to a large extent. In any case, it is clear that a lot of work remains to be done to put these good intentions into practice.

An important shortcoming of the White Paper is that it systematically underrates the legal dimension of 'good governance'. In some instances, the Commission rejects the idea of legal rules, assuming that they will lead to 'excessive rigidity' and are likely to slow down EU policy adoption. This approach is misguided and unjustified, in my view. Although the significance of legal rules must not be overrated, a solid legal basis is undoubtedly indispensable for achieving 'good governance'. A strong legal position of citizens *vis-à-vis* EU institutions and Member States will boost confidence in European governance and could, therefore, be a major contribution. For this reason, the concept of the 'rule of law' should be given more priority than the Commission assigns it in its White Paper. As a follow-up of the

98 See para. 4.

99 See Article 47 EU Charter on human rights.

EU-Charter, there should be an effort to codify general rules and principles of administrative law, with the inclusion of broadening judicial review at European level.

In anticipation of the next IGC, the Commission does not take a clear stand on several institutional issues. Such reluctance is understandable from a political perspective, but the institutional framework within which 'good governance' is to be effected remains unclear as a result. This deficiency not only hampers definition of principles of 'good governance', but also increases the risk of ambiguous, perhaps even contradictory solutions. In consequence, although difficult to achieve, a consistent, long-term vision of a future constitutional model for the EU is urgently needed. The White Paper is only a first impulse for such a model.

The Commission fails to make clear the extent to which national experience has influenced its proposals. Such experience may be of great importance for achieving 'good governance' at EU level. The existing deficiencies, as pointed out by the Commission, are often similar, at least to some extent, to the problems experienced in the Member States. Although the EU cannot be regarded as a 'state' in the traditional sense, lessons can be drawn from such experience. Why re-invent the wheel if workable solutions can be found in the Member States? Moreover, it is preferable to build on what is common in Europe, because this could boost indispensable public support for one of the key aims of the White Paper, European governance. '*Ius commune*' thus established may help to pave the way for 'good governance' at European level.

Ellen Vos

EUROPEAN GOVERNANCE: REVITALIZING THE COMMUNITY METHOD

1. Introduction

The crisis surrounding charges of fraud, nepotism and mismanagement of the Commission, which directly led to the fall of the Santer Commission, the perceived democratic deficit, the problems relating to the upcoming enlargement as well as the food crises surrounding BSE and dioxine, have all put 'European governance' high on the reform agenda. The flaws in the governance of the European Union have been a concern for many years. It was already apparent soon after the introduction of the new internal market programme in 1985,[1] that the internal market was not going to be achieved by the Commission's emphasis on mutual recognition and deregulation of the European market alone. Instead the internal market policy needed additional re-regulatory operations at the Community level.[2] In this manner the EU has increasingly entered into new policy areas, urging for, and gradually leading to, institutional reform and new institutional actors in the Community field. These developments have gradually eroded both territorial - nation-state centred - political governance and nation-state constitutionalism, questioning the legitimacy of European governance.[3]

The legitimacy of European governance was particularly debated in the face of the events mentioned above. First, confronted with the accusations of secrecy and lack of responsibility and integrity, revealed by the Committee of Independent Experts,[4] the newly appointed president of the Commission, Romani Prodi hastened to announce a thorough reform of the internal operation of the Commission. Yet, he emphasized that it was not enough simply to reform the Commission, but that it

1 COM(85) 310 final.

2 G. Majone, *Regulating Europe*, London, Routlidge, 1996.

3 See *inter alia* C. Joerges, 'The Law's Problems with the Governance of the European Market', in C. Joeges and R. Dehousse (eds.), *Good Governance in Europe's Integrated Market*, Oxford, Oxford University Press, 2002, p. 3-31.

4 See Committee of Independent Experts, *First Report on Allegations regarding Fraud, Mismanagement and Nepotism in the European Commission* of 15 March 1999, <http://www.europarl.eu.int/experts/en/default.htm>.

was necessary 'to radically rethink the way we do Europe; to re-shape Europe; to devise a completely new form of governance for the world of tomorrow'.[5]

He therefore declared the promotion of new forms of governance for the EU to be one of the Commission's strategic objectives for the next five years.[6] Prodi identified a paradox with on the one hand, the success of European integration and the internal market, enabling the EU to emerge as a world economic power capable of meeting the challenges of globalization and on the other, the loss of faith of Europe's citizens in the European institutions. In its strategic programme the Commission explained:

> 'Citizens feel remote from them and are calling for a greater say in how things are done at European level. We intend to heed their calls. The Commission has already begun to put its own house in order, and this process will be followed up relentlessly'.[7]

Underlining the need to find a new synergy between all the European Union's democratic bodies, as part of a broader improvement of European governance, the Commission proposed to strike a new balance between action by the Commission, the other institutions, the Member States and civil society. This would bring

> 'Europe much closer to the people. This means giving people a greater say in the way Europe is run; making the institutions work more effectively and transparently, notably by reforming the Commission and setting an example for other bodies; adapting the institutions to the needs of enlargement; building new forms of partnership between the different levels of governance in Europe; and ensuring an active and distinctive European contribution to the development of global governance'.[8]

After an elaborate preparation during which the Commission, acting as 'a rather imperious wizard, albeit posturing in New Age clothing',[9] had both intensive in-house discussions and research and discussions with external experts and interested parties,[10] the Commission presented its White Paper on European Governance in July 2001.[11] Central to the White Paper is the message that 'the Union must revitalize the Community method'. For the purpose of this short contribution, I shall discuss this issue.

5 R. Prodi, President of the European Commission. 2000-2005: *Shaping the New Europe European Parliament Strasbourg*, 15 February 2000, SPEECH/00/41.

6 *Idem*.

7 COM(2000) 154 final, at p. 3-4.

8 *Idem*, at p. 5.

9 D. Curtin, *The Commission as Sorcerer's Apprentice? Reflections on EU Public Administration and the Role of Information Technology in Holding Bureaucracy Accountable* (Jean Monnet Working Paper 6/01) 2001.

10 See <http://www.europa.eu.int/comm/governance/index_en.htm>.

11 COM(2001) 428 final.

2. The White Paper on European Governance

In the White Paper, the Commission first observes that while on the one hand European integration has been successful in helping to raise the standards of living, building and internal market and strengthening the EU's voice in the world, many EU citizens feel alienated from the EU's work and increasingly distrust institutions and politics or are simply not interested in them.[12] This disenchantment with EU policies and the functioning of the institutions is explained in the White Paper by, *inter alia*, the perceived inability of the EU to act effectively in situations of, for example, food scares, lack of clear communication by the Member States about the activities that the EU undertakes, and by the Member States blaming the EU for unpopular decisions, which have been taken by the EU in agreement with or even at the request of the Member States. The White Paper therefore contains a set of recommendations on how to improve the legitimacy of EU policies and its institutions. European governance should therefore be reformed *i)* to improve the openness of and participation in EU policy-making, *ii)* to restore the institutional balance *iii)* to improve the quality of its policies, to redesign rules and to promote greater use of different policy tools, in order to enhance the efficiency in policy formulation and implementation, and *iv)* to apply the principles of good governance to its global responsibilities. In this vein, five principles are affirmed as principles of good governance: openness, participation, accountability, effectiveness and coherence. These principles are 'important for establishing more democratic governance'.[13]

3. The Reinvigoration of the Community Method

Reforming European governance, so the White Paper tells us, is aimed at opening up policy-making and to make it more inclusive and accountable. The EU should therefore make better use of its powers in order to connect the EU more closely to its citizens and achieve more effective policies. This should be achieved by 'refocusing the institutions'. This should not only optimize efficiency and coordinative capacity of the institutions but also increase transparency and accountability. 'The Union must revitalize the Community method', as this would improve the quality of European governance. This means that:

> 'everyone should concentrate on their core tasks: the Commission initiates and executes policy; the Council and the European Parliament decide on legislation and budgets, the European Council exerts political guidance and the European Parliament controls the execution of the budget and the Union's policies'.[14]

12 *Idem*, p. 3 and p. 7.

13 *Idem*, p. 10.

14 *Idem*, p. 29.

In addition, the European Court of Justice would guarantee respect for the rule of law.[15] This method would, according to the White Paper, guarantee both the diversity and effectiveness of the EU and ensure the fair treatment of all Member States from the largest to the smallest. In this vein it would provide for

> 'a means to arbitrate between different interests by passing them through two successive filters: the general interest at the level of the Commission; and democratic representation, European and national, at the level of the Council and European Parliament, together the Union's legislature'.[16]

Yet, at the same time, it is recognized that there is a need to renew the Community method 'by following a less top-down approach and complementing EU's policy tools more effectively with non-legislative instruments'.[17]

4. Reinforcing the Commission's Powers

Various new governance mechanisms have indeed been developed within the Community context over the years, such as comitology, soft law, flexibility,[18] as well as partnership, social dialogue, the open method of co-ordination[19] and agencies. Joanne Scott and David Trubek mention, for example, novel ways to expand participation of civil society in policy-making, the co-ordination of action and actors at many levels of government, the possibility of co-ordinated diversity and decentralization, deliberation among stakeholders, the use of soft law and the facilitation of experiments and new knowledge.[20]

It is true that the White Paper recognizes the need to make use of some forms of 'new governance', such as, 'target-based contracts', partnership arrangements, co-regulation and the open method of co-ordination. Yet, in doing so, the White Paper is quite cautious. The open method of co-ordination, for example, should not, the White Paper warns, dilute the achievement of common objectives in the Treaty. The White Paper is somewhat more lenient towards another form of new governance: agencies. It allows however only for the creation of agencies which adopt individual decisions, particularly in areas where a single public interest predominates and the tasks require specific technical expertise. And, it does not approve agencies being given decision-making powers in fields where they would have to arbitrate between conflicting public interests, exercise political discretion or

15 *Idem*, p. 8.

16 *Idem*, p. 8.

17 *Idem*, p. 4.

18 Scott and Trubek label these forms 'new, old governance (NOG)' as they concern alternatives within the Community method, see J. Scott, D.M. Trubek, 'Mind the Gap: Law and New Approaches to Governance in the European Union', *European Law Journal*, vol. 8, no. 1, 2002, p. 2.

19 These are the 'true' alternatives to the Community method according to J. Scott and D.M. Trubek, *supra* note 18.

20 J. Scott and D.M. Trubek, *supra* note 18, p. 5-6.

carry out complex economic assessments.[21] Moreover, such agencies should not adopt general regulatory measures.

Close reading of the White Paper reveals however that the White Paper does not really embrace new forms of governance but remains primarily 'wedded'[22] to the 'classic' Community method. Great emphasis is hereby put on the expansion of the Commission's own powers in the EU's policy formulation and foremost implementation, at the expense of the role of the Member States. It is therefore not surprising that the White Paper is criticized for being 'over-ambitious in defining the Commission's role'.[23] It is 'the institutional self-interest of the Commission and its opposition to Member States'[24] which underlies the White Paper's desire to revitalize the Community method. The proposed enhanced role of the Commission is accused of constituting 'a benevolent dictatorship', albeit a 'well-informed, highly sensitive and very open form of dictatorship'.[25] The White Paper emphasizes that it is necessary to clarify that, within the EU system, the Commission bears the main responsibility for executing policy and legislation by adopting implementing regulations and decisions. Following this reasoning, the White Paper wants to restrict the role of the European Parliament and the Council to define (wherever possible with qualified majority)[26] the essential elements,[27] leaving the Commission the task to define the technical details via secondary legislation. In addition, a simple legal mechanism should be installed which allows the Council and the European Parliament to control and monitor the actions of the Commission. The conclusion that the White Paper draws from this is critical:

> '[...] the need to maintain existing committees, notably regulatory and management committees, will be put into question. Therefore a review of existing committees would have to be undertaken and their continued existence assessed'.[28]

This proposal addresses a long-standing dispute between the Council, Commission and the European Parliament about the role of the so-called policy-making/ implementation, or comitology, committees composed of national representatives created to assist the Commission in the exercise of its implementing powers. In particular the management and regulatory committees, which have been created

21 *White Paper, supra* note 11, p. 24.

22 'Editorial', *European Law Review*, vol. 26, 2001, p. 411.

23 B. Kohler-Koch, *The Commission White Paper and the Improvement of European Governance* (New York Jean Monnet Working Paper 6/01), 2001, p. 4.

24 F.W. Scharpf, *European Governance: Common Concerns vs. The Challenges of Diversity* (New York Jean Monnet Working Paper 6/01), 2001, p. 1.

25 F.W. Scharpf, *supra* note 24, p. 7.

26 'When legally possible, the Council should vote as soon as a qualified majority seems possible rather than pursuing discussions in the search for unanimity', *White Paper, supra* note 11, p. 22. See for a critique on more resort to the majority voting, F.W. Scharpf, *supra* note 24, p. 4.

27 This was already establihed in the *Köster* case; Case 25/70, *Einfuhr-und Vorratstelle für Getreide und Futtermittel v Köster, Berodt & Co.*, [1970] ECR 1161.

28 *White Paper, supra* note 11, p. 31.

since the 1960s – being a variant on the traditional Community method –, have been argued to distort the institutional balance, as they would detract from the Commission's independent right of decision and thus from the Parliament's right of control. Institutional quarrelling on this issue inter alia resulted in 1994 in the conclusion of a modus vivendi between the institutions.[29] In 1999, summoned by the IGC in a declaration to the Amsterdam Treaty,[30] the Council eventually reviewed the existing committee procedures and adopted a new comitology Decision.[31] Although this Decision simplifies the procedures, improves their transparency and enhances the involvement of the European Parliament, committees, and in particular the management and the regulatory committees, remain involved in the implementing phase. Whereas general Council and Parliament decisions may be implemented by the Council itself (in 'specific cases')[32], or by the Member States, in many fields of the internal market policy it has become common practice that implementing powers are delegated to the Commission in combination with a committee procedure. Under the management and regulatory committee procedures this means, also under the new Comitology Decision, that in case of disagreement between the Commission and the committees, the draft decisions proposed by the Commission may or, in case of the regulatory committees, must, be referred to the Council.

5. The Fall of Committees?

The Commission now seemingly wants to get rid of, albeit phrasing it in more cautious wording, this committee-based decision-making, praised by Christian Joerges as 'deliberative supranationalism'[33] and criticized by Joseph Weiler as 'a normative disaster'.[34] The White Paper makes plain that the Commission no longer wants to be controlled by the Member States' representatives sitting on these committees: the implementing powers should be invested in the 'heroic Commission'[35] alone. In this view, the Council and the European Parliament should control and monitor the actions of this Commission, by means of a 'simple legal mechanism', without however clarifying what such a monitoring system should entail.

Certainly, in terms of efficiency and transparency, over the years the comitology practice has left much to be desired. To some extent these drawbacks have

29 *Modus Vivendi* between the European Parliament, the Council and the Commission concerning the implementing measures for acts adopted in accordance with the procedure laid down in Article 189b of the EC Treaty, (1996) *OJ* C 102/1.

30 Declaration no. 31 to the Treaty of Amsterdam.

31 Council Decision 99/468/EC, Procedure for the exercise of implementing powers conferred on the Commission (Comitology) (1999) *OJ* L 184/23.

32 In accordance with Article 202 EC.

33 C. Joerges, 'Deliberative Supranationalism' – Two Defences', *European Law Journal*, vol. 8, no. 1, 2002, p. 133-151.

34 J.H.H. Weiler, 'Epilogue: "Comitology" as Revolution – Infranationalism, Constitutionalism and Democracy', in C. Joerges and E. Vos (eds.), *EU Committees: Social Regulation, Law and Politics*, Oxford, Hart Publishing, 1999, p. 339-350.

35 F.W. Scharpf, *supra* note 24, p. 5.

been addressed by the reform of the Comitology Decision.[36] Whereas further reform may prove to be necessary - in view of enlargement and depending on the manner in which the new Comitology procedures are implemented - this does not imply, in my view, that these committees should be abolished.

6. Why Comitology Should be retained

First, from a practical perspective and in view of the problematic history of the comitology system, it seems unlikely, if not simply impossible, that Member States will agree upon the abolition of comitology[37] and leave the implementing powers to be exercised by the Commission alone.[38] Moreover, strong doubts may be expressed as to whether this proposal is consistent with the White Paper's own aim 'to renew the Community method by following a less top-down approach'.[39] Surely the role of interested parties and the general public in decision-making has been neglected for a long time. Yet, is it not also true that management and regulatory committees in particular, and hence the participation of national representatives, may contribute to such a less top-down approach in the sense of less 'Brussels' (i.e. the Commission) - and more 'Member States' participation, and therefore, citizen participation? It is from this perspective in particular that the White Paper's position on comitology must be criticized.

Over the years decision-making involving comitology has led to a more consensual approach of decision-making between the Commission and the committees. Here the dual character of these committees must be emphasized: committees are composed of national representatives who generally, but not necessarily, are civil servants. On the one hand, these committees, in their composition of national *bureaucrats*, function as a forum of interaction and co-operation between the Member States and the Commission. In this way, the significance of purely national interest has been diminished, contributing to the overall trend of greater transnational decision-making, in which national interests are replaced by technical expertise, socio-economic interests and administration. On the other hand, however, these committees, in their composition of national *representatives*, have acted as '*mini Councils*'.[40] They potentially enhance the importance of the national interests and contribute to the decline of supranational decision-making.

Participation of these committees in the executive action of the Commission therefore may be argued to create a framework for co-operative and deliberative

36 *Supra* note 31.

37 F.W. Scharpf, *supra* note 24, p. 6.

38 In this context it is for example suggested that there should be a 'structural equivalent' to comitology, see Ph. Steinberg, *Governance und Parteien – Politisierung als möglichkeit größerer bürgerschaftlicher Identifikation ein Kommentar zum Weißbuch Europäisches Regieren* (New York Jean Monnet Working Paper 6/01), 2001, p. 11. Steinberg however does not elaborate on how this 'equivalent' should look.

39 *White paper, supra* note 11, p. 4.

40 See V. Eichener, *Social Dumping or Innovative Regulation? Process and Outcomes of European Decision-Making in the Sector of Health and Safety at Work Harmonization* (EUI Working Paper SPS 92/28), Florence, European University Institute, 1992, p. 48.

multi-level policy-making,[41] and makes the action of the Commission more democratic and 'closer to the citizen',[42] whilst producing good and effective decision-making. In this vein, committees are a means of bridging between the horizontal and vertical division of powers. These committee mechanisms generally provide for co-operation between all the levels concerned and might address Member States' concerns for unnecessary Community activities. Seen in this light committees might be argued to have pragmatically secured subsidiarity. Practice, moreover, demonstrates that it may be extremely important that national positions are also taken into account in the implementing phase for reasons of proper enforcement and compliance with Community decisions. When disregarding national positions, for example, the Commission may be faced with unpleasant situations in which Member States refuse to apply and enforce Commission decisions that were adopted without their consent. This has occurred, for example, in relation to the authorization of a specific GM maize product by the Commission.[43] Here, having gone through the entire regulatory committee procedure, and faced with the impossibility of the Council being able to adopt a decision within the period prescribed,[44] the Commission had authorized the marketing of this maize,[45] notwithstanding the disapproval of most Member States.[46] Yet soon after the issuance of the authorization, the Commission was punished for not having listened to the objections of several Member States within the GMO committee against the authorization and met strong opposition in the enforcement of its decision. Austria, Luxembourg and Italy, for example, which strongly disapproved of the authorization, invoked the safeguard clause,[47] as in their view, this GM maize product constituted a danger to human health and the environment. After a cumbersome procedure within the

41 Albeit this should be supplemented by participation of interested parties, see E. Vos, 'The Rise of Committees' *European Law Journal*, 1997, p. 211-230. See also K. Lenaerts and A. Verhoeven 'Towards a legal Framework for Executive Rule-making in the EU? The Contribution of the New Comitology Decision', *Common Market Law Review*, 2000, p. 664.

42 Also K. Lenaerts and A. Verhoeven, *supra* note 41, p. 664.

43 Upon request by Ciba-Geigy – (now Novartis), in accordance with Council Directive 90/220/EEC on the release into the environment of genetically modified organisms, (1990) *OJ* L 117/15.

44 In this case, the regulatory committee procedure proved very difficult and not at all consensual; the Commission's original proposal to authorize could not obtain the necessary support in the relevant standing committee under the former regulatory committee *filet* procedure as strong objections were advanced by several national representatives. In the Committee, six Member States voted for authorization (34 votes), four voted against (21 votes), with four abstaining (27 votes) and one submitting an invalid vote (5 votes). See Bradley K.St.C, 'The GMO-Committee on Transgenic Maize: Alien Corn, or the Transgenic Procedural Maze', in M.P.C.M. van Schendelen (ed.), *EU Committees as Influential Policy-makers,* Aldershot, Ashgate, 1998, p. 207-222.

45 Commission Decision 97/98/EC on the marketing of genetically modified maize in France, (1997) *OJ* L 31/69.

46 K.St.C. Bradley, *supra* note 44.

47 Austria and Luxembourg invoked the safeguard clause of Dir. 90/220 EEC, *supra* note 43, whilst Italy used the safeguard clause of the Novel Food Regulation, Reg. 258/97/EC (1997) *OJ* L 43/1.

GMO committee, decision-making by the Commission and the Council appeared impossible and no decisions were adopted,[48] herewith allowing Austria, Luxembourg and Italy to continue their practice of prohibit the import of the GM maize product onto their market.[49] Where the White Paper aims at effective decision-making and better policies, it is therefore essential that Member States are consulted in the implementing phase. This seems particularly compelling where the White Paper itself admits that there is a need for better application of Community rules at the national level.[50]

Hence both from a practical and normative perspective, deliberative interaction with the Member States by means of committees appears to be vital. Comitology pluralistically structures regulatory policy even in its implementing phase.[51] Management and regulatory committees force the Commission to take account of the national situations where the enforcement will take place and to take objections advanced by committee members more seriously than would be the case with merely advisory committees. Consequently, they should be retained.[52] As set forth above, this is not to say that there would be no need for these committees to be reformed. Particularly in view of the upcoming enlargement and consequently the increasing number of committee members it will be necessary to rethink the organizational structures of the committees and to introduce a system of sub-committees or working groups.

7. Concluding Remarks

In conclusion it is submitted that the White Paper's promised land of new forms of European governance appears rather disappointing. It is true that the White Paper embraces limited forms of some innovative models of governance, such as regulatory agencies and the open method of co-ordination. Whilst on paper the White Paper seems indeed willing to commit itself to renewing the Community method, in

48 Press Release by the European Commission, of 16 April 1998, IP/98/358. Proposal for a Council Decision concerning the provisional prohibition of the sale in Austria of genetically modified maize (Zea mays L.) with the combined modification for insecticidal properties conferred by the Bt-endotoxin gene and increased tolerance to the herbicide glufosinate ammonium COM(98) 339 final and Proposal for a Council Decision concerning the provisional prohibition of the use and sale in Luxembourg of genetically modified maize (Zea mays L.) with the combined modification for insecticidal properties conferred by the Bt-endotoxin gene and increased tolerance to the herbicide glufosinate ammonium, COM(98) 340 final.

49 In the future, this situation is no longer likely to occur. For the Commission's statement to the new Comitology decision promises that in sensitive cases, the Commission will avoid going against the predominant position which emerge in the Council. Declarations on Council Decision 1999/468/EC, 3rd Commission statement, (1999) *OJ* C 203/1.

50 *White Paper, supra* note 11, p. 25.

51 C. Joerges, Economic Order – Technical Realization – the hour of the executive: Some legal historical observations on the Commission White Paper on European Governance (New York Jean Monnet Working Paper 6/01), 2001, p. 17.

52 Verhey states that only the advisory committee should be retained, L. Verhey, 'Good Governance: Towards a European *Ius commune*?', in this volume.

practice its proposals come down to a return to the classic method. The White Paper's focus on the reinvigoration of the classic Community method, and its emphasis on the role of the Commission 'as the lone hero of European policy-making and implementation'[53] have therefore been argued to express a profound 'lack of understanding of the preconditions of successful multi-level governance in Europe'[54] and to deny the need for transnational partnership between the authorities of the various levels of governance. It is in this light, that the proposals of the White Paper, in particular those in relation to the Community method, need to be reconsidered.

53 F.W. Scharpf, *supra* note 24, p. 8.

54 *Idem.*

Criminal Law

André Klip

CONDITIONS FOR A EUROPEAN *CORPUS JURIS CRIMINALIS*

1. Introduction

Recently the feasibility of a European criminal law system came up in the discussion on various levels and *fora*. For a long time such a discussion was impossible within the institutional framework of the European Communities or European Union. The predominant view, on the basis of the EC Treaty, was that criminal law remained within the exclusive sovereignty of the States and that the European Communities have no competence at all in this field. With the establishment of a third pillar under the Treaty on European Union things have changed. In these times of change I would like to evaluate what conditions must be in place in order to have a European system of criminal law. What are the issues and questions that must be decided? Is it necessary to have a general system of criminal law for all crimes, or is it more likely that a limited catalogue of European crimes will be sufficient? These are questions, among others, which will be dealt with below.[1]

Given the interdisciplinary character of the topic my remarks will sometimes go beyond the field of criminal law alone. Since institutional and legislative aspects play a role I will also mention a few things that relate to constitutional law, international law and human rights. This is new and perhaps even frightening for criminal lawyers. Most colleagues in criminal law seem to be very reluctant to get to know 'Brussels'. Such a defensive attitude does not seem to be very productive. Whether you like it or not, it is likely that Europe will have its influence on all aspects of criminal law.

1 What I will not do: take the existing proposals for a *Corpus Juris* as a starting point. However, this proposal of the European Commission, of course also influenced my way of thinking. On reflection, I think that many of the conditions I have formulated relate to the fact that they have neither been fulfilled under the current European system nor envisaged under the *Corpus Juris*. See M. Delmas-Marty and J.A.E. Vervaele (eds.), *The Implementation of the Corpus Juris in the Member States*, vols. I-IV, Antwerpen, Intersentia, 2000-2001.

2. Why Conditions?

In my view it is necessary to raise the questions of the conditions for the establishment of such a system before the first steps towards building such a system are taken in practice. In fact this is as fundamental as the building of a house starts with the basement and subsequently ground floor and further floors will be constructed. To start off to build parts of the house without having the basement structure in place may lead to serious consequences. The house thus constructed may very soon fall to pieces or it will lean over in an unplanned direction. Similar rules apply to the establishment of a legal system, which also must be viewed in its entirety. It would, for instance, not make sense to establish a European Public Prosecutor if it has not been determined whether this institution will bring cases before a national or a European criminal court.

In this sense it cannot be denied that the European Union sometimes neglects the logical order of the steps it takes. It has created a European Police Office. Without, however, creating a European legal context in which it can operate. On a supranational level the collection, storage and analysis of data related to criminal activity now takes place. The data comes, however, from the national police services and will be returned to it. This forms an incomplete structure which only requires additional lines of communication between national police services and the new European Police. In a situation in which the police do not have the capacity to respond to all crime, it is important to be aware of the fact that the establishment of more agencies with competencies in criminal law, as well as an additional layer of legislation, also has negative effects in the sense that it complicates co-operation and may make it even more time consuming.

3. A Sharp Division between European and National Competencies

A first question we will have to deal with is the question of whether it would not be better to regulate all criminal law on a European level. This would have the advantage of having a uniform system throughout Europe and thereby evade all questions of legislative competencies, as well as other incompatibilities between a European and various national legal systems. It cannot be emphasized often enough that the more extreme options carry the attractiveness of a clearer structure.

If we were to make a distinction between European and national criminal law, numerous questions of division will come up. Regarding the chances of being introduced, as will be seen below, it is already doubtful whether a limited Code of European Crimes fulfils the conditions for introduction at the moment. This is even more so the case for a general and exclusively European criminal law system. Apart from that it is politically totally unacceptable at this stage of European integration.

It is essential that a clear division is made between the European competence in criminal law and national competence. Various questions will be raised regarding this issue. Are we envisaging a common criminal European code, as well as a common European Code of Criminal Procedure? Or do we foresee a common law in some fields,[2] while respecting national regulation in other? Do we want to establish a European Criminal Court?

Starting from the point that it is neither necessary nor appropriate to Europeanize all criminal law, we are immediately faced with the question: What will be European and what can be left to the Member States? I could imagine a European Criminal Code dealing with a limited number of crimes. I have tried to formulate three cumulative criteria, which I will further explain:

1. crime is by nature of a transnational character;
2. crime is related to European policy/legislation (or otherwise common to all Member States) in other fields of law;[3]
3. the prevention, investigation and adjudication of such a crime on a national level would encounter more difficulties than prosecution on a European level.

Ad 1. The requirement of a transnational character symbolizes that the *locus delicti* must be in more than one EU Member State. In theory, this can be the case for quite a number of crimes. A burglar may steal property in one country and sell it in another. However, this is not a typical characteristic of the crime of theft. This is, for instance, different with the crime of money laundering, which in practice almost always takes place with the use of borders between states. Money, illegally gained in the commission of a crime in one country will be transferred to another country and pop up there as legally obtained profits. It is therefore necessary to limit the number of crimes and only select for a European level those crimes that are in practice by nature transnational. Another example is trafficking in human beings.

Ad 2. The requirement of the nexus with European legislation in other fields of the law means that it facilitates a coherent system of law enforcement whereby the use of criminal law is weighed against and combined with the application of other fields of law. Thus is it possible to evade incompatibilities between for instance a general European policy on asylum and admission of third country nationals and the national implementation and enforcement of criminal law. A criticism of this criterion is that it is not fixed in the sense that a subsequent application of criminal law may follow from the extension of powers in other fields. To complicate matters further, one can apply such criteria in two ways, by including them in the definition of the crime, or by allowing their use to be at the discretion of the prosecutor when deciding whether to prosecute.

Ad 3. The third condition is linked to aspects of investigation and prosecution as well as the execution of any penalties imposed. In that sense European prosecution must facilitate and contribute to the enforcement of law. This has to do with requirements of efficiency, but can also be regarded as an expression of the principle of subsidiarity. This basically comes down to the following: if a problem

2 I will use the expression 'a common law' in order to indicate the law that will be common to all EU States. In doing so, I evaded the use of 'community law'. It is not intended to draw any parallel with Anglo-Saxon common law.

3 In this respect one could think (among others) of crimes related to the European Customs Union, to EC fraud, to the illegal smuggling of immigrants, as well as to the Euro.

can be solved on a national level, there is no need for European initiatives. Earlier I already pointed out the possible adverse consequences of an additional layer of legislation. More legislation bears the risk that it may undermine the effectiveness of legislation. The larger the number of different legal texts in existence, the greater the danger that they will lead to ambiguities and a situation in which practitioners do not know which instrument should be applied.[4] In addition, one must be aware of the fact that the European Union is not the only supranational legislator in the field of criminal law. Although less productive in quantity than the European Union, the United Nations also take initiatives in the field of criminal law. It is therefore relevant for the EU Member States to take into consideration whether EU or UN legislation should be preferred.

There is a reason to apply the three criteria in a cumulative way. There will be a number crimes that will fulfil the transnational requirement and that of subsidiarity. In this respect one could think of crimes related to drugs, trade in weapons or cybercrimes. Drugs offences would for instance not qualify for European legislation because there is no general drug policy. The crimes must also not have been dealt with by another supranational criminal legal system, such as with international crimes (e.g. ICTY/ICTY/ICC).

As a negative criterion one could say, more or less, that local crime does not qualify for regulation at a European level. In addition, it seems logical to leave crimes related to a perception of moral issues that differ extensively among the Member States, to the national legislator. If for instance one Member State allows individuals, under certain conditions, to be assisted in committing suicide, it would be inappropriate to criminalize the matter on a European level. In other words: criminalization on a European level may not run counter to liberalization on a national level. Another example of what should not be a European crime is the disturbance of public order when European (or other political) summits are being held. In the past (Amsterdam 1997, Gothenburg 2001, Genoa 2001) summits of the European political leadership have encountered a fair number of vandals, resulting in crimes related to the disturbance of public order and the demolition of property. As such, this must be regarded as a local problem. It is not the public order of the European Union at large that is threatened. Proposals to specifically criminalize the disturbance of these summits serves no other purpose than to convey a moral message.[5]

Would the fact that one Member State decriminalized specific behaviour automatically mean that another Member State may not prosecute the same offence? Not in general, but it might be so in concrete cases of extraterritorial jurisdiction. For instance, according to German criminal law, a German woman who is having an abortion performed abroad may be prosecuted, regardless of whether the law of the state where the abortion is performed allows or criminalizes such action. In a European context, such imperialism and imposition of norms upon others should be ruled out. In a European Union guided by the principle of mutual recognition,

4 Who can tell us whether a Joint Action is still a binding legal instrument?

5 Proposal for a Council Framework Decision on Combating Terrorism.

unilateral means to influence the law of others should be abolished. In fact, we are discussing a different relationship, that of the State-State within the European Union. This ought to be distinguished from the State-EU relationship. However, we can learn from these experiences. Similar mechanisms may take place in a dispute about criminalization between a Member State and the European Union.

This new division between 'federal' and 'state' crimes creates new legal and practical problems. On a theoretical level it would be possible to make sharp distinctions. However, it is unlikely that crimes and criminals will stick to this theory in practice. This may lead to additional problems. An example:

Let us imagine we have criminalized participation in a criminal organization on a European level. The suspects in question have committed various crimes against the financial budget of the EC by falsifying customs documents in at least six member states. In addition they corrupted, threatened and intimidated some customs officials in order to achieve their goals. One custom official was even killed with the aim to intimidate the others. In sum, more than one crime has been committed.

Should all of these crimes be dealt with on a European level? I do not think so. We must be very selective in upgrading a national crime to a European crime. In my view there is no necessity to criminalize murder/manslaughter on a European level. As such the murder is not related to anything European. That could be different with the criminal organization as such: this organization aims at profiting from European legislation and transnational trade. However, this may not apply to other criminal organizations active in other fields of crime. The result of this is that not only must a distinction be made on the legislative level, but also on the level of prosecution and adjudication in practice.

Various problems result from the introduction of federal crimes and state crimes: How to deal with the competencies of the European prosecutor and national prosecutors? It is one thing to agree upon criteria, but it is another thing to decide whether they apply. Would European jurisdiction be exclusive? And if so, what mechanism/what authority would decide that a crime belongs exclusively to the European jurisdiction? Following from this is the need for the formulation of a transnational *non-bis-in-idem*. European prosecutions must form a bar to national prosecutions and vice versa in order to prevent two prosecutions in respect of the same case. The provisions in the Statute of the International Criminal Court and the ICTY and ICTR Statutes could be used as an example here.[6] Thus the main

[6] 1. Article 10 ICTY Statute reads: 1. No person shall be tried before a national court for acts constituting serious violations of international humanitarian law under the present Statute, for which he or she has already been tried by the International Tribunal.
2. A person who has been tried by a national court for acts constituting serious violations of international humanitarian law may be subsequently tried by the International Tribunal only if: (a) the act for which he or she was tried as an ordinary crime; or (b) the national court proceedings were not impartial or independent, were designed to shield the accused from international criminal responsibility, or the case was not diligently prosecuted.
3. In considering the penalty to be imposed on a person convicted of a crime under the present Statute, the International Tribunal shall take into account the extent to which any

questions are whether there is a priority of jurisdictional principles and whether an international principle of *non-bis-in-idem* should apply.

Whether the European jurisdiction is exclusive or not deals with legal and factual aspects. The legal aspects relate to how to divide the competencies between national and European authorities, as well as to hierarchy.[7] In the Statutes of the ICTY and ICTR this has been provided by introducing the principle of primacy. This more or less means that both States and the tribunal may initiate criminal proceedings, but that the tribunal may decide in individual cases that the case will be deferred to the competence of the tribunal and that national proceedings will be terminated. Also a complementary system of jurisdiction could be provided. In such a system the main responsibility for prosecution would first lie with the States. Only if States, for whatever reason, do not act, a task would arise for the European prosecutor. This example is drawn from the Statute for the ICC. The question is whether this leads to anything new for the European Union. Concerning the prosecution of crimes related to fraud against the financial interests of the EU, we have had a system in which the principle task lies with the States. However this did not lead to a substantial number of prosecutions.

The consequences of overlapping jurisdictions can be quite negative for the accused (or convicted person) as well as for the interests of a fair administration of justice. The Court of Appeal in Köln (*Oberlandesgericht Köln*) recently lodged the first request for a preliminary ruling with the Court of Justice on the interpretation of the Schengen Executive Convention.[8] It concerns a case in which article 54 of that Convention must be interpreted. Does that article preclude a second prosecution before a German court when according to Dutch law the matter can no longer be

penalty imposed by a national court on the same person for the same act has already been served.
Article 20 of the ICC Statute reads: 1. Except as provided in this Statute, no person shall be tried before the Court with respect to conduct which formed the basis of crimes for which the person has been convicted or acquitted by the Court.
2. No person shall be tried by another court for a crime referred to in Article 5 for which that person has already been convicted or acquitted by the Court.
3. No person who has been tried by another court for conduct also proscribed under article 6, 7 or 8 shall be tried by the Court with respect to the same conduct unless the proceedings in the other court: (a) were for the purpose of shielding the person concerned from criminal responsibility for crimes within the jurisdiction of the Court; or (b) Otherwise were not conducted independently or impartially in accordance with the norms of due process recognized by international law and were conducted in a manner which, in the circumstances, was inconsistent with an intent to bring the person concerned to justice.

7 It is remarkable to see that the Council of Europe also experienced difficulties in determining a ranking order in the application of jurisdictional principles. See Council of Europe, *Extraterritorial criminal jurisdiction*, Report of the European Committee on Crime Problems, Strasbourg, 1990.

8 Request of the *Oberlandesgericht Cologne* of 30 March 2001 for a preliminary ruling in the criminal proceedings against *Hüseyn Gözütük*, Case Number C-187/01, (2001) *OJ* C 212/10; Reference for a preliminary ruling by the Rechtbank van Eerste Aanleg te Veurne by Judgment of 4 May 2001 in criminal proceedings brought against *Klaus Fritz Brügge*; civil party: *Benedikt Leliaert*, Case Number C-385/01, (2001) *OJ* C 348/15.

prosecuted because it is already settled? Is it relevant that the form of settlement is unknown under German law? All aspects of *non-bis-in-idem* are in dispute: what exactly is prohibited; what is twice; and what is *idem*, what are the same facts? Especially the transnational application of *non bis in idem* suffers from these problems.[9]

Whenever crimes are being defined on a European level, it is not only relevant to draft definitions of specific individual crimes, but to provide for a European general part of criminal law as well. Who commits a crime, what is an accomplice, what is participation in the crime, what is an attempt? May legal entities be prosecuted? Are we going to include broad accountability: preparation of crime/ conspiracy/criminal organization. What kind of mens rea or intent is required? If you do not develop a general part, you will see that definitions of crimes will contain 'general part elements'. Another consequence is that the determination of criminal responsibility (and finally conviction or acquittal) may depend on the forum and not on the *locus delicti*. In the end, this will lead to practical and dogmatical chaos.

4. The Need for a Common Political Discussion/Public Opinion

In a democratic society the content of the law is open for discussion in public. At times issues will come up concerning parts of the legislation. It is astonishing to see that such a European public debate is completely absent. This is strange on the one hand because of the growing influence of European legislation on the life of the citizens of Europe. On the other hand it is logical. Issues concerning European legislation and politics are very complex. The media seem to be baffled by its complexity and hardly pay any attention to institutional issues. The general public does not understand how the EU functions, let alone how the legislative process works or what the current political issues are. In addition, the general public will only participate in a discussion in one language.

The result is that discussion on Europe, its legislation and its future plans, if at all, takes place within one state, with some exceptions where Member States share the same language (IRL/GB, NL/B, D/A, F/B). The general public of the European Union as a whole does not play a role. In practice, the public is excluded from participation and discussion only takes place within European committees. I find participation of people other than state officials in a European discussion important because that will contribute to the acceptance of European legislation and European authorities. If not, we run the risk that people will regard European initiatives as alien, intrusive or foreign and for that reason will not co-operate with or support them. In the field of criminal law this is essential for its legitimacy. If the European Union does not succeed in obtaining the respect of the large majority of its citizens, there is a fair chance that the norms it produces will not be respected.

9 See J.A.W. Lensing, *Ne bis in idem in strafzaken; een rechtsvergelijkende en internationaalstrafrechtelijk oriëntatie*, Preadvies voor de Nederlandse Vereniging van Rechtsvergelijking 2000, no.60, see also the interventions, in no.61, 2001.

Other dangers must be prevented. The two most important are the danger of static law and the danger of disharmonization. The larger the European Union gets, the more difficult it will be to obtain a consensus on new legislation and on new policies.[10] It is very likely that the consequence will be an extremely static situation, in which it is very difficult to alter whatever legislation. In addition, the more the EU regulates, the less space there is for experiments with new ways of combating some forms of crime. The larger the EU gets, the more pressure there will be to eliminate deviating policies and legislation in specific States. If you were to allow one State to deviate, the whole idea of harmonization will be lost, because each State will have points on which they do not agree with the prevailing European view.

5. A Common Cultural Background/Similar Expectations of the Role of Criminal Law in Society

Despite many ties through the centuries in religion, culture and politics, views on the place and role of criminal law in society differ tremendously in the Member States. Extreme views can be found in the European Union on the prominence of criminal law. Whereas in one country the use of criminal law in response to undesirable human conduct is only admitted if all other means have failed (the principle of *ultimum remedium*), other States may appreciate the symbolic and moral deterrence of criminal law. These differences are fundamental, because they deal with the question of whether criminal law should regulate a certain issue at all. In fact this is the key issue why it is so difficult to come to an agreement on a common European criminal law.

Similar clashes come up when we raise the question of whether minimum (or automatic) sentences make sense or not. Where in one system, the ruling view is that a standard minimum penalty will have the most deterrent effect (clear and predictable consequences) in order to prevent people from committing a certain crime, another system may wish to leave the imposition of a sentence entirely to the discretion of the judge in order to take all relevant circumstances of fact and the accused into account. Also the type of sanction can be in dispute. Under the current European system many directives and regulations provide for an additional sanction of exclusion for a certain period for those who have defrauded the financial interest of the Community. Opinions on these points may get emotional. One party may regard the view of the other as leading to injustice or as a totally inadequate or ineffective response of the State to a severe problem. The following examples may be given where opinions in Member States differ:

- abortion
- assisted suicide
- evading military service
- prosecution of legal entities

10 In my opinion this is a danger that exists regardless of whether we have a democratic system or maintain the current undemocratic European legislative process.

- speed limits for motor vehicles
- use of alcohol and drugs
- whether being under influence of alcohol or drugs constitutes a defence
- possession of weaponry
- discrimination on grounds race/sexual preference/political or religious opinion
- conspiracy
- minimum sentences
- life imprisonment

These seem to be a few of the hot potatoes of the EU.

Differences on these issues can not easily be overcome by means of legislation. In order to develop common European ideas about the role, impact and expectations of criminal law it is necessary to develop a European public opinion. I must admit that the chances for such a development are small. It takes time to find compromises and develop something new that will leave earlier national ideas behind. In addition, the lack of a common language leads to the fact that no public discussions take place throughout Europe as a whole.

A European Institute for Research in Crime ought to be established. Currently EU legislation is drafted without any research into the necessity of it. One of the current characteristics of European responses to crime is that it takes place without any research and is always legislative in nature. Whenever a criminal problem seems to appear on the horizon a legal instrument is immediately drafted and takes binding effect.[11] Although the awareness of responsibilities regarding the suppression of crime must be appreciated, as well as the willingness to respond in an unbureaucratic way, numerous initiatives must be qualified as overreacting,[12] inconsistent,[13] counterproductive,[14] unnecessary,[15] unfounded[16] and lacking a legal

11 A cynical remark would be that new legislation is the only response that the European Union can come up with regarding all alleged problems.

12 A local Belgian problem (Dutroux) was transferred onto the level of the European Union, see Joint Action of 24 February 1997 concerning action to combat trafficking in human beings and sexual exploitation of children, (1997) *OJ* L 63/2.

13 It is unclear who should be in charge of combating international fraud within the EC/EU. First this was dedicated to Europol, subsequently it was the task for UCLAF/OLAF, then the EU Convention emphasized the responsibility of the Member States and lastly some voices want to establish a European prosecutor who would deal with the matter, however without relieving other authorities of the task.

14 The existence of various authorities, both on a European as well as on a national level, trusted with the same task, leads to additional problems. Co-ordination is required in order to prevent double work, conflicts of competencies and jurisdiction need to be solved and there is a fair risk that no open communication takes place.

15 EU Convention on fraud against the interest of the community. This crime could already be prosecuted on the basis of existing national criminal legislation. All forms of necessary international co-operation (extradition/judicial assistance) are applicable with regard to fraud.

basis.[17] It is not possible to predict what a European summit will come up with in relation to combating crime, but is certain that they will do so. Legislation according to the 'Pavlov's dogs' principle ought to be prevented. Criminal law is not a simple solution to complex problems. For effective law enforcement it does for instance not make a difference that certain offences can be prosecuted as 'terrorist offences'.[18] What is important is that the behaviour can be prosecuted at all, regardless of the label under which that can be done.

What we need is a realistic view on crime in society and on what can be achieved in society with the use of criminal law. To convey to the public that it is possible to eradicate crime is not a realistic notion. It gives ground to high expectations on the part of the public that can never be fulfilled. It also leads to a situation where the methods and means to combat crime will never be sufficient. This is logical because if you formulate a goal which is out of reach, you will simply not reach it. We therefore need to define what we want to reach with criminal law. This would include, in my view, an acceptance of a certain level of crime in order to be able to better combat crime. Politicians ought to convey to the public the notion that there will always be a certain level of crime. Of course we would like to lower that level as much as possible. However, to think that it is possible to eliminate all crime does not demonstrate a capacity to understand the realities of life. It might be relevant to observe that, in general, experts in criminal law expect less of the effects of criminal law than others do.

6. A Democratic System

This seems to be self evident but in light of the experience of the European Union in the past it is certainly not a superfluous requirement. Legislation may only enter into force if approved by a freely elected and representative parliament. The current practice regarding third pillar legislation in which binding instruments may be introduced without having been approved by a parliament is unheard of. In doing so, the European Union applies standards that fall short of that required at a national level. Legal instruments under the third pillar may acquire binding force without the consent of the European parliament and national parliaments. This gives far too much uncontrolled power to the governments represented in European Council. This requirement coincides with the requirement of a demarcation of the competencies of the European Parliament and national parliaments.

Democracy also provides for requirements in aspects other than the legislative process. The performance of the European police and the European prosecutor must be supervized by democratic procedures. This can be found in all democratic

16 For instance the idea of the Tampere summit that judgments should be mutually recognized throughout Europe. This is already possible on the basis of Council of Europe Conventions of 1970 and 1983, as well as an additional EC Convention of 1987.

17 There was no legal basis for the establishment of the European drugs Unit in 1993. Likewise, there is no legal basis for Eurojust under the current EU legislation.

18 See Proposal for a Council Framework decision on combating terrorism, 19.9.2001 COM(2001) 521 final, 2001/0217 (CNS).

systems. Police and prosecution are accountable to the Minister of Justice. In the context of Europe, this could mean that they are accountable to the Commissioner for Justice. He or she will be held politically responsible for the functioning of the police and prosecution. The Commissioner for Justice therefore must have the competence to fire officials.

This means for instance that the practice of scattered or non-existing accountability that exists regarding Europol must come to an end. Europol is only accountable to the collective of the Council of Ministers. Each individual minister is accountable to his own national parliament. The result is that nobody is accountable for the whole.

7. A System Protected by Human Rights Safeguards

After fifty years of existence of the European Convention on Human Rights it would be unthinkable to have a European criminal justice system that lacked the protection of that Convention. There is a risk that rights that were already protected under the ECHR in respect of national states before the establishment of the European Union must be 'won' again in order to obtain the same protection as regards the European Union. It is therefore a self-evident necessity that the ECHR or a convention with a similar level of protection as well as providing a similar efficient supervisory mechanism will be applicable to all aspects of European Criminal Law. This contains two basic elements:

1. the scope of protection of the ECHR is determined by the ECHR and not by EU organs or legislation and
2. accountability of the European organs for their behaviour.

The first condition deals with the case law of the European Court of Human Rights on the question of when someone is under a 'criminal charge' within the meaning of Article 6 ECHR. In *Öztürk* and other cases the European Court of Human Rights held that 'criminal charge' has an autonomous meaning, and must be interpreted independent from the name given to the relevant field of law by its legislator.[19] This requirement will mainly have serious consequences for two fields of law. Competition law under the EC Treaty must, on the basis of the criteria formulated in the *Öztürk* decision, be considered as falling within the definition of criminal law. Also a number of administrative sanctions may qualify as criminal law in the sense of Article 6 ECHR.

The second requirement introduces the application of the ECHR to acts of organs of the EU. This is important because under the current system of the ECHR, complaints can only be declared admissible if directed against a State party. In its current text the ECHR does not provide for complaints against the EU or its

19 ECHR, 21 February 1984, *Öztürk against Germany*, Series A-73, par. 53.

organs.[20] This is an undesirable situation because it brings an important field of law outside the protection of the Convention and would mean that citizens have fewer fundamental rights when confronted with the EU than when confronted with acts of each individual state. This would amount to a step back in the protection of human rights. This can be compensated by concluding a Protocol to the ECHR introducing a complaint against the European Union. The acceptance by the European Court of Human Rights of complaints directed against all EU Member States seems to be less attractive because the Member States are only indirectly responsible.

8. The Necessity for one Legal Language

Law is inherently related to language. Legal terminology has a certain meaning because of a certain connotation in the legal system. When translated into another language, a translation that seems to be appropriate at first glance may miss the connotation of the system from which the term originates. Only in theory is it possible to have the law written in all twelve (or even twenty in a few years to come) languages and still convey the same meaning. Everyone who has ever studied the implementation or translation of (formally) identical legal texts into national law or other languages will have noticed that the law may change as soon as it is translated or implemented into another legal system. In this context it seems wise to provide European criminal law in one language only. Of course this is not a new idea: Latin performed this function for many years under the Roman Empire and even succeeded to remain of importance until the present day. Also the French legal system and French as a legal language played such a role in a much shorter period during the days of Napoleon. We therefore need to opt for a Latin of our time. It seems logical to give the English language this role.

This certainly has negative consequences. It means that part of the law is no longer available in the mother tongue of the public. This is a serious consequence and raises questions regarding the principle of *lex certa* and the accessibility of the law for the public. However, I do not think that a defence: 'I could not read the European Criminal Code, so I did not know that I was not allowed to ....' ought to be admissible. In my opinion the use of one legal language is limited to the use of one legally binding language. It does not mean that the law may not be translated into other languages. It should still be translated and made available. This is a situation that is already in existence as regards treaty law. Many multilateral conventions are binding only in a limited number of languages. For instance conventions of the Council of Europe appear in English and French only, whereas United Nations conventions are binding in Arabic, Chinese, English, French, Russian and Spanish.

20 A.H. Klip, 'The Decrease of Protection under Human Rights Treaties in International Criminal Law', *International Review of Penal Law, 68,* 1997, p. 291-310.

9. What Level of Co-operation is Necessary?

One of the alleged advantages of a common European criminal law is that international co-operation would no longer be necessary. This is not the case. It will stay in existence, however, it may obtain a different form and change its character. Due to the fact that one of the criteria to criminalize certain behaviour on a European level is its transnational character, it is logical that evidence and suspects will be found in different states. This is nothing new in comparison to the existing situation and it is unlikely that this will ever change.

The character of co-operation might change if the introduction of eurocrimes were to be backed by a European Criminal Court. Then a kind of hierarchical relationship may be established. If not, there is not much difference to the existing legal situation. The fact that the definition of crimes is common to all states neither takes away the necessity of co-operation nor facilitates its functioning.

10. A Common Interpretation and Enforcement of European Criminal Law

To start off with a negative reasoning of the necessity: A common mechanism to interpret and enforce European Criminal Law is necessary, otherwise it would not make sense to have a common system at all. Common interpretation and enforcement can be ensured by the establishment of common European institutions. It follows from this that a European police, a European prosecutor and a European Criminal Court should exist. The European Criminal Court would be exclusively competent to interpret the European criminal legislation. In cases in which national (or other) courts have to interpret European criminal legislation they would be bound by the case law of the European Criminal Court.

In a harmonized system it would seem logical that the enforcement of sanctions must be ensured under the same conditions for all. This means that a common penitentiary system must be set up and that European rules on early release, parole and pardon would have to be developed. The principle of equal treatment requires such measures. If the execution of sanctions was not Europeanized, everything achieved in defining the law, the prosecution and adjudication of it would have been lost, when for instance different rules on early release are applied. A convicted person in Spain might then be released after completion of half of the sentence, whereas his 'colleague' who received the same penalty but had his sentence executed in the Netherlands would face a much more severe regime and be released after completion of two thirds of the sentence. How could the differentces in the penitentiary institutions be dealt with? One year in a Spanish prison may be much more severe than one year in a Dutch prison. Again this shows that developing a common legal system deals with many issues other than simply drafting legislation in theory and on paper.

Is criminal law different from other fields of law in the sense that it deserves special treatment?
Harmonization or unification of law has taken place within the European Union/ European Community in various fields of law. In some case in fields of law in

which not all conditions mentioned above had been fulfilled. This raises the question of whether criminal law is different from other fields of law in the sense that it deserves some form of special treatment. What we intend to do here has some features of harmonization, but is entirely different: a new supranational legal system is about to be created.

More than any other field of law, criminal law affects and reflects the emotions of people. It channels natural feelings of revenge to the benefit of society. It represents the morals of society by prohibiting what is unacceptable and by allowing freedom in other areas. In a more concrete way, whereas European community law deals with the freedoms awarded to citizens, criminal law deals with the limitations of freedom. This is an entirely different approach and this means that rules drafted in the field of the internal market under community legislation cannot be transferred to criminal law.

11. The Method of Achieving a European *Corpus Juris Criminalis*

In the European context with so many different views on almost all issues, nothing seems to be more difficult than to draft a common code on such a highly sensitive thing as criminal law. In order to give it a chance it is therefore absolutely necessary to establish a representative drafting commission. This commission should be representative of the Member States, but should not represent them. In my view a classical method should be followed. The nomination of a drafting commission, consisting of professors of criminal law. The character of the members on the commission is more than a mere detail. What we need in such a commission is an overview of existing legal systems, but also a vision towards a new European system with the ambition that it will last for a few decades. The commission must be given a clear mission and sufficient time. To be more specific: good legislation requires more time than the current legislative process in Brussels is willing to give.

It is obvious that a new European criminal law cannot be a copy of any existing criminal law system of one of the Member States. The drafting commission must be willing to enter new waters and to leave national systems behind. This will be a difficult task. However, it is important to develop a criminal law system as a whole, because only by developing an entire system is one able to put various aspects into context. Thus a completely different method is proposed than the current European strategy, by which not an entire system is developed but rather, small steps are taken every 6 or 12 months, following a European summit. As a consequence of that, a certain European criminal legal system evolves, but this is more as a result of a large number of uncoordinated small steps (resulting from compromises), than the result of what the European Union or each of the individual Member States had in mind.

12. Conditions must be fulfilled before Implementation

This condition also seems self evident. However, on a European level various steps have been taken before there was a legal competence to do so. The European Drugs

Unit was established as a forerunner of Europol, more than two years before a convention on the establishment of Europol was concluded. A 'provisional judicial network' was established in 2001, anticipating the formal legal basis in 2002. This European practice, which would be unacceptable under each national legal system, must come to an end.

13. Why would we do it?

This is a question that more or less forms a precondition for plans for harmonization. I have dealt with this on other occasions and expressed my doubts.[21]

14. Conclusion

On evaluation of the application of all these conditions for a European *Corpus Juris Criminalis* I seriously doubt whether Europe has already achieved the situation where such a common legal order is any more than a Utopian ideal. The protection of the rights of the citizens of Europe and the need to combat crime are too precious to get lost in embarkations towards an harmonized system without having identified its goal.

21 See 'Harmonization and Harmonising Effects in Criminal Law', in J.F. Nijboer and W.J.J.M. Sprangers (eds.), *Harmonization in Forensic Expertise, An Inquiry into the Desirability of International Standards for Scientific Evidence*, Thela Thesis, Amsterdam, 2000, p. 67-78; 'Harmonisierung des Strafrechts - eine Idee fixe?', *Neue Zeitschrift für Strafrecht*, 2000, p. 626-630; A.H. Klip, 'Nederlands Strafprocesrecht en Europese Harmonisatie', in C.H. Brants, P.A.M. Mevis and E. Prakken (eds.), *Legitieme strafvordering*, Antwerpen, Intersentia, 2001, p. 205-214.

Sabine Gleß

WHAT SHOULD BE THE CONDITIONS FOR A EUROPEAN *CORPUS JURIS CRIMINALIS*?

1. Introduction – Discussion of A. Klip's 'Conditions for a European *Corpus Juris Criminalis*

In the debate surrounding 'European Criminal Law,' two extreme points of view mark the scale of opinions:

One extreme position - let us fix it on the very right of the scale - asks for a repatriation to the national level of all powers related to criminal law.[1] All EC-regulations and directives that have the effect of harmonizing criminal law should be abolished; conceivably even the third pillar of the European Union, the close co-operation in Justice and Home Affairs, should be (at the very least) reduced.

Advocates of the other extreme point of view - on the very left of our scale - think only a common European Judicial Area can give an adequate answer to crime nowadays.[2] For them, the question of whether this common European legal space should be created on the basis of European Community Law or on the grounds of strong common measures taken in the third pillar of the European Union seems merely a question of taste.

In between these two extreme positions we find all sorts of approaches, including closer co-operation, harmonization and even a model penal code for economic or 'euro-'crime.

The early André Klip, i.e., the work of André Klip that I read when venturing into the discussion on a European criminal law a few years ago, leaned very much

1 E.g. P.-A. Albrecht and. S. Braum, 'Defiencies in the Development of European Criminal Law', *European Law Journal,* 1999, p. 293 *et seq.;* M. Köhler, 'Rechtsstaatliches Strafrecht und Rechtsangleichung' in G. Bemmann and D. Spinellis (eds.), *Festschrift für Mangakis,* Athens, Sakkulas, 1999, p. 751 *et seq.*

2 E.g. U. Sieber, 'European Unification and European Criminal Law', *European Journal of Crime, Criminal Law and Criminal Justice,* 1994, p. 86 *et seq.;* K. Tiedemann, 'Europäisierung des Strafrechts', in K.-F. Kreuzer, D.-H. Scheuing and U. Sieber (eds.), *Die Europäisierung der mitgliedstaatlichen Rechtsordnungen,* Baden-Baden, Nomos, 1997, p. 133, 134 *et seq.*, 143 *et seq.*

to the right side of our scale, harshly criticizing the European influence on criminal law.[3]

Thus, when I received the invitation to discuss André Klip's presentation on 'Conditions for a European Corpus Juris Criminalis'. I was very honoured, but on second thought, I became somewhat suspicious. Knowing his position, I asked myself: Why was I chosen to discuss his presentation. Was I a 'Europeanist' or seen as one?

And in fact, writing my comment I realized that I find myself more to the left side of our scale, I am of the opinion that (national) criminal law cannot and should not be immune to European law. European Community law and - naturally - third pillar acts should have an influence on all national law. Such an impact is the consequence of the - commonly accepted - concept of the EU after the Amsterdam Treaty.

The André Klip of today can be located a bit more towards the middle of our scale, too - accepting the idea that there could be a 'federal European Penal Code'.

However - according to his view - provisions of a European Penal Code would have to meet strict requirements, and 'negative criteria' should be developed to disqualify certain 'crimes' from being regulated on the European level - in other words - from being harmonized.

2. Crimes not to be Regulated on the EU-Level

As one example for disqualification he proposes 'crimes related to a perception of moral issues', namely assisted suicide.

But this very example already shows the difficulty or rather the impossibility of negative criteria (with the effect of fighting off harmonization), because of the (dynamic) influence of European Community law on national criminal law:

If one Member State legalizes assisted suicide for the incurably ill when performed by a physician, the Member State has created a new medical service, which, in principle, must be protected by the EC-freedom to provide services. Such a service is - in general - allowed to move freely in the EC. Thus it will be available in all other States. We have already experienced this scenario in the context of abortion, which can be legally obtained everywhere in the European Union except for Ireland. When a number of organizations provided information to Irish teenagers on legal abortions abroad (namely in England and in the Netherlands), the Irish state banned their activities. Thereupon, the organizations challenged the ban in Luxembourg before the ECJ, arguing that the ban violated the freedom to provide services in the EU. The same would, or rather could, happen to assisted suicide, too.

Legal harmonization forms - even in the area of criminal law, a necessary part of the EU. It has never been disputed that EC rules in private or commercial law also affect criminal law - to the extent necessary to ensure that economic freedoms are guaranteed uniformly in all Member States. We have seen this effect in cases such as the 'Auer' case, where Community law prevented the prosecution of an

3 See A. Klip, 'Uniestrafrecht is op hol geslagen', *Nederlands Juristenblad*, 1997, p. 663 *et seq.*

Austrian veterinary practising his profession with an Italian diploma in France without prior consent of the local veterinarian association.[4]

As ties within the Union have grown closer, the influence on national criminal law has grown stronger, especially after the ECJ held in the 'Greek Maize' case[5] that Member States have an obligation to protect the Community's financial interests, even by means of criminal law - and then, as we all know, the real debate started.

3. 'Minimum-Incrimination-Approach'

To this debate André Klip added - with his presentation today - a very intriguing idea: I would like to call it the 'minimum-incrimination-approach': Klip's demand is for an end to national imperialism in the form of incrimination in the European Union.

Professor Klip's example is the German woman who is having a legal abortion performed abroad and who nevertheless may be prosecuted in Germany. Abortion is one of the acts that will be prosecuted if a German national (or rather: a German women) commits it abroad and then returns home. The jurisdiction is established on the basis of nationality.[6] According to Professor Klip's view, the establishment of a jurisdiction based on nationality appears imperialistic if the act committed is legal in the territory in which it is committed.

This 'minimum-incrimination-approach' holds a lot of valuable aspects for the building of a 'European Judicial Area': If the people of one Member State decide that a certain act is not to be punished on their territory, no other Member State may prosecute its own nationals if they go there and act according to the law of that State, even if the people of the actor's home state think the act deserves punishment. Especially because of that difference of judgment (on rather sensitive areas like abortion and assisted suicide), this approach could in fact help start the building of a European criminal legal culture.

And in some respect, this is an approach aimed at a harmonization of criminal law on a minimum level - through the back door: If one Member State decides to decriminalize a certain act, all its neighbours would be bound by the decision.

4. Résumé

Calling for harmonization himself (albeit not coming from a supranational level, but from the national level), I found André Klip's and my position not too far away from each other.

I agree on most of the other aspects Professor Klip raises: He rightly points out that - after creating the third pillar - (many) criminal lawyers seem to have forgotten the concept of the criminal law as an 'ultima ratio' of the state and tend

4 ECR 1983, p. 2727 *et seq.*

5 ECR 1989, p. 2965 *et seq.*

6 See § 5 No. 9 German Penal Code.

towards an 'over-activity' and - what we call - a *Breitbandkriminalisierung* in Germany.

I especially agree with his opinion on the absence of a democratic basis behind European (criminal) law and the implications of this absence for a real 'European Penal Code'. There is a dangerous lack of public discussion and democratic control over European lawmaking, a problem which will increase with the enlargement of the Union.

To me it appears that the different positions in the debate on 'European Criminal law' - on the extreme right or the extreme left side of our scale - rest on different conceptions of democracy and on rather different premises regarding the relationship of state sovereignty and the competence to make criminal law.

To the advocates of the 'national position,' the competence to adopt criminal law is at *the very core* of state sovereignty. They doubt whether this competence can be delegated at all without giving up statehood itself. However, if such an assignment to a supranational level could be done, i.e., could be done without creating a new state, the entrusting states, according to this position, would have to do so explicitly and with the explicit consent of the people. None of the existing acts that allow the EC-Commission to co-ordinate the Member States' activities against crime (such as art. 280 TEC post-Amsterdam) could be the basis for such competence.[7]

Advocates of the 'European position' take a more pragmatic view: The Member States have empowered the EC, for example, to hand out subsidies in certain areas. To them, such an empowerment also implies the power to ensure an orderly administration, i.e., the EC may also punish defrauders if necessary.[8] This side does not see a 'democracy' or 'State-theory-problem' in a European competence to adopt criminal law. Even if a 'European Fraud Law' would in the end lead to a total harmonization of all national criminal laws, ultimately creating one European Judicial Area, the 'European side' would be happy that the job is done.

Recalling the original question: 'What should be the conditions for a European *Corpus Juris Criminalis*?', I would take a rather pragmatic stand: On the premise that we can (no longer) fight off the European influence on (national) criminal law, we should instead focus on the question of how the European system could be changed in order to ensure that the European influence on (national) criminal law is grounded in a democratic decision-making process at the European level. If this condition were fulfilled, the people of Europe could accept a European Penal code.

7 See *supra* footnote 1. For further information see: S. Gleß and H.E. Zeitler, 'Fair Trial Rights and the European Community's Fight against Fraud', *European Law Journal*, 2001, p. 219 *et seq.*

8 See K. Tiedemann, 'EG und EU als Quelle des Strafrechts', *Festschrift für Roxin*, Berlin-New York, Walter de Gruyter, p. 1412.

Ecotax

Stefan Ubachs

TOWARDS AN ECOTAX-SCHENGEN?

1. Introduction

Over the years, many Member States of the European Union have introduced environmental taxes in their fiscal system. The share of environmental taxes in total tax revenue is increasing,[1] and in some Member States one can even observe some form of an ecological tax reform. But what has the European Union done itself? Surely, the European Community has introduced a number of fiscal environmental policy instruments.[2] There is, however, still no European ecotax; neither does there seem to be a co-ordinated European fiscal environmental strategy. The most well-known example of Community failure is probably the attempt to introduce a harmonized CO2/energy tax in all Member States. Since 1992, little progress has been made in introducing this tax. An important reason is the need for unanimity in the Council as far as fiscal matters are concerned; the CO2/energy tax is currently still frustrated by a Spanish and British veto. It is therefore highly questionable whether the energy tax will be adopted by 2002, as the Commission indicated in May 2001.[3] Last year, the Commission made a proposal to introduce a European kerosene tax on commercial aviation. It is likely that that the same will happen to this proposal.

In this paper, I will first discuss the possibility for a European ecotax based on qualified majority. Secondly, I will set out some criteria, which in my opinion have to be met in order to create an effective ecotax. Finally, I will discuss to what extent the proposed CO2/energy tax and kerosene tax meet these criteria.

1 European Environmental Agency, *Environmental taxes: recent developments in tools for integration*, Environmental issues series, no. 18, Luxembourg, Office for Official Publications of the European Communities, p. 7.

2 For instance the different minimum excise duty rates for leaded and unleaded petrol, Directive 92/82, *OJ* 1992 L 316, or the Eurovignette which was introduced in July 2000.

3 A Sustainable Europe for a Better World: A European Union Strategy for Sustainable Development, COM(2001) 264 final, 15 May 2001, p. 10.

2. Environmental Taxation and EU law

2.1. Environmental Taxation and the EC Treaty: the Legal Basis for a European Ecotax

The first step in creating effective environmental taxes is to adopt a general Community strategy on environmental taxation. First of all, one has to assess the legal basis for a general framework for environmental taxation. Secondly, one has to be certain that the desired effects of the tax (which in many cases will be a reduction in the demand for polluting goods) will be constituted. Therefore, it is also necessary to analyse the economic effects of environmental taxation. But let us first look for the legal basis for a European environmental taxation framework.

The most important *fons iuris* of the Community, the EC Treaty, does not contain any provisions on environmental taxation as such. However, there are some provisions in the EC Treaty that are relevant for environmental taxation issues.[4] Article 2 of the Treaty, describing the task of the Community, states that the Community shall have as its task '...to promote throughout the Community a harmonious, balanced and *sustainable* development of economic activities, ... *sustainable* and non inflationary growth, ... and improvement of the quality of the environment'.

This means that the Community should take the environmental consequences of economic activities and growth into account. Title XIX of the Treaty (articles 174-176) deals with environmental issues.

Article 174, para. 2 of the Treaty states that in Community policy on the environment 'environmental damage should as a priority be rectified at source and that the polluter should pay'. One way to realize the polluter pays principle is to impose an ecotax on activities/products that cause harm to the environment. According to article 175, para. 2 provisions primarily of a fiscal nature shall be taken by the Council, acting unanimously on a proposal from the Commission and after consulting the European Parliament, the Economic and Social Committee and the Committee of the Regions.

Since most environmental taxes are indirect taxes, article 93 of the Treaty is relevant as far as environmental taxes influence the functioning of the internal market. Article 93 requires the same procedure as article 175, para. 2, so any harmonization based on article 175, para. 2 can only be constituted if the Council agrees unanimously.[5]

As far as environmental incentives in the field of direct taxation are concerned, article 94, which makes approximation of national legislation possible in the interest of the internal market, is relevant as well.[6]

4 For an overview of provisions in the EC Treaty relevant for ecotaxes, see K. Borgsmidt, 'Ecotaxes in the framework of Community law', *EC Tax Review*, 1999-4, p. 228-240.

5 See W. Schön, 'Tax competition in Europe – the legal perspective', *EC Tax Review*, 2000-2, p. 104-105.

6 See W. Schön, *supra* note 5, p. 101.

The requirement that fiscal measures can only be taken if the Council agrees unanimously has frustrated the adoption of a European ecotax to date. If the number of Member States increases in the next couple of years, decision making on tax issues will most likely be even more difficult. The more Member States, the more likely it is that one of them will use its veto. This is most certainly a problem in creating a European system of environmental taxation. How can this 'unanimity problem' be solved?

2.2. *From Unanimity towards Qualified Majority?*

The first possibility to overcome the 'unanimity problem' is of course to change the EU Treaty in such a way that qualified majority replaces the unanimity requirement. However, since unanimity is required for such an alteration of the EU Treaty, it is unlikely that this solution for the unanimity problem will succeed. To overcome the problem, one has to look for a different solution. This solution is in my opinion available, and it has been used successfully before, albeit in a different way.

Towards an Ecotax-Schengen

In the 1980s, some Member States wanted to lift intra Community border controls. However, it was not possible to do it within the existing Community framework, because not all Member States wanted to take such a measure. The Member States that did want to lift the border controls,[7] managed to reach their goal, albeit not within the existing Community framework, but on an intergovernmental basis. Since the adoption of the Schengen Convention in 1990, eight other Member States have joined the list of signatories. In the Treaty of Amsterdam, it was decided that the so-called Schengen acquis would be incorporated into the EU Treaty starting from 1 May 1999.

More recently, something similar happened with the introduction of a single European currency, the euro. The last stage of harmonization of the economic and monetary policies in the framework of the Economic and Monetary Union consisted of the establishment of a European Central Bank, the fixing of exchange rates and the introduction of a single currency. The United Kingdom and Denmark did not want to participate. A solution for this problem was found in granting them the possibility not to participate (in the form of a protocol annexed to the Treaty). There would not have been a single currency if there had not been the possibility for Member States not to participate in the introduction of a single currency.

2.3. *Closer Co-operation*

Since the adoption of the Treaty of Amsterdam, a possibility has been introduced for a group of Member States to co-operate more closely if for whatever reason the unanimity in the Council, which would be required to establish a Community measure on the subject, cannot be reached. The conditions that have to be met are

7 Belgium, France, Germany, Luxembourg and the Netherlands.

laid down in article 11 of the EC Treaty and in Title VII of the EU Treaty. The closer co-operation must in particular:

- cover an area which does not fall within the exclusive competence of the community;
- be aimed at furthering the objectives of the Union;
- respect the principles of the Treaties;
- be used only as a last resort;
- involve a majority of Member States.

If these criteria are met, the Council, acting by qualified majority, authorizes the closer co-operation on a proposal from the Commission and after consulting the European Parliament. A Member State can however refuse to allow a decision to be taken with qualified majority for reasons of national political importance. If that happens, a qualified majority in the Council can refer the matter to the Heads of State or Government, which must act unanimously.

If one considers environmental taxation, for example an energy tax, one can, in my opinion conclude that the conditions set out in article 11 of the EC Treaty are met:

- taxation is an area which does not fall within the exclusive competence of the Community;
- environmental taxation is aimed at furthering the objectives of the Union, since article 2 of the EC Treaty states that the Community shall have as its task 'improvement of the quality of the environment';
- if the environmental taxes are designed carefully, they will certainly respect the principles of the Treaties, notably the principles of free trade and fair competition. A certain degree of harmonization of environmental taxes will most probably lift existing trade barriers that result from the different national environmental taxes and tax rates in the Member States;
- closer co-operation is used as a last resort; the Commission has been trying for almost ten years to pass a proposal to introduce an energy tax, without success;
- 14 out of 15 Member States agree with the introduction of a European energy tax, based on the Commission's last proposal, so a majority of Member States are involved.

Recent developments show that in the European Parliament and in the Commission the option of closer co-operation in the field of environmental taxation is being considered.

In its strategy paper 'Tax policy in the European Union – Priorities for the years ahead'[8] the Commission stated:

[8] COM(2001) 260 final.

> 'As regards indirect taxation, the possibility of enhanced co-operation could provide a way forward in the area of environmental and energy taxation. A majority of Member States have indicated their strong desire to make progress in this area'.

On May 30, a written question on the matter was submitted to the Commission by Member of Parliament Alexander de Roo.[9] On the question of when the Commission intended to take steps to propose a European energy/CO2 tax on the basis of the enhanced co-operation clause, Commissioner Bolkestein answered:[10]

> 'As the communication *Tax policy in the European Union – Priorities for the years ahead*[11] states, the option introduced by the Amsterdam Treaty which is designed to allow closer co-operation between sub-groups of like-minded Member States could also be considered in certain cases. When indirect taxation is concerned the possibility of closer co-operation might be the way forward for environment and energy taxes'.

Commissioner Bolkestein added, however, that using the closer co-operation clause must not undermine the functioning of the internal market, become a trade barrier or affect the jurisdictions or rights of Member States that do not participate.

Will the use of the closer co-operation clause undermine the functioning of the internal market? To the contrary: in the past, harmonization of indirect taxes has proved to be a successful tool in realizing an internal market.[12] Harmonization of environmental taxes will therefore, in my opinion, contribute to the creation of the internal market. If harmonization of environmental taxes cannot be realized within the framework of article 93 or 175 of the EC Treaty, using the closer co-operation clause is the second best solution. In my opinion, the fear that this solution will constitute a trade barrier, is also not justified. Trade between Member States that do participate in the 'Ecotax-Schengen' framework will benefit from it. Trade between a participating Member State and a non-participating Member State will not be affected, provided that the Ecotax-Schengen framework is designed carefully. In fact, the situation between a participating Member State and a non-participating Member State will not be much different from the current situation, in which every Member State has its own environmental taxes with its own, different rates (or no environmental taxes at all).

Therefore, by using the closer co-operation clause there could be the possibility to create something like an 'Eco-Schengen' consisting of a group of EU Member States that impose a system of harmonized environmental taxes. One day, the 'Eco-Schengen' acquis will perhaps, just like its illustrious predecessor, become part of the acquis communautaire and will be integrated in the EU Treaty.

Having set out the legal basis on which a European environmental tax framework can be constituted, let us now look more closely at how these environ-

9 Written question P-1725/01 by Alexander de Roo (*Verts/ALE*) to the Commission, 30 May 2001.

10 Answer given by Mr Bolkestein on behalf of the Commission, P-1725/01EN, 12 July 2001.

11 COM(2001) 260 final.

12 One can think of the harmonization of the value-added tax and the harmonization of excise duties.

mental taxes should be designed in order to have the desired economic effects. After having set out a general economic framework, the proposed CO2/energy tax and the kerosene tax on commercial aviation will be discussed. Do these proposed taxes make a difference to the environment or are they just 'greenspeak'?[13]

3. Optimal Environmental Taxation: defining an Effective Ecotax

Recently, the Commission announced in its report 'A Sustainable Europe for a Better World: A European Union Strategy for Sustainable Development' that one of its headline objectives is to make sure that the EU meets its Kyoto/Bonn commitment.[14] One of the measures at EU level to reach this objective, is the adoption of the energy tax directive by 2002. Within two years of this, the Commission is planning to propose more ambitious environmental targets for energy taxation aiming at full internalization of external costs.[15] The full internalization of external costs is obviously an ambitious policy goal. Which economic conditions should be met in order to reach this goal?

3.1. An Effective Environmental Tax should be Regulatory in Nature

Traditional welfare economics has always paid a lot of attention to externalities. Indeed, environmental taxes are usually advanced as an instrument to internalize externalities.

External effects arise, as is well-known, from the moment that one individual can succeed in enjoying the economic benefit of his activities, but at the same time is able to throw the costs (or at least part of them) onto the shoulders of third parties. The effect of such an externality will be that prices do not reflect the true social costs of the activity.[16] Environmental pollution is considered by many scholars as *the* example of a negative externality.[17] Many remedies could be thought of to cure this externality. The traditional one and the most important one is obviously the Pigouvian tax. The basic idea is obviously that the amount of the tax should be such that it reflects the true social costs of the pollution. Ideally the social costs would then also be reflected in the prices the polluting company charges for its products.

Let us now address how Pigouvian taxes may work in a (European) environmental tax policy. To cope with the basic idea of the Pigouvian tax the policy maker could install a regulatory charge with the aim of influencing the behaviour of potential polluters.

13 See K. Deketelaere, *European environmental tax law and policy: greenspeak!*, Dordrecht, Kluwer Academic Publishers, 2000.

14 COM(2001) 264 final, p. 10.

15 COM(2001) 264 final, p. 10.

16 R. Van den Bergh, 'Le droit civil face à l'analyse économique du droit', *Revue Internationale du Droit Économique*, 1998, p. 234.

17 See e.g. M. Faure, 'Economic aspects of environmental liability: an introduction', *European Review of Private Law*, 1996, p. 86-109.

The regulatory environmental charge is in fact a practical translation of the Pigouvian tax. The way this usually works is that at the policy level a certain environmental goal is identified after which a certain target for the regulatory charge is chosen. Ideally the target for the charge is chosen in such a way that alternative (less polluting) solutions are offered to the polluter. This means that if one would consider e.g. a regulatory charge on consumption, this only makes sense if the charge is applied to so-called elastic goods. If the consumer would, notwithstanding the charge, have no alternative consumption possibilities, he may have no other option than to continue with the consumption of the polluting product, assuming that it is not possible to reduce demand.[18] Hence, the effectiveness of such a regulatory charge is very much related to the possibility of having less-polluting alternatives available or the possibility to reduce demand.

As soon as the target for the charge has been defined (taking into account alternatives), next the optimal amount of the charge should be fixed. The amount of the charge will be dependent upon the environmental target chosen. Indeed, environmental policy usually starts with the setting of target standards.[19]

This target will determine the optimal quality of a certain environmental component. One could e.g., within the framework of the discussion on climate change, agree that the European Union has to reduce CO_2 emissions[20] to, say, X megaton. Then economists would argue that on the basis of trial and error an environmental tax rate can be fixed which best corresponds to the environmental target chosen.[21] The disadvantage of this approach, whereby the regulatory charge is linked to a certain target, is that some polluters may not be reached by the tax (e.g. because the charge is linked and limited to specific products, services or production methods) although they do contribute to the externality.

These charges with a primarily regulatory nature have the attainment of a specific environmental target as their main goal. When, in common language, people discuss 'environmental taxes' they usually refer to these regulatory charges. It is important to stress that with these regulatory charges budgetary effects or goals play only a minor role. In its purest form one could argue that the regulatory charge should even be budget neutral. If the charge on a certain product, production method or service is a success, the logical consequence should be (given alternatives - see above) that the demand for those products or services which the charge is targeted at should reduce. Ideally the demand for the product to which the charge applies should become zero, whereas the demand for (less-polluting) alternatives will increase. The end result of such a regulatory charge would be that the demand for a certain product, service or production method would be so low that in the end

18 This may be the case if the good is one of the 'bare necessities' of life.

19 Also referred to as ambient quality standards (in the American terminology) or environmental quality standards (in the terminology of the European directive on integrated pollution prevention and control - IPPC-directive of 24 September 1996).

20 In order to reach the goals set in the Kyoto protocol.

21 This approach has been proposed by Baumol and Oates. See W.J. Baumol and W.E. Oates, 'The use of standards and prices for protection of the environment', *Swedish Journal of Economics*, March 1971, p. 42-54.

no income at all is generated as a result of this regulatory charge.[22] Hence, one can argue that the fact that a regulatory charge does not lead to great benefits for the treasury should not be considered as a problem at all. Quite to the contrary, this could precisely prove that the charge has been successful since it led to the desired result of a decreased demand for the polluting activity to which the regulatory charge applied.

Regulatory versus Budgetary Charges

It is well-known that there is a fundamental difference between on the one hand the regulatory charges, just discussed and charges with a primarily budgetary goal. Charges with such a budgetary character are best compared to traditional taxes. Indeed, these budgetary charges have, just as traditional taxes, revenue raising as their main goal. Environmental effects are just a secondary goal or play no role at all. Although in common language these charges are sometimes also referred to as 'environmental taxes' one could argue that this may be somewhat misleading, since a budgetary charge does not primarily have environmental goals.[23] Charges with such a budgetary character are in fact an indirect tax on certain goods or products (often energy related, such as oil or electricity) or on a certain service (e.g. a flight with an aeroplane).[24] As far as their nature is concerned these budgetary charges (even though they apply to environmentally polluting activities or the consumption of energy) can be compared with value-added tax or with excises.

There are also charges, which take a somewhat middle position between the regulatory charges on the one hand, and the budgetary charges on the other hand. These are referred to as the charges with a 'double dividend' character.[25] These double dividend charges have on the one hand the goal of reducing environmental pollution, whereas on the other hand they nevertheless try to realize a certain amount of tax revenue. Although we just made a clear difference between regulatory and budgetary charges, in the practice of environmental policy it is difficult to draw a clear dividing line between those two. In practice many environmental charges will have this 'double dividend' character. Obviously one may note that

22 This, by the way, leads to the interesting question whether in such a scenario the policy maker should continue to leave the environmental charge in place. If the regulatory charge were abrogated one would indeed run the risk that the polluting product would become attractive again and that its demand would again increase. Therefore, even in this scenario where the demand for such a product has reduced to zero as a result of the charge in the long run the charge should remain in existence even though the revenue it brings is zero.

23 Obviously it does not make any difference from a legal perspective whether one qualifies a tax as a regulatory or a budgetary charge. From an economic perspective this difference is, however, important. Moreover, we will show that this difference is also important if one comes to the question of whether the environmental taxes are able to reach the goals set by the policy makers (the effectiveness test).

24 See paragraph 4.2 for the Commissions idea for a kerosene tax on commercial aviation.

25 For an extensive exposé on the difference between on the one hand environmental charges with a double dividend character and environmental charges with merely ecological goals see A. Paulus, *The feasibility of ecological taxation*, Maastricht, Maastricht University Press, 1995.

with one charge the reduction of environmental pollution may be the primary goal (thus resembling more the regulatory charge) whereas with another charge the policy goal which is stressed primarily will relate more to the raising of revenue (thus making this charge look more like a budgetary charge). However, there will always remain ambiguity and tension between the regulatory and revenue raising functions of taxes.[26]

3.2. Demand for Taxed Products should be Elastic

A whole variety of tax measures can be used to reduce the harmful environmental effect of certain behaviour. In principle both regulatory as well as budgetary charges could contribute to a reduction of environmentally damaging behaviour, albeit that the environmental effects only play a secondary role to the budgetary charges. Also, environmental measures in the sphere of direct taxation (such as environmental investment deduction or energy investment deduction) could lead to positive environmental effects.

The question of the effectiveness of these measures relates to a large extent to the price elasticity of the product or service on which the tax would be applied. If the demand for a certain product were inelastic, introducing an environmental tax on that particular product with the goal to reduce the consumption of that product may not be very effective. Indeed, a pure inelasticity means theoretically that a consumer will continue to consume the specific product, irrespective of its price. One can therefore conclude that the introduction of regulatory environmental charges on inelastic products or services will probably not be very effective. Products or services whose demand is inelastic may on the other hand be very well suited to a budgetary charge. Indeed: if the main goal of the charge is to guarantee revenue raising for the government, it may well be effective to apply the charge on such a product. Given inelasticity the demand for the product of service will indeed not decrease as a result of the tax and hence the tax revenue remains guaranteed.

If one interprets the polluter pays principle of article 175 of the EC Treaty in a strict way, one should tax goods with an inelastic demand anyway, even if there are no alternatives available to consumers. In my view, such strict interpretation of the polluter pays principle can only be justified if the revenues of the tax are used to stimulate the development of alternative goods. The revenues can also be used to repair damage done to the environment if one can assess what damage is actually done to the environment by the use of that specific good, which will in most cases be impossible. Using the revenues of the tax to reach completely different policy goals, for instance reduction of unemployment, will not, in the case of inelastic goods, make a difference to the environment and should therefore not be done.

If on the other hand, the demand for a specific product is elastic, imposing an environmental tax on that product or service will have an important effect on demand. The tax will lead to a price increase and as a result of the well-known law

26 So A. Ogus, 'Nudging and Rectifying: the use of fiscal instruments for regulatory purposes', *Legal Studies* , vol. 19, 1999, p. 245-266.

of demand, demand will reduce as a result of this price increase. Depending upon the price elasticity of demand and the amount of the tax, theoretically the demand for that particular product or service could even be reduced as low as zero. At the same time it becomes clear that such a product or service for which the demand is inelastic will not be very suited for a charge which primarily has a budgetary character. Indeed, if the effect of the increased price (as a result of the tax) will be that demand decreases (and may even decrease as low as zero), tax revenues will also reduce. Hence, products or services for which there is an elastic demand will primarily be suited for the regulatory charge. If at the policy level one wishes to reduce the demand for an environmentally damaging product or service, the tax on such a price-elastic product or service will most likely lead to the desired result (assuming of course that the policymaker possesses adequate information to be able to set the tax rate accurately).

After this introduction, reminding us of the policy goal of the Pigouvian taxes and the difference between regulatory and budgetary charges, let us now address the proposed European energy tax and kerosene tax on commercial aviation and first examine how, given the differences just discussed, they could be qualified.

4. Commission Proposals for Environmental Taxation

4.1. The European Energy Tax

Taxes on energy are based on three pillars: excise duties, VAT and specific levies.[27] Currently, a harmonized Community framework exists for excise duties on mineral oils[28] and for value-added tax. There is, however, still no Community wide framework for specific levies on energy products.

In 1991, the Green Parties in the European Parliament proposed the imposition of a European energy tax on fossil energy sources, in order to promote the use of sustainable energy sources. The global environmental conference in Rio de Janeiro in 1992 stressed the importance of economic instruments to protect the environment. Principle 16 of the Rio Declaration on Environment and Development states as follows:

> 'National authorities should endeavour to promote the internalisation of environmental costs and the use of economic instruments, taking into account the approach that the polluter should, in principle, bear the cost of pollution, with due regard to the public interest and without distorting international trade and investment'.

27 COM(2001) 264 final.

28 The minimum rates for excise duties have not been increased since 1992. Many Member States have increased their excise duties significantly, and these rates may differ between Member States. To avoid distortions and to promote the functioning of the internal market, it would be necessary to increase the minimum excise duties based on the European directive.

The same year, the European Commission issued a proposal for a Council Directive restructuring the Community framework for the taxation of energy products.[29] The goal of this proposal was to harmonize the taxation of energy products in the Member States in order to introduce the polluter-pays principle and to stimulate the internal market. According to the proposal, on the one hand, mineral oils, natural gas, coal and electricity would be taxed and on the other hand taxes on labour would be decreased. This European environmental tax had to be levied by the Member States. Because of the strong opposition of some Member States, the proposal was not adopted.

The Commission's intention to use fiscal instruments to promote environmentally friendly behaviour was stressed in the Community's Fifth Environmental Action Programme:[30]

> 'In order to get the prices right and to create market based instruments for environmentally friendly economic behaviour, the use of economic and fiscal instruments will have to constitute an increasingly important part of the overall approach. The fundamental aim of these instruments will be to internalise all external environmental costs incurred during the whole life-cycle of products'.

In 1995, the Commission issued a new proposal.[31] According to this proposal Member States were not obliged to impose an energy tax on energy products. However, if they decided to impose an energy tax, they would have to follow the amended proposal. Despite the optional nature of this proposal, it was, just like the 1992 proposal, rejected by some of the Member States.

In a final attempt to constitute a harmonized energy tax in the EC Member States, the Commission issued a third proposal in 1997.[32] One of the reasons the first proposal was criticized by some of the Member States, was that a tax on energy constituted a completely new tax, which in their view was inadmissible. A difference between this proposal and the two earlier proposals is that this proposal creates an integrated system of taxing energy products. The intention of the Commission is to integrate excise duties on mineral oils and taxes on energy. The Commission's last proposal creates a very flexible regime of taxing energy products. For instance, Member States have the possibility to (totally or partially) exempt energy products from renewable sources. This provision is in my opinion essential, since it increases the difference in price between energy products from renewable sources and energy products from non-renewable sources. At this moment, the environmentally friendly alternatives of renewable sources are still much more expensive to produce than energy products from fossil resources.

29 COM(92) 226 final, *OJ* 1992 C 196.

30 Resolution 93/C 138/01, *OJ* 1993 C 138.

31 COM(95) 172 final, not published; D. Raponi, 'CO2/Energy Tax Proposal', *EC Tax Review*, 1995-3, p. 161-162.

32 COM(97) 30 final, *OJ* 1997 C 139; D. Raponi, 'Common System for the taxation of energy products', *EC Tax Review*, 1997-2, p. 121-123.

According to article 15[33] of the proposal Member States *may* refund (totally or partially) the amount of energy tax on energy costs paid by a firm that exceeds 10% of the production costs. If the energy costs exceed 20% of the total production costs, however, the Member States *must* refund the total amount of energy tax on energy costs that exceed 10% of the production costs.

This system is obviously at odds with the polluter-pays principle, mentioned in article 175 of the Treaty and can also be criticized from the perspective of an optimal internalization of the externality: the larger the energy use, the lower the tax. The reason for this rather strange system is that the Commission is afraid of endangering the competitive position of European companies in the international market.[34] Moreover, this energy policy, taxing merely the small consumers and exempting the large energy consumers is probably difficult to explain to the small energy consumer, who has been encouraged for many years to use energy saving electrical devices in order to achieve a reduction of only a few kWh on his personal energy consumption.[35] From an environmental point of view, it would certainly be much better not to make this exemption. First of all, in an effective environmental taxation system there are (tax-exempt) environmentally friendly alternatives available for the polluting energy sources. If compensatory measures for some sectors are nevertheless necessary, it would be better to create for example a compensation system in the sphere of direct taxation (for example, one can think of accelerated depreciation).

33 Article 15 states as follows:
1. Member States may refund all or part of the amount of tax paid in relation to investment expenditure incurred by a firm in improving the efficient use of energy up to a limit of 50% of eligible expenditure incurred.
2. Member States may refund some or all of the amount of tax paid by a firm on any part of its non-transport-related energy costs which exceeds 10% of its total production costs. However, when the part of non-transport-related energy costs of a firm exceeds 20% of its total production costs, Member States shall reimburse the whole of the tax paid by the firm on the part of its non-transport-related energy costs which exceeds 10% of its total production costs. The net amount of tax paid by a firm following the refunds provided for in the two preceding subparagraphs shall not be less than 1% of the value of its sales.
3. Member States may also refund to the producer some or all of the amount of tax paid by the consumer on electricity and heat generated during its production in the case of electricity produced from products specified in Article 14 paragraphs 1 (b), (c) and (d).

34 *Parliamentary Works*, TK 1994-1995, 24250, nr. 3, 8-9.

35 Recently the Dutch Secretary of State for financial affairs announced in the newspaper *Trouw* of 29 December 2000 that he would be willing to introduce an energy tax for larger consumers as well. The pressure to introduce such a tax also resulted from the discussions concerning the climate change conference. One will remember that the sixth conference of the parties concerning the framework convention on climate change was held in The Hague (the Netherlands) in the autumn of 2000. The Secretary of State announced that in order to outweigh the introduction of this energy tax one could consider lowering corporate taxes. But this point of view obviously led to critical questions of members of parliament (notably by Klein Molenkamp) to the ministers of the environment and of economic affairs.

4.2. Taxation of Aircraft Fuel

Most EU Member States do not have an ecotax on aircraft fuel or on tickets.[36] Nevertheless, air-travel causes many external costs to society that are not internalized.

Taxation of aircraft fuel is governed by Directive 92/81/EEC on the harmonization of the structures of excise duties on mineral oils.[37] and by the Chicago Convention of 1944 as well as a large number of bilateral Air Service Agreements.

Article 8, para.1, b of the Directive provides a compulsory exemption for commercial aviation kerosene.[38] This exemption is in line with the Chicago Convention of 1944 (fuel on board an aircraft) and the Air Service Agreements between individual states (fuel loaded on to an aircraft); usually, all commercial aviation fuel is exempt from any fuel tax. However, article 8, para. 7 of the Directive on excise duties on mineral oils requires the Council to reconsider this exemption on the basis of a report from the Commission. In 1996, the report from the Commission was published.[39] The Commission concluded that the European Community should levy excise duties on aviation fuel as soon as the international situation would allow the levying of a tax on all air carriers, including carriers from non-member states. This idea is reflected in the proposal for an energy tax.

Article 13, para. 1 (c) of the proposal for a Directive restructuring the Community framework for the taxation of energy products states that aircraft fuel for the purpose of air navigation other than private pleasure-flying is exempt from taxation, for as long as aircraft fuel is obliged to be exempted under international obligations. Article 13, para. 2 however allows Member States to limit the scope of this exemption to international and intra-Community air transport. A Member State is, in other words, allowed to tax aircraft fuel used for domestic flights. Quite important is the fact that article 13, para. 2 of the proposal gives Member States the possibility to waive the exemption for aircraft fuel for non-private use if the Member State has entered into a bilateral agreement with another Member State.[40]

In March 2000, the Commission published a new report on the taxation of aircraft fuel, which confirmed the 1996 conclusions.[41]

36 Only Sweden used to have a tax on domestic air transport until 1997.

37 Council Directive 92/81/EEC, OJ L 316, 31.10.1992. See on this directive: A.J. Easson, *Taxation in the European Community*, London, The Athlone Press, 1993, p. 143-166.

38 According to the Court of Justice, the Swedish tax on domestic flights was incompatible with this provision (C-346/97, ECR 1999, I-3419, *Braathens Sverige AB v Riksskatteverket*).

39 COM(96) 549 final.

40 In that case these Member States may apply a level of taxation below the minimum level set out in the Directive.

41 COM(2000) 110 final.

5. Ecological Effectiveness of the Proposed Taxation of Energy Products and Taxation of Aircraft Fuel

5.1. Regulatory or Budgetary?

The Commission clearly has not opted for a pure Pigouvian system of environmental taxation. This can be understood from a practical perspective. Above I already indicated that the Pigouvian taxes only provide a fool-proof solution to internalize the externalities caused by environmental pollution if strong assumptions are met. The effectiveness of Pigouvian taxes depend indeed upon the heavy assumption that the tax authorities have the necessary information to set the tax rate adequately. However, although environmental taxes will therefore almost never be used as the sole instrument of environmental policy, many legal systems, such as the EU legal system use taxes as one of the environmental policy instruments.

One would therefore expect that if taxes are used to control the behaviour of potential polluters, then the obvious alternative of the regulatory charge (which comes close to the Pigouvian environmental tax) would be chosen. When one considers the proposal, one cannot assess with certainty if Member States should impose a regulatory or budgetary charge. However, article 2, para 2 of the proposal states as follows: 'When implementing this Directive, Member States shall endeavour to avoid any increase in their overall tax burden. In order to attain this objective Member States shall endeavour, in particular, *to reduce at the same time statutory charges on labour.*' If the Commission intends to reduce charges on labour permanently by imposing a tax on energy products, the only way to realize this would be by imposing a budgetary charge (or a double dividend charge with a preference for the budgetary effect).

Moreover, the Commission refers in the preamble of the proposal for an energy tax to the White Paper on growth, competitiveness and employment.[42] In this White Paper, the Commission proposes to reduce statutory charges on labour. In chapter 9.4 (Possible compensatory measures) the proposed CO2/energy tax is specifically mentioned as compensatory measure for a reduction of charges on labour. This strengthens the impression that the main aim of the energy tax is to raise money and that the environment comes in second place at best.[43]

As far as the taxation of aircraft fuel is concerned, one can observe something similar. In the Commission's report on taxation of aircraft fuel, the Commission notes that

> 'the significant revenues accruing from such a measure would allow Member States to reduce other taxes and charges, notably those on labour as recommended in Article 1 of the Commission Proposal for the taxation of energy products'.[44]

42 White Paper on growth, competitiveness, and employment: The challenges and ways forward into the 21st century, COM(93) 700 final.

43 See K. Deketelaere, *supra* note 13, p. 365.

44 COM(2000) 110 final, p. 5.

If the Commission intends to reduce charges on labour permanently by imposing a tax on aircraft fuel, the only way to realize this would be by imposing a budgetary charge. In that sense one could argue that the proposed European environmental taxes are in fact no different from traditional taxes such as income tax, corporate tax or value added tax. In fact, only the object differs.

5.2. *Examining Price Elasticity and Presence of Alternatives*

This is important as an introduction to a test of the effectiveness of the proposed European environmental taxes. It shows that this effectiveness can only be assessed if one gets some idea of the elasticity of the demand for the products or services on which these taxes apply. However, examining the price elasticity of the demand for specific products or services is a highly complicated matter. Moreover, usually the demand for most products or services will be neither totally elastic nor totally inelastic. It is in most cases likely that this elasticity takes a middle position. One can illustrate this with a couple of points indicating the issues that have to be taken into account when the price elasticity of the demand for specific products or services is assessed.

One has to stress, for example, that the price elasticity will depend upon the availability of suitable alternatives for the product or service on which the tax applies. As an alternative I consider, for the purpose of this analysis, another product or service which would be available in the market with identical or almost identical properties as the product or service to which the tax applies. If an alternative of that kind is available the consumer will react to a price increase (as a result of the environmental tax) by substituting the damaging product or service (on which the tax applies) by another (more environmentally friendly) product or service. One can take the example of energy taxes. If an energy tax were only to apply to electricity resulting from power stations based on coal, then the demand for this type of electricity will reduce when an alternative is available to which the tax does not apply, such as electricity produced by windmills.[45] In the particular example the product in both cases (electricity) is identical; only the way in which the product is made differs.

As for the kerosene tax on commercial aviation, the presence of alternatives is less obvious. As far as domestic flights and other short distances are concerned, the availability of alternatives is in most cases no problem; someone travelling from Amsterdam to Maastricht could easily travel by train or car instead of travelling by aeroplane. Things become less obvious when one wants to travel from, for example, Amsterdam to Sydney. Can a journey of say, 2 weeks by boat be considered an alternative for a 20 hour flight by aeroplane? In fact, the most likely 'alternative' will be not to make the journey at all. It is, therefore, questionable if one should tax long-

45 Obviously we assume here that the price of energy produced from coal + the environmental tax is still higher than the energy produced as a result of windmills. To make this example realistic (given the current price of energy produced by windmills) the environmental tax in the example should be set adequately high.

distance flights (unless one interprets the polluter-pays principle in a strict way). One the other hand, an aircraft fuel tax might be a good instrument to reduce the number of domestic and other short distance flights.

6. Concluding Remarks

The European Union has not yet been able to create a solid environmental taxation system. A major obstacle in passing the proposal for a European energy tax is the requirement of a unanimous Council decision on the subject. Unanimity has never been achieved on the matter. This problem could, most likely, be solved if the closer co-operation procedure were to be used in the field of environmental taxation. In that case, a group of Member States could constitute an 'Ecotax-Schengen' of Member States using the same harmonized system of environmental taxation.

However, using the closer co-operation procedure would only be the first step in the direction of an effective European system of environmental taxation. If one examines the Commission's proposals for an energy tax and an aircraft fuel tax, one notices that these taxes have primarily a budgetary character, meaning that achieving an as high as possible tax revenue is the primary goal. Ecological effects are only a secondary goal. If the Commission really wants to create environmental taxes that do regulate the use of energy and aircraft fuel, the aim should be to create taxes aimed at the reduction of the use of energy or aircraft fuel.

Furthermore, the presence of alternatives is important. If one wants to create an effective environmental tax, an alternative for the product must be available. If an alternative is available, it is likely that consumers will use the 'good' alternative instead of the 'bad', polluting product that is taxed. As far as the energy tax is concerned, in many cases alternatives are available. One can think of environmentally friendly produced electricity as an alternative for electricity produced by coal operated power stations.[46] For the aircraft fuel tax, things are less obvious: for long distance flights, there will, in most cases be no reasonable alternatives. It is, therefore, questionable if one should tax those flights. On the other hand, an aircraft fuel tax might be a good instrument to reduce the number of domestic and other short distance flights.

46 Environmentally produced electricity should in that case of course be exempted from tax.

Michael Rodi

ENVIRONMENTAL TAXES

The idea of ecological taxation has been fascinating economic theorists and some politicians for quite a while. Comprehensive ecotax systems have been designed.[1] Today a growing number of different environmental taxes have been implemented, especially among OECD countries.[2] Even though reality is not always in line with pretentious goals indicated by titles such as 'Ecological Tax Reform'[3] this development requires further studies to focus on two problems: the need for harmonization on the European level and specific ideas on the design of ecotaxes and their adequate place in the concert of environmental policy instruments.

1. Why should the European Union engage in Environmental Taxation?

Only some minor aspects of environmental taxation have been harmonized on a European level so far; thus the question on whether the European Union should take further measures in this respect is still debated.

1.1. European Tradition of Indirect Environmental Policy Instruments

The Commission of the European Union has been convinced for quite a while now that environmental taxes should be introduced or harmonized on a European level.[4]

1 See e.g. D. Gee, 'Economic Tax Reform in Europe', in T. O'Riordan (ed.), *Ecotaxation*, London, Earthscan Publishing, 1997, p. 81 *et seq.*

2 See for a survey OECD, *Environmental Taxes in OECD Countries*, Paris, OECD, 1995, p. 13 *et seq.* and OECD, *Economic Instruments for Pollution Control and Natural Resources Management in OECD Countries: A Survey*, Paris, OECD, 1999, p. 56 *et seq.*

3 See in general M. Kohlhaas, 'Green Budget Reform', in K. Schlegelmilch (ed.), *Green Budget Reform in Europe*, Berlin, Springer Verlag 1999, p. 23 *et seq.* and M. Rodi, 'Ecological Tax Reform in Germany', *Bulletin for International Fiscal Documentation*, 54, 2000, p. 486 *et seq.*

4 See Commission Proposal for a Council Directive introducing a Tax on Carbon Dioxide Emissions and Energy, COM(92) 226 as amended by COM(95) 172, not published, and a revised proposal, COM(97) 30.

As these efforts, being opposed by some member states, have not been successful so far it seems appropriate to reconsider the reasons for this engagement.

From the beginning European Environmental Policies were strongly based on flexible, indirect and especially economic instruments. Thus it was easy to implement new and increasingly more popular mechanisms like the environmental impact assessment, the environmental information claim or the eco-audit-system. Modern environmental policy has to consider a broad range of instruments, including policy fields, which traditionally follow their own logic – like agriculture, traffic and transport. This demand, which is legally reinforced by Article 6 of the EC Treaty, does not only apply to finance mechanisms like ecological subsidies[5] or environmental liability[6], but also to taxation as an old and indispensable part of state activities.

1.2. Constitutional or Domestic Policy Function

As for the states it is not a question, whether to have or not to have taxes, their interest should be to modernize their tax system, reducing taxes with undesired impacts and furthering taxes with desired impacts or side effects.[7] But it is well known that there is nothing more traditional and rigid in the legal system of states than taxes. Every change is heavily opposed by certain pressure groups or parts of the public.[8] In this situation it might be interesting to delegate the competence to a higher level of decision making in order to surpass resistance. This phenomenon, described by *Petersmann* as the 'constitutional or domestic policy function' of international legal systems[9] can be illustrated with the EC law on state aid. It has generally been agreed for a long time that states offer too high amounts of financial aid disturbing internal and external competition while binding important parts of the budget. Under these circumstances it was a good idea to transfer the task of

5 See for that A. Gilpin, *Environmental Economics. A Critical Review*, Chicester. Wiley, 2001, p. 150 *et seq.*; OECD, *Subsidies and the Environment. Exploring the Linkages*, Paris, OECD, 1996; OECD, *Improving the Environment through Reducing Subsidies*, Paris, OECD, 1998.

6 See for that B. Bartsch, *Liability for Environmental Damages: Incentives for Precaution and Risc Allocation*, Tübingen, Mohr Siebeck, 1998 and the Commission´s White Paper on Environmental Liability, COM(2000) 66.

7 This can be reinforced by achieving further goals like reduction of unemployment in line with the 'double dividend' idea, see for that European Environmental Agency, *Environmental taxes: recent developments in tools for integration*, Environmental issues series No. 18, November 2000, p. 16 *et seq.*; OECD, *Greening Tax Mixes in OECD Countries: A Preliminary Assessment*, Paris, OECD, 2000, and the contributions of D. Gee, P. Bohm, P. Ekins, T. Barker and D. McCoy, in T. O´Riordan (ed.), *Ecotaxation*, London, Earthscan Publishing, 1997, p. 77 *et seq.*; critical of that the recent empirical study of Ch.M. Scholz, *Environmental Tax Reforms and the Double Dividend. A Theoretical and Empirical Analysis for Germany*, Tübingen, Mohr Siebeck, 2000, p. 49 *et seq.*

8 For the reasons see M.S. Andersen, 'Designing and Introducing Green Taxes: Institutional Dimensions', in M.S. Andersen and R.-U. Sprenger (eds.), *Market-Based Instruments for Environmental Management*, Cheltenham, Elgar, 2000, p. 31 *et seq.*

9 E.-U. Petersmann, *Constitutional Functions and Constitutional Problems of International Economic Law*, Fribourg, University Press Fribourg Switzerland, 1991, p. 210 *et seq.*

state aid control to the Commission, which developed an increasingly strict regime not basically debated by the recipients of the aid.[10]

Similarly it was clear from the beginning that taxes and especially indirect taxes posed severe problems to the functioning of the common market. For this reason Article 90 et seq. ECT were installed. The conflict between the market freedoms and regulatory taxes is even more apparent, so from there another argument for the harmonization of environmental taxes can be derived.

1.3. The Perspective of own resources

De lege ferenda it could be argued that environmental taxes might be a suitable instrument to reinforce the European Union's own resources. This idea has been advocated by the Commission for nearly 20 years now with regard to an energy tax[11] and later the CO2/energy tax.[12] Thus, by achieving a sort of 'double dividend', market and competition distortions could be overcome, while this instrument would perfectly fit into the system of European environmental policy instruments.

Still it shall be noted here that many questions regarding legal feasibility and practical advantages have still to be discussed in detail. The inclusion of an ecotax into the system of own resources according to Art. 269 ECT would reduce political flexibility as an environmental policy instrument. The Commission itself has pointed out uncertainties regarding predictability and stability of the revenue and possible different burdens for the member states.[13] For these reasons according to Art. 9 of the proposal for a Council Decision on own resources 2002[14] the possibility of new autonomous own resources has to be examined further.

2. Which Taxes should be harmonized?

2.1. Tax Object and Tax Base

The notion of ecotaxes should be understood in a broad sense as tax schemes that have an environmentally relevant impact and thus can be used as environmental policy instruments.[15] Then of course, quite a lot of different, more or less important, ecotaxes can be identified in the member states, ranging from levies on plastic bags or disposable cameras to excise taxes on fertilisers.

10 See for that M. Rodi, *Die Subventionsrechtsordnung*, Tübingen,Mohr Siebeck, 2000, p. 98 *et seq.* and p. 141 *et seq.*

11 COM(83) 270, p. 6; COM(83) 315, p. 18.

12 Commission Report, *Financing the European Union*, Luxemburg, Office for Official Publications of the European Community, 1997, p. 47; Annex 2 of the Commission report on the operating of the own resources system *Financing the European Union*, October 1998, with relation to the proposed CO_2/energy tax.

13 Commission Report, *Financing the European Union*, Luxemburg, Office for Official Publications of the European Community 1998, Annex 2, p. 4 *et seq.*

14 COM(99) 333.

15 M. Rodi, *Umweltsteuern. Das Steuerrecht als Instrument der Umweltpolitik*, Baden-Baden, Nomos, 1993, p. 33 et seq.

As the tax system should be easy to assess and understand, the practice of ecotaxes should concentrate on taxes that are ecologically relevant. Moreover, European harmonization should focus on taxes that have special relevance to the common market. For these reasons there are two policy fields that qualify for ecological taxation in general and ecotax harmonization in detail: energy (production and consumption) on the one side and traffic and transport on the other side.[16] Regarding the liberalized energy and transport law there is a special need to implement ecological concerns. Ecotaxes are an appropriate way to achieve this as these policy fields are characterized by multiple emission sources that are difficult to deal with by command and control instruments. To a certain degree this is also true for new ecologically oriented policies in the field of agriculture.[17]

2.2. Tax Systems and Tax Techniques

2.2.1. Regulatory versus Budgetary Taxes

A central differentiation is often made between regulatory taxes, which have a specific environmental target as main goal, and those taxes, which are primarily budgetary in nature.[18] From there it is argued that only regulatory taxes are suitable instruments of environmental policies and environmental taxes stricto sensu.

This argument is somewhat misleading. On the one hand it is difficult to decide, whether regulatory or budgetary goals are predominant. On the other hand it is a central task of modern environmental policies to implement ecological objectives into all relevant policy areas. In line with that the 'greening' of the whole tax system is a challenge.[19] Given the fact that modern states have to be financed mainly by taxes it is evident that taxes with positive (side) effects should at least partly substitute neutral ones or those with undesired impacts. Thus a 'double dividend' can already be earned at the revenue rising side of taxes. Above all tax burdens have to be moved from labour to e.g. energy.

16 As much as 95% of environmental tax revenue in Europe comes from the energy and transport sector, see European Environmental Agency, *Environmental taxes: recent developments in tools for integration*, Environmental Issues Series, No. 18, November 2000, p. 8; for the effectiveness of taxes in these sectors see OECD, *Behavioral Responses to Environmentally-Related Taxes*, Paris, OECD, 2000.

17 European Environmental Agency, *supra* note 7, p. 10 argues that efficient prices are needed in the field of energy, transport and agriculture because of high externalities.

18 See K. Määttä, *Environmental Taxes. From an Economic Idea to a Legal Institution*, Helsinki, Kauppakaari Oy, 1997, p. 210 *et seq.*; K. Määttä, 'Regulatory Taxes: Theoretical Considerations' (in this volume); S. Ubachs, 'Towards an Ecotax-Schengen?' (in this volume).

19 P.M. Herrera Molina, *Derecho Tributario Ambiental. La introducción del interés ambiental en el ordenamieto tributario*, Madrid, 2000, p. 46 *et seq.*; OECD, *Environmental Taxes and Green Tax Reform*, Paris, OECD, 1997, p. 17 *et seq.*

2.2.2. Direct Taxes and Tax Subsidies

Direct taxes are fiscal taxes as a rule, aiming at raising revenue while taking into account the different individual ability to pay. Still environmental tax schemes can be implemented there, e.g. by denying tax deductions for individual traffic to work, special depreciation rules for environmentally relevant investment or special tax treatment of reserves for possible future environmental damages.[20] But there are two main reasons against 'greening' direct taxes: on the one side direct taxes should be as clear and easy to understand as possible – thus regulatory elements should be avoided altogether. On the other side environmental elements in the field of direct taxes are, as a rule, tax subsidies; and as direct taxes are characterized by progressive tax rates normally, nobody can convincingly explain, why rich people need or deserve higher incentives to act in line with general goals of environmental policies (regressive effect of direct tax subsidies).

In general tax subsidies should be used only in exceptional cases. It is contrary to the polluter-pays principle to give preferential treatment to those who agree to pollute less, e.g. by reducing emissions. From an economic point of view tax subsidies are only acceptable if the behaviour leads to positive externalities. For example this may be the case when farmers contribute to a rich and beautiful landscape.

2.2.3. Tax Differentiations

Tax differentiations are a success story. Minor differentiations of the mineral oil tax between leaded and unleaded fuel were sufficient to sweep leaded fuel from the markets. Consequently, many countries apply this method not only to the amount of sulphur content of mineral oil, but also to other tax schemes: vehicle taxes or waste charges and taxes are prominent examples. Tax neutrality can be achieved within one financial instrument.

2.2.4. Indirect Taxes

Finally the advantages of indirect taxes (like e.g. electricity tax or other consumption taxes) should be stressed. They are not only easy to administer, but are also able to ensure that the tax burden will be allocated to the person whose behaviour is responsible for the externalities. From a fiscal point of view it is evident that indirect taxes play an important and still growing role in state finances. So why not combine fiscal necessities with ecological advantages?

20 See e.g. P.M. Herrera Molina, *supra* note 19, p. 301 *et seq.*

3. The Tax Dilemma and Ways out

3.1. EU Competencies in the Field of Environmental Taxation

For about 10 years now the Commission has been trying to introduce a harmonized CO2/energy tax - without success.[21] It is caught in the unanimity trap: Because environmental tax legislation on a European level touches the fiscal sovereignty of the member states unanimity is required regardless of whether this is based on the harmonization competency (Article 93, 94, 95 II ECT) or on environmental policy competencies (Art. 175 II ECT).

But there are quite relevant ways to escape the unanimity trap: on the one side the idea of an 'ecotax Schengen' gets more and more popular.[22] On the other side there are important exceptions from the unanimity requirement: ecotaxes and -charges in the field of traffic and transport can be based on Article 71 I lit. d ECT (e.g. road pricing systems)[23] and in the field of agriculture on Article 34 II 1, 37 ECT (e.g. taxes to reduce the use of environmentally harmful chemicals). Certainly, the revenue of those sectoral ecotaxes cannot be part of the general budget, but has to be spent on projects within the same policy area.

3.2. Ecotaxes as Part of a Modern Environmental Instrument Mix

Modern environmental policies are no longer based on single instruments. The idea of an environmental policy mix is part of the Commission's position.[24] Thus the question is no longer, whether ecotaxes should be introduced (they do exist anyway), but rather how to combine them with regulatory law, consensual and economic instruments (like subsidies or emission trading).

3.2.1. Regulatory law

For constitutional reasons the legislator has to provide minimum standards of environmental quality. From their certain strict requirements regarding individual behaviour can be derived. Regulatory law cannot be replaced in this field. For example, a chemical substance should be forbidden if it is proven that it damages health. Taxation is not sufficient in this case.

On the other hand regulatory law should be rather flexible beyond this borderline and allow room for individual decision-making. Here, economic instruments of environmental policies can promote internalization of external effects and thus lead to a more effective allocation of economic resources.[25] It has to be stressed in this

21 See for the development European Environmental Agency, *supra* note 7, p. 28 *et seq.*

22 See European Environmental Agency, *supra* note 7, p. 8; S. Ubachs, *supra* note 18.

23 See the Commission's *White Paper on Common Transport Policy*, COM(2001) 370 and directive 62/1999/EC ('Eurovignette II').

24 See e.g. COM(2000) 576.

25 See for the advantages of market based instruments versus regulation: OECD, *Taxation and the Environment. Complementary Policies*, Paris, OECD, 1993, p. 18 *et seq.*

respect that these requirements can also be achieved within the framework of the so-called command-and-control-law, e.g. by applying compensation rules: exemptions from strict emission standards are granted, if the operator of a plant provides for further reduction at other sites.

In relation to regulatory law there are specific advantages of ecotaxes, when individual behaviour is not covered by permit-procedures or in cases of manifold small emission sources. Again, this provides an argument for ecotaxes in the field of energy consumption and traffic and transport.

In most circumstances regulatory environmental law and ecotaxes are not mutually exclusive. Environmental taxes may prepare or reinforce regulation.[26] This idea has already been introduced with the German water effluent charge (*Abwasserabgabe*) in the 70s.[27]

3.2.2. Subsidies (Structural Funds)[28]

As a well-established policy in the framework of GATT/WTO and the European Union, state aid should be restricted as it burdens the budget and is contrary to the polluter-pays principle, as indicated above. This is true for direct subsidies as well as for tax exemptions. In this light, state aid is indicated e.g. if individual behaviour has positive external effects as this is the case when farmers contribute in a special way to the environment.[29] Moreover, subsidies could be used as a (temporal) incentive to observe stricter emission standards that are not yet prescribed by regulatory law.[30]

Thus subsidies and taxes could even be combined in one legal concept, as was the case with the Swedish NOx-tax.[31] The revenue of taxes on behaviour exceeding a certain standard could be used for financing subsidies for those who remain under this standard. The advantage of such a tax scheme is that revenue neutrality is achieved by definition.

It should be mentioned that the reasoning for a restricted use of subsidies not only refers to national measures. Thus the Commission should apply its standards for state aid control to its own environmental subsidies, e.g. in the framework of structural funds.

26 K. Määttä, *supra* note 18, p. 70 *et seq.* distinguishes 'independent and complementary environmental taxes'.

27 See M. Rodi, 'Country Survey Germany', in *Environmental Taxes and Charges*, Proceedings of a Seminar held in Florence, Italy, in 1993 during the 47th Congress of the International Fiscal Association, 1995, p. 79 *et seq.* and p. 160 *et seq.*

28 For a survey on subsidies for environmental protection in OECD countries see OECD, *supra* note 2, p. 49 *et seq.*

29 European Environmental Agency, *supra* note 7, p. 10.

30 This is also the underlying rationale of the Commission's guideline on State aid for environmental protection.

31 See K. Määttä, *supra* note 18, p. 112 ('performance-based refund system').

3.2.3. Emissions Trading

As a consequence of the problems of introducing a harmonized energy tax the Commission is trying to promote an emissions trading system at the European level.[32] For that reasons it is important to know how this could be combined with ecotaxes.

For several reasons emissions trading systems can only function efficiently in combination with permit procedures and in relation to relatively few sources and emissions. Thus big power plants are perfect candidates for an emissions trading system regarding e.g. CO2-emissions. On the other hand this again leads to the conclusion that ecotaxes should be applied to manifold emission sources (in addition). There is clear evidence that emissions trading systems and ecotax schemes are not alternatives, but have to be combined according to their specific advantages.

3.3. Ecotaxes need Thorough Planning and Sophisticated Design

The idea of environmental taxation has become both practical and disenchanted at the same time during the last 20 years. Idealistic supporters of purely Pigouvian ideas are in a minority position among lawyers and even economists today. But the practical and scientific challenges are no less sophisticated in times of environmental tax reforms. These have to be well planned and designed. As part of the general tax system they should rather contribute to the effort of making it more rational, transparent and easy to understand instead of further complicating it. As part of the environmental policy tool box they should be carefully designed and enforced according to their specific advantages. Ecotaxes will not solve the environmental problems, but these won't be solved without an environmental policy instrument mix including tax schemes.

32 See the Commission's *Green Paper on Greenhouse Gas Emissions Trading within European Union*, COM(2000) 87; Commission Proposal for a Directive Establishing a Scheme for Greenhouse Gas Emission Allowance Trading within the Community, COM(2001) 581 of 23.10.2001.

Kalle Määttä

REGULATORY TAXES: THEORETICAL CONSIDERATIONS

1. Preliminary Considerations

The discussion concerning, for instance, direct and indirect taxes or personal and *in rem* taxes is familiar to researchers of taxation. On the other hand, scant attention has been paid to the distinction between fiscal and regulatory taxes, even though it can be claimed that this distinction is especially worth studying today.

The purpose of this paper is to create a conceptual framework for the discussion concerning regulatory taxes. At the same time, the aim is to analyse the usefulness of the concept 'regulatory tax' both *a fortiori* when regulatory tax laws are designed and implemented, and *a posteriori* when these laws are interpreted. In other words, this brief study serves both the issues related to the legal policy-making as well as legal dogmatics. Geographically, the attention is focused on the Scandinavian legal environment, but many generalizations made in this paper could be applied with respect to other countries, too.

The central question running through all these issues is whether to apply the *continuity principle*, i.e. the same 'rules of the game' for regulatory taxes as are applied with respect to (conventional) fiscal taxes, or whether to give special weight to the regulatory character of the taxes concerned. According to the continuity principle, a new legal institution can be integrated into the legal system without preserving its special character and, thus, this new legal institution is actually treated in terms of the old ones. For regulatory taxes, the continuity principle would mean that they would be treated in exactly the same way as corresponding taxes such as fiscal duties are treated, when for instance the application of the legality principle (under constitutional law) or the prohibition of discriminatory taxation is at issue. In other words, it is the legal form of the institution that would be crucial to any examination of its legal consequences.[1]

Another option is that a new legal institution maintains its special character – at least to some extent – when it is integrated into an existing legal system. With

1 K. Määttä, *Environmental Taxes. From an Economic Idea to a Legal Institution*, Jyväskylä, Kauppakaari Oy, Finnish Lawyer's Publishing, 1997, p. 4.

respect to regulatory taxes, this would mean that they would not be treated in exactly the same way as corresponding fiscal taxes, e.g. as when the prohibition of retroactive legislation is assessed. The nature of regulatory taxes as a policy instrument would be taken into account and this approach is thus called the *principle of primary objective*. The objectives of the institution, and not only its legal form, would determine the legal consequences of regulatory taxes.[2]

2. The Need for a Concept of 'Regulatory Tax'

The need for the concept of a regulatory tax may be justified on similar grounds to the use of the concept 'tax expenditure'.[3] Regulatory taxes serve - by definition - ends which are similar in nature to those served by regulatory instruments or direct regulation. This means that a given policy regulation can be structured by using either regulatory taxes or direct regulation to meet the chosen target. Consequently, because regulatory taxes are a route for governments to pursue their policy (in different fields), they should be subject to similar evaluation and control mechanisms that are used for policy-making provided by direct regulation or other policy instruments.

It is also appropriate to recall the criticism directed at policy-makers, who failed to recognize that tax expenditures exist and to understand that they were essentially spending programmes;[4] the same threat is present in regulatory tax policy. If regulatory taxes are not evaluated by similar techniques and criteria as other regulatory policy instruments, there remains the risk that these taxes are regarded in the same light as fiscal taxes. In other words, the criteria for evaluating regulatory taxes differ considerably from those for other taxes. For instance, if regulatory taxes are regarded solely as revenue-generating taxes, there is a great danger of reaching the conclusion that these taxes are very costly to administer in relation to their yield and that the tax should be removed in spite of the fact they are primarily regulatory policy instruments. In addition, a review of regulatory policy will be more effective if all the different methods of government intervention are taken into account,[5] and the proper use of a regulatory tax concept may facilitate this task.[6]

For the concept of 'regulatory tax' also advocates the general argument that the taxpayer should, as far as possible, be able not only to see clearly what is to be taxed, but also to understand the purpose which it is intended to serve by choosing

2 See also K. Määttä, *supra* note 1, p. 4.

3 On tax expenditures, see S.S. Surrey, *Pathways to Tax Reform. The Concept of Tax Expenditures*, Cambridge-Massachussets, Harvard University Press, 1973, p. 6 and 28.

4 S.S. Surrey and P. McDaniels, *Tax Expenditures*, Cambridge-Massachussets-London, Harvard University Press,1985, p. 27.

5 See also OECD, *Tax Expenditures. A Review of the Issues and Country Practices*, Report by the Committee on Fiscal Affairs, Paris, OECD, 1984, p. 10.

6 K. Määttä, *supra* note 1, p. 39.

a particular form of tax.[7] In other words, the proper use of the concept of a regulatory tax is compatible with the *transparency principle*.[8] The other side of the coin is, however, that the legislator may take advantage of shifts in attitudes on regulatory issues, and use these shifts as the basis for labelling taxes as regulatory taxes, although they were far from instruments serving similar ends as direct regulation.[9] The explicit and actual goals of legislation deviate from each other in this case. The explicit goals are expressed openly in the preparatory drafts of legislation, but they do not necessarily correspond to the actual goals of legislation.[10] Consequently, the concept of a regulatory tax causes confusion rather than clarifies the purpose of the tax. The use of the concept can be seen as a use of persuasive definitions and, thus, as a basis for fiscal illusion in these circumstances.[11]

There may also be difficulties in implementing the concept of a regulatory tax, i.e. defining the scope of regulatory taxes is inevitably imprecise. For instance, in the preparatory drafting regulating regulatory taxes the goals may remain obscure; certain taxes have originally been introduced for fiscal reasons but regulatory considerations have recently come to be a factor which is taken into account in the structure of the tax in question; in some cases regulatory considerations have been taken into account only by amending part of the tax; et cetera. Whether, however, these difficulties would be so overwhelmingly large that the existence of the whole concept is threatened, is another matter.[12]

3. The Distinguishing Features between Fiscal and Regulatory Taxes

Theoretically, taxes can be divided into fiscal and regulatory taxes.[13] Taxes are traditionally regarded as revenue raising instruments. Their primary purpose is to generate revenue for the public sector. Value-added tax and income tax are examples of these fiscal taxes. However, nowadays more and more taxes are introduced, the primary purpose of which is to reduce conduct which is contrary to a desired policy goal by making this conduct more expensive. These regulatory taxes have also been defined as taxes that are the functional equivalent of direct regulation.[14] For instance, incentive environmental taxes can be classified as regulatory

7 See e.g. J.E. Meade, The Structure and Reform of Direct Taxation. Report of a Committee chaired by Professor J.E. Meade, London, The Institute for Fiscal Studies, 1978, p. 19.

8 K. Määttä, *supra* note 1, p. 39.

9 See also J.M. Buchanan, *Public Finance in Democratic Process. Fiscal Institutions and Individual Choice*, Chapel Hill, North Carolina, The University of North Carolina Press, 1967, p. 134-135.

10 K. Määttä, *supra* note 1, p. 9-10.

11 K. Määttä, *supra* note 1, p. 39.

12 See also K. Määttä, *supra* note 1, p. 39-40.

13 See e.g. S.S. Surrey, *supra* note 3, p. 155; S. Cnossen, *Excise Systems. A Global Study of the Selective Taxation of Goods and Services*, Baltimore-London, The John Hopkins University Press, 1977, p. 9 and 155-156; G. Huppes and R.A. Kagan, 'Market-Oriented Regulation of Environmental Problems in the Netherlands', *Law & Policy*, 1989, p. 215 and IEA, *Taxing energy; why and how*, Paris, OECD, 1993, p. 20. Fiscal taxes are also called revenue-raising taxes and regulatory taxes incentive taxes.

14 See also S.S. Surrey and P. McDaniel, *supra* note 4, p. 29.

taxes: they are created in order to steer the behaviour of polluters, whereas their revenues are of secondary importance, if revenues have any importance at all.

Taking advantage of Terra's (1988) definition concerning indirect taxes, regulatory taxes can also be defined in the following way: even if from an economic point of view a regulatory tax does not steer the conduct of regulatees - contrary to the intentions of the legislator - the legal character of regulatory taxes still requires the possibility of changing their conduct in accordance with the intentions of the legislator. In other words, with respect to the indirect taxes the legislator has to ensure that taxpayers have the possibility to take a tax into account in their pricing decisions, whereas with respect to regulatory taxes the legislator has to ensure that regulatees have the possibility to take a tax into account in their decisions about the measures by which they could change their conduct.

From the above-mentioned point of view, the *predictability* of tax treatment is of great importance in the context of regulatory taxes.[15] Otherwise regulatees do not have any opportunity to change their conduct according to the intentions of the legislator and all of the theoretical virtues of these taxes would be eroded. The requirement of predictability has two dimensions. Firstly, the legislator should take predictability into account and *implementation strategies* are of great importance here. As a general rule, regulatory taxes should not be implemented at very short notice; delays in implementation are needed to give regulatees time to react to take adequate measures.[16] Another point of view is the predictability of the decisions made by courts and other judicial bodies. If the decisions of such tribunals are made in an arbitrary way, this is not compatible with the regulatory nature of taxes concerned. When regulatees are not sure about their tax treatment, regulatory taxes become, in effect, fiscal in nature, because the uncertainty of the tax treatment is unlikely to lead regulatees to do anything to change their conduct. In this sense, *legal certainty* is a necessary, though not sufficient, condition if regulatory taxation is to work in the desired manner.[17] The predictability of regulatory tax treatment can be improved, nevertheless, by efficient *guidance* from authorities, but it has to be added that the guidance has its own drawbacks.

The dividing line between fiscal and regulatory taxes is not clear in all cases. For instance, taxes generally have two main objectives. On the one hand, income tax, which can be classified as a fiscal tax, includes in practice regulatory provisions. On the other hand, regulatory taxes often raise revenue. From this point of view, taxes are not usually purely revenue-raising or purely regulatory taxes.[18] Moreover, the distinction between fiscal and regulatory taxes has become obscured because - in particular - incentive environmental taxes are often introduced within the context

15 See e.g. European Environment Agency, *Environmental Taxes. Implementation and Environmental Effectiveness*, Copenhagen, European Environment Agency, 1996, p. 12.

16 See also D.W. Pearce and R.K. Turner, *Economics of Natural Resources and the Environment*, Baltimore, FT Prentice Hall, 1990, p. 115.

17 On legal certainty at a general level, see e.g. A. Aarnio, *The Rationale as Reasonable*, Dordrecht, Kluwer Academic Publishers, 1986, p. 3-4.

18 See e.g. IEA, *supra* note 13, p. 20. See also S. Cnossen, *supra* note 13, p. 8 according to whom excises are not normally justified for revenue purposes alone but also on other grounds.

of tax reforms. In addition, the fuel and energy taxes represent another problem connected with the distinction between fiscal and regulatory taxes. Fuel taxes are *mixed taxes* incorporating both fiscal and regulatory components. Traditionally, energy products are taxed to raise revenues but more recently regulatory, especially environmentally-related, components have been incorporated into these taxes.[19]

An essential feature distinguishing fiscal taxes from regulatory taxes is their primary goal - to generate funds. From this point of view, some further thoughts can be presented on the distinction. For instance, it is out of the question that a fiscal tax would be a non-revenue generating tax. In contrast, with regard to regulatory taxes it is fully possible that the tax is purely regulating and generates no revenue. Relevant here are - among other things - the redistributive environmental taxes, which only 'recycle' revenues from one polluter to another. In addition, regulatory taxes may be implemented as *prohibitory taxes*, which would be a functional equivalence to direct prohibitions, and which would not generate funds.

Regulatory taxes are fiscally paradoxical in the sense that they are harnessed to encourage *tax minimization*, i.e. to reduce taxable activity.[20] Of course, not all kinds of measures to avoid regulatory taxes are acceptable. Therefore, a distinction has to be made between *appropriate* and *inappropriate measures for tax avoidance* in addition to tax evasion. Appropriate measures for tax avoidance are just those measures which regulatory taxes encourage and which promote the achievement of policy goals. Inappropriate measures for tax avoidance are as such legal measures which reduce the tax burden but which do not promote the achievement of policy goals. These measures can take for instance the form of cross-border shopping of taxable products by consumers. In the case of tax evasion, the minimization of the tax burden takes the form of illegal practices, for instance the smuggling of taxable products for business purposes. It is possible to intervene against these measures by aggravation of penalties or by improving the tax control.

The purpose of fiscal taxes is to sustain the tax base, and therefore it is in the interest of the legislator that taxpayers do not go bankrupt as a result of the taxation. The matter is somewhat different in regulatory taxation. In some cases, the purpose is that the tax base erodes totally, as in the case of a tax on environmentally damaging products, which aims at a total shift to the consumption of benign products. In any case, the primary purpose of regulatory taxes is to achieve the desired policy goals, even if it would result in such things as the shutdown of some older plants. For this reason and because the threat to close down a factory is unthinkable and not credible in direct regulation some researchers have even recommended the adoption of regulatory taxes.[21]

A strong emphasis on the fiscal function (of fiscal taxes) is reflected well in the traditional requirements established for excise duties. The principal requirements of a traditional excise duty have been such features as a low price elasticity of demand

19 See also IEA, *supra* note 13, p. 15.

20 See also A. Paulus, *The Feasibility of Ecological Taxation*, Antwerpen-Apeldoorn, Maklu Uitgevers, 1995, p. 4.

21 See e.g. L.J. White, 'Effluent Charges as a Faster Means of Achieving Pollution Abatement', *Public Policy*, 1976, p. 113.

and the non-availability of untaxed substitutes for the dutiable goods. It has been considered that oil, tobacco and alcoholic drink duties all meet these criteria well.[22] By contrast, in regulatory taxation the criterion of a low price elasticity of demand cannot be imposed. In principle, the price elasticity should have no relevance when possible objects for taxation are being examined. This consideration is, however, of significance in the sense that, to achieve the policy goals, products which have a low elasticity of demand have to be taxed much more heavily than products which have a high elasticity of demand. Nevertheless, actual regulatory tax policy is another matter. Particularly in Belgium, the general philosophy of the Ecotax Law is that products can only be submitted for environmental taxation if alternative, more environmentally-friendly products are available.[23]

On the other hand, selective (excise) taxes have been criticized from a fiscal point of view for not being neutral, i.e. they discriminate among different items of consumption. A broadly based tax is held to be more appropriate for taxing consumption.[24] From a regulatory point of view this drawback of selective taxes turns out to be an advantage. Selective taxes create opportunities to change the conduct of regulatees.

In summation, given that there are different goals for regulatory and fiscal taxes, the weight of their evaluation criteria must clearly be different. As regards fiscal taxes, the *financial efficiency* is a key factor, i.e. the ability to achieve the desired proceeds as efficiently as possible.[25] Instead, the *regulatory effectiveness*, i.e. the capability of the tax to achieve the policy goals established for it as effectively as possible within a desired time schedule, is an essential feature when evaluating regulatory taxes. Related to this, the properties of a *good tax system* deviate, for instance, according to the type of the tax and its goals. In other words, there is no such a thing as a uniform good tax system, but simply many different good tax systems.

4. Regulatory Taxes are Taxes but...

The commonly-held view is that regulatory taxes are indeed, legally speaking, taxes. At a general level, it can be stated that taxes are unrequited payments: 'benefits provided by governments to taxpayers are not normally in proportion to their payment'.[26] For instance, Grabitz and Zacker (1989) have mentioned that taxes

22 See e.g. C.G.M. Sandford and P. Hardwick, *Administrative and Compliance Costs of Taxation*, Fersfield-Perrymead, Fiscal Publications, 1989, p. 155. See also IEA, *supra* note 13, p. 15, which states that governments tax energy to raise revenues largely because energy is convenient to tax, and because demand is relatively inelastic, permitting the raising of revenues without significantly eroding the tax base.

23 M. De Clercq, 'The Implementation of Green Product Taxes. The Belgium Experience', in *Environmental Taxes & Charges. National Experiences & Plans. Papers from the Dublin Workshop*, Luxembourg, Office for Official Publications of the European Communities, 1996, p. 48.

24 J.A. Pechman, *Federal Tax Policy*, New York, The Brooking Institution, 1987, p. 201.

25 See also S. Cnossen, *supra* note 13, p. 3-4.

26 K.C. Messere, *Tax Policy in OECD Countries. Choices and Conflicts*, Amsterdam, IBFD Publications BV, 1993, p. 453, who refers to the interpretation guide to the OECD classification of financial measures.

in the field of environmental protection need no further definition, since their definition in environmental law is no different from the conventional definition in public finance law.[27] This offers a good instance of the continuity principle.

The legal nature of regulatory taxes does not change as a consequence of their regulatory purpose. Examples of this are taxes on tobacco and alcohol, which have traditionally been regarded as taxes, although they are also characterized by a regulatory purpose. Another particular instance here is the protective custom duties where the fiscal function is of secondary importance. Finally, in the Scandinavian countries, the constitutional provisions concerning the legality principle do not require that the primary objective of the tax should be fiscal.

The distinction between penalties and taxes is also important with respect to our topic. As was mentioned above, the primary goal of fiscal taxes is to generate funds, whereas the primary goal of regulatory taxes is to change the conduct of taxpayers. Regulatory taxes are functionally closer to penalties than fiscal taxes. Both regulatory taxes and penalties are *preventive mechanisms,* and both appear to be used to modify social conduct of which the legislator disapproves. By contrast, fiscal taxes are not seen as having a preventive function.[28] For instance, income taxes do not aim to reduce participation in the labour force or to prevent work - although they may do so in practice - and value-added tax is not enacted to reduce the consumption of taxable commodities. The purpose of both of these taxes is rather to create a substantial and stable tax base in order to create funds for the public sector.

The convergence between legal institutions can be examined from the point of view of the distinction between *action* and *constitutive* norms. Action norms state what actions must or must not be undertaken. Constitutive norms, on the other hand, neither forbid, require nor permit certain transactions or activities. For instance, regulatory instruments in environmental policy can be classified as action norms, because there is no other choice left to the polluters than to comply or to face penalties.[29] Traditional fiscal taxes merely attach certain economic consequences to certain transactions and activities and, thus, they can be classified as constitutive norms.[30]

Nevertheless, the rough division of legal norms into action and constitutive norms hides the fact that norms exist which are directed at changing the behaviour of consumers and producers, although they do not directly forbid, require or permit certain actions. Regulatory taxes belong to this kind of norm. Therefore, a distinction can be made between *direct* and *indirect action norms*. Regulatory taxes can be

27 E. Grabitz and C. Zacker, 'Scope for action by the EC member states for the improvement of environmental protection under ECC law: the example of environmental taxes and subsidies', *Common Market Law Review,* 1989, p. 440.

28 See also A. Hultqvist, *Legalitetsprincipen vid inkomstbeskattningen,* Stockholm, Juristförlaget, 1995, p. 73-74.

29 See e.g. J.B. Opschoor and H.B. Vos, *Economic Instruments for Environmental Protection,* Paris, OECD, 1989, p. 12, and P. De Grauwe, *Economic Instruments in EC Environmental Policy,* Centre for European Policy Studies, Working Party Report No. 8, 1993, p. 15.

30 See e.g. A. Hultqvist, *supra* note 28, p. 327 *et seq.* See generally on the classifications of the legal norms A. Peczenik, *Rättsnormer,* Kristianstad, Norstedt, 1987, p. 14 *et seq.*

classified as indirect action norms, not as constitutive norms. For instance, incentive environmental taxes belong to this group of norms because they are a functional equivalent to direct regulation. However, unlike direct regulation, incentive environmental taxes leave polluters free to respond to certain stimuli in a way they themselves consider most beneficial economically.[31] Instead, petrol and motor vehicle taxes, which are primarily intended to raise funds, even though they may also have a beneficial impact on the environment, are constitutive norms.

In brief, legal institutions, which have traditionally been regarded as distinctive from each other, have approached each other in recent years. It can be claimed that the needs for comprehensive policy-making with the most appropriate instruments in each case have created pressures for this kind of development. In some circumstances, these institutions are alternative ways to solve the regulatory problems, in other circumstances, they complement each other.[32] At the same time, new solutions create new problems: in particular, *integration problems* may emerge when the range of instruments increases and, for instance, the risk of over-regulation increases.

5. The Structures of Fiscal and Regulatory Taxes

One of the first things in reviewing a regulatory tax system is the goal the tax is designed to achieve. The purpose of the tax determines - or it should determine - its structure to a significant degree and, conversely, practical constraints on the structure of the tax can determine what goals can be achieved with it. Therefore, the concept 'regulatory tax' may be useful in reforming the tax system. It shows one kind of 'ideal' benchmark in designing regulatory taxation.

Thus, the distinguishing features between regulatory and fiscal taxes can be highlighted from the point of view of the design and the setting of the level of these taxes. Concerning the *scope* of regulatory taxes the principle of comprehensiveness is all-important. For instance, an incentive environmental tax will be less than comprehensive (or '*under-inclusive*') if not all administratively feasible pollution activities are taxed and more than comprehensive (or '*over-inclusive*'), if activities which do not cause pollution are also taxed. The situation may be quite different with respect to fiscal taxes.

An example may be useful here. Vehicles for off-road use are usually exempted from vehicle taxation. This may have been an expression of the *benefit principle*, i.e. only those who use roads have to pay taxes.[33] With respect to the use of vehicle taxes as a regulatory tool in environmental policy, it makes no difference whether the vehicles are used on the roads or for off-road driving. Regulatory taxes should be levied, in principle, on all of these vehicles. On the other hand, if some

31 See also J.B. Opschoor and H.B. Vos, *supra* note 29, p. 12-13.

32 On these issues, see S. Shavell, 'Liability for Harm versus Regulation of Safety', *Journal of Legal Studies*, 1984, p. 357 *et seq*.

33 See e.g. S. Cnossen, *supra* note 13, p. 9.

vehicles do not cause the regulated problems, no regulatory taxes should be levied on them - and again - irrespective of whether they are used on roads or off-road.

The distinction between fiscal and regulatory taxes can be seen also by an examination of the justifications for *tax exemptions* in value-added taxation and regulatory taxation. In value-added taxation it is regarded as justifiable to exempt such activities from the tax which are subsidized to a large degree by the public sector. Health care provides an example of a substantially subsidized sector which has been left mainly outside the scope of value-added taxation. Levying value-added tax from these fields of activities would lead only to reciprocal money transactions.[34] By contrast, exemption of activities subsidized by the public sector from regulatory tax is comparable to exempting those activities from the obligations set in direct regulation. If some sectors were exempted from a regulatory tax it would weaken the effectiveness of the tax unless this exemption were 'compensated' by increasing the tax rate of taxable activities. As Cnossen and Vollebergh (1992) put it in their analysis of carbon taxes:

> 'There should be no exemption from the carbon excise for fuel used by the armed forces, hospitals, homes for [the] aged, scientific and medicinal purposes, or some other worthy goal or institution. The premise is that every burning of fossil fuel by man is potentially climate-threatening'.[35]

With respect to the determination of *tax liability*, administrative considerations are of central importance in fiscal taxation, i.e. the regulatory option that is usually preferred is the one which leads to the lowest administrative costs. This regulatory standard is important, of course, also with respect to regulatory taxes. However, when regulatory options are evaluated their impact on the regulatory effectiveness cannot be ignored. For instance, one tax liability option may entail somewhat higher administrative costs than another but it would be preferred if it were clearly more compatible with, for example, the principle of comprehensiveness.

For administrative reasons simple tax bases are preferable in fiscal taxation. With respect to regulatory taxes the *linkage principle* has to be taken into account and, thus, the tax should not always be related to the weight or volume of the product, but rather to harmful characteristics of the product.[36] Sometimes, it is not even possible to levy a tax on a product; it should rather be directed at the effluents or at waste products. However, at the same time the *accuracy principle* has to be taken into account: it can be required that taxes are related to such attributes as can be monitored and observed.[37] The accuracy principle has at a minimum the following dimensions. Firstly, it should be clear to the taxpayers what is and what is not taxable. Secondly, taxpayers must know how they are taxed, in particular according

34 See e.g. SOU 1989:35, *Reformerad mervärdeskatt m m*, Stockholm, 1989, p. 147.

35 S. Cnossen and H.R.J. Vollebergh, 'Toward a Global Excise on Carbon', *National Tax Journal*, 1992, p. 34.

36 See also J. Kay and M. Keen, 'Alcohol and tobacco taxes: criteria for harmonization', in S. Cnossen (ed.), *Tax Coordination in the European Community*, Deventer, Kluwer Law and Taxation Publishers, 1987, p. 107.

37 See e.g. J. Kay and M. Keen, *supra* note 36, p. 101.

to which attributes the tax is determined and what its level is in each case. Thirdly, there must be certainty as to who is taxed.[38]

The *tax level* of fiscal taxes is determined by revenue needs, whereas the level of regulatory taxes is determined, in principle, by the regulatory target, e.g. the environmental policy goal set for reducing NO_x emissions. For instance, in the latter case we can speak about incentive environmental taxes. It is another matter how well this train of thought is applied in practice. For instance, the goals may remain obscure, or sometimes it may be difficult to verify, whether fiscal or regulatory objectives are the primary goals of tax legislation.

6. An Example: Prohibiting Retroactive Regulatory Tax Legislation

The prohibition of retroactive legislation can be discussed from two points of view: *de facto* and *de jure*. Retroactive tax legislation *de facto* is legislation which in itself fulfils the prohibition *de jure*, but where the regulatee is economically and technically bound to investments, such as pollution reduction equipment, in such a way that he cannot actually avoid the tax for a while. On the other hand, if the regulatee had known about the new tax or a tax amendment well in advance, he might have made different investment decisions. The consequences of the retroactivity *de facto* can be mitigated by the legislator, for example by applying long delays in implementation.

If the prohibition of retroactive tax legislation were applied strictly, it would not be possible in any circumstances to direct the tax at chargeable events which have occurred before the tax law had been put into effect. However, particular reasons may exist which support a more flexible attitude to the prohibition. Here the *hoarding* of taxable products before the tax law or its amendment has been put into effect is of relevance. There is some evidence that the introduction and the increases in the rates of product-related taxes have encouraged a large-scale hoarding. Examples of this are the introduction of the Swedish pesticides tax in 1984[39] and the introduction of the price regulation charge on pesticides in 1986.[40] Such a hoarding effect might be regarded as undesirable on two counts: firstly, because regulatees reduce their tax burden without reducing pollution, and secondly, hoarding could lead to some health and safety risks, for instance, when households and farmers stock up pesticides before the tax comes into effect.[41]

In these circumstances, the prohibition of retroactive tax law cannot be justified by the legal protection of taxpayers. Thus, in § 13, paragraph 1 of the Finnish Act on Excise Duty Imposed on Liquid Fuels for example it has been enacted that

38 J.E. Meade, *supra* note 7, p. 18-19.

39 I.-M. Gren, 'Regulating the Farmers' Use of Pesticides in Sweden', in J.B. Opschoor and R.J. Turner (eds.), *Economic Incentives and Environmental Policies: Principles and Practice*, Dordrecht-Boston-London, Kluwer Academic Publishers, 1994, p. 155.

40 SOU 1990:59, Sätt värde på miljön! Miljöavgifter och andra ekonomiska styrnedel. Betänkande av miljöavgiftsutredningen, Stockholm, 1990, p. 455.

41 OECD, *Implementation Strategies for Environmental Taxes*, Paris, OECD, 1996, p. 26.

'(a)fter a bill has been presented to Parliament concerning the amendment of this law, the Government has the right to levy the tax and the strategic stockpile according to the bill'.

Such provisions - later referred to as a *bill procedure* - have been incorporated into all excise duties in Finland, irrespective of their fiscal or regulatory character, among other things purely in order to prevent large-scale hoarding of taxable products. Partly related to this is the aim of improving the *normative flexibility* of taxation. By imposing a tax already to be levied on the basis of a government bill it is possible to shorten the delays in decision-making and implementation usually associated with the enactment of tax laws.[42]

Levying regulatory taxes on the basis of a government bill is not compatible with their regulatory character in every respect. Difficulties may arise when the bill is not accepted by Parliament. In the case of sole fiscal taxes the repayment of levied taxes can be regarded as sufficient compensation to taxpayers. However, with respect to regulatory taxes, problems emerge if taxpayers and polluters have taken measures to reduce undesired conduct as a result of the government bill. It can be claimed that the repayment of levied taxes is not sufficient here since it should also cover compensation for the costs arising from reducing undesired behaviour. However, the settlement of these costs would be overwhelmingly difficult and, thus, their repayment practically impossible. Consequently, it is a reason to take a cautious attitude to levying regulatory taxes on the basis of a government bill.

The regulatory nature of taxes requires that regulatees always have the possibility to reduce their tax burden by reducing undesired activities. Against this background, the bill procedure would appear to be in contradiction with the regulatory nature of certain taxes. Nevertheless, the fulfilment of this requirement depends crucially on how well informed taxpayers are about the bill and its contents. It can be assumed that they do not act in an information vacuum in this respect. For instance, in some cases the *announcement effect* has been obvious in practice. When it is highly probable that the planned regulatory tax will be put into effect regulatees take measures to reduce conduct ahead of time.

The bill procedure may be supported with respect to product-related regulatory taxes for reasons of consistency. The levying of regulatory taxes as components in mixed taxes advocate the application of similar rules for fiscal and regulatory taxes. For instance, it would be artificial to prohibit the bill procedure in the case of environmentally motivated fuel taxes but then to allow it within the context of fiscal fuel duties.

In short, the levying of regulatory taxes on the basis of a government bill may be permissible - with certain qualifications - especially to minimize the hoarding of taxable products. Moreover, when the appropriateness of the bill procedure is

42 See also SOU 1989:35, *supra* note 34, p. 500 about the different delays in the legislative process. A delay in decision-making can be defined as a delay between the observation of the event, which requires regulation, and the point of time when the decision to amend legislation is made. A delay in implementation is the time lag before the new provisions are put into effect.

evaluated, it should be related to other regulatory options, like setting the tax rate according to the progressive time schedule. On the other hand, if there is no danger of the hoarding effect or any other inappropriate measures for tax avoidance in the implementation stage of a regulatory tax, the prohibition of retroactive legislation should be strictly adhered to. For instance, effluent taxes should not be directed at effluents emitted into the environment before the tax is put into effect. This may also hold for the waste tax. Irrespective of that, according to § 13, paragraph 1 of the Waste Tax Act in Finland, the bill procedure is applied. This provision was justified summarily in the draft stage as a way to increase the flexibility of taxation.[43] However, in my view the bill procedure should be restricted only to product-related regulatory taxes.

Another way to prevent the hoarding effect by 'retroactive' legislation is to direct the tax at the storage of taxable products. In the Finnish Energy Tax Reforms of 1994 and 1997 this kind of *storage procedure* was followed.[44] A storage procedure was applied to coal products which were bought by the users already before the tax was put into effect but used after that point of time. In preparing this legislation, the application of a storage procedure has been justified on the grounds of competitive neutrality. This is due to the fact that coal products can be hoarded before the tax has been put into effect, whereas users of natural gas clearly have no such opportunity.[45]

The regulatory nature of taxes concerned is not inevitably in conflict with the storage procedure. Where coal products in the storage of users are concerned, regulatees have the possibility to reduce the use of coal, even though the tax is formally interpreted as retroactive in nature. Nor is the 'violation' of the prohibition of retroactive legislation dramatic either. An example concerning the sulphur tax may clarify the issue. If the sulphur tax were levied as an effluent tax, the tax would have been directed, in effect, at the storage of fuels generating SO_2 emissions. In this respect, the effluent tax and fuel-related sulphur tax to reduce SO_2 emissions would be entirely directed at the same effluents if and only if the storage procedure is applied.

To summarize, the storage procedure as well as the bill procedure may be applied particularly to prevent the hoarding of taxable products within the context of the introduction or an amendment of an product-related regulatory tax. However, the role of the storage procedure may be rather limited for administrative reasons. For instance, it would be exceedingly difficult to settle the amount of pesticides in the storage facilities of each farmer when the pesticide tax rate is increased. Thus, the bill procedure is usually a more commendable solution. Finally, these considerations have shown that there are no particular reasons to deviate from the continuity principle with respect to the prohibition of retroactive tax legislation.

43 HE 48/1996 vp, *Hallituksen esitys Eduskunnalle jäteverolaiksi*, Helsinki, p. 20.

44 See § 21, paragraph 2 of the Act on Excise Duty Imposed on Certain Energy Sources, and § 28, paragraph 2 of the Act on Excise Duty Imposed on Electricity and Certain Fuels.

45 HE 225/1996 vp, *Hallituksen esitys Eduskunnalle energiaverotusta koskevan lainsäädännön uudistamiseksi*, Helsinki, p. 25.

7. Concluding Remarks

First of all, it can be said that one kind of *legal paradox* characterizes regulatory taxes. On the one hand, such taxes deviate significantly in nature from conventional fiscal taxes. For instance, incentive environmental taxes act as preventive mechanisms, like compensation for environmental damage or criminal law, and their primary goal is to improve the state of the environment and fiscal considerations are, if anything, of secondary importance. On the other hand, similar rules would apply to regulatory taxes as are applied to fiscal taxes. This argument has been supported by the analysis concerning the prohibition of the retroactive tax legislation. Moreover, the continuity principle is followed e.g. with respect to the legality principle, destination and origin principles in international trade and the prohibition of discriminatory taxation under EC law.[46]

The reasons for the dominant position of the continuity principle are manifold and vary somewhat case by case. However, some general arguments may be presented briefly. Firstly, the exact definition of regulatory taxes is almost impossible to arrive at. No purely objective criteria can be found to define these taxes, and the definition is bound up with the goals of legislation which are themselves often indeterminate. The explicit and actual goals of tax legislation may also deviate from each other. Moreover, the goals of regulatory taxes are obscured because there exists so many departures from 'ideal' regulatory taxes in practice. For instance, certain activities are exempted from the tax even though they should be regulated. In these circumstances, any hope of making sharp distinctions in the legal treatment between fiscal and regulatory taxes is restricted.

Another essential reason for following the continuity principle relates to the legislative technique applied when regulatory taxes are enacted. It concerns especially those regulatory taxes which are incorporated into existing fiscal taxes. Consistency and administrative considerations support the application of similar rules to both the fiscal and regulatory components of these mixed taxes. On the other hand, when regulatory taxes are implemented as their own laws, it would be inconsistent if similar 'rules of the game' were not applied to them as to the regulatory tax components in mixed taxes. In addition, especially product-related regulatory taxes are 'piggy-backed' on to the existing excise taxation procedure, which further streamlines regulatory and fiscal taxes.

Thirdly, the predictability of tax treatment argues for the continuity principle. Predictability is promoted by the use of the same concepts and definitions in regulatory tax laws as are used in regulatory laws and tax laws. Predictability requires that similar concepts are applied similarly.

Finally, the legal nature of regulatory taxes is obscured, in effect, because they are often used for revenue-raising purposes, i.e. to finance in particular the reduction of income taxes. On the other hand, there is a threat that certain new regulatory taxes, especially incentive environmental taxes, will share the destiny of alcohol and

46 K. Määttä, *supra* note 1.

tobacco taxes: they become primarily revenue sources rather than mechanisms to change the conduct of regulatees.

All these issues are connected to the emergence of regulatory taxation. In short, regulatory taxes were not created out of vacuum, but their adoption has been closely linked to both tax and regulatory legislation. Against this background, it is consistent that the continuity principle is dominant when the legal problems regarding regulatory taxes are examined.

These considerations do not mean that regulatory taxes could be adjusted to the legal system so that no amendments would be necessary in existing legislation. For instance, incentive environmental taxes create pressures to revise the scope of motor vehicle and fuel taxation. It is not compatible with the regulatory nature of environmental taxes e.g. to leave the off-road use of vehicles out of taxation if it causes pollution, and on the other hand, to tax such fuels, which do not cause pollution. This perfectly shows that regulatory tax may be a useful concept in legal policy-making even though its role in the application of tax law is minor.

Family Law

Katharina
Boele-Woelki

COMPARATIVE RESEARCH-BASED DRAFTING OF PRINCIPLES OF EUROPEAN FAMILY LAW*

1. A New Challenge for Private Law

The ongoing European integration and the increasing amount of EU directives and regulations in the field of private law have - as we all know - created a new challenge for private law: the elaboration of a uniform European private law and a truly European legal science. In line with this development the European Parliament has repeatedly called for the preparation of a European Civil Code.[1] A reply to the challenge set by the European Parliament was the development of a new field of legal comparative activity: the comparative research-based drafting of European private law. Different groups and commissions working in varying fields of private law are carrying out this pioneer work. Family law, due to so-called 'cultural constraints', has until now remained almost completely outside those activities, although without this classical field of private law the creation of an entire body of uniform European private law can never be completed. All areas of private law are interconnected in such a way that it is not possible to leave family law unharmonized and to allow it to co-exist with harmonized 'economic' parts of private law. In the recently published Communication from the Commission to the Council and the European Parliament on European Contract Law[2] it is recognized that in certain areas of private law, contracts are only one of the tools of regulation given the complexity of the relationship between the parties concerned. These areas, such as employment law and family law, are indeed not covered by the Communication but give rise to particular issues. Matrimonial property law, for example, is tightly linked to the general law of property and the law governing the marriage contract cannot be separated from the general part of the law of contracts. To date, the

* With the valuable help of Dr. Masha Antokolskaia and Dr. Gert Steenhoff, University of Utrecht.

1 See the Communication from the Commission to the Council and the European Parliament on European Contract Law, Brussels 11 July 2001, COM(2001) 398.

2 See *supra* note 1.

fragmentation of private law within the framework of harmonization projects and working on a field by field basis can only be justified by the technical impossibility of consolidating all the specialists in different fields of private law in one group. One should bear in mind that in the later stage the results achieved by those groups will have to be combined and that all the areas of private law should finally be covered. That means that if one seriously intends to work on the further harmonization of private law in Europe the choices in respect of family law are also unavoidable.

The current state of affairs in respect of European private law leads to the conclusion that all the different research activities have already reached such a far-reaching stage that a clear view of the feasibility and desirability of harmonization and unification in every field of private law has become of paramount importance. There is no doubt that under the current circumstances the time-lag in respect of family law forms a serious obstacle to the whole process of harmonization and unification of European private law.

The fact that the scientific activities in the field of family law are lagging behind the activities in other fields of private law is no coincidence. Family law scholars have often postulated a fundamental reservation towards harmonization and unification. Some of them are convinced that family law cannot be the subject of harmonization and unification because of the great differences between the national regulations in different European jurisdictions and the cultural constraints inherent in this legal field.[3] The perception that family law is unsuitable for harmonization and unification was so strong that family law scholars stood almost completely apart from the efforts made in the other fields of private law.

2. The European Dimension of Family Law

It goes without saying that areas like family law, which were long thought of as falling exclusively under the internal affairs of the member states, acquire, under the influence of far-reaching economic integration and the free movement of persons, a stronger European dimension. In the same way as the absence of uniformity in areas of private law facilitating economic activities forms an obstacle to the development of the free movement of goods, services and capital, so the absence of harmonized family law creates an obstacle to the free movement of persons and the creation of a truly European identity and an integrated European legal space. At the same time there is increasing tension between the desire to retain these areas within the national jurisdiction (justified by the EU principle of subsidiarity) and the persistent need for more uniform rules and regulations. This dilemma involves, in the first place, the political choices that are to be made by the European politicians in due time. The task of academic research is to facilitate those choices by studying advantages and disadvantages incorporated in both approaches and by delivering

3 The Communication (*supra* note 1, p. 6) even states in respect of contract law that it encompasses several areas of law, which are linked to Member States' different cultural and legal traditions.

relevant information to the politicians. In any case, we have reached the point where information in respect of the desirability, feasibility and the methods of the harmonization of family law is required. The following questions have evolved: Are there any reasons why these activities should not be undertaken? Why should family law not be involved in the overall comparative research-based process?

3. EU Legislation in the Field of Private International Law

Before an overview of the research activities in the field of family law will be provided, it is essential to look at the distinction between substantive law and private international law. Recently, EU legislation has been drafted and adopted which is, and will be, of great importance in the field of family law.[4] In the 1997 Treaty of Amsterdam the EU Member States determined that economic and political integration required, among other things, the mutual harmonization of both the law of property and procedural law. Family law is also specifically referred to in the Action Plan for the implementation of the Treaty of Amsterdam and the unification of private international law[5] has already started. The programme of measures for the progressive abolition of the exequatur in the field of civil and commercial matters adopted by the Justice and Home Affairs Council in November 2000 concerns four areas of work mainly in the field of family and succession law: (1) Brussels I; (2) Brussels II and family situations arising through relationships other than marriage, (3) property rights arising out of a matrimonial relationship and the property consequences of the separation of an unmarried couple; and (4) wills and succession.[6]

What has been achieved to date? The Brussels II Regulation on Jurisdiction and Recognition and Enforcement of Judgements in Matrimonial Matters and in Matters of Parental Responsibility for Children of Both Spouses'[7] entered into force on the 1st of March 2001. The Brussels I Regulation on Jurisdiction and Recognition and Enforcement of Judgements in Civil and Commercial Matters entered into force on the 1st of March 2002. Like the well-known Brussels Convention, the new regulation also applies to maintenance issues. On the 6th of September 2001 the Commission published a Proposal for a Council Regulation on Jurisdiction and Recognition and Enforcement of Judgements in Matters of Parental Responsibility.[8] In order to establish an area of freedom, security and justice the Council will adopt new measures in other fields of family and succession law.[9] The preparation of these

4 See K. Boele-Woelki, 'Unification and Harmonization of Private International Law', in *Private Law in the International Arena, Liber amicorum Kurt Siehr*, The Hague, T.M.C. Asser Press, 2000, p. 61-77.

5 Private international law applies to private relationships with foreign elements. Three main questions are to be decided: (1) Which court has jurisdiction? (2) Which law is applicable? (3) Which conditions must be fulfilled for the recognition and enforcement of foreign decisions?

6 (2001) *OJ* C 12 pf 15.1.2001, p. 1.

7 (EC) No. 1347/2000 of 29 May 2000, L 160/19.

8 Document 501PC0505.

9 (EC) No. 1347/2000 of 29 May 2000, L 160/19.

measures has already started. A few weeks ago the Commission published two general calls for tenders concerning comparative studies in the Member States:[10]

- on the rules governing conflicts of jurisdiction and laws on matrimonial property regimes and the implication for property issues of the separation of unmarried couples in the Member States (including similar concepts, such as registered partnerships)[11] and
- on the rules governing conflicts of jurisdiction and laws on wills and succession.[12]

According to Article 65 of the Treaty of Amsterdam the measures to be taken under the Action Plan in the above-mentioned fields of law are limited to private international law and procedural law. What are the reasons for the increasing activities in the field of private international law, in particular in the field of jurisdiction, recognition and enforcement? The answer is quite simple. The increasing free movement of persons is resulting in an almost proportional increase of cross-border family relations and the classical instrument to deal with questions of law arising from such relations is the use of private international law rules. Measures in the field of private international law in Europe, however, can only be considered as intermediate steps along the path towards the complete economic and political integration of Europe because the remedies of private international law were designed for a completely different situation in which migration and the formation of cross-border families occurred only sporadically. In my view, private international law is no longer an ultimate remedy to provide adequate solutions for the regular and intensive migration within the Europe of today. In the Joint Response of the Commission on European Contract Law and the Study Group on a European Civil Code on the above mentioned Communication on European Contract Law[13] it is rightly stated under the heading 'Inadequacies of Private International Law' that conflict of law rules generally ensure no more than that a legal situation is always subject to a national law and that even unified private international law cannot overcome the diversities of substantial national law.

Private international law still remains a makeshift solution. It is certainly true that through private international law a certain degree of uniformity can be achieved, but the differences between the substantive laws of the jurisdictions concerned are still maintained. The harmonization of international procedural law alone is thus unable to remove the obstacles experienced by European citizens travelling across the jurisdictions. Undoubtedly, the recent and planned legislation in the field of private international law is only to be regarded as a first step, also bringing the harmonization of substantive family law within sight. This requires a cautious and well-balanced approach.

10 Document 501PC0505.

11 JAI/A1/2001/002.

12 JAI/A3/2001/03.

13 See <http://europa.eu.int/comm/consumers/policy/developments/contract_law/comments/5.23.pdf>, p. 35.

4. Change of Attitude

The perception that family law is unsuitable for harmonization and unification due to cultural constraints and other peculiarities has only recently changed. Three pioneers should be mentioned here. In 1995 and 1998 two European legal scholars[14] spoke out, independently of each other, in favour of the formulation of a European or an international law of matrimonial property. The third European Conference on Family Law, organized by the Council of Europe in April 1995, noted the extreme diversity of laws relating to matrimonial property regimes in the European States; it felt that this diversity caused many difficulties in the case of marriages, in particular where there is an international element, and it further recognized that it would be useful to give further consideration, at a later stage, to the possibility of preparing a set of rules which could provide, in particular, an optional matrimonial property regime for married persons. But the time was not yet ripe and these proposals did not result in any concrete initiatives. In the same year, in 1995, the necessity of providing an insight into the differences and the similarities contained in the legislation of the Member States and the elaboration of a Restatement of European family law was advocated by the authoritative German comparative law analyst Dieter Martiny.[15] He established, among other things, that, distinct from the field of commercial law, where the development of a uniform law is being overseen by a large number of national and international organizations, the initiatives in the field of family law are not attuned to each other. But, according to him, European family law is more than a utopia. Attuning future activities to each other seems to him to be more necessary than ever, because until 1995 there was no fundamental change in the division of tasks between the international organizations and national legislators, and limited and various activities were also being developed alongside each other. Illustrative of this is that there was no chapter on family law at all in the first edition of the pioneer work on the unification of private law in Europe entitled 'Towards a European Civil Code' dating from 1994. The second edition, published in 1998, contains a chapter on family law, written by Dieter Martiny[16] with a very careful and reserved suggestion that family law could also be involved in the harmonization process.

At the end of the 1990s a whole range of articles appeared, written by German, Belgian, French, Dutch and British authors that put forward different arguments for

14 This concerns the Swedish professor A. Agell, 'Towards Uniform Spouses' Property Rights, Especially in International Marriages?', *Proceedings of the 3rd European Conference on Family Law,* Cadiz 20-22 April 1995, Council of Europe, p. 63-80, and the German Judge at the EC Court of First Instance and member of UNIDROIT's Conseil de Direction, J. Pirrung, 'Unification du droit en matière familiale: La Convention de l'Union européenne sur la reconnaissance des divorces et la question de nouveaux travaux d'Unidroit', *Revue de droit uniforme,* 1998, p. 629-640.

15 D. Martiny, 'Europäisches Familienrecht - Utopie oder Notwendigkeit?', *Rabels Zeitschrift für ausländisches und internationales Privatrecht,* 1995, p. 419-453.

16 D. Martiny, 'Is Unification of Family Law Feasible or Even Desirable?' in A.S. Hartkamp *et al.* (eds.), *Towards a European Civil Code,* 2nd ed., Nijmegen-Den Haag, Ars Aequi Libri, Kluwer Law Internationl, 1998, p. 151-171.

and against the harmonization of family law.[17] In the view of many academics the issue of the harmonization and unification of family law has become one of the 'hottest issues' of comparative legal science. Considering this development, it is not astonishing that the Dutch Royal Academy of Science has recently awarded one of the members of the research group on family law in Utrecht a fellowship for a comprehensive five-year post-doctoral research project on this subject.

Finally, it should be mentioned that journals, particularly new journals, are devoting increasing attention to European family law. Unfortunately, the interesting German journal *Deutsches und Europäisches Familienrecht*, which was established in 1999, had to end its publication activities because of a lack of sufficient subscriptions, but the Swiss journal *Die Praxis des Familienrechts* which was established only a year later will certainly fill the resulting gap. Furthermore, it is worth mentioning that the editors of the well-known German law journal *Zeitschrift für das gesamte Familienrecht* have, from 2001 onwards, been paying much more attention to the European and comparative aspects of family law by establishing an international council of collaborators[18] and even in the common law systems the interest in European developments is increasing. The new International Family Journal, for instance, was recently established to follow the international developments regarding the harmonization of family laws in Europe.

5. 'A Search for a European Family Law'

Is the harmonization of family law at the European level really impossible because of existing cultural differences, or differences in legal mentalities or internal moralities between the legal systems involved?[19] Raising this question requires that the oft-mentioned argument concerning cultural constraints needs to be elaborated. This has been done in the groundbreaking consultative report written in 1999 under the auspices of the Netherlands Association for Comparative Law entitled 'A search for a European family law.'[20] The authors submitted that the argument concerning cultural constraints should be put into perspective. The reasoning in this report involves the following arguments which I will summarize very briefly:

- The diversity of legal solutions for certain legal problems often merely represents different ways to achieve the same functional results (for example, a fair distribution of property after divorce can be achieved within systems of different community of property as well as within systems of limited community of property).

17 See the Selected Bibliography on European Family Law at the end of this contribution.

18 The Dutch Journal of Family Law (*Tijdschrift voor Familie- en Jeugdrecht*) has published, since 1999, special issues on European Family Law.

19 W. Van Gerven, 'Codifying European Private Law? Yes, if...!', *European Law Review*, April 2002, p. 158, who considers family law more controversial than contract law.

20 M.V. Antokolskaia, W. De Hondt and G. Steenhoff, *Een zoektocht naar Europees familierecht*, Report for the Dutch Association of Comparative Law, Deventer, Kluwer, 1999.

- The family law of the European countries, in spite of a certain degree of cultural constraint, is based on the same legal tradition which is rooted in Roman and later in canon law. This is also in some respects true for the common law countries.
- There is a clear tendency of convergence between the family laws of different European countries (all the countries are moving in the same direction towards, for example, liberalization of divorce and the further equality of the rights of married and unmarried parents, et cetera).
- The European values on which the EU is based give rise to a growing level of European common ground in family law (such as, for example, the equality of legitimate and illegitimate children based on the decision of the ECHR in the Marx case).
- Cultural constraints are not equally strong in all fields of family law. For instance, in matrimonial property law cultural constraints play a considerably less important role than in other fields within the ambit of family law such as, for example, adoption law or the law of affiliation. Also the need for uniform rules in these areas is more persistent than elsewhere.
- The axis of the differences between the family laws in Europe (because of the stronger religious influence in Southern Europe) lies South-North and not East-West. The level of the modernization of the family law of Eastern European countries, due to the reception of the radically modernized Soviet Family law at the very end of the last century, is comparable to that of the Scandinavian countries. That makes the participation of the Eastern EU candidates in the process of the harmonization of family law within the EU rather easily attainable.

6. Organization of the Comparative Research in the Field of Family Law

How is comparative research in the field of family law organized? What has been achieved so far?

Up until now we have had access to different systematic collections of country-by-country reports on the legal systems of Europe in the field of family law. These publications are of immense value in the research into a European family law. They provide the necessary information on national legal systems and belong to the reliable sources which are indispensable for mutual comparison. I would only like to point to the important series entitled 'Beiträge zum Europäischen Familienrecht', which is published by family law experts attached to the University of Regensburg. The series includes national reports of the various symposia that have been organized by the university since 1993.[21] Exceptionally valuable comparative

[21] R. Schwab and D. Henrich, *Entwicklungen des europäischen Kindschaftsrecht*, Bielefeld, Gieseking Verlag, 1994; *Der Schutz der Familienwohnung in europäischen Rechtsordnungen*, Bielefeld, Gieseking Verlag, 1995; *Familiäre Solidarität*, Bielefed, Gieseking Verlag, 1997; *Eheliche Gemeinschaft, Partnerschaft und Vermögen im europäischen Vergleich*, Bielefed, Gieseking Verlag, 1999 and *Familienerbrecht und Testierfreiheit im europäischen Vergleich*, Bielefed, Gieseking Verlag, 2001. The third volume (*Gleichheit im Familienrecht*, Bielefed, Gieseking Verlag,) in this

information is provided in this series. However, today's family lawyers should not confine themselves to an investigation of the family law solutions which are provided in their own national systems. The differences and similarities between the solutions give rise to the next step which should be taken, namely the harmonization of family laws, because the current state of affairs indicates that the subject matter has grown to such an extent that it transgresses national boundaries. The work which has to be done, particularly the co-ordination of research activities, the selection of the most suitable fields of family law and the identification of common grounds can only be carried out within the framework of a commission with sufficient authority in which distinguished experts from all the European jurisdictions work together. After carefully considering all these circumstances six academics recently decided to set up the standing *Commission on European Family Law* (CEFL). This occurred in Utrecht on September 1, 2001.[22] Before I delve into the structure of this Commission as well as its objectives and aims it should be emphasized that the CEFL would like to work in close co-operation with existing expert groups which are – to use the words of Van Gerven – currently 'underway to unearth, understand and rebuild a European common legal heritage.'[23] In the Joint Response it is proposed that it would be desirable to involve further legal professional groups in the process of Europeanizing private law.[24]

7. Structure of the CEFL

As to the structure and organization of the CEFL it is important to know that the Commission consists of two groups: the Organizing Committee consisting of the six members at the inaugural meeting[25] and the Expert Group.[26] The general task of the Organizing Committee is to set up the Expert Group[27] and to prepare and co-

series was published in 1997 under the editorship of Verschraegen. She was the general rapporteur on the subject of 'Equality in Family Law' at the first world congress, entiteld 'Law in Motion' which was held in Brussels in September 1996.

22 The first year of CEFL's operation will be supported by a grant from the European Commission under the Grotius Civil Programme starting on the 15th of December 2001.

23 W. van Gerven, *supra* note 19, p. 156-176.

24 Joint Response, *supra* note 11, p. 33.

25 Members of the Organizing Committee: Ferrand (Lyon – France), Lowe (Cardiff – the law of England and Wales), Martiny (Frankfurt/Oder – Germany), Pintens (Leuven – Belgium), Schwab (Regensburg – Germany) and the author (Utrecht – The Netherlands).

26 Members of the Expert Group Antokolskaia (Utrecht – representing Russia), Dethloff (Bonn-Germany), Eeckelaar (Oxford – the law of England), Hausheer (Bern – Switzerland), Hrušáková (Brno – Czech Republic), Jänterä-Jareborg (Uppsala – Sweden), Koutsouradis (Thessaloniki – Greece), Mączyński (Krakow – Poland), Martin-Casals (Girona – Spain), Meston (Dublin – representing Scots law), De Oliveira (Coimbra – Portugal), Patti (Rome – Italy), Roth (Salzburg – Austria), Savolainen (Helsinki – Finland), Schwezner (Basel – Switzerland), Shannon (Dublin – Ireland), Sverdrup (Oslo – Norway), Tadorova (Sofia – Bulgaria) and Weiss (Budapest – Hungary).

27 With respect to the profile of the members of the Expert Group the Organizing Committee decided that the member in question must be a specialist in family law, with a marked interest in comparative law. The member must be able to devote the necessary time and he or

ordinate the work of the Expert Group and the Commission as a whole. The members of the Organizing Committee will at the same time be members of the Expert Group. The Expert Group will consist of experts from all EU Member States with the involvement of experts from other European countries. Especially experts from Central and Eastern European countries will be involved in anticipation of prospective accession to the EU. In this respect there is a difference between the newly established Commission approach and that of other commissions working in the field of European private law. The CEFL will not only pay attention to each of the jurisdictions of the EU Member States but will also involve jurisdictions like Norway and Switzerland and especially Eastern European systems where family law reforms have recently taken place. On the one hand, not all of them will influence the solutions to be proposed for any given issue. On the other hand, no single national family law in Europe can offer a basic model for adaptation. The latter approach would - as the Joint Response rightly stated[28] - transgress the principle that the harmonization of family law should also be formulated from a genuinely European perspective rather than from a national point of view.

8. Code, Restatement or Principles?

What final aims can be achieved by the activities of the CEFL? What kind of output is feasible and desirable? At the current stage there are basically three main options. In this respect there are no differences to the options that are currently being considered in other fields of private law.

- Drafting a binding uniform family law for the whole EU (A chapter on family law in the European Civil Code being elaborated by Von Bar's Study Group on a European Civil Code);
- Drafting a non-binding Restatement which contains the common rules of all jurisdictions concerned;
- Drafting non-binding *Principles* for selected fields, as the Lando Commission, and the European Group on Tort Law (Tilburg-Vienna Group) do in other fields of private law.

The first option is much too far-reaching and is considered to be neither feasible nor desirable at the present time. The second and third options have been intensively discussed. However, the differences between a Restatement and the drafting of *Principles* are not always clear. The recently published European Commission Communication says that the aim of the academic work carried out in the field of European private law varies from the establishment of a binding code to *Principles*

she must preferably be able to write national reports in English on the basis of questionnaires to be drawn up by the Organizing Committee. English will be the main working language. Nevertheless, during meetings, everybody will be free to explain details in either French or German. In all probability, the final main documents will also be published in French and German.

28 Joint Response, *supra* note 11, p. 40.

similar to 'restatements' that can be used to provide reliable comparative information on the European legal situation in the area concerned.[29] And, according to the Joint Response, the concepts of a Restatement of law and of *Principles* are even interchangeable.[30] The question is whether the CEFL is only supposed to distil common rules - in this case the mere description of any deviation from existing national legal systems would suffice - or whether the Commission should not go a step further by making proposals and proposing new solutions. The members of the Organizing Committee have agreed that the main goal should be to distil common rules. However, there will be cases where the CEFL will have to propose alternative solutions and will decide to elaborate innovative 'better law'. Resorting, once again, to the wording of the Joint Response:

> Principles can overcome the existing substantial differences ... (they) are aimed not to adopt the lowest common denominator but rather must suggest the best solution to the most important issues.[31]

Drafting *Principles* on the basis of thoroughgoing legal comparison (the rules based on the common core of the different solutions to the family law problems provided in the various European jurisdictions) is seen as the most feasible and practical option. Moreover, not every field of family law is equally suitable for such *Principles*.[32] A careful selection of the most suitable field is thereby considered to be one of the most important goals to be attained.

9. Working Method

With regard to the approach and methodology to be adopted four steps can be distinguished.

The first step is the selection of the fields of family law most suitable for harmonization. The sociological and psychological impact on the political feasibility of harmonizing particular areas of family law must be taken into consideration during this selection.

The second step is to draft a questionnaire for the previously selected fields of family law. The questionnaire is deemed to provide an overview of the similarities and differences between the solutions to family law problems in various European countries. Attention has to be paid not only to the law 'in the books' but also to the 'law in action'. The questionnaire will embody the functional approach. The questions must be pertinent to all the systems covered. Every questionnaire will start with an introduction to the historical background and a look into the future.

The third step is to prepare national reports by the members of the Expert Group based on the questionnaire. It is advisable that the scientific potential of their

29 See *supra* note 1.

30 Joint Response, *supra* note 11, p. 40.

31 Joint Response, *supra* note 11, p. 40.

32 See M.V. Antokolskaia, 'Enkele gedachten over de harmonisatie van het familierecht in Europa', *Tijdschrift voor familie- en jeugdrecht*, 2002, p. 4-10.

affiliated universities and other legal institutions will be involved. For the first national report, the members of the Organizing Committee will be the experts for their particular countries. The reports of the members of the Expert Group will be discussed at the meetings of the Organizing Committee and at the meetings of the Expert Group. On the basis thereof similarities and differences within the various fields of the family law of the European countries will be surveyed.

The fourth and final step is to draft the *Principles* of European Family Law in the fields selected during the previous stage. The final *Principles* will be elaborated by the Organizing Committee and proposed to the Expert Group, which will decide thereon. If they cannot reach a decision, there should be a vote. In exceptional cases, where a compromise is impossible due to a strong minority, it should be possible to express this separate opinion along with the *Principles* or in comments. The publication of the *Principles* will be the end-result.

10. Selection of the m ost suitable Fields

With regard to the question of the fields to be chosen, it is important to avoid subjects that are highly culturally defined, such as subjects with very technical rules (e.g. affiliation). One must choose subjects tending to point in the same direction.[33] The members of the Organizing Committee have agreed to exclude, at least for the moment, matrimonial property law.[34] Although it might interest the European legislator, who may wish to create a supplementary marital property regime, marital property law is a very technical matter with great differences within Europe and it would prove to be a complicated matter to put forward any *Principles* even if there are some common tendencies. Here the CEFL could only confine itself to recommending an additional regime based on one of two systems: a community property system or a system with a differentiated community, whereas its aim is to establish *Principles*.

Due to the common tendencies in the divorce laws in Europe and in particular the Brussels II Regulation, the Organizing Committee of the CEFL has decided to begin its activities in this field and to start with the grounds for divorce and some of the consequences of divorce, such as maintenance between ex-spouses. As to the effects of divorce, the division of matrimonial property will not be included, nor the effect on parental authority. Although it is difficult not to include the division of matrimonial property, the CEFL will try to avoid this controversial area at this stage. However, it must be admitted that it is difficult to include maintenance and to exclude marital property law, because these two points are often (inter)related. Nevertheless, there must be a restriction and everything depends on the questionnaire.

33 See W. Pintens and K. Vanwinckelen, *Casebook. European Family Law*, Leuven, University Press, 2001, p. 16-23.

34 K. Boele-Woelki, 'Divorce in Europe: Unification of Private International Law and Harmonization of Substantive Law', in *Liber Amicorum Ingrid Joppe*, Kluwer, 2002 (forthcoming).

As stated, the first subject will be the grounds for, and the effects of, divorce. As to the effects, only maintenance between former spouses will be included. One can think of the following two main questions. Firstly, who has an obligation to maintain? And secondly, how long will this obligation last? Experts can, of course, bring up possible links to other fields of family law. However, the focus must be on this particular subject. The questionnaire, which was approved by the CEFL Organizing Committee in January 2002,[35] contains 105 questions and embodies the functional approach. The drafters have tried to devise pertinent questions in order to cover all the systems.

The second field will be parental responsibility and for the third field the Organizing Committee has chosen the new forms of cohabitation.

11. Major Benefits

Family law touches upon the very essence of people's daily lives as no other field does. The large-scale differences between the national legal systems within a Europe without frontiers constitute a serious impediment to attaining a common European identity in the form of European citizenship. The major benefits to be gained are the following:

- Comprehensive research-based choices will be made concerning the participation of family law in the overall process of harmonization of private law in Europe.
- The selection of the fields of family law that are most suitable for harmonization will be made.
- The involvement of the experts from the Eastern European candidate states to accede to the EU will facilitate their future integration into the EU, because the necessary preparatory activities for the harmonization of their family law in line with the overall EU harmonization process will already have taken place.
- The major benefit to be expected is the creation of the *Principles of European Family Law* that can directly serve as a model for both national and European legislators elaborating new family laws and in that way can facilitate voluntary evolutionary harmonization of family law within the EU. Further convergence of national family laws will be easily achieved. On a long-term basis those *Principles* could be used for the creation of binding uniform European family law.

12. Exploitation and Dissemination

In order to involve and reach researchers and professionals in the field of family law, several dissemination activities are foreseen which are instrumental to the success of the CEFL activities. First of all, a simple web site has been created. This site will, during the first phase, encompass the results of the project and will

35 The questionnaire is published on the CEFL website: <www.law.uu.nl/priv/cefl>.

gradually grow into a European Family Law site. The web site is accessible at <www.law.uu.nl/priv/cefl>. Another important step to be taken with regard to this dissemination is the periodical publication of the results of the CEFL research activities as well as contributions by CEFL's individual members in the form of scientific articles in the specific journals on family law and general journals on European private law. The publication of a special collection of national reports drawn up on the basis of the questionnaire surveying the similarities and differentces in the legislative solutions to family law problems in the European countries together with the analytical report on the selection of the fields of family law, which are suitable for harmonization will be of great importance. Finally, a large-scale academic conference entitled *Perspectives for the Unification and Harmonization of the Family Law in Europe* will be organized in Utrecht in December 2002. For the first time in European history, a truly international conference will take place where experts can discuss all the aspects of the development of a European family law. During this conference, the CEFL wishes to submit its activities and plans to a broad discussion involving both the supporters and opponents of the harmonization and unification process. The CEFL is furthermore very interested in the broad discussion of the first practical results of its work: a comparative synthesis made on the basis of the national reports in the field of grounds for divorce and maintenance between former spouses in order to pave the way for elaborating the *Principles*. During the conference the various arguments for and against the harmonization and unification of family law in Europe will be considered from a broad perspective:

- in the context of the far-reaching harmonization activities in the other areas of private law and the impact of the recent initiatives of the various EU bodies;
- in relation to the unification of private international law, recently undertaken by the European Commission based on the Treaty of Amsterdam;
- in the context of the relationship between national family law and European law;
- in relation to the influence of (European) human rights on national family law, more in particular with respect to the case law of the European Court of Justice in Luxembourg and of Human Rights in Strasbourg and, finally;
- in relation to the experiences and initiatives towards unification in the USA, where each state has its own family law.

13. The 'Harmonization of Family Law' Train has left the Station

The work on the harmonization of family law in Europe will only be successful if lawyers begin to 'think European' with respect to family law issues. Firstly, they should be aware of the European dimension of family law that already exists: the relation to European private international law, substantive European law and European human rights. Secondly, they should be confronted with the challenge of harmonizing the existing family laws in Europe and should be provided with the tools with which to do so. With the aid of the 'functional comparative law approach' it is possible to improve national family laws, learning from the solutions found abroad, trying to end up with 'the better law', on the basis of comparing the various national solutions. In order to be able to work towards this goal, it is of great importance to obtain information as to how the solutions found abroad work in practice, and for this purpose, it is extremely important to know or to have access to those working in this field. In addition, it is necessary to be prepared for further challenges in the field of family law relating to European integration. Just as the Brussels II Regulation has made it necessary to make a start on the harmonization of national divorce law, in the near future ongoing European legislation will make serious harmonization efforts in other fields of family law unavoidable.

The work on the harmonization and probable unification of family law will certainly last for many years. This prediction is more than realistic due to the complexity of family law and the great number of jurisdictions involved. The first academic activities in the field of the harmonization of contract law in Europe commenced at the beginning of the 1970s and we can expect the publication of the final version of *Principles on European Contract Law* during the course of 2002. Due to the long duration of the work on harmonization, it is of the utmost importance that young researchers will be involved from the very beginning in the general discussions concerning the whole process.[36]

In addition, it should be borne in mind that the harmonization of family law will provide an adequate legal basis for the further realization of free movement for Europeans and will contribute to the factual achievement of a Europe not only without trade and economic borders but also without legal ones.[37] Therefore, the harmonization of family law can be seen as an ultimate step on the road towards creating a truly people-friendly, integrated Europe as a common home for all Europeans.

Finally, it is evident that the work on the harmonization of family law in Europe has already begun. A long train has slowly begun to leave the station. Some passengers may leave and others may board as the train meanders along a route yet to be finalized and stops at stations yet to be determined. Nevertheless, all of these passengers should consider the conclusion Walter Pintens makes in his Casebook on European Family Law. He assures us that harmonization will only lead to

36 For the last decade, it has generally been accepted that dissertations in the field of private law, including family law, should include the comparative method. This method is one of the most successful methods for finding the 'better law'.

37 The activities of the CEFL, aiming at the partial/progressive harmonization of family law, will directly contribute to the policies that the Amsterdam Treaty has placed within the European Community system concerning external borders, immigration and asylum, and judicial co-operation in civil matters, creating an area of 'freedom, security and justice' in the EU. This means that the European Commission is responsible for proposing policies and actions (together with member states for five years, 1 May 1999 – 30 April 2004) and for implementing and executing them when the Council of the EU has so agreed. Other fields of European policy related to this area are more or less derived from this main policy. There are several actions and policies within the Union which can and will benefit from more harmonized family law matters: One can think of the citizens' first initiative of the Internal Market, and Employment and Social Affairs, and also the policy areas of Education and Research, since this subject contributes to some serious obstacles to the mobility of European citizens.

success if one manages to emphasize that which is common to all European legal systems and put the differences into perspective without denying them, thus creating a European consciousness in the field of family law. This can, at the same time, only be achieved if education and legal doctrine take centre stage.[38]

38 W. Pintens and K. Vanwinckelen, *supra* note 33, p. 27.

14. Selected Bibliography on European Family Law

Author(s)	Title	Reference
	2002	
M. Antokolskaia	Enkele gedachten over de harmonisatie van het familierecht in Europa	(2002) Tijdschrift voor familie- en jeugdrecht 4-10
	2001	
H. Däubler-Gmelin	Ehe und Familie in einem zusammenwachsenden Europa	(2001) Jahrbuch Bitburger Gespräche 99-109
G.-R. de Groot	Auf dem Wege zu einem europäischen (internationalen) Familienrecht	(2001) Zeitschrift für Europäisches Privatrecht 618-627
R. Herzog	Europäischer Grundrechtsschutz für Ehe und Familie	(2001) Jahrbuch Bitburger Gespräche 7-14
C. McGlynn	Families and the European Union charter of Fundamental Rights: Progressive change of entrenching the status quo?	(2001) 26 European Law Review 582-598
Pintens and K. Vanwinckelen	Casebook. European Family Law	Leuven, 2001
W. Pintens	Die Europäisierung des Erbrechts	(2001) Zeitschrift für Europäisches Privatrecht 628-648
A. Verbeke	Perspectives for an International Marital Contract	(2001) Maastricht Journal of European and Comparative Law 189-200
	2000	
E.-M. Hohnerlein	Konturen eines einheitlichen Europäischen Familien- und Kindschaftsrechts	(2000/2001) The European Legal Forum 252-260
K. Kuchinke	Über die Notwendigkeit, ein gemeineuropäisches Familien- und Erbrecht zu schaffen	Europas Universale rechtsordnungpolitische Ausgabe im Recht des dritten Jahrtausends. Festschrift für Alfred Söllner zum 70. Geburstag 2000, München, 589-612
D. Leipold	Europa und das Erbrecht	In: Europas universale rechtsordnungspolitische Aufgabe im Recht des dritten Jahrtausends, Festschr. Söllner (2000) 647-668
C. McGlynn	A Family Law for the European Union	In: J.Shaw (ed) Social Law and Policy in an Evolving European Union (Oxford, 2000, Hart) 223-241
	1999	
M. Antokolskaia, W. De Hondt and G. Steenhoff	Een zoektocht naar Europees familierecht	Report for the Dutch Association of Comparative Law (Kluwer, 1999, Deventer)
D. Bradley	Convergence in Family Law: Mirrors, Transplants and Political Economy	(1999) Maastricht Journal of European and Comparative Law 127-150

Author(s)	Title	Reference
D. Martiny	Die Möglichkeit der Vereinheitlichung des Familienrechts innerhalb des Europäischen Union	In D.Martiny and N.Witzleb (eds) Auf dem Wege zu einem Europäischen Zivilgesetzbuch (Berlin, 1999) 177-189
W. Pintens	Over de Europeanisatie van het familierecht	(1999) Tijdschrift voor familie- en jeugdrecht 238-243
1998		
M. Fallon	Droit familial et droit Communautés Européennes	(1998) Revue trimestrielle de droit familial 361-400
M. Killerby	Family law in Europe. Standards set by the Member States of the Council of Europe	In: (1998) Liber Amicorum Meulders-Klein, Brussels 351-378
D. Martiny	Is Unification of Family Law Feasible or Even Desirable?	In: Towards a European Civil Code, Second Edition, Hartkamp et al (eds) (Ars Aequi Libri, 1998, Nijmegen) 151-171
W. Pintens	Rechtvereinheitlichung und Rechtsangleichung im Familienrecht. Eine Rolle für die Europäischen Union?	(1998) Zeitschrift für Europaïsches Privatrecht 670-676
W. Pintens	Von Konstantinidis bis Grant. Europa und das Familienrecht	(1998) Zeitschrift für Europäisches Privatrecht 843-848
J. Pirrung	Unification du droit en matière famiale: La Convention de l'Union Européenne sur la reconnaissance des divorces et la question de nouveaux travaux d'Unidroit	(1998) Revue de droit uniforme 629-640
W. Schrama	De Raad van Europa en het familierecht. Een overzicht van de bijdragen van de Raad van Europa aan het familierecht	(1998) Tijdschift voor familie- en jeugdrecht 54-59
1997		
K. Boele-Woelki	The Road Towards a European Family Law	(1997) 1.1 Electronic Journal of Comparative Law
K. Boele-Woelki	De weg naar een Europees familierecht	(1997) Tijdschrift voor familie- en jeugdrecht 2-9
C. Forder	Het gezin in internationale verdragen	(1997) Rechtsgeleerd Magazijn Themis 130-144
W. Pintens and Du Mongh	Family and Succession Law in the European Union	In: R. Bonplain and W.Pintens (eds) International Encyclopaedia of Laws. Family and Succession Law (The Hague, 1997, Den Haag) 1996
M. Killerby	The Council of Europe's Contribution to Family Law (Past, Present and Future)	in: N.Lowe and G.Douglas (eds), Family Across Frontiers (Kluwer, 1996, The Hague) 13-25

Author(s)	Title	Reference
	1995	
A. Agell	Towards Uniforming Spouses Property Rights, Especially in International Marriages?	Proceedings of the 3rd European Conference on Family Law, Cadiz, 20-22 April 1995, Council of Europe, p.63-80
E. Hondius	Naar een Europees personen- en familierecht	in: Drie Treden - Over politiek, beleid en recht (De Ruiterbundel, Tjeenk Willinik, 1995, Zwolle) 173-181
G.-R. de Groot	Op weg naar een Europees personen- en familierecht?	(1995) 44 Ars Aequi 29-33
D. Martiny	Europäisches Familienrecht - Utopie oder Notwendigkeit?	(1995) Rabels Zeitschrift für ausländisches und internationales Privatrecht 419-453
W. Pintens	Droit des successions, des donations et des testaments en Europe - de la diversité à l'unité?	in: Fédération royale des notaires de Belgique, (ed) Les relations contractuelles internationales - Le rôle du notaire (Antwerpen, 1995) 532 onwards
A. Verbeke et al	European Marital Property Law Survey 1988-1994	(1995) 3 European Review of Private Law 445-482
	1992	
J. Basedow	Konstantinidis v. Bangemann oder die Familie im Europäischen Gemeinschaftsrecht	(1994) Zeitschrift für Europäisches Privatrecht 197-199
I. Fahrenhorst	Familienrecht und Europäische Menschenrechtskonvention	Paderborn, 1994 1993
R. Streinz	Gemeinschaftsrecht und deutsches Personenstandsrecht	(1993) Das Standesamt 243-249 1992
Ganghofer	Le droit de la famille en Europe: son évolution depuis l'antiquité jusqu'à nos jours	Strasbourg, 1992 1990
J.-M. Bischoff	Harmonization du droit privé: l'example du travail de la Commission Internationale de l' Etat Civil	in: Mélanges en l'honneur d'Alfred E. von Overbeck à l'occasion de son 65ème anniversaire, Faculté de droit de l'université de Fribourg, W.Stoffel and P. Volken (eds) (Editions universitaires Fribourg Suisse, 1990, Fribourg) 117-130
P. Boucaud	La protection de l'enfant en Europe	(1990) 38 Annuaire européen 21-38
M. Castillo	La protection des enfants dans la Communauté européenne	(1990) Revue du Marché Commun 361-365
F. Kaufmann	Zukunft der Familie: Stabilitätsrisiken und Wandel der familialen Lebensformen sowie ihre gesellschaftlichen und politischen Bedingungen	München, 1990

Author(s)	Title	Reference
T.F. O'Higgins	The Family and European Law	(1990) New Law Journal 1643-1646
A. Rieg	L'harmonization européenne du droit de la famille: mythe ou réalité?	in: Mélanges en l'honneur d'Alfred E. von Overbeck à l'ocasion de son 65ème anniversaire, Faculté de droit de l'université de Fribourg, W.Stoffel and P. Volken (eds) (Editions universitaires Fribourg Suisse, 1990, Fribourg) 473-498
1988		
I. Fahrenhorst	Sorge- und Umgangsrecht nach der Ehescheidung und die Europäische Konvention zum Schutze der Menschenrechte und Grundfreiheiten	(1988) Familienrechtszeitschrift 238-242 1982
M.-T. Meulders-Klein	La personne, la famille, et la loi au sortir du XXe siècle	(1982) Journal des Tribuneaux 137-144
F. Sturm	Das Straßburger Marckx-Urteil zum Recht des nichtehelichen Kindes und seine Folgen	(1982) Familienrechtszeitschrift 1150-1159
1981		
E. Jayme	Die Entwicklung des Europaïschen Familienrechts	(1981) Zeitschrift für das gesamte Familienrecht 221-226
G. Luther	Einheitsrecht durch Evolution im Eherecht und im Recht der eheähnlichen Gemeinschaft	(1981) 45 Rabels Zeitschrift für ausländisches und internationales Privatrecht 253-267
1977		
Furgler	L'evolution actuelle et les perspectives d'harmonization de droit de la famille au sein de l'Europe	(1977) 6 Diritto di famiglia et delle persona 913-938
Earlier than 1977		
P.H. Neuhaus	Europäische Vereinheitlichung des Eherechts	(1970) 34 Rabels Zeitschrift für ausländisches und internationales Privatrecht 253 -263
W. Müller-Freienfels	The Unification of Family Law	(1968-69) 16 American Journal of Comparative Law 175-218
P.H. Neuhaus	Europäisches Familienrecht? Gedanken zur Rechtsvergleichung und Rechtsvereinheitlichung	in: Festschrift Dölle II, 1963, p.419-435

Dieter Martiny

THE HARMONIZATION OF FAMILY LAW IN THE EUROPEAN COMMUNITY. PRO AND CONTRA

There have been many arguments made in favour of the harmonization of European family law, making it difficult to add anything new. In my view, the main task that we face today concerns finalizing the project and realizing it incrementally. However, since there are many reservations remaining which should be taken seriously, I will first begin by concentrating on these arguments before making additional remarks in respect of the future.

1. Pro and Contra

1.1. Family Law is Different

One argument against the harmonization of family law is simply that this part of the law is 'different' - too complicated and specific compared to other fields of law. Indeed, the mere fact that in the family law area today there is still a general debate on the need of harmonization as such, whereas in other fields, especially in the law of obligations and consumer law, there already exists highly developed proposals, is revealing. This demonstrates that a certain lag exists between general developments and the state of family law.

True, family law is a very specific legal subject. The first difference which arises relates to national family law systems that mainly have a role in cases where a family relationship is disturbed or broken. Of course, there are also matrimonial contracts. However, family law generally plays a much more modest role than, for example, general contract or consumer law. Additionally, in family law one finds general concepts such as, for example, separate or community property. Nevertheless, the rules are often very detailed, very specific and in many areas in constant flux. In many respects family law contains exceptions to the general rules of contract and property law.

There are fields like the calculation of maintenance payments, which have such a strong relationship not only with national substantive family law, but also with procedural rules and social security provisions for instance in respect of the different services available for children or incapacitated adults.[1] However, the fact that we have to deal with a very complicated field of law is certainly an indication that harmonization is a difficult task, but as such should not suggest that harmonization should be avoided.

1.2. No Need for Harmonization?

Often the argument is put forward that there is no economic need for European family law. Why should there be uniformity between the Polar Circle and the Strait of Messina? There seems to be no need for harmonization, e.g. of the law of marriage or parent and child. However, this argument is simply not true. There are millions of migrants, comprising hundreds of thousands of workers and their families moving within Europe and who are confronted with different laws. Thus, a different family law may well also affect free movement within the Community. This makes the enforcement of the resulting family obligations in Europe of practical interest. Status is also often a preliminary question for social benefits, tax law and immigration law, and there are areas of law concerning, for example, matrimonial property, which affect the obligations of spouses and have an immediate impact on commercial transactions.

For fields like transport law or intellectual property, international harmonization has been ongoing for more than a century. The development of family law naturally followed a different path. However, even the field of obligations, tort law in particular, was originally considered to be too complicated. We now realize after extensive research that harmonization seems to be at least debatable.

1.3. No Interest?

The third argument claims that no one is really interested in the harmonization of family law. Of course, the issue of harmonization for several decades has been mainly an academic idea without much practical relevance. There was a certain consensus that the concepts of family law could also be spread in some manner from one country to the other, but that this generally occurs not by international conventions, such as in other fields of law, but by unilateral actions of the national legislators and by so-called spontaneous or possibly co-ordinated harmonization.[2]

However, after some scepticism at the beginning of the 1990s,[3] and with increasingly more concrete plans in the present time,[4] a new discussion has been

1 Cf. D. Martiny, *Unterhaltsrang und -rückgriff I*, Tübingen, Mohr Siebeck, 2000, p. 152 *et seq.*

2 Cf. P.H. Neuhaus, 'Europäisches Familienrecht? Gedanken zur Rechtsvergleichung und Rechtsvereinheitlichung', in *Festschrift Dölle* II, Tübingen, Mohr Siebeck, 1963, p. 419 *et seq.*; W. Müller-Freienfels, 'The Unification of Family Law', *Am. J. Comp.* L. 16, 1968-69, p. 175 *et seq.* reprinted in W. Müller-Freienfels, *Familienrecht im In- und Ausland – Aufsätze I*, Frankfurt am Main, Verlag für Standesamtswesen, 1978, p. 79 *et seq.*

3 See A. Rieg, 'L'harmonization européenne du droit de la famille: mythe ou réalité?', in *Conflits et harmonization – Mélanges en l'honneur d'Alfred E. von Overbeck*, Freiburg/Schweiz, Editions universitaires Fribourg, 1990, p. 473 *et seq.*

awakened. The European Parliament and the European Commission has expressed interest in, for example, practical questions, such as the enforcement of maintenance obligations,[5] contact orders in respect of divorced parents[6] and the prevention of legal kidnapping. Concentrating more on these issues would be useful and required. However, at least in the long run, it seems difficult to concentrate solely on isolated questions. These have their origin in a broader context and therefore a wider approach is necessary.

1.4. Not Enough Consensus?

At times it is also maintained that in family law there is too much diversity between the different national systems so that harmonization would be impossible. Family law is often regarded and developed from a national viewpoint only. There is not such a milieu of international transactions, lawyers, organizations, or commercial arbitration, as in commercial matters, which gives unification a certain momentum. In addition, the approach taken in the Common Law and in the Civil Law countries is clearly divergent. There exist some major differences. Sometimes Scottish law can be viewed as something in-between. Having said that, however, in other fields it is generally accepted that exploring ways to bridge the different approaches should be possible and is even considered to be stimulating. It therefore does not seem to be impossible to find a common core and consensus in family law.

In the field of family law one can identify common trends. Today equality of the sexes is respected in European legal systems. Discrimination of illegitimate children is present only in some remnant questions. In every contemporary system divorce is recognized. It is hard to believe that when the original Brussels Convention on jurisdiction and recognition in civil matters of 1968 was drafted not all European Member States recognized divorce, therefore the dissolution of marriage and the consequences of divorce were almost completely omitted (cf. art. 1 (2)). Now it is quite obvious that the main problems in family law are similar in respect

4 G.R. de Groot, 'Op weg naar een Europees personen- en familierecht?' *Ars Aequi*, 44, 1995, p. 29 *et seq.*; G.R. de Groot, 'Auf dem Wege zu einem europäischen (internationalen) Familienrecht', *ZEuP*, 2001, *et seq.*; D. Martiny, 'Europäisches Familienrecht – Utopie oder Notwendigkeit?', *RabelsZ* 59, 1995, p. 419 *et seq.*; D. Martiny, 'Is Unification of Family Law Feasible or Even Desirable?', in A.S. Hartkamp *et al.* (eds.), *Towards a European Civil Code*, second edition, Nijmegen-Den Haag, Ars Aequi Libri, Kluwer Law International, 1998, p. 151 *et seq.*; D. Martiny, 'Die Möglichkeit der Vereinheitlichung des Familienrechts innerhalb der Europäischen Union' in D. Martiny and N. Witzleb (eds.), *Auf dem Wege zu einem Europäischen Zivilgesetzbuch* Berlin, Springer Verlag, 1999, p. 177 *et seq.*; K. Boele-Woelki, 'The Road Towards a European Family Law', *Electronic Journal of Comparative Law* 1, 1997, Nr. 1; W. Pintens, 'Rechtsvereinheitlichung und Rechtsangleichung im Familienrecht – Eine Rolle für die Europäische Union?', *ZEuP*, 1998, 670 *et seq.*; M.V. Antokolskaia, W. de Hondt and G. Steenhoff, *Een zoektocht naar Europees familierecht*, Deventer, Kluwer, 1999.

5 Cf. the Action Plan of the EC Council of 11/12 Dec. 1998.

6 Cf. proposal for a Council Regulation on the mutual enforcement of judgments on rights of access to children, (2000) *OJ* C 234/7.

of single parents, divorce, marriage after divorce, cohabitation, maintenance enforcement and so on.

1.5. Reform instead of Harmonization?

A more sophisticated argument against harmonization is that interesting and promising developments often have their origin in other countries, which are not members of the European Union, e.g. Australia, New Zealand or Canadian provinces. It would thus be more worthwhile to concentrate on these new trends than on harmonization at the lowest level. This argument has some merit. Harmonization undertaken for the purpose of unification merely does not seem to make much sense, particularly for those who would have to sacrifice their own, better solutions. Sometimes the fear is expressed that the Scandinavian countries would be at a disadvantage[7]. However, progress is not necessarily in opposition with uniformity. As in other fields of harmonization, one also has to take into account international developments outside the European borders; harmonization does not necessarily mean a 'race to the bottom', as there are many examples, especially in consumer law, where it is stated expressly that the given national standard of protection must not be lowered. When it is clear what a future European position will be, such clauses or exceptions will be possible. Without an explicit explanation concerning which particular points are criticized in detail, this counter argument often only means that there is not much more than the traditional belief that the own national system is the best developed and superior to others.

1.6. No Common Goals?

Sometimes it is also contended that there are no common goals in family law. Of course, development in family law is often a national one. However, there is more comparative work being carried out at present than ever before. There are common values in the European Convention on Human Rights and Fundamental Freedoms,[8] the case law of the European Court on Human Rights, especially in respect of Art. 8 of the Convention,[9] the EC Treaty and in the recent Charter on Basic Rights of the EC.[10] There are common trends, e.g. in equality of the sexes, non-discrimination of illegitimate children or the welfare of the child as the paramount consideration in child custody.

The trend for the development of rules for same-sex couples is a good example. Rules were first enacted in Denmark in 1989, then a Norwegian statute

7 See C. McGlynn, 'A Family Law for the European Union?', in J. Shaw (ed.), *Social Law and Policy in an Evolving European Union*, Oxford, Hart Publishing, 2000, p. 223 *et seq.*

8 European Convention for the Protection of Human Rights and Fundamental Freedoms of 4 Nov. 1950.

9 Cf. D. Martiny, *supra* note 4, p. 157.

10 Cf. E.M. Hohnerlein, 'Konturen eines einheitlichen europäischen Familien- und Kindschaftsrechts – die Rolle der Europäischen Menschenrechtskonvention -', *The European Legal Forum* 2000/01, München, IPR-Verlag, p. 252 *et seq.*

followed in 1993, the Swedish rules were enacted in 1995, the Belgian, French and Dutch rules followed in 1999, and the German statute in the year 2000.[11] Of course, one has to admit that the national solutions differ in some respects; in some other European countries there is still no special legislation and the acceptance of an idea can take more than a decade. In other fields one can detect a partly asynchronous development, which is not unusual. It is nevertheless astonishing that in such a controversial matter as registered partnership laws for homosexual couples legislation could be passed in so many European countries within such a relatively short period. One explanation points to the idea of non-discrimination now laid down in Art. 13 of the EC Treaty, which has had a far-reaching effect.

1.7. Other Institutions

Another argument against further harmonization on the Community level is that there are already other organizations in this field doing good work and that superfluous duplication should be avoided. Indeed the Council of Europe is already engaged in this field. Several European Conventions were prepared, for instance, on the Adoption of Children of 1967,[12] the Legal Status of Children Born out of Wedlock of 1975,[13] the Recognition and Enforcement of Decisions Concerning Custody of Children of 1980[14] and on the Exercise of Children's Rights of 1996.[15] These treaties are valuable contributions for the development of European family law.[16] The exchange of experiences and the Recommendations of the Council of Europe also stimulate reform. However, there no contradiction with further efforts should arise. Within the Council of Europe, with its 43 Member States there are more European countries represented than in the European Community - and the conventions of the Council of Europe only cover a small part of family law! The same is

11 See the references K. Boele-Woelki, 'Private International Law Aspects of Registered Partnerships and Other Forms of Non-Marital Cohabitation in Europe', *La. L. Rev.* 60, 2000, p. 1053 *et seq.*

12 Convention on the Adoption of Children of 24 April 1967, U.N.T.S. 634, 255; European Treaty Series No. 58.

13 European Convention on the Legal Status of Children Born out of Wedlock of 15 Oct.1975, Rev.dr.unif. 1975 I 278 ' European Treaty Series No. 85.

14 European Convention on Recognition and Enforcement of Decisions Concerning Custody of Children and on Restoration of Custody of Children (the 'Custody Convention') of 20 May 1980, European Treaty Series No. 105.

15 European Convention on the Exercise of Children's Rights of 25 jan. 1996, European Treaty Series No. 160.

16 See M. Harremoes, 'Le Conseil d'Europe et le droit de la famille', in R. Ganghofer (ed.), *Le droit de la famille en Europe – Son évolution depuis l'antiquité jusqu'à nos jours*, Strasbourg, Presses Universitaires de Strasbourg, 1992, p. 9 *et seq.*; M. Requena, 'Activities of the Council of Europe in the Field of Family Law', *Cal. W. Int. L.J.*, 31, 2000, p. 53 *et seq.*

true for the Commission Internationale de l'Etat Civil (CIEC) which concentrates on a relatively narrow field.[17]

1.8. Cultural Differences

The fact that cultural differences will prevent harmonization of family law is another argument against harmonization. Family law seems to be so entangled with national culture, religious traditions and customs, that it is not possible to harmonize this field of law. Why attack the cultural diversity in Europe only to make things the same? In response, one should note that the living conditions within the European internal market develop in an increasingly similar fashion and that in addition major family law trends within the European Union seem to be similar. Of course, there is still a great deal of diversity. Nevertheless, different religious influences are no longer so convincing and there is more openness to discussing different approaches. In former times the law focused on status. There is a tendency today to concentrate instead on the question of real existing personal relationships.[18] Many legal concepts only concern technical details, so that in some respects no contradictions within legal culture will arise.

Apart from that history also shows that family law concepts can be transposed from one country to another. For Roman Law and Common Law concepts this is self-evident. The recent development of statutes on same-sex couples seems to be another argument against the thesis of a cultural diversity, which allegedly blocks harmonization. Alternatively, this development also shows that more co-ordination between EU Member States is necessary. At the start of the reforms some Member States reacted to the newly created registered partnership laws by applying their national public policy clause. More disquieting, however, is the fact that the European Court of Justice did not recognize the registered partnership as a family relationship in the sense of a benefits scheme. The Court was even reluctant to apply the newly codified anti-discrimination provision in Art. 13 of the EC Treaty.[19]

1.9. The US Example

The example of the United States is presented as yet another argument against harmonization. The US experience shows that even within one nation one can get along without a unification of family law. There is some truth in this argument. However, within a country where most state laws are based on common law principles, diversity is less disturbing than in Europe, where there is greater diversity. More important, however, is that there also exist many uniform laws in the field of

17 J.-M. Bischoff, 'La Commission Internationale de l'Etat Civil (C.I.E.C.)', in R. Ganghofer (ed.), *Le droit de la famille en Europe – Son évolution depuis l'antiquité jusqu'à nos jours,* Strasbourg, Presses Universitaires de Strasbourg, 1992, p. 85 *et seq.*

18 Cf. I. Schwenzer, *Vom Status zur Realbeziehung,* Baden-Baden, Nomos, 1987.

19 ECJ 17 Feb. 1998 - Case C-249/96 (*Grant/South-West Trains Ltd.*), ECR 1998, I-621.- Cf. N. Bamforth, 'Sexual Orientation Discrimination after Grant v South-West Trains', *MLR,* 65, 2000, p. 694.

US family law dealing with, inter alia, parentage, maintenance and custody. These uniform laws indicate the existence of at least some sort of uniformity. Thus, even in the United States there is also an intense debate on a certain federalization of family law.[20]

1.10. No Legal Basis for a Harmonization

It is often held that the EC has no legal competence for a unification of family law. That is correct. There is a certain consensus that for contract law, Art. 95 EC Treaty could be a sufficient basis, but for family law no such legal basis exists. However, the fundamental freedoms are applicable in all fields of law. Today the EC already possesses legal competence under Art. 65 of the EC Treaty for international civil procedure, including family matters.[21] The so-called Brussels II Regulation on jurisdiction, recognition and enforcement in the field of divorce and parental responsibility shows that the EC is entering the field. A competence may be relatively easily added if there is enough consensus among the Member States and there are convincing concepts that call for unification.

1.11. Harmonization of Private International Law

Why is the harmonization of private international law not sufficient? In general, the Member States of the European Community ratify the Hague conventions in the field of international family law. The European Community has, so far, not enacted any legislation dealing directly with substantive private international law. The situation is different in the field of international civil procedure. In particular, the new Regulation on jurisdiction and recognition in the field of matrimonial affairs and child custody of 2000 ('Brussels II') is a step in the direction of more uniformity.[22]

This demonstrates that there is at least a need for uniformity in the field of private international law,[23] but it is not the final stage of the development.[24] There are new European initiatives that call for a much simpler recognition of custody decisions and enforcement of maintenance decisions. Of course, in applying the new instruments, possible new obstacles will be discovered and, at least in the long run, the rules of European Private International law will be amended by some other substantial rules. Experience shows, however, that despite an increasingly perfect

20 A.C. Dailey, 'Federalism and Families', *U.Pa.L.Rev.* 143, 1995, p. 1788 *et seq.*; R.M. Buxbaum, 'Family Law and the Federal System', in *Gedächtnisschrift Lüderitz,* München, Beck, 2000, p. 87 *et seq.*

21 C. Kohler, 'L'article 220 du traité CEE et les conflits de juridictions en matière de relations familiales, premières réflections', *Riv.dir.int.priv.proc.*, 28, 1992, p. 221 *et seq.*

22 Regulation on Jurisdiction and Recognition and Enforcement of Judgments in Matrimonial Matters of Parental Responsibility for Children of both Spouses of 29 May 2000, (2000) *OJ* L 160/19.

23 Even against this C. McGlynn, *supra* note 7, p. 232 *et seq.*

24 Cf. P.E. McEleavy, 'International Contact – Where Does the Future Lie?' *IFL*, 2000, p. 55 *et seq.*

co-ordination of national systems of laws, new discrepancies and complications in the application of those conflict rules emerge.

1.12. The Result is Insecure

As the results of harmonization efforts seem to be insecure some may hesitate and stop short of supporting harmonization. True, at present an exact prognosis of upcoming developments does not seem to be possible. Nevertheless, even the attempts for harmonization will stimulate research and will make the results of future regulations – however modest they may be – more convincing. Unfortunately today solutions in family law are found too often without much comparison. In conclusion, most of the counter arguments presented above have some merit, and they should be considered. The result, however, after having 'counted and weighed' these counter-arguments, is 'found wanting'.

2. Where to Start and in which Way?

Even after evaluating all these arguments and counter-arguments relatively little has been achieved. Substantive work is required, which calls for a certain consensus on the subject, the goal, the methods and technique to be followed and, of course, a substantive basis.

2.1. Definition of European Family Law

First, one should know what one is talking about when a 'European family' is at stake. For those teaching family law in a Civil Law country the answer seems to be fairly straightforward. European family law mainly should concentrate on the same fields, as the national rules, i.e. the relations between husband and wife (law of marriage in a broad sense), the parent-child relation and the protection of incapable persons. However, also in Community Law, there are rules dealing with family questions, for instance, relating to immigration and social security. In this respect there also exists some case law of the European Court of Justice. Preferably, within the national systems when Community rules are applied the definition of family relations should be the same. Such is the requirement of legal security and uniformity within the European Community – yet these questions should not be confused with family law as such.[25]

A similar borderline is to be drawn as concerns family policy. There are many European documents dealing with family questions, for instance, the situation of parents, children or the elderly. Family law questions are only mentioned incidentally. It should be clear that family law as such is not the same as family policy and social security.[26]

25 Cf. however C. McGlynn, *supra* note 7, p. 224 *et seq.*

26 But see C. McGlynn, *supra* note 7, p. 229 *et seq.*

2.2. *Harmonization instead of Unification*

At the moment it seems to be impossible to develop uniform rules in the form a codification for several countries. Not only are the national solutions different in many details, but the legal framework is quite different in the Member States. It must be stressed that there is no immediate need for the same provision to be in force in all countries of the European Community. A unification that seeks the same text for all Member States of the European Community may be too ambitious and even undesirable. However, harmonization in the form of principles, without too many details, seems to be feasible. These principles can focus on the basic rules with examples and explanations. Later, the principles can be used as a model for national statutes, but also for future European legislation in the field of family law.

The main goal of the principles should be to promote a common legal standard in the field of family law within the European Community. The principles identify the majority of solutions, the elaboration of a common core and its formulation. The content of the principles should be orientated according to the values of the Community legislation mentioned before. Legal policy also should play a certain role. In cases where there are different solutions possible alternatives should also be mentioned, and experiences with certain solutions evaluated. The principles should be detailed enough to cover the most important alternatives in the respective fields.

2.3. *The Task of Research*

One major problem will be research. At present, there is already more comparative research than was previously the case. For example, there are results of expert conferences held in a wide fora: the Council of Europe; conferences of the international society of family law; regular conferences held in Regensburg dealing with specific aspects of family;[27] regular reviews on foreign family law;[28] encyclopædias also on foreign family law; collections of translations of foreign statutes such as the German Bergmann/Ferid;[29] several books providing an overview of different systems;[30] detailed comparative studies; and there is of course existing national material on the respective family law systems. Teaching comparative family law, which may be facilitated by the publication of a new case book,[31] should not be ignored. Much of this material unfortunately is scattered over different countries of the Community and not accessible everywhere, and at times it is often outdated or

27 See D. Henrich and D. Schwab (eds.), *Beiträge zum Europäischen Familienrecht* (7 volumes), Bielefeld, Gieseking, 1994-1999.

28 A. Bainham, *The international survey of family law 2000*, Bristol, Jordan, 2001.

29 A. Bergmann, M. Ferid and D. Henrich (eds.), *Internationales Ehe- und Kindschaftsrecht*, 14 vol., Bielefeld, Verlag für Standesamtswesen, 1994 *et seq.*

30 Cf. C. Hamilton and K. Standley, *Family Law in Europe*, London, Butterworths, 1995.

31 W. Pintens and K. Vanwinkelen, *Casebook European Family Law*, Leuven, Leuven University Press, 2001.

not detailed enough. Despite the fact that the initial reforms in matrimonial law and parent and child relations of the post-Second World War period are now legal history, family law is still in a state of rapid change, making more research, collection of material and comparative work necessary. Without a system of reliable national reports on the basis of questionnaires, advancing common principles and solutions, progress will be impossible. This means that the preparation of these principles will be time consuming and also costly, thereby calling for a model for the funding of the research. One of the main tasks of the recently created Commission on European Principles of Family Law will be the development of such a practical approach. The difficulty and the extent of the task, however, make it inevitable that without a sound financial basis the formulation of common principles may well remain a fata morgana.

2.4. The Fields of Harmonization

Another major problem concerns the fields of harmonization. There is obviously some pressure in the areas with which the Community regulations deal and in the fields where there is a practical need. Nevertheless, it is difficult to find a totally convincing answer with which to begin.

As mentioned above, one subject could be marital property, as the obligations of the spouses are an important question for commercial and financial affairs, as well as for consumer transactions.[32] The idea of creating a special European marital property regime has been proposed.[33] Despite this need and the connection with activities within the internal market there is some hesitation. Of course there are basic types of separate and community property; apart from this, however, marital property is a difficult subject. The details are closely connected to contract law and also to property law and the law of succession. It must be said that harmonization of succession law seems to be even more difficult.[34]

A field undergoing relatively new developments is that of the rules on same-sex partnerships. After the implementation of the new rules a period of reshaping is to be expected. Parental responsibility and contact between parents and the child is on the agenda of the Council of Europe.[35] For the moment it appears that the prerequisites and, namely, the consequences of divorce seem to be a subject boasting a certain consensus and experience.

32 Cf. A. Verbeke *et al.*, 'European marital property law - Survey 1988 - 1994', *ERPL*, 3, 1995, p. 445 *et seq.*

33 See A. Agell, 'Towards Uniforming Spouses Property Rights, Especially in International Marriages?', *Proceedings 3rd European Conference on family law,* Cadiz 20-22 April 1995, Council of Europe, p. 63 *et seq.*

34 See A. Verbeke and Y.-H. Leleu, 'Harmonization of the Law of Succession in Europe', in A.S. Hartkamp *et al.* (eds.), *Towards a European Civil Code,* second edition, Nijmegen, Den Haag, Ars Aequi Libri, Kluwer Law International, 1998, p. 173 *et seq.*; W. Pintens, 'Die Europäisierung des Erbrechts', *ZEuP,* 2001, p. 628 *et seq.*

35 Draft Convention on Contact Concerning Children, *IFL,* 2000, p. 85.

3. Conclusion

The creation of an 'area of freedom, security and justice' in Europe should not exclude family law. In fact, the counter-arguments against a harmonization of family law generally are not convincing. There is a clear need for harmonization and to a certain extent one can identify tendencies in this direction, but the rules of private international law and international civil procedure alone are not sufficient. Nevertheless, a unification in a strict sense seems to be unrealistic and even a harmonization of family law based on the formulation of principle(s) is an ambitious and difficult task and one that is only possible with more research carried out on the national systems, together with a critical evaluation of the different solutions.

Civil Liability

Ulrich Magnus

TOWARDS EUROPEAN CIVIL LIABILITY

1. Introduction

1.1. Common Foundations

In dealing with the developments leading towards European civil liability, some introductory remarks concerning the legal history and tradition common to this continent seem appropriate. European heritage includes Roman law, which was rediscovered and interpreted at Europe's first law academy in Bologna and formed the basis of most legal systems for centuries to come. Similarly fundamental changes can be witnessed today. Europe has yet again entered into an era of awakening comparable to the Renaissance, during which long-established ideas were revived and adapted to new demands. Though perhaps buried under the framework of national states, the 'formative era of the European Union' necessitates some measure of reflection on this common European foundation.

1.2. Terminology

Civil liability comprises contractual as well as tortious liability. Since another Private Law workshop at this Conference already deals with contracts, this discussion paper will focus on the tort law aspect including strict liability. Further clarification is necessary as far as the use of the adjective 'European' is concerned. The term indicates both law set by the EU (e.g., the Product Liability Directive) as well as the whole body of private law to be found in Europe on the national levels. In using the term, this paper basically alludes to both meanings. The title of this presentation finally stresses the inherent dynamics of the development under discussion. We are presently witnessing the emergence of a system of civil liability common to all EU member States.

2. Unification of Law in Europe

The first question arising from the current trend towards a common European legal order, and which is not restricted to the field of civil liability alone, is whether such an order is at all desirable from a legal perspective. In view of the difficulty of providing a general answer, this paper will not attempt to decide whether legal unity or legal diversity is in general the more preferable approach. It suffices to identify whether there is any demand for a common system of civil extra-contractual liability.

Nevertheless, a few general arguments for a rather far-reaching unification or harmonization in Europe should be borne in mind. One such argument is the experience of the Common law world. Countries belonging to this system have found it extremely helpful to employ and develop a common set of legal rules, guided by the authoritative interpretation provided by the House of Lords[1]. Apart from that, law should always be committed to the idea of justice, which - as such - seems indivisible; there is no such thing as 'German', 'French' or 'European' justice. Legal diversity therefore does not exist when it comes down to the basic principles of justice (e.g., the idea of equality before the law and equal protection and benefit of the law). Finally, diversity is not the only safeguard of adaptability as is sometimes said; legal systems can ensure their flexibility and remain open to change by employing a number of mechanisms, including permanent law commissions and *ad hoc* reform committees.

3. The Need for a Common System of Civil Liability

There is no question that every legal system needs some form of non-contractual civil liability if *might* is not to prevail over *right*. This is also true for Europe, which needs a law of delict. It is quite another question, though, whether there is demand for a *common* law of delict or whether the numerous (and often diverging) systems of tort law presently functioning on the national levels suffice. Especially tort law thereby provides weighty arguments in favour of a common system of tortious liability.

Some of these reasons flow from EU law. To begin with, there is obviously a discrepancy between the postulate of 'an area without internal frontiers'[2] and the existence of different levels of third party liability. As long as EU citizens crossing borders within the Union without switching the means of transportation or even identifying themselves to foreign border police officers *inevitably* change the system of tortious liability when entering another Member State, the present diversity of rules must inhibit free mobility. The same is true for the free movement of goods and services since the risk of non-contractual liability and the degree of non-

1 This is also true for countries who gained independence long ago, e.g., Australia, India or Canada. The judiciary of these countries still holds English decisions as 'persuasive authorities' in high regard.

2 Art. 14 (2) [ex Art. 7a] Treaty establishing the EC' TEC/'Treaty'.

contractual compensation can vary considerably from country to country. These differences are aggravated by the fact that the international private law of most Member States basically focuses on the place of a tortious act as point of reference when determining the law to be applied in a given case.[3] This approach fails to justify why a car driver travelling the short distance from Trier to Metz is compensated differently depending on whether he was injured in Germany, Luxemburg or France. This legal patchwork resembles the German particularism of the 19th century when travellers crossing the country in stagecoaches changed the relevant law with each change of horses.

Common rules of tortious liability are also necessary in response to a number of factual developments, especially the high mobility of EU citizens and the increasing exchange of goods and services across European national borders. People travelling regularly in a certain area do not want to be confronted with differing and often even unknown rules of law, especially when it comes to the general rules of civil liability. Europe has become a homogeneous living space for its citizens. This is highlighted by the annual number of tourists travelling across Europe, the frequent dispatching of employees, the great number of students who chose to study in other parts of the continent and the exchange of visits between school children within Europe. The demand for a common system of civil liability is also underscored by the fact that additional insurance is often felt necessary in order to cover the risks created by different levels of liability and compensation when carrying out work or study stays and recreational trips within Europe.

The more Europe becomes one single living area the greater the need for uniform rules on how to behave within this area and how to compensate when some tortious act has happened.

On the other hand, there are also good arguments against unification. Justice requires not only that like things are treated alike but also the ability to distinguish where differences exist. There are different living standards and different living costs in Europe's many regions.

These factual differences have to be recognized by the law; as far as compensation is concerned tort law should reflect these differences. However, the basic rules of whether a person should be liable do not regularly depend on such differences.

A further argument against uniform tort rules could be drawn from the existing differences between the legal tradition and cultures of the European countries. However, these differences should not be overestimated. It is the experience of almost every legal comparatist that countries with different legal concepts and traditions rather often reach the same solution when concrete cases have to be decided. Moreover, most differences between the different European law families have developed or have been even intentionally created during the centuries under

3 For Germany see Art. 40 Einführungsgesetz zum Bürgerlichen Gesetzbuch (EGBGB); for France compare Audit, *Droit international privé*, 2nd ed., 1997, no. 777; for Great Britain compare Dicey/Morris, *The Conflict of Laws*, 13th ed., 2000, p. 1543 *et seq.*; for Italy see Art. 62 of the Act concerning private international law (dating 1995); for Austria see § 48 of the Act concerning private international law (dating 1978) in the version of 1999.

the reign of the idea of absolutely sovereign national states. For half a century this idea has been more and more supplanted by the idea of integration of states - not only in Europe but world-wide. Therefore, existing legal tradition and legal culture loses much of its appeal when a new tradition and culture is formed.

4. EU Competency for Non-contractual Civil Liability

Presently, the EU does not have a general and comprehensive competency to enact civil law. The European Union may only (1) regulate certain aspects of distinct areas of private law; and (2) enact general rules of horizontal application which promote legal harmonization with respect to requirements flowing from the internal market.[4]

4.1. Competency to Regulate certain Aspects of Non-contractual Civil Liability

Especially important competencies to regulate certain aspects of non-contractual civil liability exist in the fields of human health protection (Art. 152 TEC);[5] environment (Art. 174 et seq. TEC)[6] and consumer protection (Art. 153 TEC);[7] other areas comprise transport policy (Art. 70 et seq. TEC) and Trans-European networks (Art. 154 *et seq.* TEC).[8] Finally, the EU has a competency concerning the working conditions of employees,[9] which should also cover efforts aimed at the harmonization of liability in employment situations (Arts. 136 and 137 TEC).[10]

It has to be stressed that the competency concerning human health protection does not allow measures aimed at harmonization, as expressly stated in Art. 152 (4) lit. c TEC. Efforts aimed at the harmonization of civil liability with respect to improved health protection (e.g., of persons who have suffered personal injury) must therefore be based on other competencies. Art. 152 (4) lit. c TEC does not prohibit this.[11]

The competency of the EU to deal with environmental issues and consumer protection allows the introduction of common rules concerning non-contractual liability, albeit only in these special areas. Art. 153 (3) TEC as well as Art. 175 (2) TEC refer to Art. 95 TEC and thus allow the enactment of harmonizing directives aimed at health protection. This is covered by both objectives.[12] It is submitted that health protection *also* includes a system of civil liability which ensures reasonable

4 N. Reich, *Bürgerrechte in der Europäischen Union*, Baden-Baden, Nomos Verlag, 1999, p. 76 *et seq.*

5 Ex Art. 129 TEC.

6 Ex Art. 130r-t TEC.

7 Ex Art. 129a TEC.

8 Ex Art. 129b *et seq.* TEC.

9 Unlike ex Art. 117 TEC, Art. 136 TEC now also addresses the EU.

10 Ex Art. 117 *et seq.* TEC.

11 H.B. Schmidt am Busch, in E. Grabitz and M. Hilf (eds.), *Kommentar zur Europäischen Union* (updated January 2000), München, C.H. Beck, Art. 129 EGV no. 9.

12 Arts. 153 (1), 174 (1) TEC.

settlements in cases of personal injury, granting victims adequate compensation and rehabilitation.

As far as traffic regulation is concerned, it seems doubtful whether the EU could enact common rules of tortious liability on this basis. Authorization in this specific area may flow from Art. 71 (1) lit. c and d TEC, but it is questionable whether rules of tortious liability help to 'improve transport safety' or otherwise promote the purposes of traffic policy. The competency to regulate questions of traffic is aimed at the development of common terms of competition for commercial traffic in order to create an unrestricted market for professional transportation within Europe.[13] A common system of non-contractual liability for all traffic participants would probably exceed this restricted intention followed by the Treaty establishing the EEC. It is also questionable whether the safety of traffic can be improved by rules of tortious liability. Taking into account that tort law does have some influence on the readiness of persons participating in motorized traffic to avoid harm both for themselves and others, it is submitted that a broad interpretation of Art. 71 TEC would allow the EU to enact common rules of tortious liability in the field of motorized traffic.

4.2. General Rules of Horizontal Application

Aside from the predominant special competencies to regulate certain areas discussed above, a system of harmonized tortious liability may also be based on the general rules of horizontal application provided for by the TEC.[14] It must be stressed, though, that these horizontal powers (Arts. 94 and 95 TEC) are assigned to specific purposes only since they allow measures necessary for 'the establishment and the functioning of the common market' - Art. 94 TEC -[15] or which have as their object 'the establishment and functioning of the internal market' - Art. 95 (1) TEC.[16] These purposes - to serve the common market or the internal market - have a strict reference to commercial interests; both market concepts are thereby often regarded as nearly identical.[17] Harmonizing measures based on Arts. 94 or 95 TEC must be market-related and therefore directed at the achievement of homogeneous socio-

13 N.A. Frohnmeyer, in E. Grabitz and M. Hilf (eds.), *Kommentar zur Europäischen Union* (updated January 2000), München, CH. Beck, Art. 74 EGV nos. 2 + 3; S.U. Pieper, '§ 29 Der Verkehr, in A. Bleckmann, *Europarecht*, 6th ed., Köln, Berlin, Bonn, München, Heymanns, 1997, no. 2409.

14 N. Reich, *supra* note 4, p. 80 *et seq.*

15 Ex Art. 100 TEC. Compare also Art. 3 (1) lit. h TEC.

16 Ex Art. 100a TEC.

17 See, e.g., B. Langeheine, in E. Grabitz and M. Hilf (eds.), *Kommentar zur Europäischen Union* (updated January 2000), München, C.H. Beck, Art. 100a no. 23; H.C. Eiden, § 26 Die Angleichung von Rechtsvorschriften, in A. Bleckmann, *Europarecht*, 6th ed., Köln, Berlin, Bonn, München, Heymanns, 1997, no. 2112 *et seq.*, whereas M. Schweitzer and W. Hummer, *Europarecht*, 5th ed., 1996, Neuwied, Luchterhand, no. 1066 *et seq.* and P.-C. Müller-Graff, 'Die Rechtsangleichung zur Verwirklichung des Binnenmarktes; , *EuR*, 1989, p. 107 differentiate between both concepts.

economic conditions.[18] This understanding is also implied by Art. 95 (10) TEC, a protective clause dealing with interim measures for non-economical reasons. Harmonization on the basis of these general rules is thus obviously linked to the commercial sphere, which does not include the relationship between private persons, e.g., neighbourhood disputes or liability between schoolchildren. In commercial contexts, Arts. 94 and 95 TEC differ insofar as Art. 94 TEC requires a *necessity* for harmonization whereas Art. 95 TEC merely prescribes *utility*.

Different rules of liability and corresponding different levels of compensation can arguably impair the functioning of the common market.[19] A real common market or (much less so) an internal market cannot develop if regional markets governed by different legal rules continue to exist. If – for example – liability for certain enterprises were less strict in Germany than in France, this would result in differing regional competitive conditions; customers would have difficulties in comparing the performance of enterprises in both countries and real competition between German and French competitors on a European scale would be distorted.

Legal differences also inhibit the functioning of a common market by motivating participants to adopt strategies which are solely based on these disparities – e.g., avoiding offering certain goods or services in countries with a high level of compensation or long periods of prescription.

The considerations underlying the Product Liability Directive[20] demonstrate that the legislative organs of the EU acknowledge the distortive effects of different systems of tortious liability. The Directive was based on the former Art. 100 TEC (which is now Art. 94 TEC) and justified with these distortive effects. The considerations state:

> 'The Council of the European Communities, having regard to the Treaty establishing the European Economic Community, and in particular Article 100 thereof,
>
> (...),
>
> Whereas approximation of the laws of the Member States concerning the liability of the producer for damage caused by the defectiveness of his products is necessary because the existing divergencies may distort competition and affect the movement of goods within the common market and entail a differing degree of protection of the consumer against damage caused by a defective product to his health or property;
>
> (...)
>
> has adopted this Directive'.

18 H.B. Langeheine, in E. Grabitz and M. Hilf (eds.), *supra* note 11, Art. 100a EGV no. 43.

19 M.J. Basedow, 'Das BGB im künftigen europäischen Privatrecht', *AcP 200*, 2000, p. 424 *et seq.*; W. Tilmann and W. van Gerven, 'Die Kompetenzen der EU zur Schaffung eines einheitlichen Europäischen Schuld- und Sachenrechts und die möglichen Rechtsgrundlagen', in C. von Bar *et al, Vergleichende Untersuchung der Privatrechtsordnungen der Mitgliedsstaaten der EU im Hinblick auf Diskriminierungen aus Gründen der Staatsangehörigkeit sowie zur Möglichkeit und Notwendigkeit der Schaffung eines Europäischen Zivilgesetzbuches. Europäisches Parlament – Generaldirektion Wissenschaft*, Projekt Nr. IV/98/44 (o.J., 1999), p. 205, 219 *et seq.*; for the field of contract law O. Lando, 'Why codify the European Law of contract?', *ERPL*, 5, 1997, p. 525.

20 Council Directive 85/374/EEC of 25 July 1985, *OJ* L 210 (7.8.1985), p. 29-33.

This reasoning is not restricted to the issues covered by the Directive; it applies to *every* harmful activity of legal subjects participating on the common market.

Since tort law can affect all industrial and commercial activities, differences in the system of tortious liability will invite companies to establish themselves in countries where they can operate under a lower risk of liability. Furthermore, burdens suffered by competitors on a common market due to different levels of liability are aggravated if private international law rules focus on a company's registered place of business instead of the place of a tortious act. This is, for example, prescribed by German private international law where both tortfeasor and victim have their permanent residence or registered place of business in the same country.[21] A German company which injures German tourists in Portugal or Spain will thus be held liable according to German tort law whereas local companies causing identical damage will only have to face the often less onerous consequences of Portuguese or Spanish tort law. These disparities lead to distortions of competition solely for legal reasons and thus inhibit the functioning of a common and internal market. This is particularly true for tort law since the parties involved cannot eliminate or reduce differences of tortious liability with preceding contractual agreements.

A competency of the EU to enact a harmonized system of non-contractual liability in the commercial sphere and vis-à-vis consumers must therefore be acknowledged.

It has to be stressed that this competency does not authorize the Union to create a common system of non-contractual liability for cases lying *outside* the commercial sphere - e.g., for tortious acts between private persons or damaging acts of private tortfeasors vis-à-vis professionals. Here, the regulative power of the EU is restricted to the special competencies dealing with traffic, working conditions and the environment as mentioned above. Even the competency to deal with consumer protection established by Art. 153 TEC fails to justify common rules in this sphere: Art. 153 TEC requires one party involved to be a consumer needing protection and the other a predominant professional market participant; consumer protection can thus not be invoked in order to regulate the relationship between private persons.

The competency of the EU to enact a common system of tortious liability is thus restricted to the non-contractual liability of persons carrying on a trade as well as specific areas such as environment, traffic and working conditions. As far as these competencies are concerned, EU citizens are therefore only addressed in specific functions - as persons carrying on a trade, as suppliers of commercial traffic or employees et cetera. This also means that even an extensive use of these competencies would only result in a patchwork of horizontal and specialized systems of non-contractual liability. At this point it has to be stressed that the Treaty addresses nearly every aspect of life and that - since Maastricht - the EU citizen is thereby viewed as a unity rather than in terms of more or less distinguishable market activities (Arts. 17 - 22 TEC).[22] Furthermore, a mixture of horizontal and

21 Art. 40 (2) EGBGB.

22 M. Hilf in E. Grabitz and M. Hilf, *supra* note 11, Art. 8 EGV no. 2 *et seq.*

specialized systems of non-contractual liability would be unnecessarily complicated and thus rather senseless. These considerations influence the interpretation of the Treaty as far as the above mentioned competencies are concerned. In areas extensively covered by EU competencies, remaining gaps in the legislative authority should be filled by accepting an implied competency to regulate interrelated issues.[23] This is also true for the field of non-contractual civil liability.

The European Court of Justice has declared that provisions of the Treaty include competencies, 'without which (that treaty or law) would have no meaning or could not be reasonably and usefully applied'.[24]

A consistent form of non-contractual civil liability suitable for the demands of the internal market can only be reached through a single comprehensive and uniform system. Numerous coexistent and specialized provisions, which would have to include harmonized rules as far as fundamental issues such as causation, wrongfulness, fault, damage etc are concerned, would be neither wise nor workable. In view of the sum of special and horizontal competencies to regulate questions of liability laid down in the Treaty establishing the EC, it is thus submitted that the EU is competent to enact a comprehensive system of non-contractual civil liability.

5. Non-contractual Civil Liability in the Decisions of the European Court of Justice

The European Court of Justice has frequently, and in different contexts, addressed questions of non-contractual civil liability, particularly in view of Art. 288 (2) TEC.[25] The Court has thereby circumscribed certain fundamental issues of tort law - e.g., causation,[26] damage[27] and contributory negligence.[28] This legal practice of the European Court of Justice has not yet developed into an independent and coherent system of non-contractual civil liability, but important foundations of such a system have been set up. It seems essential to include these core elements in future European developments. With respect to the limited scope of this paper, it must suffice to indicate the existence of these structures; a detailed analysis of the Court's decisions is not possible at this point.[29]

23 N. Reich, *supra* note 4, p. 370; A. Bleckmann, in A. Bleckmann, *supra* note 13, no. 800.

24 Judgement of the Court of 29 November 1956, *Fédération Charbonnière de Belgique v High Authority of the European Coal and Steel Community* (Case 8-55), English Special Edition 1955 page 292 (299) ' EuGH Slg. 1956, 2975, 312 [Rn. 15]; see also F.H. Wenig, in E. Grabitz and M. Hilf (eds.), *Kommentar zur Europäischen Union* (updated January 2000), München, Ch. Beck, Art. 173 EWGV no. 26.

25 Ex Art. 215 (2) TEC.

26 EuGH Slg. 1979, 30.91 (*Dumortier Frères, verb.* Rs. 64, 113/76; 176, 239/78; 27, 29, 45/79).

27 EuGH Slg. 1976, 1 (*Produits Bertrand,* Rs. 40/75); EuGH Slg. 1994 I 341 (*Grifóni II,* Rs. 308/87).

28 EuGH Slg. 1985, 3539 (*Adams,* Rs. 154/83).

29 Compare U. Magnus and W. Wurmnest, *Casebook Europäisches Haftungs- und Schadensrecht* (forthcoming 2002) and W. Wurmnest, *Das Haftungs- und Schadensrecht in der Rechtsprechung des EuGH* (Diss. Hamburg, forthcoming 2002).

6. The Development of General Principles of Non-contractual Liability

Once the demand for a common system of non-contractual liability in Europe is recognized and the basic competency of the EU to legislate in this area is acknowledged, the question arises as to how this system should be enacted.

A first step is to describe the objective. The end of the envisaged harmonization should be marked by a common and binding text which reflects the basic codifiable principles of non-contractual civil liability in a clear and systematic form without regulating each and every detail. A common and binding text in all languages of the Union is necessary for reasons of clarity, publicity and transparency of the law. Since the Codex Hammurabi was chiselled into a market pillar, it is not enough to enact law merely through tradition or custom. Even Common law is based on written law reports which reflect the legal wisdom developed by the judiciary. The objective must therefore be the development of a document formulated in legal terms - this could be a treaty, a directive or a regulation - which comprises the basic rules of tortious liability.

Once this objective is agreed upon, it is also clear that a patchwork of legislation - as enacted by the EC thus far, e.g., with the Product Liability Directive - will not suffice. It is necessary to develop a systematic compilation of the whole body of non-contractual civil liability. It must also be remarked that this work cannot be done by the activity of the European Court of Justice since the Court is only concerned with certain aspects of general tort law.

Finally, it is submitted that this task does not have to be accomplished in one single step. The 'Lando-model', by which general principles are developed by a group of independent academics working on the basis of a comparison of the European legal systems (similar to a European Restatement, albeit including a search for the best solution) also seems to be a suitable *modus operandi* for the development of a common system of tort law.[30] In a second phase, the merits of these principles would be open for general academic and professional discussion on a European scale, followed by a third phase which would involve the political and legislative process leading to their enactment. In the field of tort law, the European Group on Tort Law (the former Tilburg Group) set itself the task of developing European General Principles of Tort Law some time ago.[31] The Group consists of academics specialized in tort law from nearly every Member State of the EU.[32] Eastern Europe is represented by interested academics from countries willing to contribute to the work of the Group. Eminent academics from Switzerland, the United States, South Africa and Israel complete the team, giving precious input from heterogeneous legal systems well familiar with (the internal) harmonization of law. Some results of the

30 The Lando-Group has already accomplished large parts of this task for the field of contract law, *see* O. Lando and H. Beale, *Principles of European Contract Law* (Parts I and II), The Hague, Kluwer Law International, 2000.

31 See J. Spier and O. Haazen, 'The European Group on Tort Law and the European Principles of Tort Law', *ZEuP*, 1999, p. 469.

32 Germany is represented by the author of this discussion paper.

work are already published.[33] The Group will present a comprehensive compilation of the European Principles of Tort Law in the near future.

7. Elements and Principles of Tortious Liability

7.1. Introduction

Most legal systems both inside and outside Europe share a large number of mutual elements of tort law. Though it is true that these elements do not always have the same significance in each legal order, they are nonetheless the source from which a common system of tortious liability can be developed.

7.2. The Function of Tort Law

From a formal perspective, tort law defines the conditions under which a person who has suffered harm can demand compensation from another person in the absence of a contractual or other special relationship which would otherwise determine the legal status between the parties involved. This definition demarcates the border between the general risk of having to carry the consequences of harmful events *individually* and situations which allow victims to shift these negative consequences to others who subsequently have to carry the economical burden of these harmful events. This borderline does not have a predetermined natural course. It is rather determined on the basis of valuations which are not fundamentally different but may at least vary in detail from society to society. These valuations include - on the one hand - the interest of the victim to receive protection and compensation and - on the other hand - the interest of the tortfeasor in free and unrestricted activity and in the development of his personality. The predominant objective of tort law in Europe is thus to secure an adequate level of protection and a reasonable compensation for victims *without* unnecessary restrictions of the tortfeasor's freedom of action.

At the same time, tort law has some preventive effect and influence on the conduct of persons due to the impeding sanction of enforceable damages as well as the defence of contributory negligence. It must be stressed that preventive and punitive aims are pursued to very different degrees in Europe. Whereas English law emphasizes that the law of tort does (and indeed: should) fulfil punitive and - more

33 J. Spier (ed.), *The Limits of Liability: Keeping the Floodgates Shut*, The Hague, London, New York, Kluwer Law International, 1996; J. Spier (ed.), *The Limits of Expanding Liability: Eight Fundamental Cases in a Comparative Perspective*, The Hague, London, New York, Kluwer Law International, 1998; H. Koziol (ed.), *Unification of Tort Law: Wrongfulness*, The Hague, London, New York, Kluwer Law International, 1998; J. Spier (ed.), *Unification of Tort Law: Causation*, The Hague, London, New York, Kluwer Law International, 2000; U. Magnus (ed.), *Unification of Tort Law: Damages*, The Hague, London, New York, Kluwer Law International, 2001; B.A. Koch and H. Koziol (eds.), *Unification of Tort Law: Strict Liability*, The Hague, London, New York, Kluwer Law International, 2002.

often - preventive functions,[34] German law is far more reserved as far as these elements are concerned.[35]

All in all it can be said that tort law is not limited to one single aim; it rather serves a larger number of different regulative aims, among which compensation is certainly regarded as the most important.

7.3. *Reasons for Delictual Responsibility*

It is generally accepted throughout Europe that delictual responsibility for harm suffered by another person necessarily presupposes a special reason. Furthermore, all legal systems agree that delictual responsibility is not based on a single principle. A common heritage is *fault-based* liability, which was the predominant reason for liability during the Age of Enlightenment and in the first phase of industrialization. Fault-based liability still is an important - albeit not exclusive - reason for delictual responsibility. Whoever fails to behave according to the standard required of the average person in a certain situation must bear the responsibility for the consequences.[36]

Another strong and increasingly important pillar of tortious liability is the responsibility following from the pursuit of certain especially dangerous activities and from certain dangerous objects or things. Fault is thus not necessary; persons who create or control an increased potential of risk are therefore automatically responsible for the harm caused by the source of this risk. Among European legal systems, there are significant differences in the evaluation of the factors which are recognized as sources of special danger. Whereas most EU Member States regard the operation of a motorized vehicle as a source of high danger which makes the keeper or registered user liable regardless of fault,[37] this is not the case in Great Britain and Ireland. Here, compensation for harm caused by motorized traffic is subject to fault, even if the principles employed by the judiciary are fairly strict.[38] Another question answered differently in many countries concerns the analogous application of recognized strict liability regimes to similarly dangerous circumstances. This is strictly rejected by the German judiciary,[39] whereas the Austrian Supreme Court has allowed it;[40] the Italian Codice Civile even expressly recognizes

34 See P.H. Winfield J.A. Jolowicz, *On Tort* ,15th ed., London, Sweet& Maxwell, 1998, p. 2.

35 See N.H. Lange, *Schadensersatz,* 2nd ed., Tübingen, Mohr Siebeck, 1990, p. 9 *et seq.*; K. Larenz, *Schuldrecht,* Münich, Ch. Beck, 1987, § 27 I: Prevention is 'erwünschtes Nebenprodukt'; H.J. Mertens, in *Münchner Kommentar zum Bürgerliches Gesetzbuch,* 3rd ed., 1997, vor §§ 823-853 nos 29 *et seq.*: 'Sekundärfunktionen'.

36 See M.J. Domat, *Les loix civiles dans leur ordre naturel,* Paris, Nyon, 1689, liv. II, tit. VIII, s. IV §§ 1, 3 for an early explanation: *Liability for 'imprudence, légereté, ignorance de ce qu'on doit savoir, ou autres fautes semblables'*.

37 E.g. in Germany (§ 7 *Strassenverkehrsgesetz*), France (Art. 1384 Cc) and Austria (EKHG).

38 See Nettleship v Weston [1971] 2 Q.B. 691 (driving school pupil was regarded as negligent for failing to employ the care of a diligent - experienced - driver).

39 BGHZ 55, 229; BGH VersR 1972, 1047.

40 OGH SZ 21/46; 48/131; *ÖJZ* 1992, 584.

liability for a dangerous activity ('attività pericolosa'), as long as the tortfeasor cannot prove the observance of every possible care.[41]

Finally, responsibility for one's personal sphere of living is also recognized as a reason for liability in some systems. Under English and French law, persons who have certain (normally harmless) objects in their care or sphere of influence are therefore often held liable without fault for harm caused to third persons.[42]

All things considered, liability depends not only on causation but also on the requirement of a special justification. This justification is always given in cases of fault as well as in many situations characterized by special dangers; it may also result from responsibility for one's personal sphere of living.

7.4. Protected interests

It is trite knowledge that many European legal systems do not recognize a clear catalogue of absolutely protected rights and interests: French law operates with the famous general clause contained in Art. 1382 CC which grants compensation for *every* kind of harm. Under Common law, the different interests of victims are protected by specific rules of tort law. An intermediate approach is followed by the German Bürgerliches Gesetzbuch which enumerates by way of example the most important legal interests in § 823 (1) BGB. It must be noted, however, that the latter solution was not alone guided by factual or legal considerations; it was also the motive of national demarcation which led the German draftsman to reject the model provided by Art. 1382 Code Civil and to adopt the enumerative list contained in § 823 (1) BGB instead.[43]

These differences are only superficial. It is generally accepted in all European legal systems that tort law does not provide protection for each and every loss. There is agreement that damages are only granted for the impairment of such legal positions that every member of a given society can reasonably expect to be preserved. These positions include the integrity of the person, of belongings and of absolute rights which have to be respected by everybody, e.g., real/property rights and intangible rights. The protection of pure economic interests is regarded as problematic and granted only under certain conditions. There are nevertheless also some differences in detail. Personality rights are protected in varying degrees –

41 Art. 2050 ital. Cc.

42 For France see Art. 1384 Code Civil (strict liability for the 'gardien' of an object); for Italy see the similar provision in Art. 2051 Cc; for England see Rylands v Fletcher (1868) L.R. J3 H.L. 330 (strict liability for dangerous objects or substances which escape from land and cause harm to others).

43 See, e.g., Motive II p. 22 for compensation of non-pecuniary loss: 'Durch allgemeine Anerkennung eines Entschädigungsanspruches wegen Verletzung eines nicht vermögensrechtlichen Interesses würde dem Richter jene dem deutschen Rechte fremde Souveränität seiner Stellung gegenüber dem Streitverhältnisse beigelegt, welche erst bei der Berathung der C.P.O. nach reiflicher Prüfung als bedenklich erfunden und deshalb verworfen wurde'. It is mainly French law which was meant with 'dem deutschen Rechte fremde(n) Souveränität'. For a detailed discussion of the genesis of § 253 BGB see U. Magnus, *Schaden und Ersatz*, Tübingen, Mohr Siebeck, 1987, p. 312 *et seq*.

some countries such as Great Britain[44] and Austria[45] only grant protection for certain aspects such as a name and image rights whereas other countries such as France[46] and Germany[47] recognize a comprehensive general right of personality (German: *allgemeines Persönlichkeitsrecht*) which provides for a higher level of protection in some cases, e.g., concerning truthful press coverage on private matters.[48] Grey areas are thereby admittedly unavoidable and - to a certain degree - even necessary in order to secure the flexibility and adaptability of legal systems vis-à-vis future developments.

7.5. *Causation*

One of the most important conditions of tortious liability is the element of causation. Adequate causation of harm is usually a precondition of liability. In essence, causation is dealt with similarly throughout Europe despite varying dogmatic concepts. In Belgium, causation is established merely on the basis of the conditio sine qua non rule; the system is thus a proponent of the theory of equivalent consideration (German: *Äquivalenzlehre*).[49] Common law is guided by the concept of remoteness.[50] Other systems - such as Germany and Greece - endorse the theory of adequate causation (German: *Adäquanzlehre*).[51] Yet another approach is chosen by Dutch law which first answers the question of causation on the basis of the conditio rule but then modifies the result (and thereby actually decides) with the help of a number of policy considerations.[52] To some extent - and despite their terminology -, adequate causation and remoteness actually follow along the same lines. The Dutch approach therefore represents the true common core of causation in Europe.[53]

44 J. Salmond and R.F.V. Heuston, *On the Law of Torts*, 21st ed., London, Sweet & Maxwell, 1996, p. 32 *et seq.*; P.H. Winfield and W.J.A. Jolowicz, *supra* note 34, p. 46 *et seq.*

45 See B. Schilcher and W. Kleewein, 'Landesbericht Österreich', in C. von Bar (ed.), *Deliktsrecht in Europa*, Köln, Heymanns, 1993/1994, p. 34.

46 See the French Act of 17.7.1970.

47 BGHZ 13, 334.

48 For Germany see BVerfG NJW 2000, 2191.

49 H. Cousy and A. Vanderspikken, 'Causation under Belgian Law', in J. Spier (ed.), *Unification of Tort Law: Causation*, The Hague, London, New York, Kluwer Law International, 2000, p. 23.

50 For a detailed description of this concept see P.H. Winfield and J.A. Jolowicz, *supra* note 34, p. 195 *et seq*, 207 *et seq*.

51 For Germany see BGHZ 7, 198 (204); BGHZ 57, 141; BGH NJW 1995, 127. For Greece see K. Kerameus, 'Causation under Greek Law', in J. Spier, *Unification of Tort Law: Causation*, The Hague, London, New York, Kluwer Law International, 2000, p. 75. In essence, Austria also follows these lines, although the test of adequate causation is not regarded as a question of causation but rather as a separate limitation of imputation: see H. Koziol, *Österreichisches Haftpflichtrecht*, Bd. I , 3rd ed., Wien, Manz, 1997, p. 91, 235 *et seq*.

52 See Art. 6:98 Nieuw Burgerlijk Wetboek of 1992.

53 See J. Spier and O. Haazen, 'Comparative Conclusions on Causation', in J. Spier (ed.), *Unification of Tort Law: Causation*, The Hague, London, New York, Kluwer Law International, 2000, p. 134.

7.6. *Wrongfulness*

Most European systems demand that the harm in question was caused by wrongful conduct. This means that a legal order regards certain events or results as prohibited by law and allows victims to take preventive measures (e.g., self-defence). On a dogmatic level, it is nevertheless disputed whether wrongfulness is actually a separate element of tort law. French and Belgian law regard wrongfulness as part of the basic element of 'faute' – more specifically as its objective component.[54] Different opinions also exist concerning the point of reference of wrongfulness. In some systems, it is the conduct which must have violated rules set by law in order to trigger liability (e.g., under Austrian law).[55] Other systems focus on the result of harmful behaviour when dealing with wrongfulness (e.g., Germany).[56] Yet other systems do not see the need for a general element of wrongfulness at all; this is true for English law, which defines prohibited behaviour separately for each and every tort.[57]

Additional difficulties arise as soon as strict liability comes into focus. Here, the activity is dangerous and yet *allowed*; no judge will thus grant an injunction against a neighbour who wants to use a vehicle or accept self-defence against a person who is about to drive away only because the potential victim fears being run over one day. That said, no one has to suffer injury in motorized traffic just because this is an activity allowed by the law; whereas potentially endangering behaviour may be admissible, this does not encompass injuries which can result from these activities. The problem of wrongfulness therefore is most relevant in the field of legal justifications which exclude liability for harm caused. These justifications are basically dealt with in a very similar way throughout Europe and most often include consent on the side of the victim as well as self-defence, acts in a state of emergency and allowed self-redress on the side of the tortfeasor.[58] The factor of wrongfulness will thus play a role in a common European system of tortious liability – at least when it comes to the exclusion of liability (defences).

In this context, *von Bar* has made the interesting proposal that a common European law of delict should do away with wrongfulness and legal justifications

54 See G. Viney, 'Le "Wrongfulness" en Droit Français', in H. Koziol (ed.), *Unification of Tort Law: Wrongfulness*, The Hague, London, New York, Kluwer Law International, 1998, p. 57; H. Cousy, 'Wrongfulness in Belgian Tort Law', in H. Koziol (ed.), *Unification of Tort Law: Wrongfulness*, The Hague, London, New York, Kluwer Law International, 1998, p. 31.

55 H. Koziol, *supra* note 51, p. 140.

56 BGH NJW 1996, 3205; H. Thomas, in P. Bassenge, *Palandt; Bürgerliches Gesetzbuch*, 61st ed., München, Beck, 2002, § 823 no. 32 *et seq.*

57 See W.V.H. Rogers, 'Wrongfulness under English Tort Law', in H. Koziol (ed.), *Unification of Tort Law: Wrongfulness*, The Hague, London, New York, Kluwer Law International, 1998, p. 39 *et seq.*

58 For Germany see §§ 227 *et seq.* BGB; for France see J. Flour and J.-L. Aubert, *Les obligations 2. Le fait juridique*, 6th ed., Paris, Colin, 1994, p. 107 *et seq.*; for Great Britain see P.H. Winfield and J.A. Jolowicz, *supra* note 34, p. 844 *et seq.* ('defences'); and for Austria see H. Koziol, *supra* note 51, p. 168 *et seq.*

altogether and rather introduce a system of general defences instead.[59] Since this category would mainly include the above mentioned legal justifications as well as contributory negligence, disclaimers and time limitations, it would not amount to much more than a change of terminology, thereby merging rather disparate elements.

7.7. *Fault*

Though liability may also result from other causes, it is a common core of European tort laws that fault - in any case - leads to liability. Persons who have harmed others in a way open to reproach must generally bear the consequences. This is regulated by codified law - e.g., in Art. 1382 Code Civil, § 823 (1) BGB, § 1295 ABGB, Art. 2043 ital. Codice Civile and Art. 6:162 Nieuw Burgerlijk Wetboek - and is also true for Common law, which has developed both a general rule of 'negligence' and demands 'negligence' as a precondition of liability in many torts.[60] It is also generally accepted that liability does not result from each and every negligent causation of any sort of harm. Instead, liability is limited - e.g., by focusing on certain legal interests (as in Germany), by demanding the violation of a duty of care (as in England)[61] or by the requirement of a direct relationship between the harm caused and the harmful activity (as in France).[62]

It is also generally accepted that any legal reproach for a given behaviour depends on an objective standard. Culpable behaviour can therefore result from harmful acts guided by intention as well as by a failure to comply with the behaviour which can be expected of a well-informed and reasonable person in a similar situation.[63] In a given case, the relevant standard of care will also depend on the concrete factual circumstances. This amounts to an objective standard of negligence based on the individual situation and is illustrated by an example taken from road traffic - bad sight (e.g., due to nightfall), a strongly curving road and a wet highway surface will evidently require a different style of driving than a dry and straight road in broad daylight.

Personal characteristics (both handicaps as well as additional capacities) are only of limited importance. The delictual capacity of minors and mentally incapable

59 C. von Bar, *Gemeineuropäisches Deliktsrecht*, Bd. II, Münich, Beck, 1999, no. 490.

60 For details see P.H. Winfield and J.A. Jolowicz, *supra* note 34, p. 90 *et seq.*

61 In England, certain legal interests are protected by particular torts whereas negligence demands the violation of a duty of care; see P.H. Winfield and J.A. Jolowicz, *supra* note 34, p. 90 *et seq.*

62 See G. Viney, *Les obligations. La responsibilité: conditions*, Paris, L.G.O.J., 1982, no. 273.

63 For Germany see H. Kötz, *Deliktsrecht*, 8th ed., Neuwied, Luchterhand, 1998, p. 47; for France see J. Flour and J.-L. Aubert, *supra* note 58, p. 93-94; for Great Britain see P.H. Winfield and J.A. Jolowicz, *supra* note 34, p. 171 *et seq.* Austrian law is more subjective in certain aspects; for details see H. Koziol, *supra* note 51, p. 203 *et seq.* For a recent comparative survey see G. Brüggemeier, *Prinzipien des Haftungsrechts*, Baden-Baden, Nomos, 1999, p. 62 *et seq.*

persons thus depends on subjective factors such as their insight into the consequences of their behaviour.[64]

These rare subjective impacts on fault and the objective approach to negligence described above pose the question of whether wrongfulness and fault should indeed be regarded as separate categories or whether they should not rather be combined to form one condition of liability (e.g., imputation). On the one hand, both areas certainly partially overlap as far as negligence demands the definition of general requirements - set by the objective legal order - to be met by the tortfeasor. On the other hand, both elements address different issues insofar as the legal justifycations discussed above, questions of intentional behaviour and the requirement of delictual capacity are involved. It is thus submitted that the imputation of tortious acts in the field of civil law should involve a *separate* examination of the objective components (e.g., the objective standard of behaviour and special legal justifications) as well as the subjective components (intention and tortious capacity), depending on their relevance for the case in question. The terminology employed for this procedure is therefore irrelevant. It is also clear that the proposed approach does not amount to one single question but rather to a number of different aspects which should be dealt with separately.

7.8. Damages

The greatest differences in the European concert of tort laws can probably be found in the area of damages and their compensation. There is a mutual starting point - the damage caused should lead to as much compensation as possible (restitutio in integrum)[65] - but even at this early stage many exceptions have to be noted, e.g., the fact that the level of compensation under Austrian law often depends on the degree of fault (§§ 1323, 1324 ABGB).[66] Similar difficulties exist as far as the definition of damage is concerned; the core elements correspond, but many borderline problems are solved differently. Basically, every (imputable) impairment of legal interests in the sphere of the victim amounts to a relevant damage, but this wide definition hardly serves to solve particular problems in given cases. Differences thus exist concerning the question whether and under which conditions non-pecuniary loss entitles victims to compensatory damages - e.g., whether the death or grave injury of a close relative should be compensated or whether other injuries of a victim's feelings (e.g., due to the death of a pet) are damages which require compensation. Further differences can be found on the borderline between pecuniary and non-

64 See, e.g., §§ 827/828 BGB; Art. 917 of the Greek Civil Code; Art. 2046 ital. Codice Civile; for Great Britain see P.H. Winfield and J.A. Jolowicz, *supra* note 34, p. 832, 839 *et seq*. A different approach is followed by Art. 489-2 of the French Code civil.

65 For Germany see § 249 BGB; for France (réparation intégrale) see G. Viney, *supra* note 62, no. 247; for Great Britain see P.H. Winfield and J.A. Jolowicz, *supra* note 34, p. 757.

66 See H. Koziol, *supra* note 51, for a discussion of these exceptions.

pecuniary loss; cases involving working capacity not put to economical use or the loss of spare time (leisure) are thus solved differently.[67]

Great differences also exist in the determination of the amount of compensation, especially as far as the method of computing the loss of income in cases of permanent personal injury is concerned. In England, a very standardized method is used which takes into consideration the expected income of the victim ('multiplicand') as well as a cleansed period of duration ('multiplier') based on average life expectancy.[68] In other EC Member States, the focus is more on the circumstances of the individual case. This is true, e.g., for Germany.[69]

Strong divergences also exist in the determination of non-pecuniary loss in cases of personal injury. The amount of compensation granted for the loss of an eye varies in EC Member States from 3.000 to 30.000 Euro and for quadriplegia from 5.000 to 250.000 Euro.[70] The same is true for the level of compensation granted for mental trauma due to the death or grave suffering of a close relative; victims may be denied compensation altogether (as a rule, in Germany), they may receive a fixed sum (as in England)[71] or flexible - but fairly high - amounts (as in France).[72]

Harmonization of the level of compensation in Europe seems especially important in the area of personal injury. Substantial differences in compensation of the non-material consequences of serious injuries - which are felt equally by most victims - cannot be justified. Not even the different costs of living in EC Member States can explain these huge differences in the compensation of non-material loss since they are not that substantial. Moreover, compensation for pain and suffering also has other functions besides pure compensation.

7.9. Contributory Negligence

Another common feature of European tort law is the possibility of reducing damages because of contributory negligence.[73]

Contributory negligence is basically established if the victim fails to comply with the behaviour that can be expected from a reasonable person in order to

67 See U. Magnus, 'Comparative Report on the Law of Damages', in U. Magnus (ed.), *Unification of Tort Law: Damages*, The Hague, London, New York, Kluwer Law International, 2001.

68 Ogden Tables; see also *Page v Sheerness Steel* [1999] 1 A.C. 345.

69 For details concerning the German approach see G. Schiemann, 'Ersatz des Entgelts für unselbständige Arbeit, in J. von Staudinger (ed.), *Kommentar zum Bürgerlichen Gesetzbuch mit Einführungsgesetz und Nebengesetzen*, 13th ed., Berlin, Sellier-de Gruyter, 1998, § 252 no. 33 *et seq*.

70 See the comparative survey in D.T.M. McIntosh and M. Holmes (eds.), *Personal Injury Awards in EC Countries. An Industry Report*, London, Loyd's of London, 1990, p. 16-17.

71 Sec. 1 A Fatal Accidents Act: £ 7.500 (for bereavement).

72 About FF 100.000 for the death of a spouse.

73 For Germany see § 254 BGB; for France see J. Flour and J.-L. Aubert, *supra* note 58, p. 124, 149, 170; for Greece see Art. 300 of the Greek Civil Code; for Great Britain see sec. 1 (1) Law Reform (Contributory Negligence) Act 1945; for Italy see Art. 1227 Codice Civile; for the Netherlands see Art. 6:101 Nieuw Burgerlijk Wetboek; for Austria see § 1304 ABGB; for Portugal see Art. 570 Código civil.

safeguard his own interests or - in the words of the eminent English judge Lord Denning: 'A person is guilty of contributory negligence if he ought reasonably to have foreseen that, if he did not act as a reasonable, prudent man, he might hurt himself'.[74] Since the person who has suffered injury is always (as a victim) concerned with the damage, contributory negligence is an important theoretical and - very often - also a relevant practical issue in many tort law cases. It is also an important instrument to influence the behaviour of potential victims and provides incentives to prevent harmful events.

Contributory negligence usually leads to a reduction of liability, the amount depending on the circumstances of the given case. Factors involved in the apportionment of damages include causation, fault and risk both on the sides of the victim and the tortfeasor, resulting in a distribution in the form of quotas. The principle of so-called culpa compensation - the complete denial of compensation in cases of contributory negligence - is hardly ever found today (Portuguese law prescribes this principle in cases of contributory negligence in the area of strict liability and presumed fault liability).[75]

Differences can also be discerned as far as the contributory negligence of minors is concerned. Some systems (e.g., Germany[76] and - as a rule - Austria)[77] demand tortious capacity and corresponding insight; contributory negligence of minors thus follows along the same lines as their delictual liability in general. Other systems (e.g., Great Britain) do not focus on strict age limits. Even very young children may therefore contribute to the negligent behaviour if they fail to comply with the specific standard of care relevant for children of their age.[78] In certain situations, yet other systems ignore contributory negligence of children completely. This is true for France as far as children under the age of 16 participating in public traffic are concerned. Elderly above the age of 70 and persons with a handicap of more than 80% are treated similarly.[79]

It seems necessary to develop common principles of contributory negligence in Europe, especially in the field of road traffic.

7.10. Vicarious Liability

Every system of tortious liability has to determine the conditions under which a person can be held liable for harm caused by others, especially by persons acting under his authority. In the great majority of European legal systems, vicarious liability for harm caused by others is established if a person makes use of somebody in his own interest (e.g., vicarious liability of the employer for harm caused by his

74 *Jones v Livox Quarries Ltd* [1952] 2 Q.B. 608 [615].

75 See Art. 505, 570 (2) Código Civil.

76 G. Schiemann, in J. von Staudinger, *supra* note 69, § 254 nos 39 *et seq.*

77 H. Koziol, *supra* note 51, p. 371 *et seq.*

78 P.H. Winfield and J.A. Jolowicz, *supra* note 34, p. 240-241. The same is true for tortious capacity under English law, which operates without strict age limits; see P.H. Winfield and J.A. Jolowicz, *supra* note 34, p. 832.

79 See the Loi Badinter: Act Nr. 85-677 of 5.7.1985.

employees).[80] Most European legal systems therefore do not differentiate according to whether these persons were well selected and supervized or not.[81] Under German law[82] and (to a certain extent) Austrian law,[83] the master (*Geschäftsherr*) may exculpate himself by providing proof of adequate selection and supervision. German jurisprudence has developed various ways of avoiding this rule,[84] which shows that a norm like § 831 BGB is unsuitable for a common European law of delict.

The conditions of liability for the tortious acts of others are fairly homogeneous throughout Europe. The test used to determine the master-servant relationship focuses on two elements – (1) the tortious act must have occurred during an assignment or within the general duties performed by the servant on behalf of the master; and (2) vicarious liability is excluded in cases where the servant was an independent contractor.

Another possible form of vicarious liability is the liability of parents and guardians for children or other persons put under their care. This category also includes liability of hospitals, specialized institutions and prisons for the actions of their patients, wards or prisoners. Quite different opinions exist as to whether (and under which conditions) those persons charged with custody or supervision should be liable vis-à-vis third persons.[85]

7.11. Time Limitation/Prescription

Prescription is a very important practical issue in the law of delict. European rules on prescription vary between one year in Spain[86] and 30 years in Luxembourg;[87] other countries prescribe three years,[88] five years,[89] six years[90] or ten years.[91] Time limitation usually begins with the harmful event, though some legal systems require knowledge of both the injury and the identity of the person liable to make compensation.

It is submitted that time limitation is yet another area which should be harmonized in order to develop a free and unrestricted internal European market.

80 See Art. 1384 (5) of the French Code civil; Art. 2049 of the Italian Codice Civile; Art. 6:170 Nieuw Burgerlijk Wetboek. For Great Britain see P.H. Winfield and J.A. Jolowicz, *supra* note 34, p. 693 *et seq.*

81 See the rules of French, Italian, Dutch and English law mentioned under note 80.

82 § 831 BGB.

83 Art. 1315 ABGB.

84 See thereon the recent work of H.G. Brüggemeier, *supra* note 63, p. 111 *et seq.*, 123 *et seq.*

85 See thereon C. von Bar, *Gemeineuropäisches Deliktsrecht*, Bd. I, Münich, Beck, 1996, p. 144 *et seq.*, 179/180.

86 Art. 1968 (2) Código Civil as the usual time limitation in tort law.

87 Art. 2262 Code Civil.

88 E.g., Germany (§ 852 BGB).

89 E.g., Greece (Art. 937 of the Greek Civil Code).

90 Great Britain (sec. 2 Limitation Act 1980).

91 France (Art. 2270-1 Code Civil).

8. Perspectives

The differences between the current laws of delict in Europe are - on a more detailed level - numerous and substantial. This brief survey of the basic elements of a possible European system of tortious liability has nevertheless shown that there are certain fundamental values common to most legal orders. The practical demand for a common system and the legal authority of the EU necessary to enact common rules are certainly given. Many of the differences in detail do not result from compelling reasons following from special local or other factual circumstances. They are rather - to a great extent - consequences of the epoch of nationalistic demarcation during which civil law was understood as an expression of national sovereignty and identity. Socialist law is thereby certainly a very striking example, but even the draftsmen of the German Bürgerliches Gesetzbuch were to some extent guided by the idea of creating something different from the French Code Civil.[92] For Europe, the era of separate national development has finally come to an end. The expansion of the EU due to the admission of new Member States will undoubtedly increase the pressure to replace the ever-growing legal diversity by a common set of rules. In the area of non-contractual civil liability, it seems feasible, and indeed fruitful, to develop common general principles of a European system of tort law. These principles should thereby be structured with due regard to their global use instead of focusing on special European characteristics. This should not be too difficult since all legal orders with world-wide influence are basically represented within the EU.

The work of the European Group on Tort Law can already provide some foundation for the necessary unification of European tort law.

92 See *supra* note 43.

Ton Hartlief

HARMONIZATION OF EUROPEAN TORT LAW. SOME CRITICAL REMARKS

1. Introductory Remarks

Professor Magnus's interesting paper is undoubtedly of great importance for the discussion on the further harmonization of civil law. Magnus 'detests' the patchwork of European tort law and appears to be a 'believer' in harmonization. In his paper he argues that:

- there is a need for the harmonization of tort law;
- the European Community is competent to enact a comprehensive system of non-contractual civil liability; and that
- the Lando-model by which general principles are developed should be applied and should be followed by a political and legislative process.

My contribution to the discussion today will be to make some comments on

- the arguments in favour of the harmonization of tort law and
- the consequences of harmonizing tort law.

But I would like to start by discussing the functions of tort law and the differences in the various European countries in the field of tort law. Magnus addresses these issues in the second part of his paper.

2. Functions of Tort Law and the Differences in the Various European Countries

The predominant objective of tort law is to find a balance between an adequate level of protection for the victim on the one hand and the interest of the tortfeasor to act in freedom on the other hand. That's the question in tort law: freedom or protection?

Though this objective is common to all European countries, it is possible that the actual balance chosen in one European country differs - sometimes even strongly - from the balance in another European country.

In this context Magnus points to legal diversity in for instance the field of:

2.1. Responsibility for the Pursuit of certain Dangerous Activities or for certain Dangerous Objects

There are indeed significant differences in the evaluation of the factors which are recognized as sources of special danger. This is illustrated by motor vehicles. Whereas in some systems they are recognized as being dangerous and consequently they require the application of a specific regime, this is not the case in Great Britain and Ireland. In these countries a fault-based regime still exists.

2.2. Damages and their Compensation

According to Magnus, the greatest differences can be found in the area of damages and their compensation. Differences exist concerning the question of whether, under which conditions and to what extent victims are entitled to compensation for non-pecuniary loss. The same applies to the entitlement of close relatives to damages and to the compensation of non-pecuniary loss and even to the determination of the amount of compensation in general. According to Magnus harmonization of the level of compensation in Europe seems especially important in the area of *personal injury*: substantial differences in compensation of the immaterial consequences of serious injuries - which are felt equally by most victims - cannot be justified.

2.3. Reduction of Damages due to Contributory Negligence in General and Especially in the Field of Road Traffic.

Differences can also be found when the issue of the reduction of damages due to contributory negligence *in general* and in the field of road traffic accidents *in particular* is raised. Examples can be found in the French Loi Badinter and the Dutch Supreme Court decisions regarding the contributory negligence of victims of motorized traffic accidents.

2.4. Time Limitation/Prescription.

Furthermore Magnus points to substantial differences in the field of time limitation or prescription.

Given these and other differences the question arises as to whether harmonization is desirable. Magnus's answer is in the affirmative.

3. The Arguments in Favour of Harmonization

3.1. Differences in the Field of Tort Law Amount to Distortions of Free Competition

His predominant argument is that different rules of liability and different levels of compensation can impair the functioning of the common market. If, for instance, the liability of certain enterprises were less strict in Germany than in France this would result in differing regional competitive conditions. Customers would find it difficult to compare the performance of enterprises in both countries and real competition between German and French competitors on a European scale would be distorted. Legal differences will inhibit the functioning of the common market because participants would be motivated to adopt strategies which are based on these disparities and they would avoid offering certain goods or services in countries with a high level of compensation or long periods of prescription. According to Magnus, differences in the systems of tort law will invite companies to establish themselves in countries where they can operate under a lower risk of liability.

3.2. The Perspective of Transboundary Accidents

Furthermore Magnus points out that harmonization is desirable from the perspective of transboundary accidents. People travelling regularly in a certain area do not want to be confronted with differing and often unknown legal rules. In other words: why should a German victim in Spain be less protected by the Spanish tort law system than he would be at home?

3.3. Magnus opposes Legal Differences as such

More implicitly Magnus in my view opposes legal differences as such. I believe his argument is that we live in a European living space and there is no such thing as French, German or Dutch justice. This is illustrated by Magnus's statement that the harmonization of the level of compensation in Europe is especially important in the area of personal injury since substantial differences in compensation of the immaterial consequences of serious injuries cannot be justified. Obviously in Magnus's view there is something like a European justice.

4. Putting Magnus's Arguments to the Test

I would now like to put Magnus's arguments to the test. Firstly I would like to comment on Magnus's argument that harmonization serves the functioning of the internal market.

4.1. Differences in the Field of Tort Law Amount to Distortions of Free Competition

In questioning that argument I would like to put forward that - to my knowledge - there is a lack of empirical evidence.

Is there - for instance - any empirical evidence that certain European countries are set aside by industrial enterprises since their tort law system is more generous to victims than other systems?

And is there any empirical evidence that certain European countries are willing to attract industrial enterprises by introducing a system of tort law that is more lenient to tortfeasors than the systems of, for instance, neighbouring countries?

I think that this is not a very realistic scenario since most industrial enterprises will depend on the export market. Their exposure to product or service liability will not depend upon the law of the state of their establishment but in fact upon the law of the state where the harm occurs.

Wouldn't it be wiser, to expect that other conditions like tax levels, public services, labour conditions and infrastructure would have a more significant impact than the tort law system?

Secondly I believe that as a consequence of Magnus's view, the harmonization of civil procedure and the social security systems were desirable since the actual meaning or importance of tort law systems depends not only on matters of substance but on other conditions as well. In a country with a *high* level social security system for instance, the need to make use of the tort law system is substantially less important than in countries with a *low* level social security system. Differences in the field of civil procedure can also - at least to some extent - explain the difference in the actual importance of tort law systems in various European countries. Taking this into account, the focus on uniform rules of tort law seems less productive than Magnus suggests.

More importantly, in Magnus's view the importance of tort law for the internal market is over-estimated. When it comes to the functioning of the common market safety regulation is a much more effective incentive than the tort law system. National product safety regulation can indeed amount to a trade barrier and as such distort free competition. Taking this into account product-safety regulation by the European community is, from the internal market perspective, much more important than uniform product liability rules.

In the end, it needs to be stressed that for the functioning of the market it is not necessary, let alone possible, to create total equality in competitive conditions. And let us be honest, even if the whole body of tort law were harmonized there would still be considerable differences in energy sources, access to raw materials et cetera.

In short: I'm not convinced of the need to harmonize tort law from an internal market perspective.

4.2. *The Perspective of Transboundary Accidents*

But I'm not convinced of the need to harmonize tort law from the perspective of transboundary accidents either. In his paper, Magnus argues that people travelling regularly in a certain area do not want to be confronted with differing and often unknown legal rules. In my words: why should a German victim in Spain be less protected by the Spanish tort law system than he would be at home?

Magnus adds that the demand for a common system of civil liability is also underlined by the fact that a need for additional insurance is often felt in order to cover risks created by different levels of liability and compensation when conducting work or study stays and recreational trips within Europe. In *my* opinion the need for additional insurance does not automatically correspond to a common European *need for harmonization*. The need to obtain additional insurance when travelling to other countries merely shows that there are differences in the *preferences* of European citizens.

A German victim in Spain will be less protected by the Spanish tort law system than he would be at home probably because Spanish people are not willing to pay the price for extra protection.

A German victim that wants more protection in Spain than the Spanish tort law system can offer him, should indeed find additional insurance coverage on a first party basis. That is *exactly* the right answer to differing preferences: those who seek extra protection abroad, can take additional insurance coverage and in doing so will pay the price.

Harmonization would make the preferences of one binding on another. In that case Brussels would know what's good for us all! That's paternalism!

Even in these years of high mobility it is in my view not very convincing to base the harmonization of tort law on any need arising from transboundary accidents. Why – for instance – should national traffic liability law suffer as a result of a European-felt and transboundary accident-based need for a common system of traffic liability? If transboundary accidents are of such a problematic nature that legislative action should be taken, it seems much more appropriate to restrict that action to these transboundary accidents.

4.3. *Magnus opposes Legal Differences as such*

I've already pointed out that Magnus seems to oppose legal differences as such. I've given Magnus's statement that the harmonization of the level of compensation in Europe is especially important in the area of personal injury as an illustration. According to Magnus substantial differences in the compensation of the immaterial consequences of serious injuries cannot be justified. Obviously, in Magnus's view there is something like a European justice. I would say that Magnus's example of the level of non-pecuniary loss is just another example of differing preferences which are sometimes based on philosophical grounds, sometimes on varying expectations as to the quality of life, sometimes on the level of social security or on a combination of these arguments. In my opinion there is indeed such thing as Belgian, French or German justice. I agree with Magnus that legal diversity does not exist when it comes to basic principles of justice like the idea of equality before the law but diversity shows itself when the question arises whether liability without fault can be established, whether wrongful birth claims can successfully be brought to court or whether the victim's close relatives should be entitled to compensation for non pecuniary loss.

I'm not ready to sacrifice the possibility of differing preferences to a quest for a European justice.

5. The Consequences of Harmonization of Tort Law

Finally I would like to make some brief remarks on the *consequences* of the harmonization of tort law. In my opinion, one of the major consequences will be that as a whole tort law will be stricter than before. In other words: it will expand further.

From a Dutch perspective for instance there is reason to believe that after harmonization:

- more persons will be entitled to damages than under the current situation, for example the employer of the victim;
- close relatives will be entitled to compensation for non-pecuniary loss whereas that is almost impossible under the current situation;
- the level of compensation for intangible consequences of serious injuries will be higher than under the current situation.

Can such an expansion of liability law really be motivated by the necessary prevention of the distortion of free competition or by the need for a common system for transboundary accidents?

As a consequence of harmonization a new balance between protection and freedom needs to be found: less freedom, extra protection. Extra protection that will be passed on in higher prices for services and goods. Is all this really desirable?

6. Concluding Remarks

My answer to that question will not come as a surprise. In my opinion, the harmonization of tort law is not desirable at this stage as far as those fields, where national preferences play a vital role, are concerned.

I've already given my point of view that we should save our energy for the regulation of safety rather than for the harmonization of liability rules and that in cases where the transboundary accident perspective requires legislative action that action should indeed be restricted to transboundary accidents.

Contrary to Magnus, I do not believe in the harmonization of tort law; contrary to Magnus, I love *patchwork*!

Pierre Widmer

SWISS TORT LAW ALSO IS EUROPEAN TORT LAW

1. Pleading for a harmonizated European Tort Law

First of all, I would like to thank the organizers of this conference for inviting me to participate, as a Swiss lawyer and distant descendent of William Tell, in a discussion from which I could - albeit not on a scientific level, but at least to some extent politically - feel excluded. Thus, I appreciate even more being invited and participating in a discussion among 'real Europeans'. On the other hand, I must say that after having heard the very critical and not particularly *ius commune*-oriented comments of the previous speaker, I have the firm impression that my attitude towards a harmonized, or even unified, European law is considerably more positive than is the case with my Dutch colleague. And I am certainly not the only Swiss person who feels like this.

2. Swiss Tort Law as 'European Mixture'

It is true that Swiss law, like most of the other systems of this continent, has its roots in the same Roman tradition and in the resumption of this tradition *'alla Bolognese'*, as Ulrich Magnus has very accurately shown in his paper. In fact, there was a time - and a rather long time, namely from the early Middle-Ages up to the first World War -, during which Swiss law, cantonal first, then unified on a federal level, was as European as the national systems of its neighbours and most other continental countries. The Swiss Civil Code of 1911 (which entered into force on 1st January 1912), and more particularly the Swiss Code of Obligations (subsequently quoted as SCO) - which goes back to 1881 - and within this Code of Obligations, the chapter on Tort Law, are to a large extent modelled on the same Roman patterns, or - more precisely - on the Roman models in the shape they had taken following the French legal evolution on the one hand, and the German on the other hand. Thus, one could also say that the Swiss Civil Code (SCC) of 1911 is to some extent already a 'European mixture'; this twofold inspiration is particularly obvious in art. 41 SCO which combines the French general clause of Article 1382 CCF (para. 1) with the extreme specificity of § 826 BGB (para. 2) - a provision that, in principle, makes sense only in a system based on distinct legally protected positions as provided by § 823 BGB.

It was only during the 20th century and even more so after the European Communities (EC) and subsequently the European Economic Space (EES) were created, that the Swiss Confederation began to become an island which finally, after the negative vote in the referendum on adherence to the EES in 1992 – and notwithstanding the fact, that, geographically, Switzerland was, *still is and in all probability will also remain* situated in the heart of Europe –, may sometimes appear more remote from the old continent than are the real islands beyond the Channel.

3. Brussels'most devoted 'Parrot'

However, such distance from Europe and the EU is essentially a psycho-political one, as in legal aspects we are among the most devoted emulators and parrots of the Brussels' legal production, sometimes even with more commitment than certain member States – we simply call it '*subsequent autonomous implementation*'. Occasionally, we even practise '*anticipated obedience*' as we did in 1984 in the case of Product Liability where the Swiss Federal Court introduced this concept into Swiss law – somewhat *praeter legem,* but – half a year before the European Council adopted its Directive after some ten years of hesitation. Thus, a Swiss lawyer does not really have to feel marginalized in relation to European law.

4. The domestic Reform of Swiss Tort Law as Preparation to 'Europeanization'

The second reason why I feel quite at ease in this particular circle is that the reform and the unification of tort law is currently an important and immediate topic in Switzerland as well. I hesitate to boast of this here: but in this field, again, we have somewhat anticipated the present European movement. Our reform has been under way for almost 100 years: for 34 years it has been on the political agenda of the Swiss government, and *13 years ago it entered into an operative stage.* At the end of last year a first draft of a 'General Part of Tort Law' – to be inserted in chapter II ('*Obligations resulting from Unlawful Acts*') of Part One of the SCO – was submitted to interested parties in a consultation procedure and can be downloaded from the Internet.[1]

It goes without saying that in this project we are trying to keep as close as possible to the general evolution in Europe. On the other hand, and with all due modesty, we hope of course that perhaps one or two ideas coming from a country, previously better known for its banking secrecy, its watches, cheese and chocolate than for innovative legal concepts, may contribute in a fruitful way to the debate on a continental level. One such idea could perhaps be the general clause for strict liability to which I will return in a moment ...

1 <http://www.ofj.admin.ch/index.html>; rubric: Business & Trade/Revision of Liability Law.

5. Familiar Federalist Problems

It is a fact, however, that the paper presented by Ulrich Magnus deals with certain topics on which an outsider to the EU should be very cautious to take a stance, because they refer to questions that are typically communitarian, like the problem of the legislative competency of the Union in the field of private law in general and in that of tort law in particular. I would not dare to give an opinion on this problem and on the correct interpretation of the EC-Treaty in this respect – although the kind of problem is not completely unfamiliar to a Swiss lawyer: Indeed, we have had similar debates on the delimitation of competencies between Confederation and cantons, and we have come to comparable solution and principles. This is, for example, the case where federal law infringed on procedural law which is still a matter reserved for the cantons. One of these principles states that the federal legislator may set procedural provisions '*insofar as they are absolutely indispensable to ensure the correct application and enforcement of substantive federal law*'. This concept is very close to what the ECJ held in *Fédération Charbonnière de Belgique v. High Authority of the European Coal and Steel Community*, quoted by U. Magnus.

6. A Common Market requires a Common Tort Law

But, independently from this 'federalist' problem, and also independently from diverging political projects for the deepening and development of the EU, I can express a view on the need for a uniform, or at least, harmonized system of tort law. It seems quite evident to me that in an area with such intensive commercial, social and cultural exchange as the European Union, a common system of private law, at least in the fields of contract and tort, is something which imposes itself. This also corresponds to the Swiss experience, and it is certainly not a mere coincidence that the law of obligations, including tort law, was the first major piece of former cantonal law to be unified – some thirty years before the Civil Code dealing with the other parts of private law could be realized. On the European level, we are again confronted with a similar question, insofar as the legislative competence of the Union seems to be limited to the commercial sphere, except where it can be deduced from a sectoral competence relating to the protection of the environment and the consumer.

Now, one could try to argue that almost each case of liability affects the environment in one way or another, and that most persons involved in such cases are also consumers. But – taken more seriously – it is undoubtedly a relatively strong argument to point out that a coherent system of tort law cannot reasonably be limited to such very narrowly defined sectors and that a basis of general principles has to be uniform for all types of liability.

In this respect, I cannot but support most strongly the ideas and suggestions of our rapporteur. The following slight criticisms and reservations – which Ulrich Magnus already knows, because we have often discussed these issues together – are therefore in no way directed against his concept as a whole, but refer to some specific aspects where opinions diverge at present and could also continue to diverge under a harmonized European regime.

7. Policy and Functions of Tort Law

As to the functions of tort law, my impression is that the preventive effect is frequently overestimated. Firstly, because tort law by definition always intervenes too late: it can only come into play once damage has occurred and prevention has manifestly failed. Secondly, the prevention aspect recedes into the background the more one adopts - as Ulrich Magnus suggests should also be done in a harmonized European tort law - a largely 'objectivized' concept of fault that leaves only very little space for subjective elements of the personality of the tortfeasor to be taken into consideration. It seems quite evident that where I cannot escape liability for fault even with my best efforts, because my physical and/or psychic capacities do not correspond to the abstract standard of the *'bonus pater familias'* or *'reasonable man'* (which increasingly tends to mutate into that of a '*Superman*') - the preventive effect of liability will be extremely limited. That is why I continue - even being conscious of my rather isolated position - to advocate a more subjective orientation of fault based liability, a concept which becomes more easily acceptable and can, so to say, be better 'afforded' from the moment that you accept strict liability in a sufficiently broad field so that there is no longer any need to distort the notion of fault in order to achieve liability on that basis.

As far as the (policy) reasons for tort liability are concerned, I fully support what Ulrich Magnus says of the requirement of a *'special reason'* (O.W. Holmes) which has to justify the shifting of the damage from one person - the victim - to another - the person responsible -, and I agree also with his concept of the two pillars represented by fault based liability on the one hand, and strict liability for dangerous activities on the other. I am slightly more hesitant to follow him in respect of what he calls *'responsibility for one's personal sphere of living'*; the examples given, in particular the French responsibility of the *'gardien de la chose'* (which originally was only a specific form of fault based liability)[2] but also certain types of hybrid (or 'grey zone') liabilities in Swiss law (as for example that of the owner of a piece of land or of buildings and other constructions)[3] are - in my opinion - highly problematic. Specifically because there is no plausible *'special reason'* to shift the damage from the person who has immediately suffered it to the *gardien* or the owner of an object or building if no reproach or blame can be addressed to them - but rather only because they own an object which is not specifically dangerous or simply have it in their custody.

8. 'Wrongfulness' as a Key-element of Tort Law

The limited time does not allow me to comment on the other fundamental prerequisites of liability enumerated and explained by Ulrich Magnus: damage, wrongfulness and causation. The only annotation which I cannot help putting forward is that *'wrongfulness'*, even if apparently unknown in certain national

2 Art. 1384 CCF.

3 Art. 679 SCC and 58 SCO.

systems like the French and Belgian, turns out - if not as concept, at least in its essence - to become a key-element of a tort law which tries to limit its effects to certain interests that deserve more protection than others. The core-problem in this respect is that of so called *'pure economic loss'*. So I cannot but fully agree with our rapporteur in his conclusion that - in one way or another - such a limiting factor has to be kept in the system, and that attempts to banish unlawfulness will probably result in a purely semantic exercise.

9. While Strict Liability has to be developed, Fault remains an Indispensable Tool to Reasonably Limit Liabiality

My main concern however remains the question whether and to what extent it will be possible to establish - in a harmonized European tort law regime - an adequate balance between fault based liability and strict liability. Up to now, it has proven to be rather difficult to find a common basis for a form of liability related to activities which present a qualified high risk. And the idea of allowing the judge in such cases to determine liability independently from fault, at least where activities of a similar degree of dangerousness have already been put under such a regime, still seems far from being acceptable for all Europeans. The main argument generally put forward against such a general clause of strict liability is that it would compromise legal certainty. To which one can only retort that legal certainty is by no means better ensured by a notion of fault degenerated into a synonym of the violation of a retrospectively invented 'duty of care'.

An idea which could perhaps be discussed further and more in depth, is to proceed by applying to the area of strict liability something along the lines of the famous *'Cassis de Dijon'* principle. We could for example decide that where an activity is the object of a strict liability in more than, let us say: five or six member States of the EU (or in comparably civilized countries), a similar regime could also be adopted by a judge in another member country. To propose such a comparative approach would at the same time constitute an incentive for judges to look more frequently beyond the garden-fence of their national law.

10. Strict or Soft Law

As to the form of a European tort law: the final goal is of course to achieve a European civil code. But it could perhaps be advisable, having regard to the previously mentioned psycho-political aspect, not to start from the very beginning with a formally binding European Code, but try a somewhat softer set of rules, as for example a *Restatement* or a *Model Law* or just *'Principles'* (like those of UNIDROIT for international commercial contracts)[4] which could inspire the communitarian as well as the national legislator.

4 See: <http://www.unidroit.org/english/principles/contents.htm>.

11. Strict Liability is also a Part of Tort Law

A word more on the terminology: Defining his topic, Ulrich Magnus tells us that his paper *'will focus on tort law, including strict liability'*. With all due respect, I have to react to this way of presenting things, because what at first glance looks like a simple question of semantics, in reality hides a problem that has shown itself to be quite virulent. *'Including strict liability'* suggests that strict liability would not be automatically and from the very beginning included in tort law, and that you have to say expressly the contrary if you want it to be treated on the same level. I think that this a very important point, namely that we should accept that strict liability is certainly another and quite different type of liability compared to fault based liability, but that nowadays it is also a perfectly equivalent concept, and not only an exception in respect to fault based liability, as too many lawyers and professors still seem to think.

12. Convergence of Legal Systems versus Legal Folklore

This leads me, in conclusion, to express my hope that the harmonization of tort law in Europe, even being a rather demanding job, will continue to progress, slowly perhaps, but constantly. The praise of 'diversity' and the presently very fashionable idea that there should be a constant competition between legal systems may be stimulating for scholars, but it seems rather doubtful that the man and woman in the street, entrepreneurs and consumers, feel the same joyful excitement when confronted with different regimes each time they cross the borders between European countries which otherwise do no longer exist. We are assisting the old controversy of the 'vocation of our time for legislation' – the eternal confrontation between the Thibaults and the Savignys about *'den Beruf unserer Zeit zur Gesetzgebung'*, that once again takes place, but now on a European level.

In any case, even if we succeed in achieving a harmonized or unified European legal framework, one thing is absolutely certain: this supranational system will not be carved in marble for all eternity, but will also continue to develop and to adapt itself to the changing needs of society.

And, after all, it may perhaps be a consolation for the defendants and amateurs of diversification and legal folklore that, even under a more or less unified European law, it would still remain true that where you have two lawyers you have at least three opinions.

European Contract Law

Jan Smits

THE FUTURE OF EUROPEAN CONTRACT LAW: ON DIVERSITY AND THE TEMPTATION OF ELEGANCE

1. Introduction

The European Commission has recently published a Communication on European Contract Law.[1] This document can be seen as the starting point of a new era in the discussion on a uniform law of contract for Europe. Up until now, this discussion was to a large extent characterized by its academic character: whether a uniform contract law for Europe should be possible and what its contents should be, has been debated in the scholarly literature of the last decade. These questions did, however, not become important issues for European politics or even for legal practice. Thus, the calls by the European Parliament of 1989[2] and 1994[3] that work on a European Civil Code should begin, were not answered by the Commission or the Council for a long time. It was only with the Tampere European Council of 1999 that times began to change. In the Presidency Conclusions of that Council,[4] 'an overall study on the need to approximate Member State's legislation in civil matters in order to eliminate obstacles to the good functioning of civil proceedings' was summoned. Independent of that, the European Parliament commissioned a study on a European civil code that was published in 1999.[5] Now, the 2001 communication - which can be seen as the implementation of the Tampere conclusions - invites all interested parties to give their opinion on the future of contract law in Europe. These parties include consumers, businesses, professional organizations, public administrations and the academic world. This will probably lead to a political

1 Communication from the Commission to the Council and the European Parliament on European Contract Law, COM(2001) 398 final.

2 (1989) *OJ* C 158/400.

3 (1994) *OJ* C 205/518.

4 The Tampere summit was held on 15 and 16 October 1999; SI (1999) 800. Also see <http://europa.eu.int/council/off/conclu/oct99_en.pdf>.

5 Study of EU private-law systems in relation to discrimination and the creation of a European civil code, European Parliament, JURI 103 EN (October 1999). This study was directed by Chr. Von Bar.

debate on the desirability of and the way to establish a uniform contract law for Europe.

This turn in the debate does not imply that the role of academia has become less important. To the contrary. Now more than ever should academics be critical of the path upon which the European Commission will embark. Only then can a necessary counterweight to an over-stretched belief in the feasibility of uniform law in the field of contract be provided. This paper tries to provide such a counterweight by stressing that the present 'generalizing approach' toward European contract law (this is the approach that seeks to formulate 'principles' of private law with a view to have national legal systems replaced by these) is not the right way to establish a common law for Europe. Instead, diverging tendencies should be stressed. A plea for such *divergence* can be found in section 3 of this paper. To understand what this plea for divergence is all about, a small historical survey of the development of contract law over the last few centuries is, however, also necessary. Only with this survey is the idea behind the generalizing approach of contract law to be understood properly. Thus, in section 2, a survey of *convergence* in European contract law over the last centuries is given. This sketch is preceded by an account of the present generalizing approach toward European contract law.

2. Generalization in Contract Law: Present Approach and Historical Development

2.1. The Emergence of European Contract Law over the Last Decade

The debate on European contract law as we have seen it emerge over the last decade is driven by at least two separate forces. To my mind, the most important of these is the coming into being of an academic debate on the feasibility and possible contents of a European contract law.[6] Not only have we seen the publication of textbooks on European contract law[7] and the launch of several scholarly projects, such as the Casebooks for the Common Law of Europe project,[8] the Trento Common Core project[9] and the study group on a European Civil Code,[10] we have also witnessed

6 For an overview of this debate see, among many others, J. Smits, *The Making of European Private Law*, Antwerp-Oxford-New York, Intersentia, 2002 and C. Schmid, 'The Emergence of a Transnational Legal Science in European Private Law', *Oxford Journal of Legal Studies*, 10, 1999, p. 673.

7 Notably H. Kötz, *Europäisches Vertragsrecht*, Tübingen, Mohr, Bd. I, 1996 (translated as *European Contract Law*, vol. I, Oxford, Clarendon Press, 1997); B. Markesinis, W. Lorenz and G. Dannemann, *The Law of Contracts and Restitution: a Comparative Introduction*, Oxford, Oxford University Press, 1997; cf. A. Hartkamp *et al.* (eds.), *Towards a European Civil Code*, second edition, Nijmegen, Den Haag, Ars Aequi Libri, Kluwer Law International, 1998.

8 The volume on contract law is set to be published in 2001. See for the project W. van Gerven, 'Casebooks for the common law of Europe; presentation of the project', *ERPL*, 4, 1996, p. 67.

9 On which M. Bussani and U. Mattei (eds.), *Making European Law*, Trento, Università degli studi di Trento, 2000. Two volumes, both on contract law, have now been published: R. Zimmermann and S. Whittaker (eds.), *Good Faith in European Contract Law*, Cambridge, Cam-

the publication of various sets of principles of contract law.[11] In overlooking all these initiatives, it seems as if the desire of Zimmermann 'to concentrate one's attention, for once, (...) on proximity and similarities'[12] rather than on differences, is satisfied in much of the present day writing on comparative law. Although most of the time differences among the legal systems are still recognized, the desire in most of these projects is indeed to find commonalities and to look at differences as exceptions to common cores.

The other important factor is the ever greater use of directives as an instrument for the harmonization of contract law. Thus, since 1985 a whole range of directives has been issued. These directives concern in particular protection of consumers in the field of doorstep selling,[13] consumer credit,[14] package travel,[15] unfair contract terms,[16] distance contracts[17] and sale of goods[18] as well as regulation of self-employed commercial agents,[19] timeshare,[20] electronic commerce[21] and combating late payment in commercial transactions.[22] An ever-greater part of contract law is thus governed by European legislation.

bridge University Press, 2000 and J. Gordley (ed.), *The Enforceability of Promises in European Contract Law*, Cambridge, Campbridge University Press, 2001.

10 On which C. Von Bar, 'Le Groupe d'Études sur un Code Civil Européen', *RIDC*, 2001, p. 127. Also see the Vienna Tilburg project on principles of European tort law, on which J. Spier and O. Haazen, 'The European Group on Tort Law ('Tilburg Group') and the European Principles of Tort Law', 7 *ZeuP*, 1999, p. 469.

11 *Unidroit Principles of International Commercial Contracts*, Rome 1994; O. Lando and H. Beale (eds.), *Principles of European Contract Law*, Parts I and II, Combined and Revised, The Hague, Kluwer, 2000; G. Gandolfi (ed.), *Code européen des contrats*, Milano, Giuffrè, 2001.

12 R. Zimmermann, *The Law of Obligations*, Cape Town, Juta, 1990, xi. Cf. K. Zweigert and H. Kötz, *An Introduction to Comparative Law*, thrird edition, Oxford, Clarendon Press, 1998, p. 40 who also argue for a *praesumptio similitudinis* in doing comparative law research.

13 Directive to protect the consumer in respect of contracts negotiated away from business premises (85/577; [1985] *OJ* L 372/31).

14 Directive for the approximation of the laws, regulations and administrative provisions of the Member States concerning consumer credit (87/102; [1987] *OJ* L 42/48).

15 Directive on package travel, package holidays and package tours (90/314; [1990] *OJ* L 158/59).

16 Directive on unfair terms in consumer contracts (93/13; [1993] *OJ* L 95/29).

17 Directive on the protection of consumers in respect of distance contracts (97/7; [1997] *OJ* L 144/19).

18 Directive on certain aspects of the sale of consumer goods and associated guarantees (1999/44; [1999] *OJ* L 171/12).

19 Directive on the co-ordination of the laws of the Member States relating to self-employed commercial agents (86/653; [1986] *OJ* L 382/17).

20 Directive on the protection of purchasers in respect of certain aspects of contracts relating to the purchase of the right to use immovable properties on a timeshare basis (1994/47; [1994] *OJ* L 280/83).

21 Directive on certain legal aspects of information society service, in particular electronic commerce, in the Internal market (2000/31; [2000] *OJ* L 178/1).

22 Directive on combating late payment in commercial transactions (2000/35; [2000] *OJ* L 200/35). All the above directives have been reproduced in Dutch in J. van Erp and J. Smits (eds.), *Bronnen Europees privaatrecht*, Den Haag, Boom Juridische uitgevers, 2001.

For the purpose of this paper, it is important to have a closer look at the Principles of European Contract Law (PECL) in particular. It does not come as a surprise that the PECL have had a favourable reception in (at least) academic circles. For the two main factors that have driven the development of contract law in Europe leave a vacuum. On the one hand, there is the academic debate as such, in which similarities and differences between the various European legal systems are discussed - though without much impact on legal practice. On the other hand, there is the very real impact of European directives on national legal systems. One can maintain that the most successful part of present day European contract law is made up of these directives - they have led to a true harmonization, be it of an often non-consistent,[23] sometimes disturbing[24] and definitely fragmentary[25] nature. In between the two, there is a vacuum that can be filled up by principles. These are based on comparative law research, but have definite practical aspirations. According to the drafters of the Principles of European Contract Law (PECL), the principles can - among other functions - provide a 'general contract law infrastructure' for European directives.[26] In doing so, the PECL build a bridge between comparative scholarship and practice, in which the European directives have to be applied.

But there is still another reason for the favourable reception of the PECL. Laying down the law in general principles seems to fulfil the desire of many jurists and lawyers to present the law in a concise and elegant way. *Vis-à-vis* the chaotic mass of comparative law materials - sixteen European legal systems,[27] all with their own structure, legal culture, terminology, detailed statutory rules and case law - any attempt to distil general principles is welcomed. This is particularly true for one type of provision of the PECL: those that try to lay down the common core of Europe's national legal systems (the greater part of the PECL's provisions). Other articles provide us with a 'progressive' development from that common core - giving these provisions a different character, namely much more the drafters' view of what the future law in Europe *should* be, instead of trying to restate the *present* law.[28]

This approach of distilling principles from one or more legal systems can be characterized as a generalizing approach. It tries to leave out as many details as possible in order to describe the law in a consistent, smooth and elegant way. Other

23 Also recognized in the Commission's Communication on European Contract Law, p. 15-16.

24 See in particular G. Teubner, 'Legal Irritants: Good Faith in British Law or How Unifying Law Ends Up in New Divergences', *MLR,* 61, 1998, p. 11 (on the disturbing effect of the Unfair Terms directive on English law).

25 O. Remien, 'Über den Stil des europäischen Privatrechts', *RabelsZ,* 60, 1996, p. 8: 'a few Brussels bricks here and there'. In general on the use of directives: P.-C. Müller-Graff, 'EC Directives as a Means of Private Law Unification', in A.S. Hartkamp *et al.* (eds.), *Towards a European Civil Code,* 2nd ed., Nijmegen, Den Haag, Ars Aequi Libri, Kluwer Law International, 1998.

26 O. Lando and H. Beale (eds.), *supra* note 11, xxii.

27 Those of the 15 European Member States, of which the United Kingdom has two legal systems, namely English law and Scots law.

28 For the distinction between the two, see O. Lando and H. Beale (eds.), *supra* note 11, xxiv.

examples of this approach include the work of the study group on a European Civil Code. Within this group, attempts are also made to distil common denominators from the various legal systems.[29] In the European Commission's Communication on European Contract Law, one of the options for future EC initiatives in contract law is to replace existing national law with a set of principles or another set of rules.

To get a good insight into this increasingly important approach, it is necessary to sketch the origins of this generalizing approach toward contract law. This can be done via a small historical excursion.

2.2. Historical Background of the Present Approach (National Legal Systems)

2.2.1. Orthodox Contract Doctrine: a General and Consistent Contract Law[30]

The generalizing approach toward the law of contract - that is the approach that describes contract law as a consistent whole and as founded on general principles - is the prevailing view in Europe's national legal systems. In present day contract law systems of the European countries, it is rarely debated that there is a general set of rules and principles that is applicable to all contracts and that is consistent in structure and outlook. The way I see it, this 'general part of the law of contract' exists of a combination of structure and principles. Contract law is structured according to the chronology of the contract itself: it contains rules on consecutively formation, contents (including interpretation) and (non-)performance. This structure is adhered to for all types of contracts, including those where formation exists in a simple handing over of the goods (as in real contracts) or where the contents of the contract is to a large extent made up of mandatory law. Apart from this structure, contract law is usually looked at as governed by three general principles: freedom of contract, binding force and absence of formalities (consensualism).[31] Again, these principles are presented as underlying all types of contracts. They are also presented as a consistent whole: every contract with *these* desired contents is in principle binding for the parties because the will thereto has been freely formed.

This idea of a consistent general part of contract law is best identifiable in the continental Civil Codes and in civil law textbooks. It has found its apotheosis in the German Bürgerliches Gesetzbuch of 1900 with its 'General Part' of Book I and its classification of legal acts and contracts. This structure has been taken over by various other codes. Thus, the layered structure of the Dutch Burgerlijk Wetboek of 1992 implies that the more general provisions on legal acts of Book 3 precede the more specific provisions on contracts in Book 6, Title 5 and the even more specific provisions on special contracts in Book 7. The provisions on legal act and contract

29 Cf. Chr. Von Bar, 'Konturen des Deliktsrechtskonzeptes der Study Group on a European Civil Code - Ein Werkstattsbericht', *ZeuP*, 2001, p. 515. Also see <http://www.ecc.kub.nl>.

30 The following is a summary of J. Smits, 'Eenheid en verscheidenheid in het contractenrecht', *R & R*, 27, 1998, p. 10.

31 Cf. Asser-Hartkamp II, *Algemene leer der overeenkomsten*, Deventer, Tjeenk Willink, no. 34 *et seq.*; see below for references to other textbooks.

together make up for the general part of contract law that is applicable if it is not departed from in more specific provisions.

Also in textbooks (and thus in legal education), contract law is usually treated as a whole of general and specific rules, the premise being that a consistent and uniform *general* law of contract is at the basis of every specific contract type. Thus, many continental textbooks discuss 'the contract' as a general concept next to 'the general principles' of contract.[32] But this unified structure of contract law also exists in the common law.[33] Also the few 'European' textbooks adhere to this approach.

The reasons for this way of discussing contract law seem to be self-evident. If for example defects of consent were only regulated for a sales contract, it would mean that uncertainty existed as to their applicability by way of analogy to other contracts or to other legal acts. Apart from efficiency (only the diverging provisions need to be regulated for the special contract), a reason for the legislator to create a general part of contract law is this evasion of uncertainty and the creation of transparency.[34] In legal doctrine it is (apart from simply adhering to the code's structure) in particular the wish to offer as logical a structure as possible.

How has this general and consistent doctrine come about? Wightman has stated that 'Contract is unusual in having an integrated structure which fits all the various topics together as aspects of the same thing'.[35] That calls for a further investigation.

2.2.2. Generalization in Contract Law: a History of Modernism

It is well known that contract law as it existed in Roman times and as it was received in Europe, was characterized by many different types of contract.[36] Only when a contract could be accommodated within one of these categories could the creditor enforce it. This implied that real contracts (such as bailment, gratuitous loan and pledge) stood next to consensual contracts (like sale, lease and partnership), oral contracts (*stipulatio*) and written contracts. Each and every contract type had its own rules; general rules did not exist, let alone was there a general principle that *every* contract (*pactum nudum*) was enforceable. In other words: until the 16th century or so, there was no general or consistent law of

32 J. Ghestin, *Traité de Droit Civil, La Formation du Contrat*, 3rd ed., Paris, L.G.D.J., 1993; F. Terré, P. Simler and Y. Lequette, *Droit civil: les obligations*, 7th ed., Paris, Dalloz, 1999, no. 16 et *seq.*; J. Esser and E. Schmidt, *Schuldrecht, Bd. I: Allgemeiner Teil, Teilband 1*, 8. Aufl., Heidelberg, Beck, 1995; K. Larenz, *Lehrbuch des Schuldrechts*, Bd. 1, *Allgemeiner Teil*, 14. Aufl. München, Müller, 1987; Asser-Hartkamp II, *supra* note 31, no. 8 *et seq.* and no. 77 (cf. no 1: 'We will therefore discuss in this book the rules applicable to all contracts').

33 Cf., e.g., G. Treitel, *The Law of Contract*, 10th ed., London, Sweet & Maxwell, 1999.

34 These two reasons were explicitly mentioned in making the new Dutch Civil Code: see *Parlementaire Geschiedenis Boek 3*, Deventer, Kluwer, 1981, p. 157-158 and *Boek 6*, p. 47.

35 J. Wightman, *Contract: A Critical Commentary*, London, Pluto Press, 1996, p. 13.

36 See, among others, R. Feenstra, 'Pact and Contract in the Low Countries from the 16th to the 18th century', in J. Barton (ed.), *Towards a General Law of Contract*, Berlin, Duncker & Humblot, 1990, p. 197 and in particular J. Gordley, *Natural Law Origins of the Common Law of Contract*, in J. Barton (ed.), *Towards a General Law of Contract*, Berlin, Duncker & Humblot, 1990, p. 367.

contract. The question of whether the existing types of contract had anything in common simply did not arise.[37]

This diversity gradually disappeared after 1600. It is interesting to note that this occurred under the influence of general philosophical ideas. Preceded by Humanist influence of authors like Donellus (1527-1591) and Cujacius (1522-1590), it was in particular Descartes (1596-1650) who with his *Discours de la Méthode* (1637) made the great breakthrough toward a Modernist worldview. Descartes and his disciples not only strove toward absolute certainty in the field of the natural sciences (compare Galileo and Newton) and political theory (Hobbes), but they wanted to systematize the whole world *more geometrico*. This implied that all irrelevant ('arbitrary') details would be eliminated from the period in which these existed: thus, universal principles could be set free from their context and be given a universal character.[38] Toulmin has called this the abstraction of problems from their specific situation in space and time[39] a typical characteristic of the theory-centred philosophy of Modernism.[40] It was 'a quest for reason, unity and universality of values, laws and knowledge'.[41]

The law of contract was not untouched by this development. From Spanish scholasticism via Grotius (1583-1645) and Samuel Pufendorf (1632-1694), a general theory was planted underneath the specific contract types. In accordance with the mathematical method, an axiomatic system of natural law was developed with a claim to absolute validity. Van der Walt notes:[42]

> 'Many theorists wanted to ensure that choices among competing rights are constrained by clear and unambiguous principles, so that judicial judgment could be separated from the uncertainties of political rhetoric and metaphysical theory. The lawyers of the Enlightenment were, in a word, looking for a legal science in which certainty was guaranteed through method. Ever since the Enlightenment this implied that the legal story (...) would have to be transformed from a religious fable into a scientific dissertation'.

Present day contract law can only be properly understood if it is realized that this quest for reason, unity and universality that began in the 16th century still continues. The 'project' of Enlightenment[43] still exists where there is a search for

37 J. Gordley, *supra* note 36, p. 372: 'The Romans had worked out these rules *ad hoc* without trying to explain why a given transaction should be binding on consent, on delivery, or through a formality'.

38 S. Toulmin, *Cosmopolis: The Hidden Agenda of Modernity*, New York, Free Press, 1990, p. 31.

39 S. Toulmin, *supra* note 38, p. 22.

40 S. Toulmin, *supra* note 38, p. 11.

41 C. van Peursen, *Na het postmodernisme*, sixth edition, Kampen, Kok Agora, 1995, p. 21 (original in Dutch).

42 A. van der Walt, 'Marginal notes on powerful(l) legends: Critical perspectives on property theory', *THRHR*, 58, 1995, p. 402.

43 Cf. J. Habermas, 'Die Moderne – ein unvollendetes Projekt', in J. Habermas, *Kleine Politische Schriften*, Frankfurt, Suhrkamp, 1981, p. 444. Cf. A. MacIntyre, *Whose Justice? Which Rationality?*, London, Duckworth, 1988, p. 254: 'the overambitious rationalist metaphysical constructions ...'.

rational principles for the whole of the law of contract with a claim to permanent validity. It is then not even relevant *which* principles are derived. That, for example, a principle such as the general enforceability of contract was detached from the details that were regarded as irrelevant (thus: did not fit into the idea that each and every contract validly entered into should be enforceable), was understandable from a viewpoint of the development of commerce, but it was not essential to the Modernist method itself.

This scholarly worldview was perfected in the centuries that followed. Through the work of Thomasius (1655-1728), Wolff (1679-1754), Domat (1625-1696) and Pothier (1699-1772), private law was more and more presented as a deduction of universal norms. But of course its apotheosis was in 19th century Germany. The legal method of the Pandectists became nearly the same as the method of mathematicians.[44] Thus, in Savigny's *System*,[45] with the introduction of the legal relationship ('Rechtsverhältnis') and of the legal act ('Rechtsgeschäft') as new *genus*, the pyramid of concepts was further underpinned by abstractions that legal practice did not need. Most of the national textbooks of the 20th century only elaborated this further. The separate types of contract, each of them governed by their own rules, have become a uniformly structured and consistent set of principles of contract law.

It should be stressed that the above development was not restricted to the European continent. Also in English law, the existing casuistry was eliminated, albeit much later than in the civil law countries. Until Blackstone's systematic *Commentaries on the Laws of England* (1765-1770), contract law lacked a structure. There was only a list of claims (actions) that was 'something of a nightmare'[46] from an educational point of view. Classic Roman law and English law thus indeed breathed the same air.[47] It was only with the influence of the Analytical Jurisprudence of John Austin (1790-1859) that a general theory of contract law could come into being, in particular thanks to authors like Pollock and Anson.[48] Gordley is right to state that:[49]

> 'These authors describe general contract law without trying to relate it to the law of sales, the law of leases, and so forth (...). (They) were unable to bridge the gap between their general principles of contract and the laws of particular contracts. Consequently, their efforts to develop systematic contract doctrine were concentrated on the general law of contracts which bulked ever larger in the treaties as time went on'.

44 On Savigny's mathematical method: see L. Winkel, 'l'Histoire du droit, exemple d'une science interdisciplinaire', *Sartoniana*, 1996, p. 133.

45 F. von Savigny, *System des heutigen Römischen Rechts*, Berlin 1840-1849, e.g. vol. I, 1840, Veit, p. 334 *et seq*.

46 G. Samuel, *The Foundations of Legal Reasoning*, Antwerpen, Intersentia, 1994, p. 72.

47 F. Pringsheim, 'The Inner Relationship Between English and Roman Law', *Cambridge LJ*, 1935, p. 347.

48 F. Pollock, *Principles of Contract at Law and in Equity*, Oxford, Oxford University Press, 1876 and W.R. Anson, *Principles of the English Law of Contract and of Agency in its Relation to Contract*, Oxford, Oxford University Press, 1879.

49 J. Gordley, *supra* note 36, p. 446.

This does not mean that these details do not play a role in adjudicating concrete cases, but it does mean that they have been eliminated from the description of contract law at the national level. The general theory of contract thus serves three purposes: to know, teach and determine the positive law.[50] It is not only descriptive, but also prescriptive: it shows how the law should be and thus points the way for legal practice.

This process of the generalization of contract law is still going on. It takes place in at least two different ways.

First, the concept of contract is broadened to other relationships. Where the general part of contract law was developed on the basis of the common characteristics of the existing types of contract, this general theory is now more and more being applied to the 'relationships' of marriage and company. This is also pleaded for by the American 'contrarians'.[51] Within marriage, there should be more place for contracting about various things (arbitration, regulation of holidays or even length of the marriage).[52] According to them, the use of the 'neutral' contract law would make it possible to eliminate the favourable position of the man compared to the woman.[53] Thus, marriage is just another type of contract, governed by the general part of contract law. In the US, it has also been defended that a company should be looked at as a 'nexus for a set of contracting relations'[54] between shareholders, managers, employees and creditors. These would have a greater incentive to create efficient relationships if they can do so themselves if compared to the alternative of statutory intervention. The present statutory separation of property (of shareholders) and management (of managers) is regarded as too interventionist. To them, buying shares in a company is just another case of contracting.

Of more interest for the purpose of this paper is the second way in which the general part of contract law is still being broadened. While in previous times the generalization was from specific contracts to a general contract law *within one legal system*, with the drafting of principles of European contract law, an abstraction from national legal systems as such has begun to take place. The generalization has now begun to take place at the European level. This is still a quest for 'reason, unity and universality' and thus still an expression of a theory-centred contract law. Trying to draft principles of European Contract Law (or any other initiative aiming at distilling rules or principles from national legal systems) is part of this Modernist tradition.

This is not the place to criticize the idea of generalization in contract law as such. This has been done by Savaux, who has stated that the general law of contract is nothing but a 'droit commun des amphitheâtres et des livres.' According to

50 See É. Savaux, *La théorie générale du contrat, mythe ou réalité?*, Paris, L.G.D.J., 1997, p. 25 *et seq.*

51 R. Hillman, *The Richness of Contract Law*, Dordrecht, Kluwer, 1997, p. 79 *et seq.*

52 R. Hillman, *supra* note 51, p. 86 *et seq.*

53 L. Weitzman, *The Marriage Contract*, New York, Free Press, 1981.

54 W. Bratton, 'The "Nexus of Contracts" Corporation: A Critical Appraisal', *Cornell LR*, 74, 1989, p. 407. Cf. F. Easterbrook and D. Fischel, *The Economic Structure of Corporate Law*, Cambridge Mass., Harvard University Press, 1991.

Savaux, the general part offers 'une cóherence, des régularités que la simple réalité brute ne livre pas'.[55] Collins is of the same conviction for English law, telling us that 'students learn in their early years a misleading and almost irrelevant set of rules'.[56] The remainder of this paper is devoted to a more specific criticism of the use of principles as a way to describe European contract law.

3. A Critique of Generalization: Why the Use of Principles is not the Right Way Toward a New Ius Commune

Now that the method of drafting principles has been put into a historical perspective – it should be seen as a direct consequence of the quest for rationality and unity that began in the 16th century – it seems appropriate to ask whether this method is still the right one with which to build a future European *ius commune*. This seems to be the prevailing view, held by Zimmermann[57] and many others. What is questioned in this paper, is whether this presentation of contract law in Europe as a general and consistent whole is not a surrender to 'the temptation of elegance' that Lord Goff has spoken of in his famous Maccabean lecture of 1983.[58] In this lecture, Goff questioned the use of systematization in the law: the more elegantly and concisely the law is formulated, the more convincing the rule is, but it then also becomes less effective. For, according to Goff, 'the law has to reflect life in all its untidy complexity'.

In the following, several arguments against the use of principles in European contract law are presented. These arguments all amount to the notion that present day contract law in Europe is too divergent to have it unified by way of principles. Still, the various arguments are different in character.

3.1. First Diverging Tendency: the Abstract Character of Principles and the Importance of Recognizing Differences among Legal Systems

My first objection against the use of principles is directed toward their excessively abstract character.[59] In a national legal system, one can ask whether the general part of contract law is not *too* general in view of the great variety of specific contracts. What does an international joint venture, the purchase of peanut butter in a supermarket, a building contract and a labour contract have in common? Their commonalities only exist at a very abstract level. The same is true of European

55 É. Savaux, *supra* note 50, p. 9. Also see J. Smits, *supra* note 31, p. 10.

56 The subject is of 'sublime irrelevance': H. Collins, *The Law of Contract*, second edition, London, Butterworths, 1993, p. xi.

57 R. Zimmermann, 'The Civil Law in European Codes', in D. Carey Miller and R. Zimmermann (eds.), *The Civilian Tradition and Scots Law*, Berlin, Duncker & Humblot, 1997, p. 278.

58 R. Goff, 'The Search for Principle, Maccabean Lecture in Jurisprudence', in *Proceedings of the British Academy*, vol. LXIX, 1983, p. 169, p. 174 (reprinted in W. Swadling and G. Jones (eds.), *The Search for Principle*, Oxford, Oxford University Press, 1999, p. 313).

59 The following is partly based on J. Smits, *The Good Samaritan in European Private Law*, Deventer, Kluwer, 2000.

principles. The drafting of these inherently forces us to leave out as many differences between the national legal systems as is reasonably possible with the consequence that they no longer give us much information on what the European position actually is.

This can be illustrated by Article 2:301 PECL on negotiations contrary to good faith. It is well known that the various European systems differ as to whether such liability should exist. Generally speaking, in the civil law countries such liability is recognized, be it under different conditions and with different remedies available in each individual country. English law, however, abstains from accepting a general principle to negotiate in good faith (although it may be willing to accept pre-contractual liability by virtue of an implied contract or negligence).[60] In Article 2:301 PECL, the following common denominator is provided:

> '(1) A party is free to negotiate and is not liable for failure to reach an agreement.
> (2) However, a party which has negotiated or broken off negotiations contrary to good faith and fair dealing is liable for the losses caused to the other party.
> (3) It is contrary to good faith and fair dealing, in particular, for a party to enter into or continue negotiations with no real intention of reaching an agreement with the other party'.

It is beyond doubt that this provision in a sense states the European common core. Both the civil law and the common law position are definitely stated correctly in section (1). Section (2) is however a real trade-off between the two legal traditions. On the one hand, the civil law is satisfied by the rule that conduct contrary to good faith may lead to liability, even *before* there is a contract (although it does leave open when exactly this is the case - a question that is answered differently in each civil law country). On the other hand English law is stated correctly as well in the sense that if good faith and fair dealing does not require English contracting parties to negotiate in a certain way, liability will simply not arise under this provision. Thus, the article probably fully grasps neither the civil law nor the common law mentality. There is much more to these systems than just the commonality stated here. It is a *thin* description as opposed to a *thick* one,[61] as is also the case with many other provisions of the PECL.

This analysis of the PECL can be supported by philosophical insights. Presenting law through principles is what Clifford Geertz has called a 'skeletonization of fact': moral dilemmas are reduced to abstractions. Legrand rightly quotes Friedman where he says that to reduce the law in this way is very much like the work of the old system builders (of Modernist times, indeed) that 'took fields of living law, scalded off their flesh, drained off their blood, and reduced them to bones'.[62] Many details (that actually amount to national *practical wisdom*) are thus left out in an exercise that is primarily concerned with looking for

60 For details, see R. Zimmermann and S. Whittaker (eds.), *supra* note 9.

61 G. Ryle, as quoted in C. Geertz, 'Thick Description: Toward an Interpretive Theory of Culture', in *The Interpretation of Cultures*, New York, Basic Books, 1973, p. 3.

62 Friedman, cited in P. Legrand, 'Against a European Civil Code', *MLR*, 60, 1997, p. 59.

consensus: making common principles is inherently a quest for the common denominator. This approach seems to have become the prevailing one of some leading comparatists. The well-known textbook of Zweigert and Kötz indeed departs from this 'praesumptio similitudinis': in their functional approach, the comparatist can only be satisfied if his research leads to the conclusion that the systems he has compared reach the same or similar practical results.[63] From a pure scholarly point of view, there is nothing wrong with this because it may help us to better understand the law. But if these principles or 'similar results' are subsequently used in a *political* way and prescribed to national communities (where they replace national legal systems), the warning of Paul Feyerabend becomes of paramount importance:[64]

> 'A society that is based on a set of well-defined and restrictive rules, so that being human becomes synonymous with obeying these rules, forces the dissenter into a no-man's-land of no rules at all and thus robs him of his reason and his humanity (...). Remove the principles, admit the possibility of many different forms of life'.

The principles approach is thus directed toward the finding of an intermediate position. It may very well not be the *best possible rule* that prevails, but the rule on which consensus can be reached, indeed leaving out the 'flesh and blood' of national legal systems.[65]

Here, it is important to note that the present indeterminacy of national contract law at the level of rules (the too general character of contract law) does not prevent the national courts from doing justice on the basis of the value judgments (the 'national morality') that underpin each national private law system. These judgments should - in the end - be decisive for the outcomes that the courts reach. And in national legal systems, they probably *are* decisive, because of the simple fact that the courts are aware of their own national culture (if you like: morality, *Volksgeist* or *mentalité*) in which the rules are embedded. That these judgments often do not come to the surface at the level of black letter law, does in this respect not pose a true danger for the parties' interests (although it *is* a danger from a viewpoint of a transparent and consistent national private law). This is different however if the private law rules are cut loose from their national cultural anchor and presented as European principles that are able to replace national systems. Such a venture can only be undertaken if the distilling of common denominators goes hand in hand with the development of a uniform European mentality.[66]

To sum up: replacing national legal systems with European principles will not lead to unification, but will most probably have the opposite effect. National experience in adjudicating cases will be destroyed, leaving national legal practice

63 K. Zweigert and H. Kötz, *supra* note 12, p. 40.

64 P. Feyerabend, *Against Method*, third edition, London, Verso, 1993, p. 162-163.

65 R. Hyland, 'Comparative Law', in Patterson (ed.), *A Companion to Philosophy of Law and Legal Theory*, Cambridge Mass., Blackwell, 1996, p. 190 calls this 'reductionism'.

66 Cf. P. Legrand, 'Against a European Civil Code', *MLR*, 60, 1997, p. 60: 'What point, then, is a unitary text of reference in the absence of a unitary rationality and morality to underwrite and effectuate it?'

with no other alternative but to apply abstract norms in a European legal culture that it probably does not know and that possibly does not exist. This can only have adverse effects on legal certainty and legal unity in Europe. Thus, there will only be unification at the abstract level (providing us with a 'thin description'), not in practice itself.

3.2. Second Diverging Tendency: the Influence of Directives on National Contract Law

A second objection against the use of Principles as a means of creating a European *ius commune*, is of a much more practical nature. It takes as a starting point the harmonized law that is already there by way of European directives. Undoubtedly, this part of European private law is the most successful in the sense that here a true harmonization has already taken place.[67] This harmonization leads away from the generalizing approach because contract law is governed less by general principles and ever more subdivided into separate parts, each having their own rules.[68]

This gradually leads to something that is systematically entirely different from national contract law as we know it. As we have seen in section 2, German, French, Dutch and English contract law are now more or less supposed to be governed by general principles: common rules govern the formation of contracts, govern the remedies of the contracting parties, govern the way of interpretation et cetera, *regardless* of the type of contract involved. The Europeanization of these national legal systems through directives leads to the contrary: not a *uniform*, but a *diverse* contract law in which, for example, important remedies in case of breach of consumer contracts for the sale of movable goods[69] are governed by different rules than these same remedies in the case of other contracts (commercial contracts or consumer contracts *not* for the sale of movables). Likewise, the rules governing unfair terms in consumer contracts[70] are different from the ones governing unfair terms in other types of contracts, as there will be in the near future specific rules on the payment of debts for commercial transactions,[71] not covering consumer transactions. One could also point at the formation of distance contracts[72] or at the time of formation of contracts by electronic means,[73] both regulated in a different way than other contracts. This tendency toward divergence is reinforced by the fact that it is the European Court of Justice that has the final word on the interpretation of these directives.

67 Be it with its own disadvantages. Cf. J. Smits, *supra* note 6, Chapter 1.

68 Cf. J. Smits, 'Editorial: A Principled Approach to European Contract Law?', *Maastricht Journal*, 7, 2000, p. 221.

69 Directive 1999/44 on sale of consumer goods and associated guarantees.

70 Directive 1993/13 on unfair terms in consumer contracts.

71 Directive 2000/35 on combating late payment in commercial transactions.

72 Directive 97/7 on the protection of consumers in respect of distance contracts. According to art. 6 of this directive, a consumer can still withdraw from the contract within 7 working days after delivery of the good.

73 Directive 2000/31 on electronic commerce.

It is highly surprising that the Principles of European Contract Law do not take this *fragmented* approach into account and try to cover *all* contracts in a very generalized way, reminiscent of the national private law systems as they have existed for several centuries. Even most of the directives that were issued before the publication of the PECL have not been taken into account by the drafters. The directive on sale of consumer goods as it had to be implemented by 1 January 2002, which provides a detailed set of rules specifically for consumer sale of movables (including a hierarchy of actions), of course gives a much more accurate picture of what a European contract law looks like than the PECL (that still adopt the principle (*sic*!) of free choice of action in art. 8:101).[74] The other way around, it seems that in drafting directives, the system and terminology of the PECL are not taken into account either.

3.3. *Third Diverging Tendency: Consumer Contract Law and Business Contract Law. The Double Structure of the Law of Contract*

A third argument that carries us away from the general approach of drafting general principles for a European Contract Law, exists in the recognition that over time two sorts of contract law have come to exist in the various national legal systems. These are on the one hand a consumer contract law and on the other a specific law of contract for professional parties.

Apart from the influence of European directives on contract law (mostly in the field of consumer protection), in the national legal systems a separate consumer contract law has come to exist as well. This was put into place by specific statutes (in particular in the field of general conditions - like the German AGBG, the French art. L 132-1 ff. of the Code de la Consommation and the English Unfair Contract Terms Act - and consumer sale), and also by the national courts that tend to protect individual consumers to a much greater extent than they protect professional parties in interpreting contract terms, applying good faith, et cetera.

The emergence of a specific consumer contract law as distinct from a business contract law does not come as a surprise. Already in 1952, Kessler pointed to the ambiguous character of contract law:[75] on the one hand it guarantees that parties are able to contract in freedom by attributing binding force to contracts validly entered into. On the other hand, it also regulates this freedom by not allowing *every* contract to be enforceable. This *double structure* of autonomy and intervention could also be phrased as one of economic rationality (efficiency) on the one hand and social rationality (distributive justice) on the other.[76]

74 Although the action for price reduction and the concept of fundamental non-performance have been laid down in both the PECL (art. 9:401 and 8:103 jo. 9:301) and the directive.

75 F. Kessler, 'Freiheit und Zwang in nordamerikanischen Vertragsrecht', in *Festschrift für Martin Wolff*, Tübingen, Mohr, 1952, p. 67 *et seq.*

76 Cf. Chr. Joerges, *The Europeanization of Private Law as a Rationalization Process and as a Contest of Disciplines*, EUI Working Paper Law No. 94/5, 15.

Thus, part of contract law is governed by the morality of trade.[77] If parties contract in order to make profit, this has considerable influence on their contractual relationship. In trade, one usually does not contract in order to obtain specific goods, but the contract is a means to a goal: the making of profit. If the debtor does not perform, it is only a case of bad luck: the loss should be foreseen and is usually covered by insurance.[78] If parties search for this economic rationality by making a commercial contract, the law should adjust to their wish. Thus, interpretation of contract terms should take place as literally as possible and the role of good faith should be restricted. Nineteenth century contract law was developed for this type of contracts.[79]

This morality of trade is to be distinguished from the morality of the welfare state. There, making profit is not the goal of contracting, but it is to arrange for 'living, working, life and health'.[80] If the professional party does not act in conformity with the contract, the well-being of the individual may be threatened. Here, the law *has* to be paternalistic to serve its function. This new type of contract law is still in its infancy and should be further developed for both moralities distinguished here deserve to have their own contract law. What does a contract with which one wants to make profit have in common with one to ensure enjoying the comfort of having a house to live in or having medical insurance? What has marriage in common with buying shares in a company?

If a European private law consisted of principles as envisaged by the Commission on European Contract Law, this double structure of contract law would not come to the surface. The PECL are intended to have value for any type of contract, regardless of who the parties are.[81] Again, this type of generalization conceals the conflict between the two types of contract law. This may be done deliberately in order to give the principles universal value, or, in the words of Epstein about the people that contract law gives rules for:[82]

> 'These people are colorless, odorless, and timeless, of no known nationality, age, race or sex. These people are self-conscious abstractions known to be false as representations of people in the world, and useful precisely because they are so detached from any grubby set of particulars (...). There is a cold, practical logic behind this remorseless search for abstractions. (...) This massive oversimplification of the social universe treats all persons as though they are as fungible as the letters of the alphabet, and thus ignores or rejects every effort to force the common law to take into

77 J. Wightman, *supra* note 35, p. 96 *et seq.* distinguishes in this respect between 'personal' and 'commercial' contract.

78 Cf. J. Wightman, *supra* note 35, p. 97.

79 Cf. however H. Collins, 'Formalism and Efficiency: Designing European Commercial Contract Law', *ERPL*, 8, 2000, p. 211.

80 'Wonen, werken, leven en gezondheid': see J. Vranken, *Mededelings-, informatie- en onderzoeks-plichten in het verbintenissenrecht*, Zwolle, Tjeenk Willink, 1989, nr. 27.

81 This is different with the Unidroit Principles of International Commercial Contracts of 1994, although their contents is virtually identical to the PECL.

82 R. Epstein, *Simple Rules for a Complex World*, Cambridge Mass., Harvard University Press, 1995, p. 73-74.

account the difference between an individual worker of limited means and a huge industrial corporation'.

But even if done deliberately, the effect of it in the European context is doubtful. As I have stated already in section 3.1, I do understand why, within one national legal system, courts are able to work with these abstractions: because they know about the national mentality underlying it. They know in their national context when the morality of the market becomes more important than the morality of the welfare state. This is the case because the double structure of efficiency and distributive justice has led to a specific national fragile equilibrium that is in accordance with the socio-economic constellation of the country involved. This common socio-economic constellation is missing in Europe, which probably makes principles too abstract a tool with which to build a European private law.[83]

3.4. Fourth Diverging Tendency: the Diversity of Sources of European Private Law

Another tendency that leads rather to divergence than to unity in contract law, has to do with the sources of which European private law is made up. These sources are of a very diverse character. Apart from European directives (and possibly regulations in the years to come), European contract law is made up of national rules on contract law, international conventions, case law of the ECJ and even of the ECHR, and a whole lot of other, more informal sources like commercial customary law, standardized general conditions, arbitral awards and standardized rules of professional organizations like the International Chamber of Commerce. This variety of sources is not represented adequately by laying down the present state of the law in static principles - even if these are 'designed to provide maximum flexibility and thus to accommodate future developments', as the drafters state.[84] Looking at principles as able to replace Europe's national legal systems is adhering to the view that principles are the best way to describe the law. This may be true for some European systems, but definitely not for all. It is in any event not true for English law.

This diversity of sources implies (at least as long as there is no centralist imposition of principles upon the European Member States) that the provisions of the PECL may not be regarded by lawyers as the best provisions with which to adjudicate cases or by jurists with which to describe the state of the law. Indeed, most of the articles of the PECL lay down the classic concepts of contract law. They do not pay much attention to solutions for more recent problems in the contract law of the national legal systems. I think, for example, of cases where contractual provisions are applied to the relationship between a contracting party and a third

83 Here, I agree with G. Teubner, *supra* note 24, p. 11, who suggests that the dividing lines in the law of Europe should not be the national frontiers, but the production regimes.

84 O. Lando and H. Beale (eds.), *supra* note 11, xxvii.

party, as in the case of 'drittfinanzierte Erwerbsgeschäfte'[85] and in the case of profiting by third parties from non-performance or invoking contractual defences against third parties. I also think of problems related to the *Vormerkung* (and related concepts in other legal systems) and of the legal consequences of a contract as envisaged in art. 6 of the directive on distance contracts during the period within which the consumer can still withdraw. Here, the PECL could indeed play a prominent role in showing the way toward just decisions - but they do not.

3.5. Fifth Diverging Tendency: Multiculturalism

A final reason why the imposition of principles may not be the best way of proceeding toward a European Contract Law is again of a more theoretical nature, but with important practical consequences. Here, I can only hint at it. It is that today's Europe is not only diverse as to the different legal systems that are part of it, but that also *within* the Member States, the concept of fairness and law differs many times. I am referring to the fact that as a result of the immigration of large groups of foreigners over the last decades, there are now, within the European Union, many different ethno-cultural groups with their own views of what is fair. This does not only apply to family law, but also to the law of contract: there *is* an Islamic view of when contracts should be binding and why this is so (just as there is a common law- and a civil law view). Fairness nowadays is a pluralistic concept, or as Michael Walzer puts it:[86]

> 'There is no single set of primary or basic goods conceivable across all moral and material worlds - or, any such set would have to be conceived in terms so abstract that they would be of little use in thinking about particular distributions'.

The making of *general* principles, destined to govern all these different sets, is not in line with this cultural diversity. This has as a practical consequence that a future European Contract Law has to take these differences into account. The imposing of principles cannot contribute to this goal since principles are inherently unable to represent diversity, unless they are indeed - as Walzer puts it - 'abstract.'

4. The Temptation of Elegance or a Celebration of Diversity?

The objections against the use of principles in European private law as formulated in the above can be summarized by referring to Lord Goff. To make principles for European contract law *and* to have the ambition to have these replace the national legal systems is indeed to give in to the 'temptation of elegance.' Principles do not reflect the difficult and complex law in an adequate way. Or, to quote Goff again:[87]

85 P. Heermann, *Drittfinanzierte Erwerbsgeschäfte*, Tübingen, Mohr, 1998. Many legal systems face similar problems with this concept.

86 M. Walzer, *Spheres of Justice: a Defense of Pluralism and Equality*, New York, Basic Books, 1983, p. 8.

87 R. Goff, *supra* note 58, p. 174.

> '(...) it is better to have a feast of contrasting sources, festering with ideas, than a single hygienic package, wrapped in polythene, insulated (...) from differences in analysis and on points of detail (...)'.

The above is not to deny that with the PECL, an important step in the development of a common law for Europe has been taken. To have - as we do now at the beginning of the 21st Century - a text on which eminent scholars from all Member States of the European Union could agree, is a good starting point for further discussion on the future content and shape of a European Contract Law. It is in this idea of a *common text* with which the various national legal orders can be compared and from which inspiration can be drawn, that the great value of the PECL lies.[88] To have a more ambitious view of a principles project - as the drafters of the PECL have because, according to them, at least one of the main functions of their principles is to serve as a 'precursor' for a future European Code of Contracts[89] - is an over-stretched ambition. There is great use in *drafting* principles for scholarly purposes, but looking at them as a precursor for an *imposed* law, is not in line with the needs of today's Europe. Instead, we should celebrate diversity in a future common law for Europe.

88 On this point of the common language, also see M. Hesselink, *The Principles of European Contract Law: Some Choices Made By The Lando Commission*, Deventer, Kluwer, 2001, p. 25.

89 O. Lando and H. Beale (eds.), *supra* note 11, p. xxiii.

Stefan
Grundmann

COMMENTS ON JAN SMITS' 'THE FUTURE OF EUROPEAN CONTRACT LAW: ON DIVERSITY AND THE TEMPTATION OF ELEGANCE'

The paper itself is a temptation, elegant and of high interest. I sympathize to a certain extent with the main thrust of the paper. In my view, however, other dangers that a Code based on European Principles of Contract Law would engender are still more important. And also the result that I would advocate is somewhat different.

1. Smits' Thesis

The main thesis of Smits' paper which I shall discuss is that a European Code on the basis of general principles of contract law would have adverse effects. Smits is not really sympathetic to national Codes based on generalization and general principles either, but he is convinced that because of the underlying common tradition, national legal communities can handle such codes successfully. Smits is clearly against a European Code based on generalization and general principles, because generalization has its problems anyway and cannot be handled on a Community level because the underlying tradition is lacking. In a rather hidden passage, Smits tells us that he would have no objections against Community measures if based on a more pointillist approach, i.e. a contract by contract approach (see footnote 83). It is not completely clear whether he even advocates this approach (which I believe to be the case) or whether he would rather opt for as few Community law measures as possible.

I will take up this last proposal - contract by contract legislation on a Community level - first, then give some impressions on whether cutting back on generalization may not also have its problems. Finally I will briefly state what I think are the chances of the Commission's Communication on European Contract Law of 2001 to which Jan Smits' paper and its title refer.

2. A Contract by Contract Approach on the Community Level

A contract by contract approach in legislation already exists on the Community level. It is the law made up of directives. Smits himself sees them as 'the most successful part of present day European contract law' (p. 242).

If, however, the main proposition is to use a contract by contract approach then discussion of this corpus of directives is of prime importance. As the author of a commentary on the whole of this corpus (*Europäisches Schuldvertragsrecht*, 1999) and as one of the founders of a European Society which frequently discusses this corpus (Society of European Contract Law, SECOLA, www.secola.org), I am certainly sympathetic with this goal. Then, however, an in depth discussion of the corpus of directives, the lex lata in Europe on contracts, is the order of the day. It is needed and very much so in Jan Smits' approach. Or in Voltaire's words: If you are opposed to an idea you must strengthen its counterparts. And obviously Voltaire advocated this with enormous political success.

The natural starting point for any in depth studies would be commentaries on the whole area (apart from that by Connor Quigley, *European Contract Law*, (1997), see *Europäisches Schuldvertragsrecht* already mentioned), the same is true for monographs or concepts. Taking Smits seriously, one should not primarily deplore potential tendencies but study and thus strengthen the existing law and, if needed, improve it gradually. One should certainly use empirical data which already exist and which show that the cross border trade within the Community almost tripled within the decade in which contract law harmonization had its full breakthrough (and cross border trade to other countries only increased 'normally'; see figures cited now in ERPL 2001, 505). One should very much question whether European Community contract law is really fragmentary. There is already an extensive discussion on this question and if one rejects a generalizing approach a core question is whether the selection is sound. It is not the full picture if only those authors who repeat that European Contract Law is fragmentary are cited. There is also opposition based on facts. First, from a rather pragmatic point of view: Areas with large volumes and strong cross border elements are the main criterion of choice. Therefore there is quite substantive harmonization for banking contracts (about 16% of Europe wide gross income), public procurement contracts (about 11%), insurance law, perhaps not so much insurance contract law (about 9%), for contracts in the motor-vehicle and computer industry and in tourism (all about 5%), partly in directives, partly in block exemptions. All other industries do not even amount to 5%. From another pragmatic point of view: There seems to be an automatic reaction to real scandals (or perceived scandals) in cross border contracts. And this renders it more acceptable to recognize other laws as equivalent. This reaction mechanism worked, for instance, in the case of the time-share directive (e.g. *Gran Canaria* cases, with much German participation). From a more theoretical perspective: There is a clear tendency in Community legislation and in the Court of Justice's case law to prefer information rules over mandatory substantive rules. The reason is simple. The former may cure the problems in the contract relationship, typically differing information levels, without taking away the parties' capacity to design the product themselves and according to their own preferences (see Fleischer,

Informationsasymmetrien, (2001); Grundmann/Kerber/Weachterill, eds., *Party Autonomy and the Role of Information in the Internal Market*, (2001)). And there is a clear split, again both in Community legislation and in the Court of Justice's case law, between regulation and enabling law. It is questionable whether European Contract Law is fragmentary if it regulates almost exclusively consumer weakness and (other) public interests and if at the same time it regulates this area to an extent which almost completely exhausts these areas for the national legislators. There is virtually no consumer and public interest regulation in Germany which is not based on European standards. European Contract Law today does not cover the enabling part of contract law, it exhausts, however, the regulation part of contract law - at a minimum standard (see *Zeitschrift für Handelsrecht* 1999, 635). And it may be sound to legislate only on this regulatory part - and perhaps only at a minimum standard - on the Community level and leave the rest - the more stringent regulation and all default rules - to national legislators.

3. Questioning General Concepts and Principles in Contract Law

Another potential view of Smits' paper would be concerned with his attack on generalization. Smits' philosophical outlook is impressive, it is indeed clear that post-modern philosophy clearly showed how relative systems are and that they broke down periodically - also in the realm of the mind. Nevertheless, the enormous practical advantages of system and generalization and also the disciplining effect of it are also beyond doubt.

This point can, however, be discussed again more closely with respect to existing EC Contract Law. The interesting thing here is that apparently we face the opposite trend to what Smits advocates is the EC legislation in directives. A tendency towards generalization is clearly also visible here today. One of Smits' examples is consumer contracts vs. commercial contracts. I personally believe that consumer contracts follow and should follow general private law principles, and that the information rules needed are often needed for the market as a whole, not only for consumers. I cannot explain this here (see *Archiv für civilistische Praxis* 202 (2002) 40), two things, however, are clear: The sales directive as the last core measure was intended as a measure modernizing national contract law generally, more than any other EC measure before. And a directive which adopts solutions virtually identical to those adopted by the UN Convention on international (commercial) sales cannot be explained as being driven by needs which are particular to consumers only.

The other examples given by Smits do not seem completely convincing to me either. The Roman law of 'actiones' seems to have brought many legitimate claims to a halt.

The third example given, diversity of legislators, is indeed a very important issue, perhaps even the core issue. Yet, this is a completely different issue. It is different because it is not concerned with the question of how much generalization, or otherwise, is needed for the law itself but who is best equipped to regulate on these questions.

Before commenting shortly on this core question, let me point out one important argument supporting Smits' basic line of arguments: General, all-encompassing, principles on a centralized level (for instance, in federal legislation) that claim priority over the rule on a decentralized level (for instance, in member state legislation) would be a phenomenon as yet unheard-of in the contract law of large entities. They do not exist in the United States nor did they exist in the centuries of a Roman law-influenced common law of Europe (*ius commune,* gemeines Recht). The general principles are, and were always, applicable only on the basis of subsidiarity. Otherwise, many are convinced, we would not have had the evolution and dynamics of contract law that we have had.

4. Chances of a Merely Optional – and probably Generalizing – Code

This brings me to the chances of a merely optional code. The importance of general principles on the federal level as a basis of scientific discourse is accepted - by Smits, by me and probably anybody in this hall.

A Code of general principles on a federal basis which can be chosen could bring much of the main advantages of centralized rule making, i.e. standardization and gains in transaction costs. Smits is probably right that an optional European Code with more detailed rules will be chosen more readily, legal security will be higher. This does not decide the question of whether this should be done contract by contract, as is apparently the case in international rule setting today, or whether this can be done for the whole of contract law, as was intended by the master minds behind the UN Convention on international sales.

The whole scenario changes fundamentally if freedom of choice is taken out. We live in a world where innovation - including legal innovation - is of prime importance. Think only, over the last few decades, of the invention of consumer protection, of the law on standard contract terms, of networks of contracts vs. privity or also of e-commerce and internet law. The huge advantage of decentralized legislation is the much higher potential for experimentation and thus innovation. Even the kind of legislation we have today on a Community level has a lot of this potential because elements fostering decentralized decision making are to be seen in the principle of supremacy of information rules and in the minimum harmonization approach. The main danger of a European Code substituting national laws built on the basis of general principles is at least as much its potential petrifying effect as the lack of legal security in its application.

Hector
MacQueen

A RESPONSE TO 'THE FUTURE OF EUROPEAN CONTRACT LAW: ON DIVERSITY AND THE TEMPTATION OF ELEGANCE'

Jan Smits has written a characteristically thoughtful and thought-provoking piece which, if I may say so, also does not eschew entirely the virtues of elegance, at least in presentation and argument. There is much in his paper with which I can largely agree, but there are also more general questions on which I must, with respect and considerable tentativeness, disagree with him.

Let me begin with some points on which we can agree.

1. Single Markets and Diverse Laws: a UK Perspective

A Scots lawyer does not find it too difficult to assent to the proposition that it is not a necessary condition for the creation of a single market that it be governed by a single law. That has been the condition of the single market of the United Kingdom since the Union of the Scottish and English Parliaments in 1707, and still today within the United Kingdom there are quite distinct Scottish and English legal systems (to say nothing of the legal system of Northern Ireland). At the conference where the oral version of this response was presented, it was objected that there was no parallel between the Scottish/English Union of 1707 and today's European Union. But the text of the articles of the 1707 Union are quite clearly concerned with much more than simply the creation of a single Crown and Parliament (Articles II and III). The root of the Union was economic and commercial. Article IV says that 'all the subjects of the United Kingdom of Great Britain shall from and after the Union have full freedom and intercourse of trade and navigation to and from any port or place within the said United Kingdom'. Article VI lays down that 'all parts of the United Kingdom for ever from and after the Union shall have the same allowances, encouragements and drawbacks, and be under the same prohibitions, restrictions and regulations of trade, and liable to the same customs and duties on import and export'. Articles VII-XV make provision for a uniform tax regime, while Article XVI sets up a common currency and Article XVII a common weights and measures system. Article XVIII goes on to provide for 'the laws concerning regulation of trade, customs and excises to be the same in Scotland and England', but otherwise preserves Scots law, albeit making it alterable by the new Parliament of Great Britain. However, the Article distinguishes between public and private law in this regard, with the former being liable to change simply to make them the same throughout the United Kingdom, whereas change to private law cannot be made 'except for evident utility of the subjects within Scotland'. The lengthy Article XIX makes elaborate provision for the preservation of the court systems of England and Scotland, and Article XXV states that prior laws contrary to or inconsistent with the other Articles shall cease and become void from and after the Union.

It is thus clear that, while the drafters of the 1707 Union sought to create a single market in Great Britain, they did not see more than a limited legal union as a necessary step towards that end. Nor was this because they were unable to contemplate the possibility of a single law within England and Scotland. The possibility of legal union was first opened up in 1603, when the Scottish King James VI inherited the throne of England in the Union of the Crowns, and a good deal of energy was expended by various parties upon the project for the remainder of the seventeenth century.[1] The limitations set down in the 1707 articles reflected this century of experience and thought on both sides of the Anglo-Scottish border.

The 1707 Union was undoubtedly successful in establishing a single market in Great Britain. What is also interesting, however, is to observe both what happened within the areas in which the 1707 articles enabled the creation of similar or the same laws, and developments in those areas which were left as they stood at the time. By and large, 'single market law' can be identified from that experience as including tax, welfare, companies and business associations, employment, intellectual property, financial services including insurance, and consumer protection. In all these areas today it is clear that we can talk about United Kingdom law.[2] The fields where Scots and English law remain distinct to this day are in the classical private law subjects: persons, family, property and obligations, and interfaces between these latter two, such as rights in security and trusts.[3] Even within these subjects, moreover, a good deal of convergence has taken place, most notably in the law of delict and in particular negligence,[4] but also in large parts of contract law.[5] This has not been a one-way process: just as Scots law has moved in

1 See B.P. Levack, *The Formation of the British State*, Oxford, Clarendon Press, 1987, and, more recently, A Wijffels, 'Le débat sur une unification des droits anglais et écossais au lendemain de l'accession de Jacques VI/Ier au trône d'Angleterre', *Tijdschrift voor Rechtsgeschiedenis*, 68, 2000, p. 357 (an English translation of this will appear in 6 (3) *Edinburgh Law Review*, 2002).

2 Indeed, increasingly since 1973, European Community law.

3 See in general K.G.C. Reid and R. Zimmermann (eds.), *A History of Private Law in Scotland*, Oxford, Oxford University Press, 2000.

4 H.L. MacQueen and W.D.H. Sellar, 'History of negligence in Scots law', in E.J.H. Schrage (ed.), *Negligence: The Comparative Legal History of the Law of Torts*, Berlin, Duncker & Humblot, 2001.

5 H.L. MacQueen, 'Scots and English law: the case of contract', *Current Legal Problems*, 54, 2001, p. 205.

an English direction in a number of respects, so English law can be seen developing to become closer to Scots law.[6]

I say no more about this here, other than to observe that the United Kingdom does provide a still-working example of how a reasonably large and active single market can develop, thrive and function despite internal diversity of law. Since the laws of both England and Scotland have developed fairly pragmatically since 1707, whether development was legislative or judicial, their history over that time can reasonably be examined to see what problems were thought to require a unified response, and what diversity could be left alone. Of course, the lessons to be drawn from this experience for the much larger and more complex task of creating a single market in Europe are limited; but the evidence is at least interesting and compels the asking of questions which are relevant to the issues we face now. At least in contract, the fact that the relevant Scots law, developed over the last 300 years by jurists and judges, is quite similar in many respects to the results of the Lando Commission for a European Contract Law, is certainly worth noting.[7]

2. Contract Law as a Generalization

My other points of agreement with Jan Smits may be more briefly stated. I think his remarks about the history of contract law as one of generalization of an idea to cover more and more specific types of relationship is probably correct. But, unlike Smits (I think), I believe that the generalization of contract law has been a valid development and that it has been helpful to bring a number of distinct relationships under one overall basic conceptual umbrella, in particular because an essential feature of contract law is its default nature, i.e. it applies when the parties themselves have made no provision or when there is no more specific law dealing with the point in issue. Thus the fact that employment is a contractual relationship has enabled the courts in England and Scotland to apply contract law ideas in that field recently and produce a major development, the implied obligation of mutual trust and confidence, which has been beneficial for both employers and employees.[8] Insofar as Directives deploy a fragmented and incoherent approach to contract law, without any clear reasons for doing so, this should in my opinion be discouraged. Certainly it is one of the objectives of the Lando Commission to provide a model upon which Directives can build in future.

All law is necessarily an at least slightly artificial way of structuring the world, to enable us to plan our arrangements for the future so far as we can, and to resolve our disputes, when they occur, by means of some common standards. I agree that as far as possible these structures and standards should correspond with what happens in the world (although not perhaps in *all* its untidy complexity); but so far

6 E.g. the development of a principle against unjust enrichment in the law of restitution, or the abolition of privity in the Contracts (Rights of Third Parties) Act 1999.

7 See H.L. MacQueen, *Scots Law and the Road to the New Ius Commune*, Maastricht, Ius Commune Research School, Netherlands, 2000.

8 See *Malik v BCCI* [1998] AC 20; *Macari v Celtic FC* 1999 SC 628; D. Brodie, 'Legal coherence and the employment revolution', *Law Quarterly Review*, 117, 2001, p. 604.

as contract is concerned, the idea that promises should be kept does seem to fit with the way we do things, and the way we want things done, in the western world generally.[9] Having expounded general contract law for many years to professional audiences from commerce, industry and government, I can say that I have never been told that it was, by virtue of its abstract and general character, irrelevant to them and their various professional experiences: rather the reverse, to judge from the way they and their representatives keep coming back and asking for more!

But certainly the ongoing process of generalization must be carefully watched, and there may well come a time in the development of the law when parts of the law have to be subject to be reassessment and perhaps put out into the rain or brought under a new covering. Thus, for example, I increasingly think that consumer contracts may have to be given their own generalization away from contract law, which would thus be confined to commercial and purely private individual relationships. I would agree that analysis of marriage through contract law is not especially helpful. But this is not the occasion to pursue such questions in depth. All I would say is that the consumer, or indeed inequality of bargaining power, is far from being ignored in the Principles of European Contract Law (PECL) prepared by the Lando Commission: the principle of good faith and fair dealing prevails over freedom of contract (Article 1:102, 1:201) and includes a duty to co-operate (Article 1:202); standard form contracts are regulated (Article 2:104); excessive benefit or unfair advantage invalidates a contract (Article 4:109); un-negotiated unfair terms are avoidable, even in non-consumer contracts (Article 4:110); a contract becoming excessively onerous must be adapted or terminated (Article 6:111); and clauses excluding remedies for non-performance may not be excluded if that would be contrary to good faith and fair dealing (Article 8:109). So PECL by no means treats all contracts as involving merely economic actors who are all the same, and the text does strive to take account of social differences so far as relevant to contract law.

3. Compromising in the Search for the 'Best' Rule

Finally, Jan Smits is right to say that documents such as PECL and, indeed, the European Directives are compromises, often representing intermediate positions between the various possibilities exemplified by the various national laws. But at least so far as concerns PECL, this does not mean that the search for the best possible rule is given up or itself compromised. As I have experienced the deliberations of the Lando Commission, the arguments leading to the apparent compromises are rarely in defence of national positions or merely in quest of the common denominator, but are indeed about what is the best rule, tested against known problem situations and practice legal and commercial, and enabling the text

9 This may raise the problem of multi-culturalism, referred to briefly in Smits' paper. I am not sure how far one can go with the recognition of multi-culturalism in law: in the end it seems to be an argument as much against national as *supra*-national law, possibly involving a return to the medieval idea of a personal law.

to be presented in a way that makes its intended meaning as clear as possible in varying national contexts and cultures.

4. Flesh and Blood in PECL: Adding to Diversity

This point allows me to make a transition to the areas on which I disagree with or differ from the conclusions offered up by Jan Smits. His anxiety about fleshless, indeed bloodless, abstractions, while perhaps justified in the case of Directives, seems a little stretched beside the actuality of the PECL, which contains, apart from the texts of the principles themselves, a commentary on these texts, generally lengthy with numerous examples (often based upon actual cases from the various national systems of Europe and beyond), together with admittedly brief notes on the national laws. Thus PECL actually draws upon the existing diversity in order to help the user come to grips with what the principles are about and what they are trying to do. National laws are not suppressed; reference to them and their experience is essential to understanding PECL fully. Indeed, for many involved in PECL, it is rather important that the principles are 'soft law', coming into effect only when chosen by contracting parties or when invoked in international commercial arbitrations. So PECL adds to, rather than detracts from, diversity; at the same time, where that diversity is an impediment to cross-border activity in particular, it points the way forward to solutions.

5. The Cross-Border Problem: the Internet E-Commerce

The point about cross-border activity can be taken further. National law is seldom at its happiest in dealing with such matters unless it can pretend that the whole transaction is an entirely domestic one. This is becoming less and less possible. It is commonplace, but nonetheless true, that we live increasingly in a European, a global economy, and that we transact, both commercially and privately, across national frontiers. The Internet is extending the possibility of such transactions dramatically. The E-Commerce Directive seems to me to show the need for a common contract law to deal with this. Its articles 9-11 tell us a great deal about procedures to be followed by those supplying goods and services across the Internet, but the consumer will know nothing from these texts about when she is entitled to hold the supplier to obligations of delivery.[10] It will not please her to be told that it depends on which law of contract applies to the transaction. How much better if there was a clear answer, or at any rate a set of clearly stated principles by the application of which an answer could be reached.

10 There have been at least two recent cases in the UK where this was an issue. In September 1999 the Argos webpage mistakenly advertized at a price of £ 3 TVs normally selling at £ 399 and received a rush of orders. Argos refused to deliver and at least one customer was said to be willing to sue for breach of contract. This however seems to have come to nothing. In January 2002 Kodak's UK website advertized at £ 100 a digital camera normally retailing at £ 330. Over 5,000 orders were placed and after a dispute Kodak finally agreed to deliver the cameras.

6. The Search for Principle(s)

Finally, Jan Smits more than once invokes the words of the distinguished English judge, Lord Goff of Chieveley, in support of his arguments against principles. But some caveats must be entered in relation to this material. It is worth noting straightaway that the Maccabean Lecture from which the quotations are taken is entitled 'The Search for Principle'.[11] The lecture argues that this search is a job upon which both judges and jurists must engage, albeit by performing rather different roles. The overall context of the lecture is clearly one not hostile to, but rather strongly supportive of, the creation and development of legal principles. It is after all Lord Goff, more than any other judge, who has been responsible for the recognition by English law of the principle against unjustified enrichment. Without principles, there can be no law, only a wilderness of single instances. Law is a combination of principle with specific responses to specific situations: 'precedent is the cement of legal principle'.[12] But in general he sees the jurists as rather better than the judges at identifying and formulating the general principles of the law, because they are less focused upon the decision of actual cases.

Lord Goff's understanding of the importance of legal principles emerges very well in his famous speech in *Kleinwort Benson v Lincoln City Council*,[13] the case which abrogated the barrier to recovery of payments made under mistake of law in the English law of restitution (unjust enrichment). His historical analysis of the mistake of law rule shows that it was originally perceived as resting on sound legal policy and also achieving 'practical justice' (a phrase much favoured by Lord Goff).[14] But once scholars had shown how the English law of restitution depended upon the principle against unjust enrichment, and the courts had accepted that proposition, the mistake of law rule was doomed. This was 'because a blanket rule of non-recovery, irrespective of the justice of the case, cannot sensibly survive in a rubric of the law based on the principle of unjust enrichment'.[15] Also important was the recognition of a change of position defence within the unjust enrichment principle, because this allowed appropriate play for the factors which had hitherto supported absolute non-recovery under the mistake of law rule. Here we see general arguments about principle, coherence and system being given full play. Later in his speech, discussing whether English judges merely declare or actually make law, Lord Goff explains how judges must decide cases on the basis of the law as it is understood to be. But:

11 As is also the Festschrift in honour of Lord Goff, by W. Swadling and G. Jones (eds.), *The Search for Principle*, Oxford, Oxford University Press, 2000. The volume reprints the Maccabean Lecture in an appendix.

12 R. Goff, 'The search for principle', *Proceedings of the British Academy*, 69, 1983, p. 184.

13 [1999] 2 AC 349.

14 The best-known example of its use is in the disappointed beneficiary case, *White v Jones* [1995] 2 AC 207 at 259-60.

15 At 373.

> 'in the course of deciding the case before him he may, on occasion, develop the common law in the perceived interests of justice, though as a general rule he does this "only interstitially", to use the expression of O W Holmes J in *South Pacific Co v Jensen* (1917) 244 US 2095, 221. This means not only that he must act within the confines of the doctrine of precedent, but that the change so made must be seen as a development, usually a very modest development, of existing principle and so can take its place as a congruent part of the common law as a whole. ... Occasionally, a judicial development of the law will be of a more radical nature, constituting a departure, even a major departure, from what has previously been considered to be established principle, and leading to a realignment of subsidiary principles within that branch of the law. ... Bearing these matters in mind, the law which the judge then states to be applicable to the case before him is the law which, as so developed, is perceived by him as applying not only to the case before him, but to all other comparable cases, as a congruent part of the body of the law'.[16]

All this, I would suggest, confirms Lord Goff's belief in the importance of principles as well as practical justice in law. Principles provide stability and 'congruence' (for which we might reasonably read 'coherence'). But principles may change and new ones emerge, requiring shifts of other principles, in response to the requirements of practical justice. None the less, the overall internal congruence of the law thus modified needs to be maintained. Also notable in this speech of Lord Goff, as in so many others, is the process of cross-checking with other legal systems, civil as well as common law, testing whether the principles and outcomes being established in England are in line with those found elsewhere.[17]

A further interesting example from recent English case law in which Lord Goff was involved, albeit only in concurring with the leading speech of Lord Nicholls, is *Attorney General v Blake*,[18] in which the House of Lords recognized for the first time the remedy of account of profits for breach of contract ('restitutionary damages'). The breach of contract was a traitor's unauthorized publication of his memoirs, the profits £ 90,000-worth of royalties on sales of the book. The principle that damages for breach of contract compensate for the loss of the innocent party (here the British Government, which had employed the traitor) was of no use in this case, since there was no meaningful loss to the Government today in the publication of events forty to fifty years ago. Lord Nicholls, however, identified instances in the previous law where a 'just response' to a breach of contract was to deny the wrongdoer retention of its profit from the breach. This remedy was appropriate only in exceptional cases, of which this was one, where ordinary remedies were inadequate. But to grant the remedy would not 'contradict some recognized principle applied consistently throughout the law to the grant or withholding of an account of profits'.[19] Lord Steyn's speech, while founded on the consideration that 'practical justice strongly militates in favour of granting an order for disgorgement', also sought 'a principled basis to develop the law in a way which covers this case and other cases sharing

16 At 378.

17 At 374-5.

18 [2001] 1 AC 268.

19 Per Lord Nicholls of Birkenhead at 285.

materially similar features'.[20] It cannot be said that either Lord Nicholls or Lord Steyn was particularly successful in finding the principle or principles explaining the law resulting from the *Blake* case - Lord Nicholls admits that 'no fixed rules can be prescribed',[21] while for Lord Steyn they are 'best hammered out on the anvil of concrete cases'[22] - but the concern to be principled, or at least not inconsistent with principle, even when avowedly engaged in judicial innovation, is clearly apparent in both speeches.

Overall, therefore, neither Lord Goff nor English lawyers more generally should be seen as implacably hostile to principle and systematization in law. Rather, their attitude seems to show a sense that principle is important to the clarity and predictability of law, but should not be allowed to inhibit or cramp its responses to a changing world. I do not think, however, that the English judges would be enthusiastic about rendering principles of contract in legislative or codal form, although in *Kleinwort Benson* Lord Goff does pay tribute to 'the pioneering work' of the American Restatement of the Law of Restitution (1937) in initiating 'the blossoming of scholarly interest in the development of a coherent law of restitution ... in the common law world'.[23] Personally, I shall be satisfied if the Lando Commission does likewise for contract in the European law world.

In conclusion, then, I would suggest that the search for European principles of contract law is not misplaced and that, at least as so far as concerns the Lando Principles, some of the criticisms made by Jan Smits are. At the present stage in the development of European law, the Lando Principles seem rather to add to the present diversity, but to show a possible way forward at the very least for cross-border transactions, perhaps being best seen in their present role as 'soft law'.

20 At 291.
21 At 285.
22 At 291.
23 *Kleinwort Benson v Lincoln City Council* [1999] 2 AC at 372.

Civil Litigation and Legal Culture

Remco van Rhee

CIVIL PROCEDURE

Civil procedure is one of the most history laden branches of the law. In many countries on the European continent, this procedure still has a distinctively Romano-canonical flavour (in my opinion, this is even the case in Germany, although P.H. Lindblom in a recent article in the *European Review of Private Law* ('Harmony of the legal spheres. A Swedish view on the construction of a unified European procedural law', *ERPL* 1997, p. 11-46), does not seem to agree with my point of view. Consequently, the significance of many of the modern rules can only be evaluated fully by a study of their long history. Strangely enough, most legal historians (just as their colleagues in the area of positive law) have not shown much interest in the study of procedure. As a result, modern treatises on the history of procedure are scarce, especially if one compares their number to studies dedicated to the history of other areas of the law.

A study of procedure in the past may shed extra light on many issues, for example on why the majority of civil lawsuits are still slow and costly even though attempts have been made to change this situation for at least seven centuries. The first paper in this section by Professor K.W. Nörr contains (amongst other things) valuable information for the framing of a programme of research, for example as regards delay in civil procedure. From the perspective of the study of procedural delay, the *ordine isonomico* and *ordine asimmetrico* dichonomy as proposed by Giuliani and discussed by Professor Nörr, may play an important role.

The two remaining papers discuss two different periods in the history of procedure and show the changing attitude of the legislature to procedural reform. The paper by Professor A.A. Wijffels depicts a legislature who has taken the traditional approach to procedural reform by focussing on the rules of procedure. It evokes the conviction of the late 18th and early 19th century lawmaker that good rules result in an expedient and affordable procedure. The aim of the legislature, therefore, is the search for beneficial rules. It imposes short time-limits and restricts any means of procrastination and delays at the different stages of the proceedings. Additionally, it relies to a certain extent on the faithful application of the rules by the judge and the litigants (or their counsel).

The study of procedural reforms in the past shows, however, that rules which are good in themselves are not a guarantee for a quick and inexpensive procedure. More than once rules which could have furthered expediency and reduced costs (i.e. 'good' rules) have been applied in such a manner that the benefits they might have brought were nullified. This was either the result of their (intentional or unintentional) misinterpretation by those who had to work with them, i.e. the bar and the judiciary, or of their outright abuse.

An example of the first situation can be found in the 19th century State of New York. In 1848 New York witnessed the introduction of a code of procedure (named the Field Code after its main drafter), which aimed at curbing the evils of common law and equity procedures. The Field Code introduced a single procedure for both jurisdictions. However, due to the conservative attitude of members of the bar and the judiciary many of the new rules were misinterpreted and, as a result, old practices dating from before 1848 were retained. Consequently, the new rules did not bring the reforms so desired by the legislature (at least not immediately).[1]

An example of the outright abuse of rules may be found in the area of 'exceptions' or preliminary defences of continental civil procedure. The rules governing this area of the law aimed at guaranteeing that preliminary defences were introduced in a particular order (in various countries this is still their aim) and decided on in separate rulings before the defence on the merits. They made sure that issues which should be addressed in the initial stages of the proceedings could be addressed in these stages. The rules prevented, for example, a defendant pleading that the court lacked jurisdiction after having introduced his defence on the merits. This was beneficial because a successful preliminary defence would make proceedings on the merits superfluous. Nevertheless, defendants interested in using delaying tactics could abuse these rules, for example, by putting forward a long list of preliminary defences they knew would not meet with success in order to have the court refute these defences in a series of separate rulings and, thereby, cause delays. This was, indeed, what happened in practice.[2]

The conviction that good rules do not necessarily result in an expedient and affordable procedure is reflected by the last paper printed in this section, i.e. the paper by Professor W.D.H. Asser. Professor Asser claims that the introduction of new rules in order to reform the procedure will only be successful if these rules meet the needs and interests of all parties concerned. He further claims: 'Instead of regarding the proceedings in court as a battlefield both parties should see it as a joint responsibility to enable the court to render justice or, if possible, to settle the dispute in some other way'. It is a change of attitude that reformers should concentrate on, something which was advocated in England by Lord Woolf. Lord Woolf's proposals for reform of English civil procedure were enacted in 1999. According to these rules the parties and the court should co-operate in deciding an

1 On the Field Code, see my article in D. Heirbaut a.o. (ed.), *Handelingen van het XVe Belgisch-Nederlands Rechtshistorisch congres*, Antwerp, Kluwer, 1998.

2 On exceptions, see C.H. van Rhee, '"*Exceptiones dilatoria*" and "*peremptoriae*": from Roman Law to Modern Civil Procedure in the Netherlands', in *Viva Vox Iuris Romani*, Essays in honour of J.E. Spruit, Amsterdam, Gieben, 2002, p. 297-313.

issue at law. It is Lord Woolf's conviction that although the rules should be changed, changing them alone is not enough. In his paper Professor Asser subscribes to this point of view.

It is my conviction that the issues addressed by Professors Asser, Nörr and Wijffels have considerable significance for those involved in bringing about the harmonization of civil procedure, either in a European context or on an even larger scale.[3] Taking note of past experiences may help in avoiding some of the pitfalls of the past and, therefore, contribute to the framing of a truly satisfactory procedure. Let us hope that we do not need to wait another seven centuries before the introduction of such a procedure.

3 For harmonization in Europe, see M. Storme (ed.), *Approximation of Judiciary Law in the European Union*, Antwerp, Kluwer, 1994. For harmonization on a world-wide scale, see the *Principles and Rules of Transnational Civil Procedure* drafted by the Working Group for the Preparation of Principles and Rules of Transnational Civil Procedure, set up jointly by UNIDROIT and the American Law Institute (<http://www.unidroit.org/english/procedure/main.htm>).

Daan Asser

LESS CONFLICTS AND MORE CO-OPERATION IN CIVIL PROCEDURE

The recent reform of the German *Zivilprozeßrecht*, which will come into effect as of 1 January 2002, has been based on the following considerations

A. Problem
Der Zivilprozess muss durch eine grundlegende Strukturreform bürgernäher, effizienter und transparenter werden. Die Verhandlungskultur, die Funktion der Rechtsmittelzüge und der Gerichtsaufbau genügen den berechtigten Ansprüchen der rechtsuchenden Bürgerinnen und Bürger sowie der Wirtschaft nicht mehr. Zudem kommen auf die Zivil-justiz durch die zunehmende Verrechtlichung des Alltagslebens, den rasanten Fortschritt der Informations- und Kommunikationstechnologien und nicht zuletzt durch die Vereinheit-lichung des europäischen Rechtsraums neue Aufgaben zu, die sie – angesichts der Haus-haltslage der Länder – ohne zusätzliches Personal bewältigen muss.[1]

1 B. Lösung
Die angestrebte Qualitätsverbesserung und Effizienzsteigerung innerhalb der Ziviljustiz kann nur mit einer grundlegenden Strukturreform erreicht werden. Die Reform enthält folgende Schwerpunkte:
- Institutionalisierung des Schlichtungsgedankens im Zivilprozess durch die Einführung einer Güteverhandlung *(amicable settlement,* § 278-279),
- Erhöhung der Transparenz und Akzeptanz richterlicher Entscheidungsfindung durch eine stärkere Betonung der richterlichen Aufklärungs- und Hinweispflichten, - Einführung des originär zuständigen Einzelrichters beim Landgericht (§ 348-348a),
- Abbau von streitwertabhängigen Zugangsbarrieren zum Rechtsmittel durch Einfüh-rung eines Abhilfeverfahrens und einer Zulassungsberufung gegen bisher unan-fechtbare Urteile sowie Abschaffung der Streitwertrevision,
- deutlichere Funktionsdifferenzierung der Rechtsmittelebenen durch die Umgestal-tung der Berufung in ein Instrument zur Fehlerkontrolle und - beseitigung (a complete new Book 3; § 511: appeal only if the court of first instance has given leave to appeal; review, no rehearing; § 526 unus iudex; introduction of rehearing by the first instance court if the right of "Rechtliches gehör" has been violated, § 321a),
- Einführung einer beschleunigten Erledigungsmöglichkeit für substanzlose Berufungen sowie
- Wegbereitung für eine weitere Harmonisierung der Verfahrensordnungen.

Similar considerations have been the basis for the modest Dutch reforms which will come into effect on the same date of 1 January 2002.[2]

Although the German considerations speak of '*Verhandlungskultur*' i.e. the trial-culture, I doubt whether both the German and the Dutch reforms will really change the prevailing attitude and culture which has existed in the litigation practice of both countries for a long time. Of course, some changes and even some important changes may occur, but on the whole I don't think that one can speak of a fundamental reform in either case (except for the *Berufung*, the appeal in Germany whose character is indeed fundamentally changed). In this paper I will dwell on the subject of attitude and culture in civil proceedings.

Thinking of civil procedure reform we have to recognize the problem of the proceedings themselves being one of the main obstacles on the road to modernization. Any reform in this field will have to cope with the question of how to change the traditional attitude of the participants in legal proceedings - both parties and judges - in such a manner as to create a less discordant atmosphere. Traditionally both parties play the role of opponents, which is, of course, perfectly natural in respect of the dispute giving cause to the action. It is inherent in our way of dealing with disputes since the Romans that we consider a conflict in terms of the law. Confronted with a dispute between two parties, lawyers immediately build a *case* out of it. We tend to regard the dispute as a case, as we have been taught to do since the teaching of Roman law began. Consequently we start looking for similar cases in order to find the applicable rules and if necessary we do some distinguishing which enables us to apply them. More than once we manipulate and mould the facts to that effect. Facts are less important than rules. Civil proceedings, at least in the continental Roman Law tradition, tend to emphasize the so-called legal consequences and to neglect the facts, or rather: the reality behind what we call facts. It is, in fact, all part of a rich tradition of debating and rhetoric. We are trained in this marvellous art in our law schools and faculties. This impressive heritage of at least two millennia of legal thinking is a part of our culture.

But far from being a civilized exercise in debating, litigation is, as a matter of fact, a fight over the very rights and interests of the opponents themselves. Much depends on the outcome of this fight and the stakes are high, apart from the costs involved in the operation. Consequently, there seems to be a natural tendency of both parties to employ all possible means to win their case. If they find a procedural way to victory they will use it and the lawyer who neglects such an opportunity may find himself at the end of the day being held liable for malpractice. The aspect of the advocate's liability very much complicates the matter because it means that the advocate has a selfish interest in finding every suitable opportunity achieve success.

The word litigation refers to the Latin word *lis*, which means strife, dispute, quarrel. Hence our tradition in civil litigation is one of parties opposing each other,

2 The reforms concern mainly the first instance. However, the Dutch Government have announced that the possibility of introducing more fundamental changes is being studied by a working party consisting of three experts in this field.

quarreling, trying to win their case by any means that are not forbidden. Both parties will not confine their debate to the rights and obligations concerning the claim itself, but they will also rely on procedural methods to fight each other. Clean and technical warfare is the impression most civil proceedings will give. As a result, civil proceedings tend to accumulate conflicts instead of solving them, and this might well be regarded as one of the main reasons why proceedings regularly take so many years to come to an end.

Furthermore, litigation is embedded in the system of law, which means that right from the beginning the conflict is brought to the level of legal arguments and reasoning. The parties build their strongholds and defences in view of any possible litigation, even if they would eventually prefer a negotiated settlement to litigation. The expectations and chances of winning the case in court frequently dictate the outcome of negotiations, as we all know. Therefore, when a conflict appears to be inevitable both lawyers and clients tend to prepare for battle rather than looking for any solution which may prevent the worst possible outcome: lengthy and costly proceedings in court. Even in a pre-trial stage, such as discovery, one discerns the smoke of gunfire. Both parties attempt to gain as much ground as possible in order to obtain the most favourable starting position in the proceedings to come. As a result, complicated and lengthy, and hence costly, pre-trial proceedings prevent ordinary people from exercising their fundamental right to present their case to the court. The Woolf reforms of civil proceedings in the High Court of England and Wales have brought considerable relief in this respect by introducing a new form of disclosure of documents under strict surveillance of the court.

Can we change things and if so, how could we achieve change? We could, of course, rely on the traditional way we change the law: by simply introducing new laws. We impose new rules on all parties concerned and we believe that they will apply them to the effect that changes are brought about. This will, I believe, only be successful if the new rules meet the needs and interests of all parties concerned.

First we have to consider the relationship between both litigants. Litigation between two parties can be regarded as a certain stage of development of their legal relationship. This relationship may have given rise to the conflict, *e.g.* a contract or a marriage. However, it may also happen that the conflict has arisen without any such specific relationship existing in advance, *e.g.* when the cause of action is the recovery of damages caused by a traffic accident. Before the accident took place there was no relationship between the parties concerned, but I would assume that the accident itself created a legal relationship in respect of the liability for the damages. If the damages are not settled amiably there is a conflict in this legal relationship. Sometimes the cause of action concerns the question of whether any legal relationship exists at all, which may be the case if the defendant denies that a contract has ever been made between him and the claimant or if he denies any involvement in the accident. In such events it is the mere fact that both parties are involved in litigation, that creates a kind of relationship which is, as I see it, of a procedural nature. One may conclude therefore that in litigation there is always some sort of relationship between both parties. It is that relationship which should be the starting point of, and simultaneously provide the basis for, a different approach of civil litigation. Instead of regarding the proceedings in court as a battlefield both parties should see it as a joint responsibility to enable the court to render justice or, if possible, to settle the dispute in some other way. They should bear in mind that, as far as the conduct of proceedings is concerned, their relationship provides a basis for reasonable and fair behaviour in respect of one another. Moreover they both bear a responsibility for decent procedural behaviour in respect of the court and the community as a whole.

Secondly, there is the court itself and its old and venerable traditions. On the Continent the more modern tradition is that the conduct of civil proceedings, especially in the field of factfinding, is the task of the court rather than of the parties, even though the *Verhandlungsmaxime* (the adversarial system) is still regarded as the overriding principle. The parties present their case to the court and it is up to the court to decide which information and evidence it needs to do justice. The parties should assist the court in finding the facts and the law. It is the court that decides whether it has been sufficiently informed in order to do justice, whether witnesses should be called or experts be appointed, whether it wants to collect more information or not. It is the court that examines witnesses and experts. This is, at least, the situation in the Netherlands. Everything is focussed on the court preparing its judgment. Of course, in a growing number of jurisdictions the courts are enabled or even obliged to consider whether the parties could be brought to an amicable settlement, but the main prospect is that of the court terminating the case by rendering judgment.

In the common law countries the adversarial system is traditionally much stronger than on the Continent. However, in England, the Woolf reforms have brought about a shift in the direction of the active and managing judge, whereas formerly the court was regarded perhaps more as an umpire.[3] The pure adversarial system, fostered by the members of the profession, has been replaced by a system in which the court has more power and discretion as to the conduct of proceedings and the parties are obliged to adopt an attitude of co-operation. It is not only interesting from a comparative viewpoint but also necessary for those looking for solutions in their own system to take into consideration the principles of the Woolf reforms in England. We can perhaps learn a new attitude from them which will also help us in reforming the civil procedure on the Continent. Therefore, I would like to quote the main principles:

1. The Overriding Objective

(1) These Rules are a new procedural code with the overriding objective of enabling the court to deal with cases justly.
(2) Dealing with a case justly includes, so far as is practicable –
  (a) ensuring that the parties are on an equal footing;
  (b) saving expense;
  (c) dealing with the case in ways which are proportionate –

[3] See also M. Bramley and A. Gouge, *The civil justice reforms one year on, Freshfields assess their progress*, London, 2000.

- (i) to the amount of money involved;
- (ii) to the importance of the case;
- (iii) to the complexity of the issues; and
- (iv) to the financial position of each party;

(d) ensuring that it is dealt with expeditiously and fairly; and
(e) allotting to it an appropriate share of the court's resources, while taking into account the need to allot resources to other cases.

2. Application by the Court of the Overriding Objective

The court must seek to give effect to the overriding objective when it-
(a) exercises any power given to it by the Rules; or
(b) interprets any rule.

3. Duty of the Parties

The parties are required to help the court to further the overriding objective.

4. Court's Duty to Manage Cases

(1) The court must further the overriding objective by actively managing cases.
(2) Active case management includes –
- (a) encouraging the parties to co-operate with each other in the conduct of the proceedings;
- (b) identifying the issues at an early stage;
- (c) deciding promptly which issues need full investigation and trial and accordingly disposing summarily of the others;
- (d) deciding the order in which issues are to be resolved;
- (e) encouraging the parties to use an alternative dispute resolution (GL) procedure if the court considers that appropriate and facilitating the use of such procedure;
- (f) helping the parties to settle the whole or part of the case;
- (g) fixing timetables or otherwise controlling the progress of the case;
- (h) considering whether the likely benefits of taking a particular step justify the cost of taking it;
- (i) dealing with as many aspects of the case as it can on the same occasion;
- (j) dealing with the case without the parties needing to attend at court;
- (k) making use of technology; and
- (l) giving directions to ensure that the trial of a case proceeds quickly and efficiently.

Here we have a declaration of principles of civil procedure which applies to both the common law and the continental procedural system. I believe that this declaration will also have a great impact on the rethinking of procedural law elsewhere. No doubt the emphasis now lays on the activities of the court. There is a clear shift towards the Continental systems.

In my view the most important issue is the co-operation of the parties and the court. Here the fundamental change of attitude and culture can be achieved. If we accept that the parties and the court have a joint responsibility for the conduct of the proceedings, we should stress that the parties should have a duty to prepare the case thoroughly before going to court and even that they have the obligation to avoid litigation as much as possible. Whether the court itself should play a role in this respect, is to be studied carefully. Court-annexed mediation is something which may be attractive, but we should bear in mind that any confusion as to the role of the judge (mediator or judge?) should be avoided. Nevertheless, from the point of view of reducing the case-load of the courts, measures should be taken to facilitate the parties to reach an amicable settlement before going to court. If we impose duties of that kind on the parties we should also stimulate them to fulfil these duties.

Measures should also be considered to the effect that the parties should have the available evidence collected and well prepared before starting proceedings instead of waiting for the judge to decide upon whom the burden of proof rests. The fact-finding process should be completed as much as possible before trial and not, as is now still the situation on the Continent, during the proceedings in court. I submit therefore that also in the continental systems, rules should be developed which introduce the possibility of something akin to the English disclosure. The court should facilitate the pre-trial and even pre-action fact-finding by making it possible for the parties to invoke the assistance of the court as regards the collecting of evidence and solving disputes in that stage, even if third parties are concerned. If a system requires the court to examine the witnesses under oath it should provide the parties with the possibility of a judge being appointed in advance to do so.

In the new English system pre-action protocols should play an important role. I think that on the Continent we should also encourage the parties to make provisions themselves, laid down in protocols, as to how the proceedings will be conducted. If speeding up proceedings is one of the main objectives of every reform of civil justice, we should bear in mind that an agreement between the parties as to the deadlines and pace of the process may have a much more compelling effect than abstract rules which provoke delaying tactics and exceptions. Moreover, the court would be much less inclined to allow exceptions to what parties have agreed upon in a binding agreement than to abstract rules which are imposed on them. One can also think of models – fixed protocols agreed upon between the judiciary and the bar – from which the parties may chose the most suitable one.

I believe that also on the Continent we should embark on the task of making civil procedure something which belongs to both the parties concerned and the court. We should further the idea of co-operation as regards procedure, with more agreements and better preparation.

In striving for unification or at least harmonization of the law of civil procedure in the European Union, we cannot escape harmonizing at least the basic principles and elements of the various systems of civil litigation. I am sure that, even if we must accept that the different traditions and cultures will stay alive in the decades to come, the overriding objectives are already the same in many countries in our part of the world and harmonization will gradually be effected. We cannot explain to people doing business all over the world why we in Europe should maintain all those differences and why every country requires you to hire expensive specialists to find - if not: to bluff - your way in court.

Alain Wijffels

A PHANTOM CODE: THE 1830 CODE OF CIVIL PROCEDURE FOR THE KINGDOM OF THE NETHERLANDS

> *'Dans la Constitution actuelle de la grande République Européenne, au milieu des rapports inévitables, qui en lient tous les peuples et tous les Gouvernements, un Code de lois et de règlements qui, isolant une nation de toutes les autres, ne conviendrait et ne pourrait convenir exclusivement qu'à elle seule, loin d'être national, serait pour elle-même le plus désastreux, et par conséquent le plus anti-national que ses législateurs pourraient imaginer de lui donner'.*[1]

In the aftermath of the Congress of Vienna, the new Kingdom of the Netherlands was set to establish its own 'national' codes. By then, both the Southern provinces and the Northern provinces were using the French codes of the Napoleonic era, although French law and institutions had been in force for much longer in the Belgian territories, and had perhaps met with a more sympathetic welcome than in the Northern Dutch areas. Whatever the unifying forces there may have been at work between the North and the South, the codification works of the 1820s proved to be an exercise in bridging not only opposing political views (which often cut through the North-South divide), but also to some degree a cultural antagonism, not in the least among the legal profession. In this paper, the emphasis will be on fundamental principles[2] governing the Code of civil procedure which was enacted

1 From a speech of Dotrenge, member of the Lower House, on 7 February 1828, arguing against those members who criticized the project of the Code of civil procedure for being influenced too much by the French Code of 1806, and thus insufficiently steeped in the 'national' legal tradition. Nevertheless, he denied that there was a close conformity between the French Code and the project under discussion (*infra* note 23).

2 One participant in the discussion after this paper was read remarked that, as concepts, the *Verhandlungsmaxime* and the *Untersuchungsmaxime* were formulated long after the statutes I discuss in my contribution were enacted. Perhaps the remark was meant to imply a degree of anachronism or even a lack of historical criticism. I have, indeed, emphasized more strongly the theoretical approach in this paper, because I plan to use the same material for different research in the future. Even so, I believe that both principles, however formulated, are

in 1830, but never came into force. Throughout the governmental and parliamentary preparation of that code, the French Code of 1806 cast its long shadow over the discussions, not only because it was seen, for better or for worse, as a model to be rejected or followed, but also because it remained by and large the system prevailing and applied during the same years in legal practice. Nevertheless, it may be useful to refer briefly to two other pieces of legislation on civil procedure which had been promulgated in the Netherlands during the previous decades: the 1786 Ordinance of civil procedure for the Austrian Netherlands and the 1799 Rules of procedure for the Batavian Republic.[3] Two 'codes' which, in spite of the different political contexts in which they saw the light, somehow reflect the reformatory spirit which was imposing itself against forensic inertia and traditionalism towards the very end of the Ancien Régime and during the revolutionary years of the 18th-century's last decade; two codes which on the whole also remained phantom

adequate hermeneutic tools for diachronically comparing patterns of civil procedure in Western legal history. My own standard (and hardly original) presentation of the history of civil procedure to undergraduate students consists in telling them that at any time in history, procedural systems in private law have attempted some kind of compromise between the policy of leaving as much leeway and initiative as possible to the litigants (i.e. whether to initiate proceedings, by defining the object of the proceedings, by deciding what evidence is to be produced, by ensuring the progress of the proceedings at every stage et cetera) and that of putting the judge in charge. These policies are but two extreme poles, never to be found unadulterated. Since the development of the Roman-canonic procedure, most legal systems in the West have laid greater emphasis on the *Verhandlungsmaxime*, though not without corrections (e.g. for inquests, or in summary proceedings); conversely, historical examples of civil procedures favouring more systematically the *Untersuchungsmaxime* (as in late-18th century Prussia) have so far not been the most successful. Nevertheless, I would myself not feel bound by the dichotomy for assessing current trends in civil procedure: indeed, I believe that the current development of having recourse to the *Untersuchungsmaxime* is a feeble and inadequate response to the contemporary challenges civil procedure is facing today, and which I briefly hint at in the final page of this paper. As a legal historian, I would, however, refrain from suggesting any models drawn from my historical experience. Possibly the age-old concept of the *trias forensis* needs to be expanded, and alternative models of interaction between the procedural actors need to be developed, both in practice and theory. This is, of course, already under way. One of my favourite concepts for formulating a fundamental principle of modern procedure is that of *Prozeßtreue*, i.e. the requirement that all actors should ensure that the means and the aim of the procedure are respected. Such a concept can also be found in non-western legal systems e.g. in the Islamic tradition, cf. H.P. Glenn, *Legal Traditions of the World*, Oxford, Oxford University Press, 2000, p. 163: '[In Qadi dispute resolution, the parties] are not free to obstruct in any way the judicial process, and are rightly seen as partners of the qadi in the law-seeking process. The process is not adversarial, in common law language, but neither is it investigative in the formal manner of civil law procedure'.

3 For the Northern provinces, a full survey ought also to take into account J. van der Linden's work and the *Wetboek op de regterlijke instellingen en regtspleging* which was enacted under Louis Napoleon's rule in 1809. In general, an edition of the surviving source-material on the various preparations and drafts of a code of civil procedure in the Batavian Republic, the Kingdom of Holland and the years immediately following the retreat of the French authorities and the creation of the Dutch-Belgian union is still wanting. Much useful information can meanwhile be gathered (up to the French annexation) in M. van Boven's book, referred to *infra*, note 11.

legislation, only ineffectually enforced, if at all.[4] Ghost legislation, however, bears just as much testimony to legal history as those more successful codes and statutes which did make it to legal practice.[5] This, in the long term, may be of some comfort to those scholars of our own time who have devoted much of their time and energy to associate their names to the codification of European law.

1. Reform of Civil Procedure in the Southern Netherlands: The 1786 Ordinance on Civil Procedure for the Austrian Netherlands (*Reglement over de Civile Rechtsplegínge voor de Oostenryckscbe Nederlanden*)[6]

The *Reglement* has traditionally been associated with Joseph II's rule as an 'enlightened despot', a (moderate) influence of the eighteenth-century School of Natural Law, and his reform of the courts' system in the Austrian Netherlands.[7] No doubt the most important innovation the *Reglement* would have introduced would nevertheless have been a uniform set of rules governing civil procedure throughout the Emperor's Netherlands. Since medieval times, the fundamental principle for the administration of justice in the Low Countries had been (at least, at first-instance level) that, in general, legal pluralism in the sense of a great diversity of substantive law *ratione territorii* (at local, regional or provincial level), *ratione personae* and *ratione materiae* (e.g. in property law, depending on the legal status of the land) was also reflected in a corresponding diversity of jurisdictions with their own style of procedure. By and large, a specific court was in place for most of the particular legal systems (*iura propria*) which coexisted and overlapped in the Southern Netherlands

4 The common opinion is that Joseph's judicial and procedural reforms (which also included new Rules of criminal procedure) were barely applied. However, Prof.em. G. van Dievoet told me in November 2001 that his earlier research, which has yet to be published, had revealed more instances where the reform was effectively introduced than has hitherto been thought. It seems less controversial that the 1799 *Reglement* was never applied (*infra* note 12).

5 For a survey of successful and less successful codification projects in 19th-century Belgium: J. Gilissen, 'Codifications et projets de codification en Belgique au XIXe siècle (1804-1914)', *Belgisch Tijdschrift voor Nieuwste Geschiedenis,* 14, 1983, p. 203-85, and specifically on civil procedure: p. 221-2, 255-6. For an outline of the Dutch history, cf. T.A.W. Sterk, 'Honderdvijftig jaar Nederlands burgerlijk procesrecht', in E. Spanoghe and R. Feenstra (eds.), *Honderdvijftig jaar rechtsleven in België en Nederland,* Leiden, Universitaire Pers Leiden, 1980, and more recently, with greater emphasis on early 20th-century discussions, C.H. van Rhee, '"Ons tegenwoordig sukkelproces", Nederlandse opvattingen over de toekomst van het burgerlijk procesrecht rond 1920', *Tijdschrift voor Rechtsgeschiedenis,* 68, 2000, p. 331-46.

6 References to the Act in this paper are to the Dutch version (Tot Brussel, By Pauwels, drucker van Syne Majesteyt, op de groote Merckt, 1786) - for which I am most grateful to Prof.em. J.Th. de Smidt. I have occasionally compared the text with the French version (which is also to be found in the *Recueil des ordonnances des Pays-Bas autrichiens,* 3e série XX [Brussels 1910], 552-83), published concomitantly but separately as *Reglement de la procédure civile pour les Pays-Bas autrichiens.* A Bruxelles, Chez Pauwels, Imprimeur de Sa Majesté, à la grand'place, 1786.

7 G. van Dievoet, 'De hervorming van het burgerlijk procesrecht door Jozef II in de Zuidelijke Nederlanden en de School van het Natuurrecht', in *Derde Colloquium van nederlandse en Belgische rechtshistorici,* Amsterdam, Centrum voor Rechtsgeschiedenis (UFSIA) en NCRD, 1979, p. 41-49.

until the end of the Ancien Regime. Over the centuries, a limited degree of uniformity had been reached through a common legal culture regarding the administration of justice fostered by the influence of civil law and, at least at the provincial level, through the practice of the provincial courts of justice. Compared to a much larger and legally diversified territory such as France, the early-modern Southern Netherlands had not experienced anything comparable to the *Ordonnance* of 1667 or even the powerful effect of the *Parlements* – the Great Council of Malines would hardly bear the comparison, even on the smaller scale of Belgium, to the *Parlement de Paris*.

The ordinary first-instance courts were therefore intimately linked to the (mostly, territorial) *ius proprium* they were called to apply. Even the provincial courts, whether as appeal courts or in first-instance proceedings, remained anchored in the provincial interests and legal institutions, and followed their own style of procedure. Joseph II's jurisdictional reform[8] severed in many respects that age-old bond between the court, substantive law and procedure. His *Reglement* on civil procedure was a further step in cutting off the traditional tie between the courts and local or particular law.[9] Indeed, the courts' constitution and legitimacy in the Emperor's new system were no longer founded on, nor culturally or politically anchored in, those local or particular interests. The contrast, however, would inevitably have been exacerbated, if the *Reglement* had been fully implemented in practice, since the new 'state' system of courts[10] following a uniform set of procedural rules would still have had to apply the great diversity of Belgian *iura propria* – which the Hapsburg rule, even under Joseph II, did not subject to unification or codification, except in a few limited areas.

Although the *Reglement* therefore fitted into a potentially fundamental reform of the administration of justice, the civil procedure introduced by Joseph II in 1786-7 was far from revolutionary. Throughout this code, the main concern which emerges is that of giving effect to the *Beschleunigingsprinzip* by imposing short time-limits for submitting documents, pleas, defences, or for introducing remedies, and by restricting any means of procrastination and delays at the different stages of the proceedings. The idea of abridging civil proceedings was hardly new. What is more remarkable is that in spite of this aim, the *Verhandlungsmaxime* continues to dominate the whole proceedings; the traditional technique for speeding up civil proceedings, *viz.* by introducing at critical stages of the proceedings specific applications of the *Offizialmaxime* or of the *Untersuchungsmaxime*, was not followed by the drafters

8 Cf. the Emperor's Edicts of 1 January 1787, which abolished most jurisdictions and replaced them with a hierarchical, pyramidal system of courts for the Austrian Netherlands, including one Supreme Court, two courts of appeal, and 63 first-instance courts.

9 It seems that in Vienna, K.A. Martini rejected most of the drafts which had been prepared in Brussels, because they contained too many rules borrowed from local customs. Instead, his project was inspired by the codification introduced in Lombardy and legislation for the Austrian *Erbländer* (J. Gilissen, *Introduction historique au droit*, Brussels, Bruylant, 1979), p. 306-307).

10 Some provisions of the Reglement nevertheless seem to continue to refer to the old jurisdictions (at a local level): §§ 335, 424, 444-5.

of the *Reglement* – indeed, the code does not even contain a title on summary proceedings.

The *Verhandlungsmaxime* is expressly said to prevail in civil proceedings, except when the law lays down that the judge will act *ex officio* (cf. the general statement in § 1). This general principle is occasionally repeated and applied in the code: e.g. in § 123, which prohibits the judge from imposing the production of any (additional) evidence on the litigants; see also § 283 (which restricts the judge's authority to press too strongly for a settlement); § 312 (on how execution may be issued on the judgement). Applications of the *Offizialmaxime* are limited in the *Reglement*: e.g. § 21 (oral proceedings in rural areas: the judge will verify whether the basic requirements are met as regards the object of the litigation, the evidence, the capacity of the litigants, and the jurisdiction of the court); § 78 (several measures in the case of proceedings involving a plurality of creditors against a debtor unable to pay); §§ 171-2 (tasks of a judge outside the jurisdiction where the case is being heard, who is assigned to proceed to the examination of witnesses); § 201 (the judge's decision to call for an expert's opinion; however, the decree will be issued after the litigants have made their submissions); § 263 (service of the judgement); §§ 374-5 (convocation of the creditors in order to ratify a provisional settlement; sanctions against a fraudulent debtor).

The *Verhandlungsmaxime* is also fundamental for deciding whether the proceedings will be oral or written: § 15 provides guide-lines for the choice, but the litigants remain largely free to select the type of procedure (see also § 17; and, for oral proceedings in general: §§ 18 *et seq.*). Closely related to the *Verhandlungsmaxime* is the *audi alteram partem* rule, which receives many applications throughout the *Reglement* (e.g. §§ 38, 40, 45, 48, 54, 140, 243, 258, 269); witnesses will be examined by the judge without the litigants being present, but the records of their evidence will be communicated to the latter (§§ 179 *et seq.*). The rule suffers only a few exceptions (e.g. § 202: when an expert's examination is required without delay).

It is less obvious how the code intended to enforce its strict provisions regarding time-limits and restrictions on attempts at adding fresh elements to the case. For the latter, it had to rely mainly on the judge's duty to reject any untimely claims or belatedly submitted evidence and remedies, or, in some cases, on their arbitrary power to impose penalties. More generally, however, any infringement of the strict rules of procedure laid down by the code was supposed to be sanctioned by nullity and possibly by the liability of the judges – hardly the most effective sanctions for discouraging chicanery and protracted procedural remedies.

The general sanctions of nullity and liability of the judge are already mentioned in the code's introductory enactment formula. The judge's liability (to pay damages) is further confirmed in §§ 278 and 451. Nullity as a remedy is organized in §§ 276 *et seq.*; § 281 provides explicitly for the superior court to hear complaints against alleged procedural errors, without stating what the remedy may be.

A more traditional procedural sanction is the inadmissibility of a submission, act, witness et cetera. This occurs on a number of occasions, e.g. regarding belatedly submitted defences after default (§ 29 in oral proceedings, § 36 in written proceedings); § 47 (new facts introduced in the plaintiff's second memorandum: the judge will not take them into account in his decision); § 53 (if the defendant fails to submit his rejoinder in time, facts alleged by his opponent may be regarded as true facts); §

271 (appeal-proceedings: new facts or evidence submitted by a litigant will not be taken into account by the appeal judge).

However, in most cases, the *Reglement* does not specify what the sanction is if its order of procedure is not complied with. This is all the more striking, since the code contains a great many provisions restricting the submission of pleas or documents (e.g. §§ 2, 7, 40 *et seq.*, 189, 361), forbidding repetitions (§§ 9, 10, 47 *et seq.*, and, somewhat patronizingly, prolixity, e.g. §§ 12, 13, 56), or imposing time-limits (e.g. §§ 35, 38, 44 *et seq.*, 51, 252). It is not always clear whether the general sanctions mentioned before would apply, nor whether, if so, that would stimulate swift and orderly proceedings. In some cases, one should perhaps assume that the submission in question would simply not be admitted or taken into account. Nevertheless, in several cases, the provision seems simply to impose a duty on the litigants (or their counsel), but no effective sanction in case of a breach seems to have been considered: e.g. § 161 *et seq.* (on the drafting of submissions of evidence, which should be restricted to facts, and should avoid any arguments about rights). Even more questionable is the procedural sanction when the code addresses a duty imposed on the judge: e.g. § 260 (general duty to hear and judge cases without delay); § 270 (the same, for the judge in appeal). In contrast, recalcitrant witnesses may incur fines and corporal punishment (§§ 174, 199)!

The lack of clear, specific sanctions for failing to follow the provisions set out in the *Reglement* are in some respects characteristic of the general tone of that code. The *Reglement* sets out a model procedure which to some extent relies on the judge's and the litigants' (or their counsels') willingness to abide by a 'code of conduct' which it partly expresses itself. It fails to establish convincing means for avoiding one of the major traditional risks of most procedural systems, *viz.* that of having less conscientious practitioners and litigants turning its own safe-guards against its main purpose of a fair and expeditious process of law. In addition, it remains to a large degree (perhaps not altogether inappropriately for a phantom-code) a skeleton codification which would necessarily rely on an additional body of rules – whether statutory, customary or based on civil law, although the issue remains unexpressed and unresolved in the *Reglement* itself – in order to be fully operational in practice. Considering, as pointed out previously, that it was a new judicial system which was meant to operate in an environment of an historically rooted and territorially fragmented substantive law, the legislator was evidently counting very much on the loyalty of the judges and the advocates towards their commitment to a due system of civil procedure.

In the introductory enactment formula, the legislator reserves the interpretation of the *Reglement* to himself; the last § of the *Reglement*, however, makes plain that major questions of interpretation may be dealt with by the supreme court (§ 451). Otherwise, the code contains several examples of specific situations where the appreciation (of facts) is left to the discretion of the judge; this is in particular true for assessing the evidence (e.g. § 148, 158).

The office of proctor was to be (gradually) abolished (§ 424), and representatives other than professional advocates were only acknowledged in a very marginal and subsidiary position. The *Reglement* provided for academic qualifications for advocates, for pupillage, and an examination before being admitted to exercise the profession (Ch.

38); corresponding requirements were expressed for those who sought a judgeship (Ch. 39).

Judgements were not to contain the reasons of the decision (§ 261), but these reasons were to be given when a remedy against the decision was sought (§§ 264, 270).

2. Reform of Civil Procedure in the Northern Netherlands: The 1799 Rules of Civil Procedure for the Batavian Republic (*Manier van Procedeeren in Civiele Zaaken, zoo voor de Burgerlyke Rechtbanken als voor de Departementaale Gerechtshoven*)[11]

Although enacted by the Assembly of Representatives of the Batavian 'sister republic' of France, the Rules of civil procedure of 1799[12] present several common features with that of Joseph II for the Southern Netherlands (territories which by that time had been incorporated into France and were fully subject to French laws).[13] The Batavian Act is clearly better formulated and expresses a superior technique of statutory drafting; it also avoids the somewhat high-handed precepts of the 1787 code. Nor does it revolutionize the system of civil procedure. The main revolution is to be found outside the code, *viz.* in the concept of a 'nation-wide' state-system of courts which was to replace the intricate structure of local and provincial courts.

11 For a brief discussion of the Reglement and its preliminaries, although mainly from the vantage-point of the organization of the courts' system: M.W. van Boven, *De rechterlijke instellingen ter discussie. De geschiedenis van de wetgeving op de rechterlijke organisatie in de periode 1795-1811*, Nijmegen, Gerard Noodt Instituut, 1990, p. 117-20.

12 The official imprint is the *Algemeene manier van procedeeren in civiele en crimineele zaaken, met de daartoe behoorende instructien voor alle openbaare aanklagers, rechtbanken en gerechtshoven in de Bataafsche Republiek. Gearresteerd by Decreet van het Vertegenwoordigend Lighaam des Bataaffschen Volks. Op den 22. Augustus 1799. Het vyfde Jaar der Bataafsche Vryheid*, In den Haag, ter 's Lands Drukkery 1799. It contains, first (p. 1-47) the 'Instructie en manier van procedeeren voor de Vrederechters en derzelver byzitters', followed (p. 49-230) by the 'Manier van procedeeren in civiele zaaken, zoo voor de Burgerlyke Rechtbanken als voor de Departementaale Gerechtshoven', then (p. 231-535) the 'Manier van procedeeren in crimineele zaaken, zoo voor de Burgerlyke Rechtbanken als voor de Departementaale Gerechtshoven', and (p. 537-567) the 'Instructie en manier van procedeeren voor het Hoog Nationaal Gerechts-Hof'. Each of these statutes contains an appendix with standard forms for specific procedural acts. The publication by the Executive of the Batavian Republic followed on 24 October 1799. The Executive's decree of publication provided for special means of publicity: (i) the full text of the different Acts mentioned previously was to be published by the Land's Drukkery in the format of an authenticated in-8o book; (ii) the book was to be sold nationwide; (iii) copies of the book were to be sent to the administrations of the departementen and to the town councils; all in addition to the usual manner of publication of statutes. In spite of the clear formulation of this decree, there has been a controversy among Dutch legal historians whether the enactment was actually issued or not (cf. thesis IX to F.C.J. Ketelaar, *Oude zakelijke rechten vroeger, nu en in de toekomst*, Leiden-Zwolle, Universitaire Pers Leiden en W.E.J. Tjeenk Willink, 1978); M.W. van Boven, *supra* note 11, p. 119, accepts that the *Reglement* was formally enacted, but says it was never introduced into practice nationwide.

13 In common with the 1787 *Reglement*, the *Manier van procedeeren* gives special attention to bankruptcies and debtors unable to pay their debts. The 1799 Batavian code contains a markedly more sustained attention towards foreign parties and litigants, and litigants residing abroad.

Here, too, a new judiciary, working according to a new standard procedure,[14] was called to apply the great diversity of Dutch *iura propria*,[15] while the prospect of national Batavian codes which would unify the various areas of substantive law could still be envisaged as a short-term goal.

The code deals separately with proceedings before justices of the peace (*Vrederechters*) and other civil courts. In both parts, the *Verhandlungsmaxime* prevails. The *Offizialmaxime* is only marginally applied in the latter, but more markedly in the proceedings before the justices of the peace. The code contains strict rules regarding the submission of documents and pleadings, and comparatively short time-limits. Procedural sanctions for non-observance of these rules are systematically stated. The Batavian law-maker obviously relied on judicial discipline to implement this order of procedure, but was less sanguine than Joseph II about imposing a swift procedure: instead of urging the litigants to abide by the time-limits and other procedural restrictions imposed in the 1787 *Reglement*, the *Manier van procedeeren* offers a standard procedure which, under urgent circumstances or at specific stages, can be speeded up[16] or, on the contrary, may give more leeway for introducing additional elements.

The *Verhandlungsmaxime* is implicit throughout the *Manier van procedeeren* in civil cases. Its predominance appears mostly indirectly: partly through the paucity of recourse to the *Offizialmaxime*, partly through the insistence at all stages of the proceedings and in most of the special proceedings provided for in separate sections of the code on the *audi alteram partem* rule.

Even so, the *Verhandlungsmaxime* is restricted overall by the code's strict imposition of time-limits and, above all, its restrictions on the introduction of new submissions or documents at a later stage of the proceedings than initially provided for (see e.g. artt. 80, 259). An exception to this rule and perhaps one of the most explicit examples of the *Verhandlungsmaxime* is art. 83(2), which allows the litigants to request the judge to stay the proceedings for a period of time. The *Offizialmaxime* appears at the beginning of the proceedings, when the judge (in a provision reminiscent of the French revolutionary approach to civil procedure) is required to propose means of conciliation between the litigants (art. 2). In some cases, the judge will issue *ex officio* a decree: e.g. when a party applied for a 'voluntary condemnation' (art. 21, though the decree may be subordinated to a hearing of third parties); also, the judge may strike out a case when the litigants are not complying with the time-limits or their submissions (a seemingly harsh measure if the failure is only due to one of the parties: see, however, the phrasing of art. 83(2)); a strong instance of the *Offizialmaxime* is art. 267, which allows the judge to call for further evidence on an issue which he feels will be crucial for deciding the case (art. 267). Special proceedings occasionally also allow the judge to take *ex officio* initiatives: e.g. in the case of *cessio bonorum*, for calling the creditors of the debtor and issuing an order after hearing them (art. 225). In some cases, the absence of a provision for the judge to act *ex officio* is more surprising: e.g. art. 9, which deals with minors under a guardian, married women and other categories who cannot normally pursue proceedings by themselves, and requires that if such a person is not duly

14 The general principle was that, apart from the written submissions and records, the proceedings would be oral: art. 265.

15 For some specific proceedings, however, special procedural rules still applied: artt. 98-102 (bills of exchange), artt. 103-106 (insurances), 118 (bankruptcy).

16 E.g. artt. 31, 54, 62, 171 *et seq.*, 262.

assisted in court, the judge will appoint a *curator ad litem* at their own request or at the request of their opponent.

The *audi alteram partem* rule, on the other hand, pervades the whole code.[17] Exceptions to the rule are usually restrictively formulated: e.g. artt. 18 (cases where the nature of the request or the urgency of the matter necessitates at least provisionally a judicial decree without hearing the other party: the article states explicitly in which proceedings such an exception to the general principle formulated in art. 17 will be allowed), 33 (requests to the judge will normally be dealt with after hearing the other party 'if it is convenient', «indien zulks doenlyk is»). Some special proceedings, such as arrests and attachments, inevitably require decrees which, pending further proceedings, will be issued without hearing the applicant's opponent (artt. 133 *et seq.*; the latter's rights will be considered in a later hearing, e.g. provided for in art. 145). In other urgent proceedings, the judge may also make provisional orders, if he thinks fit, without hearing the other parties (artt. 159 *et seq.*). Requests by a litigant to amend an error or omission, are, as a matter of course, subjected to the *audi alteram partem* rule (art. 239).

The sanction for non-compliance with the procedural requirements is usually clearly stated. It usually consists in declaring the irregular submission inadmissible. Special cases are e.g. the irregular service of a writ or order by a bailiff (art. 43: the act is void and the bailiff is bound to pay damages to the wronged party); if a plea of defence has not been duly answered, the author of the plea can request that the judge will nevertheless decide on the plea (art. 64); when documents are appended to additional memoranda, they should only refer to the new facts adduced in these additional memoranda: if they are intended to support the arguments contained in the original memoranda, the judge will not take them into account and send them back to the party before making his judgement (artt. 80 *et seq.*); art. 83 (already mentioned, *supra*); an irregularity in the enforcement proceedings of a judgement may justify an order allowing for a suspension of these proceedings (art. 314). A remedy towards obtaining the annulment of a judicial decision is provided for in art. 168.[18]

The format of the judgement does not give the reasons of the decision, apart from stating the arguments of the litigant who prevails (art. 269 and appendix No. 82).
The separate Instruction for justices of the peace as mentioned emphasizes more frequently the *Offizialmaxime*: e.g. artt. 19 (referral to another jurisdiction); 20 (proposal of submitting the case to arbitration); 38-40 (default proceedings); 42-43 (reconciliation proceedings); 71 *et seq.* (post-judgement proceedings on costs). Art. 36 restricts, at this level of jurisdiction, the interventions of professional advocates (not before the higher courts: cf. *Manier van procedeeren*, art. 8).

3. The 1830 Code de Procédure Civile/Wetboek van Burgerlijke Regsvordering

Of the five codes that had been enacted and were to become law in 1831, the civil code had proved the most arduous to prepare. Its parliamentary history is so far the

17 It would be too cumbersome to provide a full list. Examples are to be found, *inter alia*, in artt. 13, 17, 19, 32, 34, 35, 56, 72, 84 (a litigant who requires more time to produce his evidence should address a request to the judge, who would decide after hearing both parties), 86, 92 (communication of the records of examinations and counter-examinations to both parties), 166 *et seq.*, 172, 179, 184, 219, 234, 310.

18 The system of procedural 'sanctions' is organized along fairly traditional lines in artt. 49 *et seq.*; 187-188 (appeal proceedings); 323-324 (revision proceedings); see also in special proceedings: artt. 201, 211, 270. And in the Instruction to justices of the peace: artt. 38 *et seq.*

best documented and the best known to legal historians. Its architecture, conventional by post-1804 (C.c.) or post-1811 (ABGB) standards, at least avoided the mock-classicist features to be found in the 1820 project, which comprised a Book IV dealing with 'actions'.[19] By contrast, the preparation of the Code of civil procedure[20] may not have grasped the interest of the Members of Parliament to the same extent as the Civil code.[21] Polemical or scholarly writings discussing the bills related to the civil procedure during the late 1820s often tend to focus on merely technical questions.[22]

19 *Ontwerp van het Burgerlijk Wetboek voor het Koningrijk der Nederlanden, aan de Staten-Generaal aangeboden den 22sten November 1820* [I used the edition: Tweede Uitgave, benevens de ophelderende memorie, met eene voorrede van Jhr. Mr. J. de Bosch Kemper (Leiden 1864)]: «Vierde Boek. Van regtsmiddelen tot handhaving van regt», p. 343-94, artt. 3181-3630, which contains mainly procedural rules (though not, of course, a system of forms of action). For a rear-guard fight in favour of incorporating the general principles of civil procedure in Book IV of the Civil code, cf. the speech by van Asch van Wijck on the project of the Code of civil procedure (9 February 1828, in: Noordziek, *infra* [1827-8, I], p. 165). On the concept of a Book IV dealing specifically with actions, exceptions, remedies: J.C. Voorduin, *infra* note 20, p. 60 *et seq.*

20 My main sources were: J.J.F. Noordziek, *Geschiedenis der beraadslagingen, gevoerd in de Kamers der Staten-Generaal over het ontwerp van Wetboek van Burgerlijke Regtspleging, I, Zittingsjaar 1827-1828*, The Hague, Martinus Nijhoff, 1885, 2 parts; *idem, Geschiedenis der beraadslagingen, gevoerd in de Kamers der Staten-Generaal over de ontwerpen van wet tot aanvulling van gapingen in de tot stand gekomen wetboeken, Zittingsjaar 1828-1829*, The Hague, Martinus Nijhoff, 1887, 2 parts; J.C. Voorduin, *Geschiedenis en beginselen der Nederlandsche wetboeken, volgens de beraadslagingen deswege gehouden bij de Tweede Kamer der Staten-Generaal, I/1, Algemeene Inleiding*, Utrecht, Robert Natan, Akademie-Boekhandelaar, 1837, passim; and a volume of separate Bills, Amendments et cetera bound together in one volume 'Deliberatiën der Staten-Generaal over het Wetboek van Burgerlijk Regt' (Leiden UL 2005 A 18). Further source-material can be found at the *Algemeen Rijksarchief*, The Hague, a.o. 2.21.098 Nos. 31-2; and in Amsterdam (UL, Legaat Den Tex).

21 Den Tex, 'Ueber den heutigen Zustand der Gesetzgebung in Nord-Niederland', *Kritische Zeitschrift für Rechtswissenschaft und Gesetzgebung des Auslandes*, 5 1833, p. 163-86, recalled that the Code had been enacted «*nach ziemlich ruhigen und gleichgültigen Discussionen*» (p. 169). Nevertheless, it should be remembered that the discussions on the Civil code were sometimes relevant to questions of the courts' organization and procedure. For example, the parliamentary debates on guardianship during the early 1820's showed great tensions between the King's government and a large group of members of the Lower House, particularly on the nature and role of the *conseil de famille* in relation to the justice of the peace; the end result was a strengthening of judicial control over all important questions of guardianship (A. Wijffels, 'La résistance au modèle français de la tutelle dans l'"impossible" Code civil néerlandais, 1798-1838', *Mémoires de la Société d'Histoire du Droit et des Institutions des anciens pays bourguignons, comtois et romands*, 58 2001, p. 95-131).

22 I have used: S.P. Lipman, *Aanmerkingen op het ontwerp van Wetboek van burgerlijke regtsleging*, 3 parts, Leiden, J.W. van Leeuwen, 1827-8, which follows the order of the project and is fairly extensive (reviewed in *Bijdragen tot regtsgeleerdheid en wetgeving*, 3 (1828), p. 461-2); W.H. van Voorst, *Iets over het ontwerp van Wetboek van Burgerlijke regtspleging*, Haarlem, Bij de wed. A. Loosjes Pz., 1827, a collection of short essays focusing on issues rather than technicalities (reviewed *ibidem*, p. 458-61); P.J. Spinael, *Concordance des textes et indication de corrections indispensables à faire par forme de révision de rédaction dans plusieurs dispositions du Code de Procédure civile des Pays-Bas, avant sa mise en vigueur*, Bruxelles, Chez H. Remy, imprimeur-libraire, 1828, a small pamphlet referred to during the later parliamentary debates, but which, its

The 1830 Code of civil procedure was, according to common opinion, largely inspired by its French model of 1806,[23] which it was to replace in the Netherlands. Not only, as could be expected, were the Belgian lawyers much in favour of maintaining a procedural system they had become familiar with, a similar attitude was also to be found among Dutch practitioners.[24] Perhaps even more strongly than for the substantive law, it was felt that a return to principles more or less authentically related to the 'Old Dutch Law' (*Oud-Vaderlands recht*) was not a desirable option in procedural matters. Moreover, the legislative work ever since the Batavian Republic – not only the *Manier van procedeeren*, but also J. van der Linden's proposals and writings, as well as the short-lived Code under Louis-

roaring promises in the introductory pages notwithstanding, hardly addresses any fundamental questions, but contains many criticisms on translations, practical and technical features et cetera (reviewed in *Bijdragen...* 4 (1829), p. 477-8). Throughout the 1820s, French textbooks or commentaries written by Belgian and Dutch authors, but based on the French Code, were commonly used; this may have triggered J.D. Meyer's remark, repeated by Th.A. Fruin more than a century later (*Geschiedenis van de wetenschap van het Nederlandsch burgerlijk procesrecht na 1811*, Amsterdam, Noord-Hollandsche Uitgeversmaatschappij, 1937, p. 25-5), according to whom the reception of a foreign procedure was always at the expense of nationhood.

23 Cf. the introductory report on the project by Barthelemy, 6 February 1828 (J.J.F. Noordziek, *supra* note 20, p. 5; and, *ibidem*, the speech by Beelaerts van Blokland, a member of the Drafting Committee, p. 46; Dotrenge, on 7 February, *ibidem*, p. 59). Daam Fockema pointed out that following closely the French Code meant that French case-law and commentaries would continue to be used as authorities (*ibidem*, p. 29-30). In spite of the evident reliance on the 1806 Code, more research ought to be done on the possible influence of other foreign legislation. The parliamentary works indicate that there were controversies on the value of German legislation, but also on the extent to which the 1819 reform of civil procedure in Geneva, which had (partly through Bellot's *Exposé des motifs*) acquired a reputation for correcting some of the French Code's alleged deficiencies, should have been followed. In this context, it will be recalled that C.J.A. Mittermaier had regularly published articles on current legislative work, especially in the field of civil procedure, in the *Archiv für die Civilistische Praxis*, from 1818 onwards. Most of his contributions on this theme dealt with statutory developments in the German territories, but he also published brief reports on the codification of civil procedure in, *inter alia*, the Netherlands: 'Die neueste Prozeßgesetzgebung mit beurtheilender Darstellung der neuen Entwürfe für Baiern und die Niederlande under der Prozeßordnung für die Untergerichte des Königreichs Hannover', *Archiv für die Civilistische Praxis*, 11 (1828), p. 144-68, p. 229-68, p. 424-50. After Belgian independence, the Dutch King ordered the sale of the copies of the 1830 Code which had already been printed by the State's Printing Office, in the case of the French text perhaps in the hope that these would be acquired by foreign lawyers and scholars (though not Belgians...) with an interest in comparative law (Den Tex, *supra* note 21, p. 175, advertizing the prices in a footnote). It does not appear that the legal profession and academia lived up to this disinterested commercial venture.

24 One should refrain from carrying the cliché too far. W.H. van Voorst, *supra* note 22, who was a judge in the first-instance court at Haarlem, is critical of the French Code, but by no means does he reject it (on the contrary: cf. a.o. p. 1). The Belgian Spinnael, on the other hand, who was an advocate at the High Court in Brussels, and who did not shun heavy rhetorics, regretted that the French Code of 1806 served as a model, a code «qui n'est que l'ancienne forme de procédure du [C]hatelêt, plus compliquée, [et qui] était peut-être le plus mauvais thème qu'on pût prendre» (p. 3).

Napoléon's reign – had paved the way for a procedural system which could espouse many features of the French code.[25]

In perhaps excessively broad terms, it could also be surmized that the 1830 Code of civil procedure expresses the general ideology of many early-19th century codes. The Napoleonic code's bias for a mainly formal equality of the persons it governs, both in private law and in criminal law, has for a long time been a set – and certainly not unfounded – cliché and criticism. An entirely similar critical assessment can be proposed for the Code of civil procedure: the litigants are, in theory and as a matter of principle, seen as equals, with formally the same, equal access to procedural remedies. Some of the Civil code's biases which, indirectly, express its concern for protecting property and, with even greater force, landed property, are reflected in the Code of civil procedure's special precautionary and protective measures governing attachment and the enforcement of judgements.

As a result, the *Verhandlungsmaxime*, which is a convenient instrument for upholding the principle of equality in a formal sense, remains the prevailing principle throughout the code. However, there would appear to be sufficient trust in the judges' capacities and willingness to ensure that the procedural safeguards against delays and chicanery are effectively applied. Thus, there is perhaps a stronger tendency to leave a number of procedural decisions – for instance, in granting additional delays or facilities for submissions, in other words: departures, within set limits, from the codified order of procedure –, which necessarily require an assessment of the circumstances, to the judge. The legislator seemed to expect with a relative degree of confidence that the judge would generally follow within comparatively narrow margins the procedural rules set out in the code.[26] Nevertheless, the drafter's attitude towards the judiciary remained ambivalent. Some rules (which, *mutatis mutandis*, are also reflected in other contemporary codes) appear to show that, even in the context of civil proceedings between private individuals, the judiciary is not quite on a par with Parliament or the Crown as state powers.[27] The section on denial of justice, for example, which sets out the extent of the judge's personal liability towards the litigants in cases of professional miscon-

25 Nevertheless, the members of the Lower House who criticized the project of the Code often suggested that it would have been preferable, in order to achieve a truly 'national' code, to use the pre-1809 Dutch works as starting-point (e.g. Van Asch van Wijk, in J.J.F. Noordziek, *Geschiedenis der beraadslagingen, gevoerd in de Kamers der Staten-Generaal over het ontwerp van Wetboek van Burgerlijke Regtspleging, I, Zittingsjaar 1827-1828*, The Hague, Martinus Nijhoff, 1885, 2 parts, p. 52; Warin, *ibidem*, p. 54).

26 Comp. with Daam Fockema's criticism of the project, and his emphasis on the *Offizialmaxime* (J.J.F. Noordziek, *supra* note 20, p. 33-4).

27 Comp. with the speech by van Asch van Wijck on 8 February 1828 (J.J.F. Noordziek, *supra* note 20, p. 118 *et seq.*, who challenged what is perceived to be a formidable extension of the judge's discretionary powers, at the expense of the principle of legality («*de mensch moet nimmer treden in de plaats van de wet. Dit gezegde is bijna tot een gulden regel geworden in de gevoelens dezer eeuw*»). W.H. van Voorst, *supra* note 22, p. 15 *et seq.*, fears that too great a latitude in the regime of nullity as a sanction is a recipe for arbitrary decisions; he sees a similar risk in the project's provisions for allowing the judge to press for an agreement at different stages of the proceedings (p. 17 *et seq.*).

duct or wrongdoing, tends to assimilate the judge's legal position to that of a civil (or Crown's) servant by early 19th-century standards.

The 1830 Code contains 745 articles: significantly less than the French Code of 1806, and that was meant to express the legislator's aim of simplifying the rules on civil procedure. The Code contains some general rules, which are normally applicable to all ordinary proceedings; particular rules for the proceedings before the *juges de canton* (formerly justices of the peace); and particular rules for the higher courts, including inevitably, special rules for the various remedies available. The last sections of the code deal with specific proceedings.

Again, when compared to the previous (indigenous) codes enacted in the Northern and Southern Netherlands since the end of the Ancien Régime, the changes and progress in the legislative drafting technique are obvious. The 1830 code shares with its predecessors and its French model a concern for imposing time-limits and restrictions on submissions of all kinds, and insofar restricts a boundless application of the *Verhandlungsmaxime*. Nevertheless, while the litigants have to abide by these restrictions, the progress of the proceedings still depends on their initiative. Throughout, the judge's role is mostly to ensure that the order of procedure is applied, and, at critical stages, to allow limited departures from that order at the request of a litigant.

Both in the general rules of procedure and in the special proceedings, the initiative of the litigants is assumed and sometimes specifically stated. In some cases, an agreement of the litigants on both sides may even prevail over the judge: e.g. art. 161 (when the authenticity of a document is challenged,[28] the judge may appoint commissioners and experts; however, if the parties agree on who should be appointed as experts, the judge *may* follow their submission, «zal de regter daarin kunnen berusten»); similarly, art. 189 (when a survey is required, the judge will appoint three experts; however, if the parties agree that a single expert will be appointed, the judge will be bound by their decision; and if the parties agree on the person or persons who have to be appointed as experts, the judge will be bound to make those appointments).[29] Not only the judge, but in some ways the commissioners he has appointed, may sometimes defer to a litigant's request (e.g. art. 182: when a party applies to a commissioner appointed for hearing the evidence for a further delay before a witness is examined). A plaintiff's right to withdraw from the proceedings is only possible under strict condi-

28 According to P.J. Spinnnael, *supra* note 22, p. 15 *et seq.*, the Code's drafters had confused two different situations, *viz.* (a) when a litigant wants to use a document; (b) when a document on which a litigant relies is incidentally challenged as a *faux*. Lipman, on the contrary, thought that the draft Code was, in that respect, an improvement on the French system of separate proceedings (S.P. Lipman, *supra* note 22, p. 69 *et seq.*). For a discussion of the French system when it was applied in the Northern Netherlands: W.IJ. van Hamelsveld, *Manier van procederen in burgerlijke regtszaken, volgens de thans nog bestaande wet van burgerlijke regtspleging* I, Amsterdam, J.C. van Kesteren, 1823, p. 126 *et seq.*; J.-A. Rogron, *Code de procédure civile expliqué par ses motifs et par ses exemples, avec la solution, sous chaque article, des difficultés ainsi que des principales questions que présente le texte, et la définition de tous les termes de droit*, Bruxelles, Chez H. Tarlier, libraire, 3rd ed. [«contenant les changements, modifications et dispositions nouvelles, adoptés par le Code de procédure civile belge»] 1829), p. 86 *et seq.*, who, however, barely takes into account any special features in the practice of the Netherlands (his popular text-book follows the French text, and contains brief footnotes quoting the text of the draft Code of 1830).

29 S.P. Lipman, *supra* note 22, p. 86 *et seq.* criticizes the arrangement for appointing experts, but on different grounds. The system of *ex officio* or *ex parte* (*partibus*) appointments was already in use under the French Code, cf. W. IJ. van Hamelsveld, *supra* note 28, p. 186; J.-A. Rogron, *supra* note 28, p. 88 *et seq.*

tions (art. 233). The judge's control over the litigants' 'hold' over the proceedings is also illustrated in the case of an application on behalf of one side to subject the opponent to an examination (artt. 201 *et seq.*).

The *Verhandlungsmaxime* also plays an important part during appeal proceedings. One of the most striking initiatives the litigants can take is related to the at the time controversial rule that a first-instance case could under certain circumstances be brought before the appeal-judge: this could happen on behalf of the plaintiff, but if the defendant refused, the case was committed to the first-instance judge (artt. 269 *et seq.*); even more striking in that context is the provision of art. 273, which says that at any stage of the (first-instance) proceedings, the litigants may, by common agreement, decide that the procedure will be continued before the provincial court of appeal![30] (See also, for less spectacular initiatives of a litigant, e.g. art. 290, which allows the respondent in appeal to request the enforcement of the first-instance judgement, pending the appeal; art. 296, which allows the judge who is hearing an appeal against an interlocutory decision to give a final judgement in the case, inter alia, if the litigants apply for such a judgement).

For applications of the *Verhandlungsmaxime* to special proceedings, see also artt. 546 *et seq.* (rules governing the parties' right to submit their case to arbitration); 584 (presence at the removal of the seals before proceeding to an inventory); 691 (enforced delivery of an act). For examples of the right of a third party to intervene: artt. 324 *et seq.*; 378, 400 *et seq.* (but *contra* during appeal proceedings: art. 294).

However, the technique which emphasizes the *Verhandlungsmaxime* most of all is the reference to the *partie la plus diligente* (*meest gerede partij*). Throughout the code, the use of this technique effectively makes it possible for the judge to 'get on' with the proceedings (e.g. artt. 78, 96, 158, 167, 185, 187, 193, 199, 266, 306, 431, 549, 675).

Finally, it should be obvious that in this code, too, the *Verhandlungsmaxime* implies as a general principle the *audi alteram partem* rule.[31] It is equally obvious that the rule suffers exceptions in special circumstances, such as summary and provisional proceedings (artt. 245 *et seq.*).[32]

The *Offizialmaxime*, then, as one would expect, appears only incidentally. The code recognizes the judge's discretionary power to attempt a conciliation between the parties (art. 19).[33] *Ex officio*, he will notify grounds of his recusal that are known to him

30 The provision does not appear to have been very controversial. Only one section of the Lower House criticized it, because «les premiers juges pourront n'être que des juges d'instructions. Ne serait-ce pas trop les rabaisser?», an objection which the Government rejected: «Er bestaat geene reden, om niet aan partijen het vermogen toe te kennen *om vrijwillig*, in elken stand van het geding, hare zaken aan de regtsmagt van het hof te kunnen onderwerpen, en alzoo de instantie in hooger beroep af te snijden» (J.J.F. Noordziek, *supra* note 20, p. 428 and p. 558; italics in the original).

31 The principle was explicitly referred to during the parliamentary debates, e.g. in the speech by Beelaerts van Blokland, regarding the judge's decision to end proceedings after one pleading by the litigants: the application of the *Offizialmaxime* in such a case (viz. the judge's duty to examine whether the conditions for such a decision are met, even when there has been no application from one of the litigants), does not preclude the necessity to hear both parties (J.J.F. Noordziek, *supra* note 20, p. 101-2).

32 W.H. van Voorst, *supra* note 22, p. 24 *et seq.*, wishes that summary proceedings were more precisely defined, but he does believe that in may cases, such proceedings can be organized without unduly restricting the right of the defence.

33 The parliamentary discussions reflect the (legal profession's and politicians') disillusion about the early-revolutionary attempts to encourage conciliation-proceedings between the citoyens. S.P. Lipman, *supra* note 22, p. 17-8, follows that received wisdom, while at the same time approving the draft. Nevertheless, he warns of a misguided application of the principle,

(art. 30) and refer the case to the competent judge if he has no jurisdiction (art. 133; but he may refuse to adjudicate in cases involving foreigners when their litigation arises from actions or facts which have taken place abroad, art. 699). When preparing his judgement, he will examine and supply himself, if necessary, the legal grounds of his decision (art. 39; see also art. 49, 4°: the judgement must give the reasons;[34] the same applies to the decision of arbitrators). The judge can also decide several issues regarding evidence: e.g. artt. 79 and 186 *et seq.* (the court's visit to a *locus* in order to assess the damage, the state of a property et cetera; art. 200: a new visit may be decided if the report on the first visit is inconclusive); 169 (custody of documents pending the trial); 202 (examination of a litigant: it is the judge's duty to consider whether the interrogatories submitted by the opponent are admissible and do not conceal 'trick questions' («strikvragen»);[35] 139 (decree ordering the submission of written arguments).

The Code applies a wide range of sanctions (and combinations of sanctions) depending on the circumstances. Its use of nullity as a sanction has been criticized for lack of coherence.[36] Apart from a general sanction on nullity (artt. 80-83), special instances of procedural acts declared void because of infringement of the procedural requirements are (e.g.) art. 6 (summons), 224 (procedural acts *ultra vires*), 285 *et seq.* (*partim*: appeal), 524 and 537 (arrests). Similarly, irregular submissions or acts can be declared inadmissible (e.g. artt. 32. 102, 235 *et seq.*, 282 *et seq.*). The author of the irregular act can be condemned to pay the ensuing costs (e.g. artt. 83, 102, 105, 138, 144) and in several cases, be liable to pay compensation: e.g. artt. 17 (void service of a writ by a bailiff), 83 (counsel or bailiff), 106 (absent witness), 175 (author of a document submitted, who denies his authorship), 330 and 332 (unsuccessful remedy of *requête-civile*), 465 (agents for insolvent buyers at auctions), 553 (arbitrators who fail to reach a decision within the fixed time-limit), 700 (judge's refusal to adjudicate)[37] – in many of these cases, in combination with other sanctions such as fines. A warrant of arrest could be obtained as a means of pressure (e.g. artt. 175, 512 *et seq.*). Criminal penalties are mentioned for (inter alia) registrars who deliver an authenticated copy of a judgement before it has been signed by the judge will be prosecuted for forgery (art. 52); bailiffs who receive any sums above the price reached at an auction, for extortion by a public official (art. 414); debtors who violently oppose the enforcement of a judgement (art. 529). A bailiff who constantly refuses to serve a writ on a judge may be removed from office (art. 700).

offering his (Dutch) readership an entertaining anecdote of a crass abuse of the judicial power in such a case by (predictably) a Belgian judge.

34 This was already a requirement expressed in art. 173 of the Constitution. For a brief survey of a judge's duty to express the reasons of his judgement, particularly from the Batavian Republic onwards until the Dutch Code of 1838: J.J. Vriesendorp, *Ambtshalve aanvullen van rechtsgronden in het burgerlijk geding,* Zwolle, Tjeenk Willink, 1970, p. 29-35 (see also for an abridged version by the same author, the Zwolle 1981 edition *Ambtshalve aanvullen van rechtsgronden*, p. 3-6. Under the French Code: J.-A. Rogron, *supra* note 28, p. 58.

35 The latter, however, can sometimes be admissible: S.P. Lipman, *supra* note 22, p. 93-4.

36 W.H. van Voorst, *supra* note 22, p. 15-7.

37 For actions against the judge under the French Code, as applied in the Netherlands: W.IJ. van Hamelsfeld, *supra* note 28, p. 115 *et seq.*; J.-A. Rogron, *supra* note 28, p. 179 *et seq.*

4. Costs

A brief discussion of the sections on costs in the three 'codes' may serve as a summary, topical illustration of how the fundamental principles of civil procedure are articulated.

In the 1786 Edict,[38] three sets of rules can be distinguished: *(a)* First, (imperative) rules regarding the condemnation to costs, i.e. establishing which party will be condemned; under what circumstances compensation of costs is to be excluded; under which circumstances compensation will be mandatory. The *Offizialmaxime* is expressed in the rule that the judge is bound by these rules and that he is required accordingly to make a provision on costs in his judgement. *(b)* Secondly, rules regarding the assessment of costs: the litigants have to submit their costs, necessarily before the judgement (for the judgement also requires a decision on the costs); some plaintiffs are bound to offer security or to declare their indigence under oath. For these matters, the initiative lays with the litigants and the *alteram partem auditur* rule accompanies the *Verhandlungsmaxime*. *(c)* Thirdly, rules ordering the judge to fine or punish any litigant who has proceeded on manifestly unfair grounds. Thus, these sets of rules combine to ensure that any abuse of procedural remedies will be directly (*viz.* through penalties) or indirectly (*viz.* through the adjudication on costs) penalized.

In the 1799 Rules of Procedure,[39] the costs are allocated on the basis of a post-judgement decision by commissioners. The initiative for these post-trial proceedings lays with the litigant who is entitled to obtain compensation for the costs he has incurred. The proceedings require him to submit all documents regarding these costs for assessment by the commissioners. At that stage, an attempt at conciliation should take place; if it fails, the commissioners will continue the proceedings, hear the arguments on both sides and write a report to be submitted to the trial judge. The *Reglement* contains a few rules stating which costs may be taken into account. The general principles are expressed in artt. 244-5: if the litigant who is entitled to be compensated for his costs appeared as litigant-in-person, all costs may be taken into account, except counsel's fees; if the services of one or more counsel were used, only the fees of one counsel may be taken into account. In any case, the assessment is governed by the principle of accusatory proceedings, including the possibility for the party who has been condemned to pay costs to apply for a reduction; here again, at all stages, the *Reglement* holds on to the *audi alteram partem* rule. The party condemned may even challenge through separate proceedings the rightfulness of his condemnation to costs (art. 257). All these rule show that, even at this stage of the proceedings, the *Verhandlungsmaxime* prevails. In that respect, the *Reglement* contains an array of safeguards against summary assessments and enforcement, at the risk, inevitably, of protracted proceedings.

38 §§ 412-23.

39 Artt. 244-58.

The 1830 Code[40] here, too, shows its confidence in the judge's discretion: the judge *may* assess in his judgement the costs «and compensation» to be paid by one of the litigants. When this is not possible, the claimant has to present his account and to notify the opponent; the latter is then entitled to submit a counter-offer; if no agreement is reached, a decision will be reached upon 'summary' proceedings (but, as art. 540 half-heartedly states: «unless the case cannot be dealt with through such summary proceedings»!).[41] In comparison to the detailed system of the 1799 Rules of Procedure, the 1830 Code thus allowed for more leeway as to how the costs would be assessed; in general, its approach to the issue of costs is pervaded by the same general concern of providing safeguards against excessively expeditious enforcement.

5. Conclusion

In spite of an altogether different political context, and in spite of distinctive, new drafting techniques, the 1830 Code of civil procedure by and large shares a common approach with the reformatory legislation from the transition period between Ancien Régime and post-revolutionary, post-Napoleonic Restoration. They all express a concern for swift proceedings and the need to prevent chicanery — a concern which, indeed, was already expressed in the rhetoric of late-medieval and early-modern statutes on civil procedure. Joseph II's Ordinance may express this concern more strongly as a matter of policy and as a reaction against a perceived dysfunctioning of the legal system, while the 1830 Code may reflect a more confident and liberal attitude of the legislator, but on the whole, the main structure of civil proceedings remained cast along the general lines worked out by civil procedures throughout continental Europe since the late middle ages. This does not mean that civil procedure was not undergoing fundamental changes. The changes, however, are to be looked for outside the procedural system itself. The traditional principles of civil procedure proved sufficiently versatile to be instrumental to the new national legal policies. The trias forensis was still largely left to its own device, but within narrower or more stringent limits laid down by a code. One should

40 See mainly: artt. 538-41; also: art. 47, and *passim*, provisions for costs as a sanction in the case of a belated, wrongful et cetera submission. However, many aspects of costs only appear implicitly in the Code, or (as for various taxes and duties) are dealt with in other statutory documents: the cumulative effect of all these factor which directly or indirectly affect the costs of proceedings is one of the themes discussed by W.H. van Voorst, *supra* note 22, *passim* (*inter alia*, p. 3 *et seq.*, 21 (in proceedings brought before the Court of Appeal), 33 (advocates' fees); similar criticisms were expressed by the Rotterdam advocate F. Frets, 'Over het verval van de Judiciëele Praktijk', 4 *Bijdragen to regtsgeleerdheid en wetgeving*, 1829, p. 210-42. On the system applied in the Netherlands under the French Code: W.IJ. van Hamelsveld, *supra* note 28, p. 298 *et seq.*; J.-A. Rogron, *supra* note 28, p. 63 *et seq.*

41 The qualification is an addition to the original draft: J.J.F. Noordziek, *supra* note 20, p. 289, p. 689-90 (one of the sections in the Lower House expressed the criticism that the text did not specify how the proceedings would take place: «zal de proces-orde dan aan hunne willekeur [*viz.* of the litigants] of aan het goedvinden der regters staan, naar mate het geval vereischt?»), 782, 817.

never forget that the major change for the generation of legal practitioners whose professional activity stretched from the end of the Ancien Régime to the post-Napoleonic national political systems was the wholesale 'nationalization' of the court system and the introduction of uniform law – both substantive and adjective – at a nation-wide level. This had a profound influence on legal education, on the social and cultural cohesion of the legal profession, and on the perception of law and the administration of justice by the public at large. Never before, in European political and legal history, had law and state-power been so exclusively associated.

The great paradox – with the benefit of hind-sight – was that at the time, the enactment of private law, and particularly a civil code, was seen (and would long continue to be identified) as the very quintessence of the law. The civil courts, in that context, are the privileged area where, necessarily, the 'civil society' of private individuals and the state (the latter as the sole and quasi-absolute holder of coercive power within that society), were to meet. However liberal and non-interventionist the state might be in the private affairs of individuals, it imposed, or at least controlled, any breakdown of the orderly relations between those individuals by the legal standards it had itself imposed. Civil procedure was therefore organized in such a way as to leave the peaceful settlement of disputes as much as possible to the private individuals themselves, the court offering the indispensable minimum amount of coercive state-power that was necessary so as to ensure the implementation of legally binding obligations or legally recognized rights. What the French Revolution had not changed – yet – was a dominant political culture which was willing to use the law and the legal system for the purpose of changing the social and economic inequalities within the system. As, very gradually during the 20th century, the social and economic threshold to relative wealth and property was lowered in the welfare state, access to the court system became available to an ever-increasing group of litigants. The pressures on the legal system to be used for correcting social and economic inequalities have not, so far, fundamentally revolutionized civil procedure – characteristically, the means developed in order to compensate for the merely formal equality of the litigants have largely evolved outside the civil-procedural system as such: e.g. legal aid and parallel procedures before other courts and tribunals for particular areas (such as industrial law). The pressure for change, however, exists, for the long-term law reforms which have increasingly recognized more substantive rights and remedies to the ever-growing emancipated classes within a democratic society, who duly stand up to claim those rights and remedies, is putting a strain on the civil courts' system which goes far beyond a mere problem of volume of litigation. In the history of our Western societies, the legal system has by and large been able to develop because, at least implicitly, it operated on the premise that the law was for all, but justice for the few. Unless the national legal systems and the burgeoning efforts towards building a common European legal system of procedure in the areas of private law succeed in addressing the problems arising from the increasing invalidation of that premise, we shall face the first great crisis in the history of civil procedure since the late-12th and 13th century, when the prevailing archaic system of ordeals by fire and water became unacceptable to those who had to rely on an effective administration of justice.

Knut Wolfgang
Nörr

ÜBER EINIGE STADIEN DER HISTORIOGRAPHIE DES PROZESSRECHTS

1. Einleitung

Wie alle anderen Historiographien, so hat auch die Geschichte vom Prozessrecht ihre eigene Geschichte. Wenn wir die Prozessrechtsgeschichte europäisch fassen wollten, dann würde das sogenannte gelehrte oder verwissenschaftlichte Prozessrecht im Vordergrund stehen, also ein Teilbereich aus dem europäischen *ius commune* oder gemeinen Recht, um den eingedeutschten Ausdruck zu gebrauchen. Die Geschichte der Prozessrechtsgeschichte ist dann in erster Linie die Geschichte der Historiographie des gelehrten oder gemeinen Prozessrechts. Das gilt jedenfalls für die Geschichte des Zivilprozesses.

Dieses gelehrte Prozessrecht wirkte bis in die Ära der Kodifikationen hinein. Wie im materiellen, so waren auch im Verfahrensrecht an der Kodifikationsbildung nicht nur das gemeine gelehrte, sondern auch nationales oder regionales Recht beteiligt. Die Quote dieser Beteiligungen, wenn man so sagen darf, war von Fall zu Fall verschieden, das gemeinsame europäische Erbe also hier stärker, dort schwächer ausgeprägt. Die Einwirkung des gemeinen Prozessrechts konnte auch vorwiegend negativer oder kontrastierender Art sein; das bekannteste Beispiel hierfür sind die Prozessgesetzbücher des aufgeklärt-friderizianischen Preußens geworden. Natürlich spielt auch das Bewusstsein von einem gemeinsamen Bestand des Prozessrechts, gewissermaßen einer gemeinsamen Prozessrechtskultur eine Rolle; dieses Bewusstsein nahm in zunehmender Entfernung von der gemeinsamen Wissenschaftssprache, dem Latein, ebenso zunehmend ab; und die Prozessrechtsvergleichung, die sich dann zusammen mit der allgemeinen Rechtskomparatistik entfaltete, bot ihres sekundären Charakters wegen doch nur einen schwachen Ersatz.

2. Stadium: Die Entdeckung der Prozessmaximen

Aber wenden wir uns nun einigen Stadien der Historiographie des gelehrten Zivilprozessrechts zu. Die Anfänge gestalteten sich sozusagen unterschwellig, fast apokryph, aber dann doch nicht überraschend. Es handelt sich um die Natur- oder

Vernunftrechtsperiode und hier um die Art und Weise, wie man zu den Rechtssätzen gelangt ist und zu den Prinzipien, die dann das System getragen haben. Denn aus der Luft konnte man die Dinge nicht greifen, der abstrakte Gedanke, so großen Wert man auf ihn auch legen mochte, blieb doch immer im Allgemeinsten hängen. So sah man sich um nach den Erscheinungen der eigenen Zeit und den Erscheinungen der Geschichte. Rechtssätze und Rechtsstrukturen der Vergangenheit konnten sich gewissermaßen in zeitlose Empirie verwandeln. Mancher Naturrechtssatz, manches apriorische Gebilde war dann das Ergebnis. Und mit dieser Methode wurden nun auch die bekannten Prozessmaximen entdeckt oder erfunden. Wir befinden uns da an der Wende vom 18. zum 19. Jahrhundert, also zu einer Zeit, als das Vernunftrecht schon im Abklingen war. Die Maximenschöpfung — Verhandlungsmaxime, Untersuchungsmaxime — ist bekanntlich mit dem Namen des Nikolaus Thaddäus Gönner verbunden; spätere Prozessualisten haben das Maximengeflecht noch weiter unterteilt und verfeinert.

3. Stadium: Die Betonung des evolutischen Charakters der Prozessrechtsgeschichte

Prozessrechtsgeschichte als Implikat 'rationalen' Prozessrechts: so können wir die Anfänge geschichtlicher Reflexion im Prozessrecht charakterisieren. Das nächste Stadium dieser Reflexion, bald zur Blüte gereift, nimmt die Historische Schule ein. Wie ist das in Hinblick auf das gelehrte Prozessrecht genauer zu verstehen? Wenn wir uns zunächst dem Haupt der Schule, Savigny, zuwenden und seiner Einschätzung des gelehrt-gemeinen Rechts überhaupt als Gegenstand einer geschichtlichen Rechtswissenschaft, dann ist an die gewissermaßen schizoide Haltung zu erinnern, die Savigny gegenüber der Ursprungsperiode des gemeinen Rechts, dem Mittelalter, eingenommen hatte. Denn einerseits hatte er dem mittelalterlichen gelehrten Recht im vollen Bewusstsein seiner Tragweite für das große geschichtliche Programm ein vielbändiges literargeschichtliches Werk gewidmet; als er aber, auf der anderen Seite, die Arbeit an einer Rechtsdogmatik begann, übersprang er fröhlich genau dieses Mittelalter, hielt er sich nicht mehr bei den Glossatoren, Kommentatoren, Konsiliatoren, also den Vätern des *ius commune* auf.

Dieser Bruch, diese Ungereimtheit blieb allerdings auf das materielle Recht beschränkt, die Historiographie des Prozessrechts blieb hiervon unberührt. In der Historischen Schule hatte sich dem Prozessrecht auf programmatische Weise bekanntlich Bethmann-Hollweg zugewandt, der nun den evolutorischen Charakter der Prozessrechtsgeschichte heraushob und betonte. Man dürfte von der Antike bis in die Gegenwart sozusagen kein Jahrhundert beiseite lassen, keine Perioden und Phasen vernachlässigen, um zur Analyse — und zur Kritik — des geltenden Prozessrechts zu gelangen. Und wenn Schwerpunkte zu setzen sind, dann würde ihrer einer den gelehrten Juristen, den Zivilisten und Kanonisten vom 12. Jahrhundert an, sowie dem Gerichtsbrauch jener Periode gebühren.

4. Stadium: Die Entdeckung des langobardisch-frühitalienischen Prozessrechts

Hatte mit diesem Programm Bethmann-Hollweg den Blick auf die Frühzeit des gelehrten Rechts, die 'Wiege unserer Wissenschaft' gelenkt, um ihn einmal wörtlich zu zitieren,[1] so erweiterte sich alsbald das Gesichtsfeld der Prozessrechtsgeschichte auf eine zunächst so nicht erwartete Weise. Bekanntlich war das 19. Jahrhundert der Historiker und Juristen angefüllt mit dem Kampfgetös zwischen Romanismus und Germanismus, dem Getös eines Großdiskurses, dessen Ursachen hier nicht geschildert werden müssen. Für uns ist bedeutsam, dass man im Zuge dieser Auseinandersetzung, auf der Suche nach dem 'Germanischen' in der Prozessrechtsgeschichte, eine überraschende Entdeckung machte, nämlich die hohe Entwicklungsstufe des langobardisch-frühitalienischen Prozessrechts, das nun seinerseits, auf dem Wege des Gerichtsbrauchs oder der Adaption der Quellentexte, das gelehrte Prozessschrifttum beeinflusste. In Italien stand dann dieser Vorgang in steter Wechselwirkung mit der städtischen Rechtsaufzeichnung und Gesetzgebung, dem Statutarrecht.

Vorausgegangen war in dieser Forschungsrichtung Hans Karl Briegleb mit der Abhandlung von 1839 über den Exekutiv-Prozess; hieran schlossen sich zahlreiche Monographien unter anderem von Adolph Wach und Richard Schmidt und ihren Schulen an. Von Wach stammte das einprägsame Stichwort der 'prototypischen Natur' des italienischen Territorialprozesses (vielleicht hätte er heute 'paradigmatisch' gesagt). Es ergab sich hieraus von selbst eine enge Verbindung zwischen den deutschen und italienischen Prozesshistorikern, eine Verbindung, die dann mit dem Aufkommen des Konstruktivismus im letzten Drittel des 19. Jahrhunderts auch die Wissenschaft vom geltenden Prozessrecht erreichte. Eine ertragreiche Kooperation war die Folge, die weit über das gewohnte Bild gemeinsamer rechtshistorischer oder rechtsvergleichender Interessen hinausging. Auf italienischer Seite sei nur der Name Giuseppe Chiovenda genannt. Diese Symbiose, wenn man so will, nahm erst mit dem alles zerstörenden Ersten Weltkrieg ein Ende, nicht völlig zwar, aber doch in einem nur noch Reste belassenden Ausmaß. Doch sind hierüber nicht die Leistungen der italienischen Rechtshistoriker zu vergessen; es sei nur an die handbuchartige Synthese der italienischen Prozessrechtsgeschichte von Giuseppe Salvioli aus den 1920er Jahren erinnert.

1 M.A. v. Bethmann-Hollweg, *Der Civilprozeß des gemeinen Rechts in geschichtlicher Entwicklung*, VI.1, Bonn, Marcus, 1874, Vorrede p.V. – Vgl. zu unseren Abschnitten 1 bis 3, K.W. Nörr, *Naturrecht und Zivilprozeß*, Tübingen, Morhr, 1976; K.W. Nörr, 'Wissenschaft und Schrifttum zum deutschen Zivilprozeß im 19. Jahrhundert', 10 *Ius Commune*, 1983, S. 141 (*Iudicium est actus trium personarum*, 1993, S. 189).

5. Stadium: Die Zeit nach dem Zweiten Weltkrieg

5.1. Die Neuerforschung des mittelalterlichen Prozessrechts

Nach dem 2. Weltkrieg können wir eine neue Vorliebe für das Mittelalter feststellen, diesmal in Form der Erforschung des umfangreichen und teilweise noch unbekannten Bestands an Handschriften der gelehrten Rechte. Den Anstoß gab, wenn ein historiographischer Vorgang zeitlich fixiert werden soll, der Gratian-Kongress, der 1952 in Bologna stattgefunden hatte; und das Vorhaben wurde bekanntlich in erster Linie Stephan Kuttner anvertraut. Von der neuen Forschungsrichtung konnte auch das gelehrte Prozessrecht profitieren; neue Entdeckungen, neue Werksanalysen waren das Ergebnis, aber auch dogmen- oder institutionengeschichtliche Untersuchungen, die sich nun nicht mehr auf im Druck vorliegende Texte beschränkten, sondern die Handschriften miteinbezogen, so dass vor allem die Frühzeit des gelehrten Prozessrechts, das heißt die Periode vor der Standardisierung der Lehren in Form der *glossae ordinariae* und großen Summen, besser zu erkennen war.

5.2. Der Einfluss des Trivium

Es gab nach dem 2. Weltkrieg aber auch Entwürfe, die sich der Prozessrechtsgeschichte als einem Ganzen mit neuen Konzeptionen und Theoremen zu nähern versuchten; natürlich war die mittelalterliche Entwicklung hierin eingeschlossen. Der Anstoß ging vom Urthema gewissermaßen aller Regelungen und Reflexionen aus, nämlich der Rollenverteilung zwischen dem Richter und den Parteien im Prozessgeschehen. Die historische Entwicklung selbst hatte Phänomene hervorgebracht, die man dann in Modelle oder Modellteile übertragen konnte. Am wichtigsten für diesen konzeptionellen Vorgang ist die schon erwähnte preußisch-friderizianische Prozessgesetzgebung geworden; sie hatte die Bildung und Ausformulierung der Prozessmaximen zur Folge. Das Thema hat seitdem alle Sparten der Prozessrechtsdisziplin beschäftigt: die Prozessrechtspolitik einschließlich der Legislative, die Dogmatik und Systematik, die Rechtsvergleichung, natürlich auch die Prozessrechtsgeschichte. Und hier sind nun die frischen Ansätze konzeptioneller Betrachtung hervorzuheben, die wir zwei italienischen Gelehrten verdanken, nämlich Alessandro Giuliani und Nicola Picardi, die teils getrennt, teils gemeinsam ihre Einsichten geformt und vorgetragen haben.[2]

2 A. Giuliani, *Il concetto di prova: contributo alla logica giuridica,* Milano, Gioffrè 1961; A. Giuliani, 'Ordine isonomico ed ordine asimmetrico: "nuova retorica" e teoria del processo', *Sociologia del diritto,* 1986, S. 81; A. Giuliani, 'L'ordo iudiciarius medioevale, Riflessioni su un modello puro di ordine isonomico', *Rivista di diritto processuale,* , 43, 1988, S. 598; A. Giuliani, 'Prova(filosofia)', 37 *Enciclopedia del diritto,* 1988, S. 518; A. Giuliani, 'Dalla litis contestatio al pleading system', in *L'educaziono giuricidica* VI.2, 1994, S. 205; A. Giuliani, 'L'Ordo Iudiciarius medievale tra retorica e logica', in M. Bellamo (Hrsg), *Die Kunst der Disputation,* 1997, S. 133; N. Picardi, 'L'esame di coscienza del vecchio Maestro [Francesco Carnelutti], *Rivista di diritto processuale,* 41, 1986, S. 536; N. Picardi,' Processo civile (dir. moderno)', *Enciclopedia del diritto,* 36, 1987, S. 101; N. Picardi, 'Les racines historiques et logiques du Code de procedure civile',

Man kann von einer geistes- oder methodengeschichtlichen Wende der Historiographie des Prozessrechts sprechen. Untersucht wird nämlich, und dies nicht sporadisch, wie es ja verschiedentlich schon früher zu finden war, sondern in einem systematischen Anlauf, der Einfluss des Trivium – Dialektik und Rhetorik – und der sich entfaltenden Logik auf das gelehrte Prozessrecht. Vorausgehen musste dem ein intensives Studium der einschlägigen Schriften der Philosophie in ihrer geschichtlichen Entwicklung; als Ergebnis zeigt sich uns ein eindrucksvolles Bild der großen Gestalten der Rhetorik und Logik mit ihren themenbezogenen Äußerungen. Ein detailliertes Referat wäre hier nun am Platz, doch sei es mir erlassen; ich möchte aber allen Prozessrechtshistorikern besonders die Lektüre der beiden Artikel in der Enciclopedia del diritto empfehlen.[3]

5.3. *Nichtstaatlichkeit und Staatlichkeit als These Picardis*

Was uns jedoch an dieser Stelle beschäftigt, ist die Aufgabe, zu einigen Begriffen und Thesen Stellung zu nehmen, die in Verbindung mit den erwähnten rhetorik- und logikgeschichtlichen Untersuchungen zur Prozessrechtsgeschichte im engeren Sinn aufgestellt worden sind. So hat Picardi vorgeschlagen, den großen Bogen der Entwicklung von einem nichtstaatlichen zu einem staatlichen Prozess an den Begriffen *iudicium* oder *ordo iudiciarius* einerseits und *processus* andererseits abzulesen, wobei für die Nichtstaatlichkeit (*extrastatualità*) der gemeine Prozess in seiner ursprünglichen Gestalt, für die Staatlichkeit (*statualità*) hingegen der schon mehrfach erwähnte preußische Prozess des 18. Jahrhunderts als Exempel diente. Wortgeschichtlich tritt aber, und das ist Picardi entgegenzuhalten, *processus* bereits unter Innozenz III. auf, also zu einem Zeitpunkt, in welchem der gelehrte *ordo iudiciarius* seinen ersten Höhepunkt erlebt hatte, und das dem Substantiv zugrunde liegende Verb *procedere* findet sich in seiner verfahrensrechtlichen Bedeutung bereits

in *L'educazione giuridica,* V.1, 1988, S. 241; A. Giuliani and N. Picardi, *La responsabilità del giudice*, Milano, Gioffrè, 1987.

3 Hin und wieder sind gewisse methodische Einwände angebracht. Es besteht die Gefahr, dass aus vereinzelten Äußerungen des einen oder anderen Autors zu weitreichende Folgerungen gezogen werden. Zwei Beispiele seien angeführt. 1. Für den (von Giuliani so formulierten) Satz *'Quaestio facti est in arbitrio iudicis'* wird als Gewährsmann Nicolaus Vigelius angeführt (Il concetto, *supra* note 2, S. 223 *et seq.*). Aus dem Zusammenhang, in welchem dessen Texte stehen, ergibt sich aber, dass ein Vergleich zur *quaestio iuris* gezogen werden sollte, und zwar zur Verhängung von Strafen, bei welcher der Richter kein *arbitrium* besitzt, sondern strengstens an das Gesetz gebunden ist. Der angeführte Satz darf also keinesfalls so absolut verstanden werden wie es die Formulierung nahe legt. - 2. Ein gewisser Nachdruck wird auf die Wendung *'Probatio seu ordo iudiciarius'* gelegt (A. Giuliani, 'Prova', *Enciclopedia, supra* note 2, S. 529 linke Spalte, S. 530 r.Sp., S. 536 l.Sp.). Gestützt wird die Formulierung auf eine Stelle in der Dekretalensumme des Hostiensis, *De sententia* (X 2.27) *Qualiter proferri debeat.* Es handelt sich jedoch um einen Lesefehler; statt *probatio* heißt es in Wirklichkeit *prolatio.* Wir geben den Text der Summe im Zusammenhang wieder: *Qualiter proferri debeat. Et quidem rite, alioquin nulla est sententia ratione prolationis seu ordinis iudiciarii non seruati, qui consistit in sequentibus casibus. Primo: ratione prolationis seu pronunciationis nulla est sententia, si ipsam non sedendo sed stando iudex pronunciet* (...) (ed. Venetiis 1605, n. 5, col. 764).

vielfach in den von Gratian gesammelten Texten.[4] Auf der anderen Seite, am Ende gewissermaßen des begrifflichen Bogens, das heißt im preußischen Prozess, lautete das abschließende legislative Resultat des aufgeklärt-wohlfahrtsstaatlichen Verfahrenskonzepts nicht Prozessgesetz oder Prozessordnung oder ähnlich, sondern Gerichtsordnung (Allgemeine Gerichts-Ordnung für die Preußischen Staaten, 1795), ein Ausdruck, der nichts anderes als eine Übertragung von *ordo iudiciarius* ('Ordnung des Gerichts') darstellte.[5] Die Wortgeschichte löst daher erste Zweifel an dem begrifflichen Bogen aus, noch größere aber dann der Umstand, dass keine Belege aus Juristenschriften auftreten, welche auf eine Reflexion des Inhalts schließen ließen, dass mit der Verwendung der Begriffe der Gegensatz zwischen einem nichtsstaatlichen und einem staatlichen Prozessverständnis ausgedrückt werden sollte.

5.4. Gleichheit und Ungleichheit als These Giulianis

Überzeugender fällt da die Begriffsbildung aus, die wir bei Giuliani finden können. Auch für Giuliani geht es um die Verteilung der Rollen zwischen den Verfahrensbeteiligten, dem Richter und den Parteien. Und auch er stellt das gelehrt-mittelalterliche dem preußischen Prozessrecht gegenüber. Den entscheidenden Gesichtspunkt sieht er in der Gleichheit oder Ungleichheit der Stellung der drei Beteiligten. Wo Gleichheit im Prozessgeschehen herrscht, spricht er von Isonomie, vom *ordine isonomico*. Pate gestanden für diese Begriffsbildung hat ein politisches Theorem, nämlich die athenische Demokratie mit ihrer Gleichstellung von Regierenden und Regierten. Wo aber Ungleichheit herrscht, das heißt der Richter oder eine der beiden Parteien eine privilegierte Stellung einnimmt, entsteht Asymmetrie, entsteht das Gebilde des *ordine asimmetrico*. Natürlich war diese Begriffsbildung auch von Erscheinungen der Geschichte des Strafprozesses angeregt, vom Verfahren *per accusationem* hier, *per inquisitionem* dort.

Die isonomische und die asymmetrische Ordnung des Verfahrens werden zunächst als Modelle verstanden, das heißt als Muster oder Bilder, die *per definitionem* nicht mit der Realität sich decken, sie nicht eins zu eins abbilden, sondern auf irgendwelchen Extrakten dieser Realität beruhen. Wenn nun aber, in einem zweiten Schritt, der mittelalterliche *ordo iudiciarius* als *'modello puro'* der isonomischen Ordnung angesprochen wird, dann treten Zweifel und Fragen auf. Es genügt hierzu, auf zwei Phänomene des Prozessrechts hinzuweisen. Zum einen auf das richterliche Fragerecht: es war umfassendster Natur, konnte sowohl den Parteien als auch den Zeugen gegenüber, konnte in jeder Phase des Verfahrens, das heißt sowohl vor als auch nach Litiskontestation, gegebenenfalls sogar trotz *causae conclusio* ausgeübt werden. Das richterliche Fragerecht wurde bei jeder Gelegenheit betont; in der Lehre vom *officium iudicis* gehörte es zum *officium actioni deserviens*.

4 Insofern ist Fn. 9 in N. Picardi, *Processo civile, supra* note 2, zu ergänzen.

5 R. Stintzing(-E. Landsberg), *Geschichte der Deutschen Rechtswissenschaft* I, München, Leipzig, Oldenbourg, 1880, S. 13.

Zweitens erweist sich das Verfahren bei Ausbleiben des Beklagten als verräterisch. Denn im 'reinen' Modell des isonomischen Prozesses würde der Richter entweder den Kläger nach Hause schicken, da ohne den Beklagten ein Verfahren gar nicht zustande kommt, oder er würde unbesehen, das heißt ohne jede weitere Prüfung, der Klage stattgeben, weil der Beklagte keine Anstalten macht, sich gegen den Anspruch zu wehren. Aber die Realität des Prozessrechts sah ganz anders aus. Schon der technische Begriff *contumacia* zeigt uns, dass es um ein Verfahren wegen Ungehorsams, und zwar Ungehorsams gegenüber dem Richter ging. Und der Richter setzte seine Macht und seine Zwangsmittel ein, um den Beklagten zum Erscheinen zu veranlassen: durch Einweisung des Klägers in den Besitz oder im Fall des kirchlichen Richters durch Exkommunikation. Nur wenn der Beklagte zunächst erschienen war und Litem kontestiert hatte, entschied der Richter in der Sache, aber auch bloß dann, wenn völlige Gewissheit bestand (*si liquet de meritis causae*).[6] Übrigens konnten auch Zeugen zum Erscheinen durch Zwangsmittel veranlasst werden. Diese Hinweise mögen genügen; insgesamt würde ich eher den Stimmen beipflichten, die wie Mario Ascheri von einer Koexistenz der beiden Modelle, oder wie Jeroen Chorus – zugespitzt auf den gemeinen Prozess des 18. Jahrhunderts – von der '*well-balanced division of tasks between judge and parties*' sprechen;[7] letztere Feststellung kann durchaus auch für den mittelalterlichen *ordo iudiciarius* gelten.

5.5. Das richterliche Suppletionsrecht

Bei Giuliani finden wir aber noch eine weitere den mittelaltlerlichen gelehrten Prozess betreffende These. Hiernach würde die Mitte des 13. Jahrhunderts eine Zäsur mit der Folge zweier deutlich unterscheidbarer Perioden dargestellt haben. Den Ausgangspunkt für die These bildeten Beobachtungen zur Entwicklung der Logik (Dialektik) im 13. Jahrhundert; diese Beobachtungen wurden dann auf die Rekonstruktion der Beweistheorie übertragen.[8] Hierbei blieb es jedoch nicht, sondern die beiden erwähnten Modelle des Prozessrechts selbst wurden in die neuartige Periodisierung einbezogen. Für Giuliani waren die Modelle in verdichteter Form durch die bekannten Adagen '*iudex de facto supplere non potest*' beziehungsweise '*supplere potest*' repräsentiert, und so führte er im Anschluss an die Bemerkung, der mittelalterliche Prozess dürfte nicht als einheitliche Erscheinung angesehen werden, wörtlich aus: '*la metà del XIII secolo rappresenta la linea di demarcazione ideale tra le due anime dell'ordo iudiciarius*: segna infatti il passaggio dall'ordine isonomico ('iudex non potest supplere in facto') all'ordine asimmetrico ('iudex potest supplere in facto')'.[9] Aber schlüssige Belege für diesen Satz finden

6 Näheres etwa bei Tankred, Tit. 4, 1, ed. Bergmann, S. 135 *et seq.*

7 M. Ascheri, 'Il processo civile tra diritto comune e diritto locale: da questioni preliminari al caso della giustizia estense', *Quaderni storici*, 1999, S. 362; J.M.J. Chorus, 'The Judge's Role in the Conduct of Civil Proceedings', in D.L. Carey Miller (ed.), *Comparative and Historical Essays in Scots Law*, Edinburgh, Butterworth, 1992, S. 39.

8 A. Giuliani, *Il concetto di prova: contributo alla logica giuridica*, *supra* note 2, S. 117, 139, 156, 160, 164.

9 A. Giuliani, 'Dalla litis contestatio al pleading system', *supra* note 2, S. 207.

sich nicht.[10] Um ihn abzusichern, hätte man das Prozessschrifttum nach 1250 heranziehen müssen, allen voran das *Speculum* des Duranti samt den *Additiones* des Johannes Andreae und Zusätzen des Baldus. Ein Blick in diese Schriften ergibt aber, dass von einem Grundsatz, der Richter dürfe *de facto supplere*, keine Rede sein kann; diese Möglichkeit wurde nur in Ausnahmenfällen bejaht.[11] Ähnliches gilt für die Feststellung weiterer prozessualer Veränderungen während des 13. Jahrhunderts, etwa einer Preisgabe der ursprünglichen Konzeption der *positiones* und einer Abschwächung der Lehre von der Relevanz des angebotenen Beweises:[12] auch hier müssten die genannten Schriften erst herangezogen und genau geprüft werden, bevor Thesen und Hypothesen zu einschneidenden Periodisierungen der Geschichte des gelehrten Prozesses aufgestellt werden.

6. Zusammenfassung

Wenn wir unsere Lektüre der Abhandlungen vor allem Giuliani's zusammenfassen dürfen, dann stellen die vorgeschlagenen Begriffe des *ordine isonomico* und *asimmetrico* zweifelsohne eine Bereicherung des konzeptionellen Verständnisses der Geschichte des Prozessrechts dar. Die isonomische Typologisierung ergänzt überzeugend und erfolgreich die anderen Typologisierungen wie die kontradiktorische oder adversative oder parteiendispositive Kennzeichnung des Prozesses. Und die asymmetrische Typologisierung ist der allgemein üblichen inquisitorischen sogar vorzuziehen, weil unsere Typologien als solche keine Werturteile enthalten, sie wertneutral sind, in dem Begriff 'inquisitorisch' aber, ob man will oder nicht, die negative Bewertung der kirchlichen 'Inquisition', das heißt der inquisitorischen Verfahrensweise gegen Häretiker usw., mitschwingt, der Begriff also unverdientermaßen mit Argwohn betrachtet wird. Die neuen Begriffe sagen also zu. Wenn aber Feststellungen getroffen wurden, die sich auf das mittelalterliche gelehrte Prozessrecht *in concreto*, auf seine Institute und Sätze beziehen, dann erwiesen sie sich bisweilen als nicht genau genug, als weniger verlässlich, so dass man für die angeschnittenen Fragen des öfteren die Quellen selbst aufsuchen und sich die Interpretation der Texte vorbehalten muss.

10 Auch nicht in der Monographie von 1961 noch im Artikel in der *Enciclopedia del diritto* von 1988.

11 W. Duranti, *Speculum iuris II 2, De disputationibus et allegationibus advocatorum, Satis* (ed. Basileae 1574, repr. Aalen 1975, S. 751 *et seq.*).

12 A. Giuliani, 'Il concetto di prova', *supra* note 2, S. 186, S. 208. Die *positiones* wurden durch die *articuli* ergänzt, nicht jedoch fortschreitend substituiert (so aber S. 174).